Capitalists and Revolution
in Nicaragua

Rose J. Spalding

Capitalists and Revolution
in Nicaragua

Opposition and
Accommodation,
1979–1993

The University of North Carolina Press
Chapel Hill and London

The paper in this book meets the guidelines for
permanence and durability of the Committee on
Production Guidelines for Book Longevity of the Council
on Library Resources.

Library of Congress Cataloging-in-Publication Data
Spalding, Rose J.
    Capitalists and revolution in Nicaragua : opposition
and accommodation, 1979–1993 / Rose J. Spalding.
        p.   cm.
Includes bibliographical references (p.   ) and index.
ISBN 0-8078-2150-0 (cloth : alk. paper).—
ISBN 0-8078-4456-X (pbk. : alk. paper)
    1. Business and politics—Nicaragua.   2. Elite (Social
sciences)—Nicaragua.   3. Nicaragua—Politics and
government—1979– .   I. Title.
JL1609.5.B8S68   1994
322'.3'097285—dc20   93-38430
                                                              CIP

98 97 96 95 94   5 4 3 2 1

contents

tables

RAMIRO GURDIÁN Ortiz was an up-and-coming banana producer from
an elite León family when the Sandinista revolution occurred. On
a farm his father "carved out of the jungle," Gurdián had built up one
of Nicaragua's larger banana plantations and was moving rapidly up the
administrative ladder of Standard Fruit's Nicaragua operation. He was
skeptical of the insurrection that swept the regime of Anastasio Somoza
Debayle from power in 1979 and brought in the leaders of the FSLN, and
he remained aloof from the political imbroglio that followed. But in 1980,
Jorge Salazar, the president of his private sector association, the Nicaraguan Union of Agricultural and Livestock Producers (UPANIC), began
organizing a counterrevolutionary expedition and was killed by state security forces during an arms transaction. Gurdián agreed to serve as his
replacement in UPANIC. During the next ten years, he became one of the
nation's most outspoken critics of the Sandinista regime. He was arrested,
convicted, and placed on probation for violating the censorship provisions
of the 1982 National Emergency decree; his farm was confiscated without
compensation; his family scattered, leaving him as the sole continuing
resident of Nicaragua.

Ricardo Coronel Kautz was a part-time rancher and full-time administrator of the livestock enterprise owned by the region's largest sugar
mill, the Ingenio San Antonio, prior to the revolution. Son of José Coronel Urtecho, a prominent Nicaraguan intellectual who had served as a
diplomatic representative of the Somoza regime but became increasingly
disaffected, and his muse, María Kautz, a Nicaraguan of German descent
whose family had been dispossessed of its primary estate by the Somoza
regime during World War II, Coronel had developed an abiding antipathy
for the Somoza dynasty. As a top administrator of Nicaragua's most prominent agroindustrial complex, Coronel helped organize an underground
political movement among the technical staff in support of the Sandinista insurrection. In 1977 he was named to the prestigious Los Doce,
a group of twelve prominent business, religious, and intellectual leaders

who lobbied for international political support for the Sandinista cause in the final years of the insurrection. When he returned to Nicaragua after Somoza's departure, he was appointed a vice-minister of agriculture and agrarian reform. For eleven years, Coronel served in the Nicaraguan government, exercising considerable influence over the state farm sector and agricultural development policy throughout the Sandinista era.

These vignettes suggest the range of views held by Nicaraguan economic elites about the Sandinista revolution. The relationship between the revolutionary government and most of Nicaragua's traditional business elite was generally antagonistic. Yet during the same period, some endorsed the revolution and became active participants in the social transitions it produced. Others ranged in between, reaching a tenuous accommodation with the regime but retaining a critical distance.

Two broad questions shape this study. The first addresses the theoretical debate about the composition and segmentation of the bourgeoisie. This analysis explores the unity/division of the capitalist class as it interacts with other social sectors. The second focuses on the capacity of economic elites to participate in a process of social change. This discussion evaluates the capacity of the elites to contribute to or to impede equitable distribution and the collective development of the nation.

Structural analysis, which has provided the dominant theoretical and methodological framework in Latin American studies for the last two decades, typically assumes a high degree of class cohesion. According to this approach, "capital" has clear interests and needs defined by its structural position in the economy. The dominant class is found to use its resources to impose constraints on other actors, limiting the options for structural change. The state may attain a "relative autonomy" from the business sector, but this autonomy is ultimately limited by the structural dependence of the state on capital. Capital, therefore, is understood as an increasingly united, cohesive actor. To the extent that segmentation occurs within the bourgeoisie, one fraction tends to emerge as the dominant force and exercise direction over the others.

Because of the fundamental cohesion of the bourgeoisie alleged in this model, any notions of cross-class alliances between the underclass and elements of the bourgeoisie are seen as inherently flawed. The participation of capitalist partners in a reform coalition is seen as ultimately undermining the movement because they are expected to serve the long-run interests of the dominant fraction of their class. For any structural transformation to occur, this exploitative class must be removed from power.

Yet Popular Front struggles and many progressive electoral strategies have been premised on the assumption that movements for social change can draw on the energies of a range of class actors, including elements of a "nationalist" or "progressive" bourgeoisie. Both Social Democratic and Democratic Socialist coalitions have understood the necessity for a continually evolving class compromise involving a component of the private sector in their movement. Latin American Populist and Third World National Liberation movements have traditionally drawn on a multiclass coalition that, while limiting the redistributive impact of the outcome, also allows for the participation of economic elites who can insert themselves into the changing economic order.

New research traditions, such as strategic choice analysis, explore more open, less deterministic models of social change.[1] These approaches assume that actors are not fully bound by their structural positions. Participants in political negotiations are viewed as volitional agents who operate with an element of discretion, allowing the use of analytical schemes that are more dynamic and interactive. In these models, changing calculations of costs and benefits, combined with multilevel bargaining, produce highly complex and varied alliance strategies. This relatively open approach may better capture moments of "extraordinary" politics, when regimes undergo transitions and the social compact is subject to revision.

Attention to complex alliances and ongoing bargaining reopens questions about the character and political roles of capital in Latin America. These questions will become increasingly central in the study of Latin American politics in the 1990s. Throughout much of this region, the fiscal crisis of the state and the weakness of foreign financial support now move the local business elite toward the strategic center of the development debate. Finding a way to engage the resources and energies of business elites and break the cycle of capital flight, while simultaneously opening new social and economic opportunities to nonelites, will be a central challenge for Latin American leaders in the coming years.

My research on the relationship between the state, capitalists, and revolution began in 1982 when, with support from the National Endowment for the Humanities, I started a research project on the Sandinista concept of the "mixed economy." That year my annual trek to Nicaragua began. Support from the University Research Council and the College of Liberal Arts and Sciences of DePaul University allowed me to mount an ongoing research effort on the shifting dynamics of the Nicaraguan revolution.

My attention was increasingly drawn to the anomalous role of the local bourgeoisie in the revolution. Much of the material on Nicaragua during this period focused on the contra war and the conflict with the United States. Less understood were the complex, internal relationships that played a critical role in shaping the development of the revolution. To analyze the way in which the revolution unfolded, I carefully examined these internal dynamics. Given the centrality of the agricultural sector in the national economy, I concentrated on the agricultural and agroindustrial sectors. In 1985–87, I began a series of interviews with leaders of the major private sector organizations.

By the time I began my interviews, a sizable core of the prerevolutionary economic elite had left the country. The effort to better understand elite-state dynamics in the Somoza era and the impact of emigration on the revolution took me to Miami, where I conducted a round of interviews in 1988 with seventeen former and current Nicaraguan private sector leaders. The Latin American and Caribbean Center of Florida International University generously provided housing accommodations during my stay; Mark Rosenberg and Doug Kincaid provided intellectual and logistical support for this phase of my work.

Most of the research for this book was completed in 1989–90 with support from the Joint Committee on Latin American Studies of the Social Science Research Council and American Council of Learned Societies with funds provided by the Andrew W. Mellon Foundation and the Ford Foundation, and with support from the Howard Heinz Foundation. A fellowship at the Kellogg Institute of International Studies at Notre Dame provided a congenial environment in which to begin writing this book. I am grateful to generous and supportive colleagues at all of these institutions for facilitating this research.

Research in Nicaragua would not have been possible without the extensive assistance provided by Laura Enríquez, Amalia Chamorro, Peter Utting, Peter Marchetti, Eduardo Baumeister, Rodolfo Delgado Cáceres, and Paul Oquist. I am also grateful for the research assistance provided by Freddy Quesada, Carlos Molina, and Edith Muñoz. Invaluable intellectual companionship was provided at different phases in this process by Florence Babb, Martin Diskin, David Dye, Dennis Gilbert, Richard Grossman, Barbara Kritt, Shelley McConnell, Alice McGrath, Jack Spence, George Vickers, Phillip Williams, and Daniel Wolf.

Several colleagues read versions of my work as it wended its way toward the final draft. John Booth, Laura Enríquez, Ilja Luciak, Steven Sanderson, Richard Stahler-Sholk, Evelyne Huber Stephens, and Carlos Vilas deserve special thanks for their constructive criticisms, as do my colleagues Mike Alvarez and Pat Callahan. For their useful comments on the comparative framework and some of the theoretical constructs employed here, I want to thank David Collier, Sandra McGee Deutch, Francisco Durand, Jeffrey Paige, and Eduardo Silva. Lisa Milam and Veronica Diaz helped me to polish and produce the final version of the manuscript. David Perry at the University of North Carolina Press gently and efficiently shepherded the manuscript to publication, and Stephanie Wenzel proved a remarkably keen-eyed copyeditor. The usual disclaimers about responsibility for the remaining flaws in this work apply.

I also want to thank the private producers in Nicaragua who gave generously of their time to introduce an unschooled *chela* to the world of Nicaraguan business and agricultural production. Ramiro Gurdián, for many years the president of UPANIC and currently the president of COSEP, and Daniel Núñez, long-term president of UNAG, provided invaluable advice and suggestions; without their help this book would not have been possible. I am also deeply indebted to Mario Hanón and his family for their many kindnesses over the years. While most of those producers whom I have interviewed will take issue with different parts of my analysis, I hope that they will see merit in it as well.

Finally, I want to thank my patient and generous husband, William Denton, who sacrificed as much as I did to get this book written and who wasn't able to share much of the fun; my daughter Claire, who walked this long journey right by my side; and my daughter Grace, who was born just as it came to an end.

acronyms and abbreviations

ACBN	Asociación de Criadores de Ganado Brahman de Nicaragua
ADACH	Asociación de Algodoneros de Chinandega
ADAL	Asociación de Algodoneros de León
ADEX	Asociación de Exportadores (Peru)
AGROEXCO	Corporación Propulsora de Agroexportaciones
ANAR	Asociación Nicaragüense de Arroceros de Riego
ANEP	Asociación Nacional de la Empresa Privada (El Salvador)
ANPROBA	Asociación Nacional de Productores de Banano
ANPROSOR	Asociación Nacional de Productores de Sorgo
ANSCA	Algodoneros Nicaragüenses Sociedad Cooperativa Anónima
APENN	Asociación Nicaragüense de Productores y Exportadores de Productos No-Tradicionales
APP	Area de Propiedad del Pueblo
ARENA	Alianza Republicana Nacionalista (El Salvador)
ASCANIC	Asociación de Cañeros de Nicaragua
ASGANIC	Asociación de Ganaderos de Nicaragua
ATC	Asociación de Trabajadores del Campo
BANAMER	Banco de América
BANIC	Banco Nicaragüense
BANPRO	Banco de la Producción
BCN	Banco Central de Nicaragua
BND	Banco Nacional de Desarrollo (formerly BNN, Banco Nacional de Nicaragua)
CAAN	Confederación de Asociaciones de Algodoneros de Nicaragua
CACM	Central American Common Market
CADE	Conferencia Anual de Empresarios (Peru)
CADIN	Cámara de Industrias de Nicaragua

CAFENIC	Corporación Nicaragüense del Café
CANACINTRA	Cámara Nacional de la Industria de Transformación (Mexico)
CARNIC	Carnicería de Nicaragua
CAS	Cooperativa Agrícola Sandinista
CCS	Cooperativa de Crédito y Servicio
CEPAL	Comisión Económica para América Latina y el Caribe
CIERA	Centro de Investigaciones y Estudios de la Reforma Agraria
CIPRES	Centro para la Investigación, la Promoción y el Desarrollo Rural y Social
CISA	Comercial Industrial, S.A.
CNG	Comisión Nacional de Ganadería
COIP	Corporación Industrial del Pueblo
CONAL	Comisión Nacional del Algodón
CONAPRO	Confederación de Asociaciones Profesionales
CONAZUCAR	Corporación Nicaragüense de la Agroindustria Azucarera
CONCAFE	Comisión Nacional del Café
CONCAMIN	Confederación de Cámaras Industriales (Mexico)
CONCANACO	Confederación Nacional de Cámaras de Comercio (Mexico)
COPARMEX	Confederación Patronal de la República Mexicana
COPROCO	Confederación de la Producción y el Comercio (Chile)
CORDENIC	Comisión sobre la Recuperación y el Desarrollo de Nicaragua
CORFO	Corporación de Fomento de Producción (Chile)
CORNAP	Corporaciones Nacionales del Sector Público
COSEP	Consejo Superior de la Empresa Privada
COSIP	Consejo Superior de la Iniciativa Privada
CRIES	Coordinadora Regional de Investigaciones Económicas y Sociales
CST	Central Sandinista de Trabajadores
ECLA	Economic Commission on Latin America
ECODEPA	Empresa Cooperativa de Productores Agropecuarios
ENAL	Empresa Nicaragüense del Algodón
ENALUF	Empresa Nacional de Luz y Fuerza
EPS	Ejército Popular Sandinista

FAGANIC	Federación de Asociaciones Ganaderas de Nicaragua
FAO	Frente Amplio Opositor
FIDA	Fondo Internacional de Desarrollo Agrícola
FIDEG	Fundación Internacional para el Desafío Económico Global
FNI	Fondo Nicaragüense de Inversión
FNT	Frente Nacional de Trabajadores
FONDILAC	Fondo de Desarrollo de la Industria Láctea
FSLN	Frente Sandinista de Liberación Nacional
GAO	General Accounting Office (United States)
GRACSA	Grasas y Aceites, S.A.
HATONIC	Sociedad de Empresas Pecuarias del APP
IBRD	International Bank of Reconstruction and Development
IDB	Inter-American Development Bank
IHCA	Instituto Histórico Centroamericano
IMF	International Monetary Fund
INCAE	Instituto Centroamericano de Administración de Empresas
INCAFE	Instituto Nacional del Café (El Salvador)
INDE	Instituto Nicaragüense de Desarrollo
INFONAC	Instituto de Fomento Nacional
INIES	Instituto Nicaragüense de Investigaciones Económicas y Sociales
INIESEP	Instituto de Investigaciones Económicas y Sociales de la Empresa Privada
ISA	Ingenio San Antonio
JEA	Jamaica Exporters' Association
JGRN	Junta de Gobierno de Reconstrucción Nacional
LASA	Latin American Studies Association
MDN	Movimiento Democrático Nicaragüense
MEDA	Marco Estratégico del Desarrollo Agropecuario
MEDE	Ministerio de Economía y Desarrollo
MIDINRA	Ministerio de Desarrollo Agropecuario y Reforma Agraria
MIPLAN	Ministerio de Planificación
mz.	manzana (.7 hectares)
NAFINSA	Nacional Financiera, S.A. (Mexico)
OAS	Organization of American States

OCALSA	Organización César Augusto Lacayo, S.A.
PIP	Programa de Inversión Pública
PLC	Partido Liberal Constitucionalista
PLI	Partido Liberal Independiente
PRI	Partido Revolucionario Institucional (Mexico)
qt.	quintal (100 pounds)
qt. oro	100 pounds processed
SAIMSA	Servicio Agrícola-Industrial de Masaya, S.A.
SNA	Sociedad Nacional de Agricultura (Chile)
SNI	Sociedad Nacional de Industrias (Peru)
SOFOFA	Sociedad de Fomento Fabril (Chile)
SPP	Secretaría de Planificación y Presupuesto
TIMAL	Ingenio Tipitapa-Malacatoya
UCA	Universidad Centroamericana
UDEL	Unión Democrática de Liberación
UNAG	Unión Nacional de Agricultores y Ganaderos
UNAN	Universidad Nacional Autónoma de Nicaragua
UNCAFENIC	Unión Nacional de Caficultores de Nicaragua
UNO	Unión Nacional Opositora
UP	Unidad Popular (Chile)
UPANIC	Unión de Productores Agropecuarios de Nicaragua
USAID	U.S. Agency for International Development
USDA	U.S. Department of Agriculture

Capitalists and Revolution
in Nicaragua

Nicaragua's Electoral Regions

chapter 1

Capitalists and Revolution

> It is a complex problem, but we have not given up the search for ways of integrating the more-or-less large individual producers who live in Nicaragua today into a social formation in which revolutionary hegemony prevails.
>
> —Jaime Wheelock Román, *El gran desafío*

DEVELOPMENTALISTS, social theorists, and revolutionaries have long puzzled over the problematic role of economic elites in the process of social change. Much of the general literature on revolution and structural reform presents the dominant class as a homogeneous entity intransigent in its opposition to significant change. As beneficiaries of the status quo, economic elites are seen as a primary obstacle to social restructuring, often in close cooperation with foreign capital.

In recent years, however, many of the standard categories used to chart contending social forces, such as "workers," "peasants," and "bourgeoisie," seem increasingly inadequate to describe what are often highly differentiated clusters of people. Workers moving steadily into the informal sector now lack a formal employer counterpart and become self-employed; peasants have weaker ties to the land and rotate annually through a series of job categories and residences; the bourgeoisie is divided into a series of competing layers whose relative fortunes rise and fall. The inability of the traditional conceptual categories to accommodate this acute diversity calls for the use of different analytical methods and the development of new conceptual schemes. For studies of the bourgeoisie, a closer analysis of the social sectors that make up the elite is in order.

The search for the fissures within the dominant elite is not simply an analytical exercise in social dissection. This task has been a central preoccupation of proponents of social change. Underlying much of this kind of analysis has been the desire of both academicians and political practitioners to locate a "progressive" sector of the bourgeoisie. Academic analysts such as Barrington Moore (1966) claimed to find such a sector, arguing that there were circumstances under which an urban bourgeoi-

I

sie could break with traditional landholding elites and nudge the political system toward democracy. Some reform-oriented political leaders also claimed allies within the economic elite. Needing the economic capabilities, international credibility, and domestic leverage that such coalition partners would provide, these politicians searched assiduously for business leaders with whom to link arms.

Leaders of populist movements were particularly inclined to seek an alliance with a "nationalist bourgeoisie." Populism as an ideology presented no barrier to the inclusion of national elites; indeed, the overriding nationalism embedded in populism called these leaders to strengthen local economic strongholds. Cultivation of emerging industrialists often secured their support. Juan Perón's success in building an alliance with small- and medium-sized capitalists through the Confederación General Económica in Argentina has been well documented (Acuña 1991; Teichman 1981). In spite of its social base in labor, the Peronist coalition anchored the support of emerging elites in the light industry sector, firms that manufactured for the domestic market, and industries that were less dependent on imports. Since these kinds of industrialists benefited from an expanding local market, they could find common cause with unionized labor in its bid for increased earnings. Although old, established elite organizations moved firmly into the opposition, emerging elites included prominent allies.

Even democratic socialist movements typically found it necessary to court a segment of the economic elite, in spite of ideological reservations. To locate a theoretical rationale for this compromise, the concept of a "non-monopoly" bourgeoisie was sometimes employed. A non-monopoly bourgeoisie was differentiated from the hegemonic, monopoly sector by the former's unfavorable economic position and tendency to be eroded by the monopoly sector. This alliance was reinforced in dependent nations by the tension between subordinated local capital and hegemonic foreign capital. Alliances between a nonhegemonic, small- and medium-sized local capitalist faction and the peasant and worker underclass, it was argued, would undercut the foreign-oriented, hegemonic bourgeoisie and allow for a process of socialist transition.[1]

This form of social theory and consequent alliance strategy had its critics. For analysts of the bourgeoisie like Nicos Poulantzas and André Gunder Frank, the effort to locate a sector of the dominant class that could accept social change was futile and self-defeating.[2] In a monumental study of agrarian, industrial, and financial factions of the Chilean bourgeoisie, Maurice Zeitlin and Richard Earl Ratcliff add empirical support to this interpretation. Their detailed study of the social structure of the top Chilean elite in the 1960s produced "a discovery of great import: an incomparably large effective kinship unit, formed of multiply intermarried banking, industrial, and landowning families, erases any ostensible social cleavages between supposedly contending landowning vs. capitalist 'upper' classes in these economic sectors" (Zeitlin and Ratcliff 1988, 173).

Because of the presence of close family members who straddled sectoral divisions, Zeitlin and Ratcliff concluded that contradictions between top capitalists with different structural locations in the economy were muted. Clashes and divisions between capitalist sectors in the twentieth century, they argued, "arose not between ontologically real rivals, but within the bosom of the same class" (Zeitlin and Ratcliff 1988, 208). Divisions that other analysts had found to segment the capitalist class—between bankers and industrialists, owners and managers, large landowners and urban capitalists, foreign and local capital—are minimized here, since bonds of kinship ultimately were found to weave these sectors together.[3]

This discussion of the character and political predilections of the Latin American bourgeoisie reflects two competing visions. In one view, the bourgeoisie, in spite of some sectoral divisions, is essentially a unitary actor. Interpenetration through family, financial, or contractual ties overcomes any tendency toward segmentation. In the other, real differences exist within the bourgeoisie that incline different segments or clusters toward different political projects.

This book tackles the question of the unity/division of the economic elite by focusing on the elite's political interactions with the state during periods of state-led reform. Episodes of structural change put enormous pressure on both the state and the bourgeoisie. Established social hierarchies and resource allocation patterns are called sharply into question. A sense of peril propels the elite into direct political action. This moment can either increase the unity of the elite, as it attempts to defend established privileges or obtain new ones, or divide it, as different segments negotiate for an improved position relative to the others.

The way the bourgeoisie responds, I argue, depends on a series of factors. Central among these are (1) the degree to which oligarchical control over the elite has been ruptured, (2) the organizational autonomy and density of private sector associations, (3) the degree of perceived class-based threat posed by the state, (4) the extent to which the revolutionary regime succeeds in institutionalizing a new political order, and (5) the capacity of the regime to consolidate a viable economic system. The first two factors focus on the inherited character of the economic elite. The last three shift the attention to the nature of the revolutionary state.

To explore the segmentation of the bourgeoisie, this chapter briefly analyzes two types of outcomes: cases in which the bourgeoisie unites in opposition to the reform movement and defeats it, and cases in which the bourgeoisie divides and some sectors reach an accommodation with the regime.[4] Each of these subtypes will be analyzed by a review of cases in Latin America where the central dynamics diverged. Analysis of the oppositional bourgeoisie focuses on the democratic socialist regime in Chile under Salvador Allende (1970–73) and the reform regime in El Salvador (sputtering between 1979 and 1989). Information about the accommodationist bourgeoisie is drawn from the study of state-capitalist relationships under revolutionary populism in Mexico during the Lázaro Cárdenas era (1934–40) and in Peru under the Juan Velasco regime (1968–75).[5]

Not all of these experiences are conventionally regarded as revolutions, either because they were quickly reversed or because the changes actually introduced were not profound enough to warrant the label. Each of these cases did, however, entail a major effort to restructure what had been core features of the nation's social and economic order. In this sense they all qualify as major initiatives in structural change. Lessons drawn from the analysis of these experiences will be used to sketch an interpretation of the variations in state-capitalist relations and devise a framework within which to analyze state-capital relations during the Sandinista revolution.

A cautionary note is needed here before we proceed. The literature on these cases has been compiled by hundreds of scholars, most of whom have spent decades working on a single country. Because there have been so few cross-national studies of revolutionary processes and none that focus specifically on the reaction of economic elites, the task of building up this broad comparison is both daunting and perilous. Epistemological assumptions and methodologies vary from study to study. Concepts that are frequently used in this literature such as "family clans" or "oligarchy" may refer to different phenomena in different national settings. Standards used in making judgments about the degree of economic concentration may vary from case to case. For example, Chile's long experience with multiparty electoral democracy allowed it to be linked analytically to the study of Western European politics. Analysts studying the Chilean system, therefore, may be implicitly comparing the Chilean social structure with those found in Italy or France rather than those found in Peru or Mexico.

Since the same set of assumptions and standards is not applied consistently by scholars analyzing each of these cases, similar characterizations (for example, the claim that the economy is dominated by an oligarchy) may reflect rather different realities. I have attempted to look beyond the summary judgments to appraise the evidence on which those judgments are based and to use comparative statistics when possible, but my work is necessarily constrained by these limitations.

The Bourgeoisie in Opposition

Democratic Socialism and the Coalesced Bourgeoisie in Chile

Prior to the election of President Salvador Allende in 1970 and his attempt to introduce "democratic socialism,"[6] economic diversification had generated some divisions in the Chilean bourgeoisie, and the deepening of democratic processes had diminished its power. The experience of the Allende era, however, reunited the economic elite and propelled their offensive against the regime. Several characteristics of the Chilean elite and the Allende regime contributed to this outcome.

The Chilean bourgeoisie was shaped by a centralization of resources at the top and a norm of forceful organization that extended even into the middle sector of the elite. At the end of the 1960s, for example, 2 percent of all industrial establishments produced over two-thirds of all industrial output in Chile; the top five banks allocated over half of all credit (de Vylder 1976, 18).[7] Land concentration was marked. Prior to the adoption of the agrarian reform law by Christian Democratic president Eduardo Frei in 1967 there were 11,000 large, multifamily estates averaging 2,200 hectares each. These large estates represented 4.2 percent of all agricultural units but occupied 79 percent of the country's agricultural land (de Vylder 1976, 166). Zeitlin and Ratcliff's (1988, 163–64) detailed analysis of the upper reaches of the Chilean economic elite in the 1964–66 period identified 24 "kinship groups" that were located among the top stratum of bankers, corporate executives, and landowners of the country, including one large "maximum kinship group" that included 56 percent of the top bankers, 16 percent of the top corporate executives, and 30 percent of the top landowners.

In spite of a relatively sustained tradition of political democracy and

the dense organization of civil society in Chile,[8] the business elite retained significant political influence. The economic elite pressured the
state directly through leadership of political parties and indirectly through
privileged access to state institutions.[9] Six private sector associations
provided an organizational forge for the economic elite. The venerable
National Agricultural Society (SNA) was formed in 1838; leaders of this
association, in turn, formed the Society for Industrial Promotion (SOFOFA
or SFF) in 1883, after the minister of finance requested their assistance in
promoting the industrial development of the country. The National Chamber of Commerce (previously the Central Chamber of Commerce) dates
from 1858, and the National Mining Society, representing Chilean mine
owners, from 1883. Of the associations representing economic strongholds, only the Chamber of Construction and the Association of Banks
and Financial Institutions were of twentieth-century origin (Menges 1966,
344–46; Campero 1984, 312–18).[10] To defend their collective interests,
the four older associations came together in 1935 to form one central
peak association, the Production and Commerce Federation (COPROCO).
Chile's elite business associations tended to be very selective, drew
heavily from larger establishments, and had restricted internal democracy.[11]

Nonetheless, a large population of medium-sized producers had
emerged in Chile including small- and medium-sized industrialists, urban
professionals, a self-employed petty bourgeoisie, and small- and medium-
sized agricultural producers. Reflecting the norm of political pluralism,
this medium-sized economic elite had devised its own network of associations in Chile, albeit in more recent decades. The largest of the private sector organizations serving small- and medium-sized businesses,
the Chilean Trade Federation of Retailers and Small Industry, was founded
in 1938; a host of transportation federations developed in the 1940s–
60s (Campero 1984, 316–19). Unlike their larger counterparts, these business associations lacked a central organizing agency that could pull them
together, and they were not given the representational prerogatives in
government agencies that the elite institutions had acquired. Compared
with most other Latin American cases, however, these small and mid-
sized capitalists in Chile were relatively mobilized and autonomously
organized.

Allende's UP coalition was designed to divide the Chilean bourgeoisie and incorporate small- and medium-sized producers. The UP's official
campaign *Programa* opens by expressing concern about the suffering "by

workers, peasants, and other exploited classes as well as in the growing difficulties which confront white collar workers, professional people,
small and medium businessmen, and in the very limited opportunities
open to women and young people." Against this broad coalition of the
disadvantaged are placed the interests of "imperialist nations," "bourgeois
groups who are structurally related to foreign capital" and the "national
monopolistic bourgeoisie" ("Popular Unity's Programme" 1973, 255–56).

In practice, however, deep divisions remained within the coalition
about how to deal with this sector. The traditional Communist party
position had favored a broad "People's Front" that included "progressive
sectors" of the national bourgeoisie. The Socialist party, on the other
hand, raised doubts about the existence of any such progressive sector
and favored a more narrowly based coalition of proletarian forces. The
UP government, composed of Socialists, Communists, segments of the
old Radical party, and heretical leftists from the Christian Democratic
party, began without consensus on the role of the bourgeoisie. There was
agreement that the hegemonic faction of the bourgeoisie should be eliminated, both to undercut the political capabilities of the right and to secure,
through expropriation, economic resources with which to finance the new
order. But there were sharp divisions within the coalition about what to
do with the nonhegemonic faction of small- and medium-sized producers.

Allende began his presidency by avoiding that divisive issue; he sought
national consensus by focusing attention on foreign capital. In nationaliz-
ing the copper mines, he fulfilled a broad, national aspiration and secured
unanimous support within the legislature. Although the subsequent decision to impose a retroactive tax on the mining companies' excess profits
and not pay compensation was more controversial, the initial expropriation was a widely supported move that rallied even local elites against
foreign control.

The government's subsequent move to acquire control over the commercial banking system was more controversial and had a much deeper
impact on local elites. Financial institutions were often the linchpin that
held together large economic groups. Their expropriation undercut the
ability of these groups to assure capital flows to their affiliates. But the
government's willingness to pay handsomely for the buyout of existing
stockholders muted the opposition to this measure.

The UP's agrarian reform initiatives were yet more controversial, and
the majority opposition in congress prevented the government from securing more sweeping change. Forced to use the agrarian reform legisla-

tion passed previously by the Christian Democrats, the regime possessed limited redistributive capabilities.[12] Consequently, the Chilean agrarian reform program was somewhat smaller than that which took place in Mexico or Peru.[13]

The regime's most controversial property reform measures were in the industrial sector.[14] In spite of formal plans to delimit narrowly the firms that would be expropriated, and repeated official guarantees to small- and medium-sized producers that their properties would not be affected, the actual expansion of the state sector proceeded according to a different dynamic. As Peter Winn points out in his study of the expropriation of the Yarur textile factory, the Chilean revolution was not encapsulated by political leaders but often flowed from base-level initiatives. When union leaders and factory workers at the Yarur plant decided to seize the factory and called on Allende to incorporate it into the state sector, for example, Allende's resistance was eroded by labor militancy and the defection of his own cabinet officials, like the independent socialist Pedro Vuskovic who ran the powerful Economic Ministry (Winn 1986, 193–95).

Unceasing pressure to expropriate led to the rapid expansion of the state sector. Unable to get congressional authorization for these expropriations, the government resorted to the use of a little-known piece of legislation passed during the brief Popular Front government of the 1930s that allowed the government to intervene in industries producing items of "basic necessity" when labor disputes threatened to halt their operation. The "requisitioning" of such factories, followed by offers to buy, allowed the state to expand its domain. Beginning with 46 enterprises in 1970, the state sector grew to 507 firms (plus 19 banks) by September 1973.[15] This rapid expansion of the state sector to include 44 percent of industrial production by mid-1973 (Bitar 1986, 189) in spite of congressional opposition led to a constitutional crisis that contributed to the institutional breakdown of the regime.[16]

Initially, the private sector's reaction to the new government was ambiguous. There was a brief run on the banks, and stock values plunged, as some of the wealthy panicked. Some of the most prominent elites, such as key members of the Matte and Edwards families, sounded the alarm and actively conspired with the Nixon administration against the confirmation of Allende by the Chilean legislature.[17] Other bourgeois leaders, however, while not pro-UP, adopted a "wait and see" attitude toward the new government. Indeed, a few private sector organizations, such as the Chilean Trade Federation of Retailers and Small Industry, even publicly congratulated the new president on his victory. Others, like the Central Chamber of Commerce or the president of the National Mining Society, expressed a willingness to work together for economic growth and development (Campero 1984, 46; Silva 1992, 3).

The private sector responded to the uncertainties surrounding the new government with a general decrease in investment. According to calculations made by Barbara Stallings (1978, 248), the private sector's portion of fixed capital investment in industry dropped from an already low 43 percent in 1970 to only 20 percent in 1971, and declined still further to around 10 percent of the total in 1973.[18] Outside the construction sector, private domestic investment reportedly dropped 71 percent between 1970 and 1971 (Valenzuela 1978, 56).

This reluctance to continue investment did not, in the initial phase, signify open political rebellion. By the end of 1971, however, concerted opposition swept through the national bourgeoisie. Both the outcome of the April 1971 municipal elections, in which the UP vote increased to 49.8 percent of the total (Valenzuela 1978, 54), and the pattern of increased expropriations, which included the symbolically important Compañía Manufacturera de Papeles y Cartones presided over by former president Jorge Alessandri, alarmed economic elites. In December 1971, several private sector organizations representing both large and small entrepreneurs called the Encuentro del Area Privado attended by 5,000 affiliates. At this meeting, Orlando Sáenz, SOFOFA's new president, denounced the government for "breaking with Chilean tradition" and launched the Frente Nacional de la Actividad Privada to protest government policy (Campero 1984, 56–64). Unlike in Mexico, where no united private sector opposition to the revolution emerged, or in Peru, where such attempts repeatedly failed, by the end of 1971 a forceful opposition business front had emerged in Chile.

Many businesses apparently benefited economically during the 1971–72 period.[19] Although the dramatic reduction of foreign credit affected access to certain imports and major wage increases were decreed, many producers oriented toward the domestic market benefited from the sharp upsurge of domestic consumption. The economy grew rapidly at first, expanding 7.7 percent in 1971; industrial production, drawing on installed capacity, jumped 13.7 percent in the first half of 1972 (Bitar 1986, 46, 93).

Nonetheless, within a short period of time, the economic elite closed ranks against the regime and joined the effort to topple the government. The most graphic evidence of sweeping bourgeoisie opposition came in

October 1972 with the "bosses' strike." This movement was not confined to the top elite; it drew support from even small- and medium-sized capitalists who had been courted by the Allende regime. Bolstered by foreign financing from the CIA as well as private corporations in other Latin American countries (Stallings 1978, 142), 109 trade and professional associations called a national lockout that lasted for three weeks and brought the country to the point of crisis. Transportation halted, food supplies dwindled, and panic swelled. Six days into the strike, the National Command Center for Gremio Defense (Comando Nacional de Defensa Gremial) was created and charged with the task of summarizing the bourgeoisie's demands. The subsequent list of the "Demands of Chile" (*Pliego de Chile*) called for a reversal of several UP measures such as the takeover of the banking sector and Alessandri's paper company, limitations on agrarian reform, and the elimination of local price control boards. The massive mobilization of workers to defy their employers' attempted lockouts produced sharp class confrontation that was attenuated only when Allende brought the military into his cabinet in November (Campero 1984, 68–73).

In spite of the UP program and Allende's commitments, the government was unable to divide the bourgeoisie and win any appreciable segment of business support. The political homogeneity of the elite was not simply an ontological given.[20] Marveling at the inability of the government to corner some elite support, SOFOFA president Orlando Sáenz, one of the UP's most entrenched opponents and business's more effective organizers, concluded, "Allende managed things so poorly, so poorly that he wasn't able to divide the business sector" (cited in Campero 1984, 58). The coalescence of the bourgeoisie was due to the specific historical features of the case. A history of elite interpenetration at the top and a strong tradition of organizational autonomy laid the groundwork for cooperation, but the Allende regime's pattern of concessions to more radical elements on expropriation decisions, especially of smaller and medium-sized domestic firms, triggered a deepening of elite unity.[21] Although the Allende government had broadened its political base in 1971, it remained a weak, plurality government with limited penetration of the state apparatus. By 1973 the regime's political debilities had combined with a sharp economic contraction and the advent of hyperinflation to further undermine its capacity to govern. The Chilean bourgeoisie fused in its opposition and actively sought to destabilize the regime. This unity prevailed through the military coup of September 1973 into the period of military government.

Fearing that they had no future, and knowing that they could be next, even the small- and medium-sized producers rejected the government. This rejection was skillfully nurtured by larger business leaders and private sector associations who cultivated links to less prominent or politicized producers.[22] Painted in simple terms and appealing to consensual values, the bourgeois opposition deepened the political polarization of the society and fed the military's hostility to the regime—and to the democratic system that had allowed it to come to power.

This analysis suggests that democratic socialist regimes are likely to generate sweeping private sector opposition. Although the bourgeoisie may not be vociferously or uniformly oppositional at the beginning, it will tend to move toward open opposition over time, with the pace and intensity of that movement dictated in part by the pace and intensity of the regime's reform effort. The fissures and internal differentiation of the bourgeoisie will tend to dissipate as the "national" and "nonhegemonic" bourgeoisie increasingly adopts the antireform stance of the more conservative sectors. This move is fueled by a "free" press, in which conservative economic elites can project a virulently antireform message in the name of protecting liberty and individual freedom.[23] Fundamental features of democratic socialism (the close alliance between the state and a powerful working class, ideological hostility to a dominant elite, and the political freedom of opposition groups) make successful courtship of any sector of the business class very difficult for political reformers.

The Habit of Command and the Salvadoran Oligarchy

In the Chilean case, democratic development had withered the traditional social and political power of the elite, and economic diversification had increased the complexity of the bourgeoisie. This heterogeneity and stratification allowed a reform regime to emerge and introduce structural change, at least temporarily. In contrast, in the Salvadoran case the residue of oligarchical power remained relatively undiluted. Reform, in this setting, faced more formidable obstacles and was more readily circumscribed.

The concept of "oligarchy" has been much discussed and debated; it remains somewhat ambiguous. Although the term is frequently used to describe a traditional rentier class, oligarchies that survive into the mid-twentieth century must display some dynamism and capacity for skillful investment. Jiménez (1986, 22–28) defines an oligarchy as an identifiable group of families who possess concentrated economic power, social prestige and authority, and either direct or indirect control over dominant political actors. Oligarchies are typically defined by the transfer of these powers through hereditary means, with family notability dating back at least several generations.[24]

In most of Latin America's larger, economically diversified countries, this kind of concentration of political-economic-social power tended to dissipate in the twentieth century. Traditionally, the oligarchy was grounded on its control of land and the preeminence of agroexport production. With economic diversification, industrial growth, and the expansion of an industrial workforce, these rural elites tended to be displaced from power. The creation of competitive electoral systems with extended suffrage and mass mobilization also undercut the political and social privileges of traditional oligarchs. But if the oligarchical families succeeded in diversifying into varied economic sectors, particularly nodal institutions like the banking system, and if political pluralism was relatively weak, then oligarchical networks could retain considerable influence.

One concrete case of continued oligarchical power can be found in El Salvador following the collapse of the Romero government and the proclamation of a revolutionary junta in 1979.[25] Reform efforts were blocked largely through the work of an oligarchical, antireform elite that remained powerful and well organized even into the 1980s.

Scholarly consensus on El Salvador holds that an oligarchy rooted in coffee production developed in the latter half of the nineteenth century (Baloyra 1982; López Vallecillos 1979; Jiménez 1986; de Sebastián 1986; Colindres 1977). After the bourgeois revolution of 1870, this ascendant elite ruled the country directly for over sixty years, with top political positions circulating among two or three groups, including the Araujo, Meléndez, and Quiñónez Molina families (Baloyra 1982, 5). This group's direct control of government ended following the collapse of the agro-export sector during the depression and the rise of labor militancy, which was triggered by falling wages and a rural male unemployment rate of 40 percent in 1929 (North 1985, 33). Military leaders seized control of the state, and the incipient labor uprising was brutally repressed.[26] In the years that followed (1932–44), General Maximiliano Hernández Martínez governed as a personalistic dictator. The military subsequently governed the country as an institution from 1948 to 1979 by rotating top government offices among ranking military officers.

The passing of direct political control from the elite families to the military signaled a decline of the traditional oligarchy, but this economic elite remained a very potent economic, social, and political force. This powerful coffee-based network was still able to dictate the rules for the economic order and kept issues like agrarian reform off the political agenda.[27] Coffee continued to be the primary export, generating 53 percent of export earnings even as late as the 1975–79 period (Brockett 1990, 60). Key state institutions such as the Central Reserve Bank were run by this elite.[28]

Modest economic diversification [29] did not displace the coffee oligarchy; it remained a vibrant participant in the diversification process. Beginning in the 1880s, coffee wealth had been used to found a private banking system. The Banco Salvadoreño and the Banco Occidental emerged first in the 1880s. In 1934 the government created an additional bank, the Banco Hipotecario, to funnel yet more resources into the agricultural sector, and large producer associations were brought in as major partners.[30]

Profits generated from coffee production were high during much of the postwar period and allowed for the formation of a series of spinoff ventures (Baloyra 1982, 28). In addition to the banking system, coffee oligarchs diversified into the relatively lucrative processing and commercial export sectors. Data from Colindres' (1977) monumental study of the Salvadoran elite show substantial overlap between large coffee producers (those producing over 10,000 quintals in 1970/71) and large coffee exporters (those exporting over 1 percent of total coffee crop in 1974). Furthermore, according to that analysis, the country's 36 largest landowners controlled 66 percent of the capital of the 1,429 largest firms in 1971.[31] The common reference to Salvador's "fourteen families" overstates the case, but there is little debate about the claim of acute concentration of resources in pre-1979 El Salvador.

No economic elite, even one that is fully grounded in a single sector or interpenetrated through family ties, can be entirely homogeneous. Predictably, some segmentation existed within the Salvadoran elite. Salvadoran analysts like López Vallecillos (1979) divide the elite into two sectors: a traditional sector based in coffee production and banking (the "agro-financial sector"), and a sector that had also extended into industrial activities, including coffee processing (the "agro-industrial-financial sector").

Baloyra takes this segmental analysis a step further by separating the "oligarchy," which dominated export agriculture and the banking system, from "the bourgeoisie," which was dominant in industry and commerce. But even Baloyra sees the bourgeoisie as essentially following the lead of the oligarchy, not representing an independent political force. "A bourgeoisie did indeed emerge in El Salvador," he concludes, "but it remained bound to the traditional groups or at least dependent on them for the finance of major projects. The bourgeoisie remained unable to secure the resources necessary to embark on the type of economic projects that would have made it socially and politically hegemonic" (Baloyra 1982, 30).

A sector of middle-sized industrialists, commercial establishments, and agricultural producers did emerge, but this stratum represented a small portion of the strategic sectors of the economy (only 8.9 percent of coffee production, for example), and these producers were not independently organized or powerful.[32] Unlike the Chilean case, where small- and medium-sized elites had long had their own organizations and were courted by contending political parties, these mid-level elites in Salvador were characterized by their lack of effective mobilization. The limited size of the medium sector, the low levels of foreign investment in El Salvador compared with the rest of the Central American region (Bulmer-Thomas 1987, 103), and the organizational weakness of the middle elite meant that established oligarchs remained the hegemonic and largely unchallenged force in the local economy. Accustomed to power, and unaccustomed to negotiation, this elite dominated the social order. A powerful peak association, ANEP,[33] was formed in 1966 to further consolidate and bolster the power of this traditional elite.[34]

Reform moves did come, however, in 1979, in the form of a military putsch that abruptly embraced the reform proposals of a broad coalition of center-left political parties and mass organizations. Jolted into action by the Sandinista revolution in Nicaragua, military reformers founded the Junta Revolucionaria de Gobierno in October 1979 with the participation of political party leaders, intellectuals, and a handful of business elites.[35] Drawing on the recommendations emanating from the Foro Popular, a rally of reformers in September 1979, the new junta adopted a series of initiatives designed to revolutionize the social and economic systems.

The three reforms inaugurated by the government were (1) a major land reform program that was designed to alter fundamentally the land distribution patterns, (2) the nationalization of the banking system, and (3) a state takeover of foreign trade. These reforms precisely targeted the three legs of oligarchical economic power: land, banking, and trade. Recurring and rapid turnover in the governing junta between October 1979 and March 1980 reflected uncertainty about the military's commitment to reform, but by early 1980 changes had been legislated in each of these three areas.

By May 1980, over 300 agricultural estates had been seized, thus completing what is generally known as Phase I of the land reform program.[36] Land affected in this round was 70 percent pastureland; only 12 percent of the coffee crop was produced on these large estates (Reinhardt 1989, 459). From the standpoint of the coffee elite, the second phase of the reform, which was designed to break up estates of 100–150 hectares (depending on land quality) to 500 hectares where the core of coffee cultivation took place, was more threatening. Since Phase II would most affect the traditional coffee oligarchy, that segment of the plan was bitterly resisted. Phase III was a land-to-the-tiller program that would allow peasants renting small plots (up to 7 hectares) to claim that land for themselves.

The goals of this reform were exceptionally ambitious. If implemented as designed, the program was to redistribute roughly 48 percent of agricultural land to approximately 50 percent of Salvador's rural poor (Reinhardt 1989, 459–60).[37] Resistance and complications soon took a toll, however. Phase II was annulled by the dominant center-right coalition in the first legislative session of the Constituent Assembly elected in March 1982. The following year, the constitution of 1983 provided more durable protection to this sector by raising the land size threshold and delaying implementation for two years, during which time owners could reduce the size of their holdings to avoid expropriation. In the end, this part of the plan was never implemented.

The regime was slow to regularize land reform titles, and war and terror in the countryside undermined Phases I and III of the process. Beneficiaries of the land reform sometimes abandoned their land and their claims, terrorized into leaving by death squads and military threats.[38] Few beneficiaries could pay for the land they had received, so unmanageable debts burdened the participants.[39]

Ultimately, the program did allocate approximately 20 percent of the arable land to around 20 percent of the rural labor force (Strasma 1990, 5, 14–15). In comparative terms, the Salvadoran reform falls roughly in the middle of Latin American agrarian reform outcomes in the portion of land and of rural population affected, distributing more, for example, than Ecuador but less than Mexico and Peru (Thiesenhusen 1989, 10–11). The fact that most coffee land was sealed off from expropriation and that the program fell far short of its initial goals, however, suggests that traditional elites remained powerful enough to resist incursions into their domain.

From the standpoint of the traditional elite, the other two reforms were probably more damaging. In March 1980 the banks were surrounded by military vehicles, and eleven financial institutions were nationalized.[40]

Private sector representation on the board of directors of the Central Bank was also decreased from 3 of 8 members to 1 of 7 after the reform (Ramírez Arango 1985, 158).

But nationalization did not mean that the old structure was transformed. Two issues are relevant here: the compensation paid to former owners, and credit priorities of the bank following nationalization. First, to placate former owners, generous compensation was provided. In almost all banks, former owners received substantially more than the real value of their shares as determined by the evaluation commission.[41] Second, bank control and credit distribution became, if anything, yet more concentrated than they had been before the reform (Valdés 1989). Bank workers could not afford to buy into the system; they acquired no more than 10 percent of the stock, and the state retained virtually all of the remainder. Central Reserve Bank lending went heavily to the public sector (more than 60 percent of the total in 1982–85), and those private operations that received loans tended to be the large ones (Valdés 1989, 795–97).[42] The coffee sector actually increased the portion of agricultural credit that it had absorbed (from 51 percent of the total in 1979 to 65 percent in 1984) (Valdés 1989, 802). The economy still revolved heavily around coffee, and the banking system continued to reflect that reality.

For most of the traditional economic elite, the worst blow came with the nationalization of export trade. INCAFE was established in December 1979; this was followed in May 1980 with the creation of the Instituto Nacional del Azúcar. Between them, these two state trade monopolies controlled 58 percent of foreign trade in the 1980–83 period (Orellana 1985, 20). Under the new rules, coffee producers were now to be paid only in local currency at prices fixed by the state.[43] Profits were still to be made by producers with medium to high levels of efficiency, but the gap between international prices and the price paid locally by INCAFE provoked a steady denunciation by *cafetaleros* who felt victimized and maligned by the regime.[44] One member of the coffee elite reported to a North American academic, "When coffee reached $200 per *quintal*, Duarte said that was too much money. . . . He said we would just spend it on cars" (Paige 1993, 19). With producers earning less than half the FOB price in 1986, INCAFE and the Christian Democratic government became a prime target for elite hostility.

The disaffection of coffee producers and their unwillingness to keep up investments contributed to the rapid spread of coffee rust and the decline in coffee yields. By the end of the decade, this drop-off was exacerbated by the collapse of the international coffee organization and the subsequent fall in coffee prices. The coffee harvest in 1988–89 had dropped to one-third what it had been a decade before (Barry 1990, 80).[45] The coffee decline fed into the overall erosion of the Salvadoran economy. With stagnant public investment, little private investment, and droning warfare, the per capita gross domestic product declined 15.2 percent in the 1981–90 period (CEPAL 1990b, 26).

Confronting this decline was a weak reform regime. The 1979 reform movement was quickly curtailed by military countermoves and electoral defeat in 1982. The private sector peak association, ANEP, mobilized to take advantage of the frailty of the reform movement.[46] By mid-1980 this organization had not only reestablished bonds with sectors of the armed forces but had sponsored the creation of the Alianza Productiva, a politically charged private sector association composed of ANEP and several of its affiliates, two small business associations, and two associations of professionals and managers. This new organization formed a bridge between the private sector and ARENA, a right-wing political party founded in 1981. Only major pressure from the Carter and Reagan administrations, who supported these policy changes as a means of avoiding leftist revolution, prevented the edifice of reform from crumbling in 1982 when ARENA and the conservative Partido de Conciliación Nacional secured thirty-three of the sixty seats in the new Constituent Assembly. ARENA leader Roberto D'Aubuisson became president of the assembly and narrowly missed being named the provisional president of the country.

The Christian Democrat party and its perennial leader José Napoleón Duarte did not attain the presidency until 1984 or gain a legislative majority until 1985. Reformers had a precarious hold over the state apparatus and none over the military. Confronted by an economic elite that still had considerable wealth, organizational capabilities, traditional authority, and an enormous capacity for violence, the reform agenda could not be sustained. Unable to create a strong political party or to mobilize an array of mass organizations, preempted from the left and vilified from the right, reformers failed.

Right-wing legislative victory in 1988, in which ARENA secured an absolute majority in the national assembly, was a prelude to easy presidential victory the following year. With a 55 percent turnout rate, ARENA got 54 percent of the vote; under the mantle of recent ARENA affiliate Alfredo Cristiani, economic elites regained center stage. Cristiani, a political novice but former president of the Association of Processors and Exporters of Coffee, incorporated other prominent business leaders into the new government.[47] In addition to the presidency, ARENA dominated the legislature, nearly 70 percent of the mayoralties, and the court system (Miles and Ostertag 1989). Forced by the changing rules of the 1980s to play an electoral game in order to secure political power, the traditional elites funneled resources into the right-wing party and proved to be skillful strategists.

A reform movement that had been deflected for several years was now derailed. After its victory, the ARENA government moved to reverse several key reforms. A supreme court decision in 1989 had declared INCAFE to be an unconstitutional monopoly, and this program was replaced by a modest supervisory board, the Salvadoran Coffee Council. Unlike its predecessor, the coffee council did not determine prices. Former private export companies reestablished their operations, and prices were now set by the international market. The banking system was targeted for speedy privatization (although bank insolvency complicated the process); agrarian reform was formally halted, and previous land grants were decollectivized (Martínez 1989). ARENA's ideology, which combined an assertive nationalism with a commitment to neoliberal economics, promised to counter lingering reform sentiment. Having demonstrated its considerable skill in playing by the rules of electoral democracy, the elite now pushed to restrain reform through the democratic route.[48]

Structural change and redistribution in El Salvador during the reform era was not as profound as in Allende's Chile. Without an organized working class or ideologically coherent and highly mobilized leftist parties, the reform movement in El Salvador remained narrowly delimited and modest. But the Salvadoran elite reacted with perhaps even greater ferocity to the reform, not only conspiring with the military but financing its own death squads to annihilate opponents. The Salvadoran opposition was due less to the threat of unstanched expropriation of even small- and medium-sized firms, which proved so significant in Chile, and more to the continued clout of a relatively unreconstructed oligarchy. The reform movement, which succeeded in electing Duarte to the presidency only in 1984 and which had lost power by 1988, was even weaker in Salvador than in Chile, and provided little incentive for cooperation by business leaders. Furthermore, a sharp economic erosion that began immediately after the reform was launched in El Salvador fed further elite disdain and disillusionment.[49] Although the combination of factors differed somewhat in each case, in both El Salvador and Chile the bourgeoisie coalesced quickly in opposition to reform and contributed forcefully to its overthrow.[50]

Accommodation to Reform

Symbiotic Interdependence and Silent Partners in Mexico

The bourgeoisie is not always able to coordinate sweeping opposition to reform. Indeed, in several Latin American cases, revolutionary regimes not only deflected an elite opposition movement but won a segment of elite backers. The ability of a revolutionary government to gain overt bourgeois supporters, in spite of its commitment to agrarian reform, state expansion, and redistribution, is an anomalous process that deserves close analysis. It has been most evident in Latin America during periods of revolutionary populism.

Populism is a rich and contradictory ideology that emphasizes controlled mobilization of marginal groups under the leadership of an activist state. This dynamic is typically fostered by a multiclass coalition dominated by emerging middle-class forces that have a commitment to nationalism, economic growth, and a degree of redistribution. In Latin America, this model has generally been found to emerge during the "Bonapartist interlude," a period after traditional oligarchic power has been checked but before new industrial elites have consolidated their own power base (Ianni 1975, 53–54). During this phase, the state is said to attain a relative autonomy that allows it to act independently of, and even at times in opposition to, the preferences of economic elites. The state pursues either the long-term interests of capitalist development, which may not be apparent to the local bourgeoisie at the moment, or its own specific interests (Hamilton 1982, 4–25; Skocpol 1979).

During episodes when the traditional elite struggles with economic collapse or the devastation of war, the populist state can mobilize new class actors to replace it. State support is provided for priority sectors such as manufacturing, production for the domestic market, or high employment industries, and the economic elite is recomposed along those lines. The surging nationalism of the populist project generally pushes the state to check the power of foreign capital. The resulting nationalizations or expulsions of foreign firms serve the populist cause by expanding the resources and economic leverage of the state when the state acquires expropriated concerns, or by strengthening domestic producers as local businesses move into the space created by the removal of foreign operations.

Populist movements are not identical; some involve much stronger mass mobilization and higher degrees of state autonomy than others.[51] Most populist projects have ended in collapse, due to fiscal crisis and financial dependency, internal division within the state, the inability to consolidate a mass base, or a series of conjunctural factors (O'Donnell 1973; Stepan 1978, 282–316; Dornbusch and Edwards 1991). In some cases, like Argentina, military coups or countercoups signaled the demise of populism; in others, like Mexico, antipopulist forces penetrated the state, leaving populist and antipopulist forces in an uneasy cohabitation.

In the Mexican case, the old Porfirian elite of landowners, industrialists, and foreigners who had come to dominate the state in the last decade of Porfirio Díaz's presidency were thrown into decline with the departure of their leader and the following seven years of civil war (1911–17). Economic elites were not eliminated, but they lost wealth through expropriations, evictions, vandalism, and depreciation.[52] In the wake of the violence, a new elite emerged. The tattered remnants of the old bourgeoisie were joined by revolutionary chieftains who had appropriated land and capital.[53]

State-sponsored change, which had sparked and fizzled in the 1920s, began in earnest when the revolutionary coalition elected Lázaro Cárdenas to the presidency in 1934. Using legislation that limited estate size to the equivalent of 150 irrigated hectares, Cárdenas expropriated vast tracts of land.[54] Unlike many agrarian reform programs, these expropriations included land of good quality held by prominent local and foreign elites. By 1940, 47.4 percent of all cultivated land and 57.3 percent of all irrigated land had been allocated to *ejidos* (Hamilton 1982, 177).[55] Cárdenas also undercut the urban elite by rechanneling resources to labor. Real wages soared as the regime promoted strikes and legislative protections for workers.[56] The state-sponsored mass organizations, the Mexican Labor Federation (Confederación de Trabajadores de México) and the National Peasant Federation (Confederación Nacional de Campesinos) linked the popular sectors to the regime.[57]

Business elites were predictably alarmed. Producers, particularly in regional strongholds like Monterrey, retaliated and threatened lockouts in protest. Going into the lion's den, Cárdenas addressed the Employers' Center of Monterrey in February 1936, chastising business leaders for their hostility to reform. He announced: "Entrepreneurs who feel fatigued by the social struggle can turn over their industries to the workers or the government. That would be patriotic, the lockout would not."[58] In the wake of rising strikes and presidential criticism, capital flight accelerated.[59]

In spite of rhetorical clashes and state expansion, Cárdenas was hardly a simple opponent of business. The top-down developmentalists of the revolutionary government looked for ways to incorporate business into their new growth strategy. The national bourgeoisie benefited repeatedly from legislation and policy that edged out foreigners. The state itself expanded, as with the nationalization of the petroleum sector, but so did Mexican capitalists. Legislation requiring insurance companies to invest their reserve in Mexico, for example, triggered the departure of foreign-owned companies that were replaced by both state insurance companies and a rapidly mushrooming number of locally owned insurance businesses (Hamilton 1982, 205). The revolutionary populist state undercut old, inefficient businesses or those that seemed not to favor Mexican national development, and warmly embraced others that contributed to national growth.

The industrial sector was especially favored by state resources and assistance in the form of tax incentives and investment loans. Special attention was provided to small and medium industries, which flourished during this era. Given a range of supports, including tax exemptions, subsidies, investments, reduced rates for rail transportation of their cargo, and the elimination of some agricultural intermediaries, small- and medium-sized producers expanded. The number of manufacturing firms (not including artisan workshops) in the country increased from 6,916 in 1935 to 13,150 in 1940, and most of the new enterprises were small (employing on average only ten workers) (Hamilton 1982, 201–2; Mosk 1954, 316). During the 1934–38 period, the gross national product grew by 22 percent, particularly in the industrial sector, which increased 33 percent (NAFINSA 1978, 19, 24).

Seeking to consolidate a state-business alliance, Cárdenas built bridges into the business heartland. As long as it did not rebel, the bourgeoisie would be showered with praise and support. By 1939, in a speech given before the Cámara de Comercio of Saltillo, Coahuila, Cárdenas had altered his tone. He now proclaimed, "I consider your cooperation very valuable; I hold your knowledge, experience and entrepreneurial spirit in esteem; I conceive of you as a prominent factor in our progress and as promoters of our homeland's culture" (quoted in Medina 1974, 278).[60]

To enhance its penetration of a rapidly growing business sector, the state redefined the organizational infrastructure of business. Prior to the revolution, business organizations tended to be fragmented and dispersed. Reflecting the strong regional tendencies and fractured nature of the economy, these organizations operated only at the local level and had not merged into broader national federations.

Following a series of meetings with industrialists and merchants in 1917, the Mexican state attempted to facilitate steady but controlled communication with the private elite by creating two new associations—the National Federation of Chambers of Commerce (CONCANACO) and the Federation of Chambers of Industry (CONCAMIN). During the Cárdenas era these organizations were merged into a single unit and strengthened through the requirement of mandatory membership.[61] Another round of institution building occurred in 1941 with the founding of the National Chamber of Manufacturing Industry (CANACINTRA, sometimes referred to as CNIT), an association explicitly designed to serve the needs of small- and medium-sized industries that were emerging under the protection of the Mexican state.[62]

Given the requirement of participation in these organizations, few business leaders went beyond them to form associations of their own creation. One of the rare exceptions was the Mexican Republic Employers' Federation (COPARMEX), a forceful, antistate organization that dates back to the divisive 1928 debate about the Labor Code. Even this independent offshoot posed little threat to the regime. For several decades COPARMEX remained essentially a regional, Monterrey-based organization; it failed to develop a broad national base and could not compete organizationally with the larger, state-sponsored federations.[63]

Through its influence over the major private sector organizations, selective distribution of resources, state investment funds, licenses, and tax exemptions, the state incorporated the bourgeoisie as a silent partner in a state-sponsored development initiative. Mexican businesspeople were notoriously withdrawn from public political life, even to the point of eschewing party membership.[64] Because of the revolution's formal commitment to the masses and marginal groups, public alliances between the regime and economic elites would have been uncomfortable for both. Instead, linkages between the state and the bourgeoisie were generally informal and tacit rather than highly visible and overt. Through participation in state-created business associations, sectoral leaders, who tended to be drawn heavily from the largest firms and industrial groups, obtained representation on a host of government boards and agencies.[65] In turn, they refrained from organizing independently and implicitly supported the line of the political leadership.

The entrepreneur who was savvy enough to cut through the socialist rhetoric and seek contacts with political elites often flourished. Whether the fictional Artemio Cruz of Carlos Fuentes's invention, or the pseudonymous Pablo Gómez described so deftly by Larissa Adler Lomnitz and Marisol Pérez-Lizaur (1987, 37–38, 61–63), entrepreneurs who energetically sought investment opportunities and political alliances with the revolutionary regime could expand rapidly during this period of historic economic growth.[66]

This complex political configuration endured through the subsequent decades. In a study of the recent relationship between the government and business associations, Luna et al. (1987, 19–21) found that the twelve major private sector organizations in Mexico ranged along a five-point continuum from those that gave unconditional support to the government (like the National Federation of Small Property Owners) to those that made fundamental criticisms of both the political and economic systems (like COPARMEX). Most organizations ranked somewhere in between, with some, like CANACINTRA, generally endorsing the government line and pushing to have business organizations formally integrated into the PRI party apparatus. CANACINTRA became a durable base of support for government initiatives, backing legislation that recognized the state as the regulator of the economy in 1950, the nationalization of the electrical industry in 1960, restrictions on foreign investment in 1973, the government's decision to stay out of the General Agreement on Tariffs and Trade in 1980, and even the nationalization of the banks in 1982 (Alcázar 1970, 120–21; Arriola 1976, 45; Basáñez 1990, 124–25; Maxfield 1987, 4). Other organizations, like CONCAMIN, called for a gradual reduction in the economic roles of the state and increased business autonomy, but generally cooperated with the regime.

This factionalism is in part related to the overall size and complexity of the Mexican economy. Regional economic differences were marked and played a role in the internal differentiation of the business elite. For example, the Monterrey group, developing prior to the revolution and, in the case of steel, in competition with parastate enterprises, was quite independent from and often critical of the government.[67] Private elites clustered in the capital city, on the other hand, were slower to confront the regime.

Unlike in Chile and El Salvador, where traditional elites remained more autonomous and mustered broad opposition to the state, business hostility was undercut by state organizational intervention in Mexico. Through the distribution of investment, credit, subsidies, and protection, the state helped to create certain economic sectors and groups. These groups were dependent on the regime and had difficulty organizing autonomously around class needs or interests. Although expanded state roles and recurring expropriations caused consternation in some sectors, alliances and understandings forged in the aftermath of the revolution continued to facilitate cooperation and communication with others.

The Mexican regime was also exceptional in its ability to maintain economic growth, even during the period of most intense social transformation. Continually expanding economic resources made it possible to avoid a zero-sum situation in which increased assets for the state or popular sectors meant reduced resources for capital. Growth allowed for multiple beneficiaries; even those who did not benefit directly could console themselves with the prospect of future gain. The result was what has been called a "symbiotic relationship" between the state and key segments of the private sector (Camp 1989, 250–52). State stability since the 1940s has been premised on the prosperity of business; business leaders in turn have relied on the support and stability provided by PRI dominance. In sum, the Mexican state has a complex, variegated relationship with a fragmented bourgeoisie based on the assumption of shared benefit and the persistence of mutual need, even as periodic conflicts have erupted.

Private Sector Alliances in Revolutionary Peru

The Peruvian experience with revolutionary populism did not produce an enduring alliance with the bourgeoisie like that found in Mexico, but it did drive a wedge into the elite and win support in some capitalist quarters.[68] Like the Mexican case, the reform effort in Peru signaled the demise of the traditional oligarchy. Seizing control of the state, the Peruvian military launched a large-scale agrarian reform program that effectively abolished the large landowning class. Rural estates were limited by Supreme Decree #265-70-AG to a maximum of 150 hectares of irrigated land on the coast and a modest 15–55 hectares of irrigated land (depending on the province) in the highland or high-jungle region.[69] As a result, roughly 35 percent of Peru's agricultural land was transferred into the reformed sector by 1977, benefiting around 24 percent of Peru's rural families (McClintock 1981, 62).[70]

The remainder of the bourgeoisie did not rush to defend the collapsing rural oligarchy, which was "a class in the process of deteriorating" (Castillo Ochoa 1988, 195; see also Bourricaud 1966). The economic center of gravity was already shifting toward the industrial sector in Peru, and military president Juan Velasco Alvarado (1968–75) targeted the latter for special support. Some large landowners from the coast (what Gilbert

[1980] calls the "metropolitan oligarchy"] had relaxed their links to the land and diversified assets into mining, urban real estate, banking, and manufacturing.[71] Most industrialists, however, were not from oligarchical families but from a new class of relatively recent immigrant extraction.[72] Because the traditional elite had already been displaced from the economic center in Peru, agrarian reform did not produce the same tooth-and-nail resistance among the bourgeoisie that it precipitated in El Salvador.

To encourage private investment in the industrial sector, the military authorized the redemption of bonds given in payment for expropriated land at 100 percent of their face value to ex-landowners who would invest those payments in new industrial enterprises. A few landowners, like those in the Grupo Romero, used them to transfer resources into new industrial operations.[73] Tariffs on imported manufactured products also helped stimulate industrial growth, particularly in household goods. The primary growth areas of the economy during the Velasco era were manufacturing and construction (FitzGerald 1976, 63, table 35; Malpica Silva Santisteban 1989, 48).

To prevent a rupture in the relationship with emerging domestic capitalists, Velasco attempted to shift much of the burden for financing this transformation onto foreign-owned operations. The revolution was to be financed through what Becker (1983, 61–71) has called the "bonanza development" approach. In this model, the state would derive resources from the foreign-dominated large-mining sector, particularly that involved in the extraction of copper. These funds were to be spent on large-scale state investments including an oil pipeline, irrigation facilities, and turnkey projects in refining, chemical fertilizer, and fish processing.[74] By 1974, the state controlled 26 percent of the GNP and over 40 percent of production in the modern sector (FitzGerald 1976, 36). To achieve this state-led growth, some sectors of foreign capital were expropriated. Those that remained were required to adopt a profit-sharing scheme that would ultimately apportion 50 percent of the stock in their companies to industrial communities representing the workforce in their firm.[75]

As in the Mexican case, the Peruvian regime was able to undercut the traditional landholding elite and cultivate ties with segments of the bourgeoisie that benefited from the new, nationalist development scheme. The National Society of Industries (SNI) initially found common cause with the regime and was "cautiously cooperating" (Becker 1983, 258). This cooperation reached its peak in the late 1960s and early 1970s when the SNI was dominated by executives from the larger, more modern firms. Contradicting standard theory about the receptivity of small, domestic capital to populist reforms, it was the larger industrialists who were relatively open to reform in the Peruvian case. When questioned in a 1968–69 survey, for example, industrialists in multinational subsidiaries and large Peruvian consortia were more likely than their smaller counterparts to note the existence of structural problems in the economy and approve of a more dynamic role for the state (Wils 1975, 170). Building on that predisposition, a complex and sputtering understanding emerged between some of the larger industrialists and the revolutionary regime.

Bamat's (1978) close study of the Peruvian capitalist elite located several business sectors that participated in affirmative negotiations with the state. These included the association of exporters, ADEX (founded in 1973 by the large enterprise leaders from the SNI who had sought more active cooperation with the regime), which benefited from the government's active promotion of exports; the National Chamber of Commerce, which benefited from an expanding internal market and was exempt from the profit and stock sharing requirement imposed on industry; the Mining Society, which was buoyed by the massive foreign investment deal arranged by the state for southern Peru's Cuajone project[76]; and the Peruvian Institute of Business Administration, which sponsored an annual conference of executives (CADE) that drew together a number of managers, executives, industrialists, and bankers who provided support for some reforms (Bamat 1978, 212–19; see also Becker 1983, 271–72; Wils 1975, 210).[77] To "reinforce the sensible elements" in the regime, private sector leaders like Pedro Reiser, former president of the National Chamber of Commerce, served as government advisers and appointees in key economic agencies and provided a selective defense of government policies (Bamat 1978, 216).

On the other hand, many industrialists who were not in the top elite were historically skeptical of state economic interventions and resented the new rules. The regime dealt forcefully with these business critics. The National Agrarian Society, an old, elite organization that had represented the traditional oligarchy, was simply dissolved in 1972, and its assets were seized by the state. It was replaced by a state-created peasant federation, the National Agrarian Confederation, which was emphatically pro-Velasco. After several of the larger, more modern industrialists channeled their energies into the formation of ADEX, small- and medium-sized industrialists became more prominent in the SNI leadership, and the SNI became the leading critic of the military's project (Bamat 1978, 192–219;

Becker 1983, 258). The requirement of stock allocation to workers generated some harsh disputes at both the firm and the national level, and the SNI led the charge. In response, the military flexed its muscles and withdrew legal recognition of the association. As tensions built, the regime forced changes in the SNI, requiring, for example, that workers be included in its national directorate and that it change its name.[78]

As in Chile and Salvador, some disgruntled private sector leaders attempted to organize a cross-class response to the revolution. For example, two movements to create a peak association that would allow economic elites to mount a collective front in opposition to the regime were launched. Unlike the Chilean and Salvadoran cases, however, both failed in Peru.[79] Throughout the revolution, the private sector in Peru continued to be divided into more than a dozen different national organizations (Durand 1988b, 275). The regime's ability to divide and rule by playing exporters, for example, against small industrialists allowed it to prevent the consolidation of a united bourgeois front.

As in Mexico, this fragmentation is due in part to the collapse of the traditional oligarchy and the economic and ideological weakness of the emerging industrial-commercial elite that replaced it. Stratified into layers that had different needs and organizational styles, divided into sectors with often competing interests, and played against each other by regime policies that favored some over others, the Peruvian bourgeoisie was unable to form a political consensus about its relationship with the state.[80]

Also as in Mexico, economic reform was accompanied by economic growth in Peru. The gross domestic product increased by over 5 percent per year between 1970 and 1974, and by 4 percent in 1975 (McClintock 1981, 60). Continued growth both reflected and contributed to a less extreme elite opposition, at least as compared with that found in Chile and El Salvador. In spite of this success, economic and political problems eventually erupted for the regime. The rapid economic growth of the 1970–75 period subsequently dropped off, and economic performance slowed. Growth was increasingly dependent on the state sector, and the state sector was increasingly dependent on foreign financing (Stepan 1978, 284, table 7.4; FitzGerald 1979, 164).[81] Unlike in Mexico, where the expansion of the state sector proceeded gradually over the course of several decades, state enterprises expanded rapidly in Peru into industries that needed massive investments, leaving a heavier financial burden for the state to assume. Increased financial dependency made the regime highly vulnerable to external forces. By 1976 this dependency gave foreign banks and the IMF considerable influence over the model and ultimately contributed to the erosion of the revolutionary project (Stallings 1979, 242–48).[82] In contrast, during the crucial period when the Mexican revolution was consolidated, state expansion could be managed by internal borrowing. This buffered Mexican populism somewhat from foreign influences.

Operating in a relative institutional vacuum after the 1911–17 revolution, the Mexican leadership was also freer to fill the landscape with organizations of its creation. Whereas most of the private sector organizations in Mexico were established by the state, the Peruvian military confronted an array of existing associations, many of which became regime opponents. The Peruvian regime focused its energies on taming or dissolving relatively autonomous organizations. It failed to institutionalize a network of business support; it even failed to institutionalize a network of support among peasants and labor, the purported beneficiaries of the revolution. For these and other reasons, the Peruvian revolutionary regime proved less durable than that of Mexico (Stepan 1978, 304–11).

In spite of these differences, there are certain notable similarities in these two cases. In neither did the bourgeoisie as a class publicly revolt against the regime; instead, segments of this elite operated in tandem with the revolutionary project.[83] Neither had, as we found in the Chilean and Salvadoran cases, a strong, well-organized bourgeoisie capable of coordinating cohesive resistance to reform. Both of these regimes were capable of targeting sectors of the economic elite that would be incorporated into the new development model. Because of these characteristics, these regimes could, under certain circumstances, secure a cooperative relationship with key sectors of the bourgeoisie and maintain growth, even as the government attempted to restructure the social order and reallocate resources. Ultimately, this state-bourgeoisie alliance restricted the degree to which the society could be transformed; it also made some degree of transformation possible.[84]

Conclusions

There is a strong tendency for the bourgeoisie to reject revolutionary or strongly reformist regimes. The pattern of opposition, however, is not uniform. It varies in two key ways. First, differences may be observed in the breadth of private sector hostility. In some cases, like Chile and El Salvador, this opposition was sweeping and included even nonhegemonic, middle-sized businesses. In others, like Mexico and Peru, opposition was concentrated in pockets of the elite. Many business organizations stayed out of the fray; some even aligned with the regime.

The second variation is found in the depth or intensity of the opposition. Reform regimes are likely to generate resistance from those who benefit most from the status quo, but the degree of hostility ranges from spirited grumbling to concerted sabotage. In Chile and El Salvador, business organizations actively conspired with paramilitary and military groups for the overthrow of the regime. They organized a formidable campaign against the government in the press to mobilize hostility and fear, rejecting the regime's feeble attempts at dialogue. Elite opposition in Mexico and Peru never reached this level. Emphasis in the latter cases was placed on economic measures, like an investment slowdown and capital flight, which could in some measure be compensated for by a speedup in government investment.

The degree of hostility evoked depends much on the character of the bourgeoisie, the nature of the reform regime, the resources held by popular sectors, and the state's ability to institutionalize its authority as a hegemonic actor. These characteristics will be analyzed more systematically in the concluding chapter of this book. Overall, however, we can identify five kinds of variations that seem to shape the unity/division of the bourgeoisie.

First, when a traditional oligarchy remains dominant and other business leaders are predisposed to follow its lead, economic elites tend to become intransigent, implacable foes of reform; conversely, when the power of the traditional oligarchy has been ruptured, there is a greater tendency toward political fragmentation and sectoral accommodation.

Second, business elites who have succeeded in establishing a dense network of elite associations prior to the reform era may be relatively forceful critics, inured from state cooptive strategies; those that are weakly organized or whose organizations depend heavily on state resources, on the other hand, are more easily drawn into an alliance with the regime.

Third, not all of these regimes were perceived as equally threatening. Those that expropriate widely, concentrating on domestic firms, and blast the bourgeoisie with class-laced rhetoric tend to trigger fuller opposition than those that focus on the nationalization of foreign holdings and employ more inclusionary communication strategies.

Fourth, the regime's success in consolidating a new order also affected state-business relations. Weakly institutionalized regimes with fragile electoral bases and little control over key state agencies (such as the military, the courts, the legislature) invite strident opposition in the hope of triggering regime collapse; well-consolidated regimes, on the other hand, elicit begrudging dialogue from business elites who see no obvious alternative.

Finally, the performance of the economy both responds to and shapes the response of the local elites. If the economy declines precipitously and inflation reels out of control, this may propel the business sector into opposition; if the government can keep the economy from collapsing and develop a model that is perceived as viable, if not ideal, then it may be able to coax out private sector acquiescence to the new order.

The most recent revolution in the region, that in Nicaragua, blends together a complex pattern of elite confrontation and accommodation. Unlike the elite in neighboring El Salvador, the business community in Nicaragua lacked an oligarchical center. The Nicaraguan elite developed its political capabilities only relatively recently, and sectoral, regional, and strata distinctions pulled it in contradictory directions. Unlike that in Chile, the Nicaraguan bourgeoisie lacked a strong tradition of independent organization at the national level, making it more susceptible to manipulation by the state. Although the bourgeois opposition rallied under the COSEP banner, this class was never well fused; both the Somoza and the Sandinista regimes' policies and organizational efforts succeeded in peeling off some elites and drawing others into sustained negotiation.

Threats to property and social status did promote unity within the Nicaraguan bourgeoisie during the revolution, since domestic producers were targeted and, as in Chile, succeeding waves of expropriations suggested no clear boundaries to the process. This cohesion diminished, however, when the post-1988 deradicalization of the revolution opened further avenues of negotiation with the bourgeoisie. By the end of the era, the Sandinistas were actively courting elites, using language and symbols that paralleled those used in Mexico and Peru, to the dismay of grassroots revolutionaries.

During the decade of the revolution, the Sandinistas were particularly successful in the realm of political institutionalization. Much like the Mexican regime, the FSLN's ability to build a broad mass base, produce sweeping electoral victories, and consolidate control over all vital state institutions fostered elite acquiescence. However, Nicaragua's unprecedented rate of economic decline during the 1980s seriously undermined the credibility of the revolution from the standpoint of the business elite.

Economic deterioration eventually even eroded the regime's mass base. This decline encouraged elite opposition and helped bring the revolutionary period to a close.

The next five chapters detail these shifting relations between the bourgeoisie and the state in Nicaragua, probing for underlying characteristics that have shaped this dynamic. The concluding chapter weaves the Nicaraguan case into the discussion of the four cases described above to refocus on the comparative dimension.

chapter 2

From Elite Quiescence to Elite Confrontation in Prerevolutionary Nicaragua

Up to the present time, domestic private enterprise has, with few exceptions, done relatively little to develop the country's productive capacity. . . . Private enterprise . . . has often been unimaginative and unduly cautious. It has been too prone to seek either the safe investment or a quick return.

—IBRD, *The Economic Development of Nicaragua*

It was a weak agroexport bourgeoisie whose ability to put itself at the head of the nation as a social class was brutally cut off by the years of North American intervention. From 1912 to 1933, that intervention not only took over the management and control of the most important mechanisms of the emerging agricultural and mining economy, but it took away the sense of nationhood from this mentally impoverished and little educated class. This class lost the historic opportunity to consolidate itself as a national bourgeoisie.

—Sergio Ramírez Mercado,
"Los sobrevivientes del naufragio"

COMPARED with capitalists in the rest of Latin America, the Nicaraguan private elite was long characterized by its weak entrepreneurship, organizational fragmentation, and political incompetence. Although this elite was small in number, its modest proportions did not ensure political affinity or coherent organization. The Nicaraguan bourgeoisie was both heterogeneous and regionally divided, suggesting that the political organization of the bourgeoisie may respond more to historical rivalries and sectoral fissures than to the size of the national economy.

Unlike El Salvador or Peru, Nicaragua never experienced a long, unrelieved period of oligarchical rule, which might have sedimented the political authority of a branch of the bourgeoisie. Unlike Chile, it lacked a durable experience with political pluralism, which might have sparked the broad and spontaneous organization of private sector elites. Instead, the private sector organizations that sprang up in Nicaragua tended to have limited scope and little authority; they rose and fell rapidly. As in Mexico, the more durable organizations were generally those that received the favor of the regime and were given special representational status within state agencies. Fractured into a series of discrete organizations and manipulated with discretionary rewards provided by the state, the Nicaraguan elite remained politically ineffective through much of the prerevolutionary era.

By the early 1970s, however, this splintering was attenuated, and the private elite made a bid for greater political influence. Nicaraguan representatives from an array of regional and sectoral business organizations formed their first broad, national peak association in 1972. This new organization began to push for a reformulation of the character of the state and the national development model.

In spite of its growing organizational capacity, the Nicaraguan private sector was unable to emerge as the hegemonic force in the campaign to overthrow the Somoza regime. It did learn, by the end of the era, to employ collectivist strategies in high stakes confrontations with the regime, but it was swept aside by the rising momentum of a revolutionary movement under the FSLN.

The Development of the Nicaraguan Bourgeoisie

The Nicaraguan bourgeoisie historically was poor. Travel testimonials of the mid-1800s note the uncertainty of economic life in Nicaragua and the modest standard of living of its elite. Commenting on conditions in Nicaragua, historical chronicler Paul Levy concluded: "This society has one fundamental problem: it is poor" (cited in Burns 1991, 83).

Local notable families emerged, some of whom traced their family history to the *conquistadores* (Stone 1990). The ready availability of land in this lightly populated country, combined with the weakness of the state, however, allowed much of the local population to continue subsistence production, often on communal lands, instead of serving as a labor force on the estates of the elite (Burns 1991, 138–39, 235). The scarce and relatively expensive labor supply, along with the constant warfare of the postindependence period, retarded the process of accumulation.

What surplus there was in the nineteenth century evaporated in regional warfare between the Conservatives of Granada and the Liberals of

León. Competing for political control in interminable internecine feuding, the Liberals brought in U.S. filibuster William Walker, whose seizure of the Nicaraguan presidency led to intervention by neighboring countries. In the words of President Tomás Martínez, who took office in 1858 as the smoke cleared following the "Walker War": "Our fields lie bleached by the ashes of our dead; our cities lie ruined, a reminder for many years to come of the horrors wrought by foreign invaders; even now, agriculture and commerce remain paralyzed as a consequence of a recent Costa Rican invasion; the public treasury is empty; private property is destroyed; the schools remain closed. Such is the present picture, sad as it may be, of Nicaragua" (cited in Burns 1991, 223).

This economic morass began to lift with the advent of coffee. In part because of the Liberal-Conservative warfare, Nicaragua was slower to initiate coffee production than neighboring countries like Costa Rica. By the 1850s, however, the visibility of the Costa Rican success prompted Nicaraguan state efforts to push coffee cultivation.[1] President Martínez approved a package of incentives to *cafetaleros* in 1858 and the Law for Uncultivated Lands was adopted in 1859. The benefits offered to coffee growers included exemption from military service (for producers and workers for twelve years as long as peace prevailed), tax exemption on coffee earnings, exemption of import duties on agricultural machinery, the provision of inputs (seeds, plants) at cost, and subsidies for planting new crops. A port was built at Corinto in 1859 to handle increased exports (Burns 1991, 233).

To attract immigrants and open new lands, the government provided 500 mz. of land to those who would plant 25,000 *cafetos* and maintain them until they could be harvested.[2] The erosion of communal lands was accelerated, both to provide land for the new export crop and to reduce the economic alternatives available to peasants. The Liberal administration of José Santos Zelaya (1893–1909) deepened the country's commitment to coffee production by sharpening the antivagrancy laws passed in the 1840s and 1850s to increase the available labor supply and by expanding the transportation infrastructure (Barahona 1989, 15–18).

In spite of these trends, Nicaraguan elites were never fully entrenched in coffee cultivation. Whereas the Salvadoran coffee elite reigned supreme and became the direct occupants of top political positions in their country for a half-century, coffee producers in Nicaragua remained an important but not singularly dominant sector (Torres-Rivas 1989, 178). In 1929, on the eve of the depression, coffee accounted for 93 percent of export earnings in El Salvador and 77 percent in Guatemala. In contrast, a more modest 54 percent of Nicaragua's export earnings were obtained from coffee (Bulmer-Thomas 1987, 34). Compared to its neighbors, Nicaragua's export profile was relatively diversified, with bananas and timber each contributing over 10 percent of export earnings at that time.

Unlike the Salvadoran coffee elite, which expanded quickly into the banking and export trade sectors, the Nicaraguan coffee bourgeoisie confined its activities largely to cultivation. Lucrative finance and export activities were monopolized in the Nicaraguan case by a partnership of the state and foreign investors, limiting the economic terrain available to domestic producers.[3] Coffee production in Nicaragua tended to shift over time from the more populated and historically dominant Pacific coastal regions into the more mountainous interior, and Nicaraguan coffee producers were increasingly located away from the mainstream of national political life in the relatively inaccessible Matagalpa and Jinotega regions.

Perhaps a more important factor explaining the Nicaragua elite's relative impotence was the political role assumed by the United States. During the 1911–33 period, the U.S. government took control of most of the economic and military functions of the Nicaraguan state; the U.S. collector general of customs took charge of the collection and dispersal of state revenues, and the marines set up a military academy and constabulary national guard. Political power was subsequently commandeered by National Guard Commander Anastasio Somoza García, and a long era (1937–79) of personalistic and familial control was launched. This monopoly over political power in Nicaragua left other contenders, such as those enriched by coffee export, scattered on the sidelines. The coffee elite in Nicaragua was only one of several contending powers, and it vied weakly for political authority. Its relatively modest contribution to the national economy and inability to extend into banking and exports, combined with the political intrusion of the United States and the lock on power held by the Somozas, impeded the development of a hegemonic, coffee-based oligarchy in Nicaragua.[4]

The Post–World War II Era and Economic Diversification

Economic activity in Nicaragua became more dynamic and diversified in the period after the 1940s as the Nicaraguan economy became increasingly integrated into an expanding international market. This trend was reinforced by the interventions of international financial and development authorities, particularly World Bank and IDB consultants and USAID missions. In addition, expansion and diversification were supported by eclectic interventions on the part of the Nicaraguan state.[5] The most important new sectors to emerge during this period were cotton, livestock, and manufacturing.

The Cotton Boom

During the 1950s cotton boom, cotton was established as the dominant crop in the fertile Pacific region around León and Chinandega. In 1950 the international price for cotton fiber reached a historic $57.61 per qt. These prices were extraordinary; they were not seen again until the end of the 1970s. Inspired by the windfall profits to be made in cotton trade, increasing numbers of producers shifted into this sector.[6]

The ability of these producers to take advantage of this opportunity was restricted by the weakness of the transportation and financial infrastructure of the country. The World Bank mission that visited Nicaragua in 1951–52 pointed the finger at these bottlenecks and called the Somoza regime to task. The mission praised the regime for starting a program to build major highways on the Pacific side of the country but criticized the limited scope of the project and called for the construction of local access and farm-to-market roads to complement the highway system (IBRD 1953, xxviii). The mission also criticized the country's frail credit system for failing to rechannel savings efficiently into productive investments (IBRD 1953, 4), indirectly pressuring the state to relinquish its monopoly over the banking system.

Following this report, the road-building program in the Pacific region was expanded (Williams 1986, 20–24). Two new private banks, BANIC and BANAMER, were founded and helped funnel private sector profits back into other productive activities. Even the state bank responded to the new dynamic; the credit capacity of the state-owned BNN grew exponentially, and the bank became a hub of national economic growth. The development of this physical and financial infrastructure facilitated the rise of a new entrepreneurial sector of the Nicaraguan bourgeoisie, particularly in cotton production.[7] In 1951–52, 1,305 producers cultivated cotton; by 1960–61, 2,015 producers did so. This figure continued to rise, reaching 5,080 in 1965–66 (Biderman 1982, 182).

This emerging cotton bourgeoisie had several distinguishing characteristics. A large number of these producers were primarily urban professionals who bought or rented land as an outlet for entrepreneurship and speculation (Núñez Soto 1981, 30–33).[8] Their growing participation in cotton production sharpened the distinctions between the Nicaraguan class structure and that found generally in Central America. Whereas the rural oligarchy that dominated Guatemala and, to a lesser extent, El Salvador emerged from a traditional landholding elite, cotton expansion in Nicaragua followed the "merchant road" to capitalist development, drawing heavily from a professional urban class that maintained multiple occupations. Unlike Guatemala and El Salvador, where agroexport production was concentrated on larger estates, or Honduras, where banana production developed in an enclave economy, Nicaraguan agricultural development rested more fully on a foundation of locally owned middle-sized estates.[9] These distinctive local characteristics gave agricultural development in Nicaragua a less dualistic twist than that found in much of the region.

In part because of the intense regional divisions in the country and the weakness of the transportation system, the cotton and coffee sectors tended to evolve as distinct entities with little overlap between them. Unlike their more traditional counterparts in coffee production, Nicaraguan cotton producers were quick to adopt technological innovations. Whereas the yields of Nicaraguan coffee producers lagged far behind the average rates for the region, yields for the country's cotton producers were among the world's highest.[10] Nicaraguan *algodoneros* experimented with seed varieties and fertilizer use and turned readily toward mechanization (Belli 1968, 46–48). They represented a new type of producer in Nicaragua, one who was more dynamic, less risk averse, and more technologically sophisticated.

Although bitter regional disputes among elites were suppressed under the authoritarian rule of the Somoza dynasty, economic diversification sharpened the sectoral differentiation of this class. In the 1960s, two additional sectors, livestock and manufacturing, grew rapidly. As with cotton, their development was supported by the international market and international development consultants and backed by the Nicaraguan state.

Cattle Sector Development

Following its 1951–52 visit, the IBRD mission recommended the construction of a modern slaughterhouse with refrigerated storage to replace the inefficient export of live animals, and it endorsed the establishment of several new milk processing plants capable of producing condensed or powdered milk for export (IBRD 1953, 141–45). In the years that followed, both recommendations were implemented.

The Nicaraguan state became increasingly interventionist in support of livestock development. The expansion of the BNN and the creation of INFONAC in 1953 gave the Somoza regime conduits through which to funnel resources into the cattle sector. When INFONAC was founded, it provided the only significant source of medium- and long-term loans in Nicaragua. It served as an important conduit of foreign credits, securing over 9 percent of all resources in the financial sector by 1964 (Vichas 1967, 81–82).[11]

INFONAC signaled its vision by financing the Matadero Modelo, a beef export facility that opened in 1957–58. This facility was the first USDA-approved packing house in Central America, giving Nicaragua a jump on beef exportation for the region. The relatively low cost of land in Nicaragua provided a "comparative advantage" for the production of range-fed cattle, and the rise of hamburger chains in the United States raised the demand for inexpensive, lower-quality hamburger that range-fed cattle could satisfy (Williams 1986, 77–98). By the 1960s Nicaragua's cattle industry had been largely integrated into the U.S. beef market.[12]

As a result of these domestic and international interventions, the livestock sector grew rapidly. The value of beef exports rose from US$3 million in 1960 to US$44.5 million in 1973. At their 1974 peak, earnings for Nicaragua's beef exports surpassed even those for its coffee exports and were second in value only to cotton (Biderman 1982, 177). Land used for pasture expanded sharply during this period, rising from 1.5 million mz. in 1960–61 to 4.1 million mz. in 1978–79. Whereas a little over 70 percent of the agricultural land was used for pastureland in 1960–61, over 80 percent of the agricultural land was so used in 1978–79 (FIDA 1980, 1).

The Growth of Manufacturing

New primary sector activities created related opportunities in agroindustry and international trade. During the 1960s, for example, the cotton sector was increasingly integrated into a network of industries and markets both inside and outside Nicaragua. Backward linkages were developed with industries and commercial firms that provided inputs into cotton production. Sales of fertilizer, pesticides, and agricultural machinery soared, and local firms were increasingly involved in the production and distribution of these products. Forward linkages were also developed for the processing of the fiber, the extraction of cottonseed oil, the export of unprocessed cotton, and textile production.[13] Not only did the agricultural bourgeoisie become more dynamic and diversified, new industrial and commercial sectors also developed rapidly.

National economic policy became more proactive and began to favor industrialization. To stimulate industrial expansion, the Nicaraguan government approved the 1956 Ley de Inversiones Extranjeras that encouraged the entry of foreign capital (*La Gaceta*, March 10, 1956). Following the assassination that year of Anastasio Somoza García and the assumption of the presidency by his oldest son, Luis Somoza Debayle, the regime deepened its commitment to industrial growth. The 1958 Ley de Protección y Estímulo al Desarrollo Industrial declared industrial development to be of "general interest" and provided an array of tax and tariff concessions to both established and new industries (*La Gaceta*, March 12, 1958).[14]

The formation of the CACM in 1960 and the Alliance for Progress development programs further stimulated industrial and commercial expansion.[15] On the recommendation of the U.S. government, the Corporación Nicaragüense de Inversiones was created in 1964 with financing from USAID.[16] By 1966 three-fifths of the organization's loans had gone to industrial enterprises (Lethander 1968, 359). Many of these projects were joint ventures involving foreign banks, Latin American-based transnational corporations, and local industrialists, including members of the Somoza family (Dosal 1985, 91; Wheelock Román 1980b, 181).

Local financing also supported industrial development. In the 1960s, the domestic banking system shifted credit toward the secondary sector. In 1960 only 18 percent of bank loans went to the manufacturing sector, less than half those received in agriculture. Lending to the manufacturing sector rose in the early 1960s, however, exceeding 24 percent in the 1962–65 period. By the mid-1970s, loans for the industrial sector often surpassed those for agriculture. (See Table 2.1.)

Financial support from international agencies, the state, and the banking system combined with changing trade policy to fuel industrial expansion. Nicaragua's annual GDP growth rate in the 1960–70 period was a formidable 6.9 percent, the highest in the region (Weeks 1985, 50). The industrial sector spearheaded this expansion, growing a phenomenal 15 percent annual average in the 1960–65 period, and a still-remarkable 8.9 percent annual average in 1965–70 (Weeks 1985, 64). At an overall average annual growth rate of 12 percent during the 1960s, Nicaragua's industrial sector expanded much more rapidly than that in any other Central American country. As a result of this dramatic growth, this sector assumed a significant role in the national economy. Whereas only 12 percent of Nicaragua's GDP was derived from manufacturing in 1960, this rose to 22 percent in 1975 (Weeks 1985, 135).[17]

As a result of these surge areas, the Nicaraguan economy grew rapidly,

Table 2.1

Financial System Loans to the Private Sector by Economic Activity, 1960–1979 (Percent of Total)

Year	Agriculture	Livestock	Natural Resources	Manufacturing	Construction
1960	40.3	12.6	0.0	17.8	0.0
1961	43.6	11.8	0.0	19.1	0.0
1962	38.6	12.8	0.0	25.0	0.0
1963	38.2	12.2	0.0	23.7	0.0
1964	35.7	14.4	0.0	23.7	0.0
1965	30.3	16.2	0.0	24.4	0.0
1966	29.9	15.7	0.6	23.0	0.5
1967	31.0	15.1	0.5	21.7	0.4
1968	31.1	13.9	0.4	19.7	0.3
1969	30.5	12.1	0.4	20.4	0.5
1970	31.3	12.1	0.9	22.0	1.6
1971	28.7	12.0	1.2	22.1	1.5
1972	26.1	12.5	0.9	22.7	1.3
1973	22.8	15.7	0.7	23.1	1.8
1974	21.9	14.0	0.8	22.7	2.0
1975	20.2	12.4	1.1	24.3	2.2
1976	18.1	11.3	1.0	22.4	2.1
1977	20.5	10.7	0.6	19.9	0.9
1978	21.9	9.7	0.6	20.7	0.8
1979	22.6	8.2	0.3	26.2	0.8

Source: BCN (1979, 29).

though unevenly, during these decades. In the early 1950s the GDP growth rate surpassed that of all other Central American nations with the exception of Costa Rica; in the early 1960s it topped even the Costa Rican rate, rising more than 10 percent per year. (See Table 2.2.) This growth rate provided resources for the local bourgeoisie that were historically unprecedented.

Economic Groups and the Commanding Heights

The rise of new economic sectors was intimately associated with the rise of a series of "economic groups." These groups were composed of a network of investors bound together in what Strachen (1976, 3) calls a "fiduciary atmosphere" of relatively open disclosure and trust. At the apex

Table 2.1 (continued)

Year	Housing	Commerce	Services	Other
1960	6.0	12.1	0.0	11.3
1961	5.1	11.9	0.0	8.4
1962	6.2	10.6	0.0	6.8
1963	6.4	13.9	0.0	5.7
1964	6.8	12.7	0.0	6.7
1965	8.4	13.0	0.0	7.6
1966	7.8	11.2	2.1	9.3
1967	8.1	9.9	2.7	10.7
1968	10.6	8.5	2.4	13.1
1969	11.6	8.4	2.8	13.3
1970	13.1	10.2	4.1	4.8
1971	14.4	10.9	4.7	4.4
1972	14.6	11.2	4.9	5.7
1973	12.1	12.0	4.8	7.1
1974	14.7	12.9	4.2	6.8
1975	16.2	11.0	4.5	8.1
1976	18.0	13.2	4.7	9.2
1977	20.1	16.9	4.1	6.3
1978	20.5	14.7	4.0	7.2
1979	18.6	15.1	3.3	4.9

of the Nicaraguan bourgeoisie were three rapidly expanding and highly diversified economic groups that emerged in the 1950s (Strachen 1976; Wheelock Román 1980b, 148–76). Two were formed by private entrepreneurial networks; the third was built around the Somoza family's business operations. An important part of the innovative economic activity in Nicaragua of the 1950s and 1960s was orchestrated by these groups.

The principal economic groups were centered on the private banking system that emerged in the 1950s. The BANAMER group was organized around the nation's largest private bank and included investments in sugar, cattle, rum, large-scale commerce, construction, land development, food processing, and the apparel industry.[18] The BANIC group had a less extensive realm of operation but included not only the Banco Nicaragüense but also a notable swath of cotton and coffee production, cotton gins and

Table 2.2

Average Annual Real GDP Growth Rates in Central America (Percent)

Country	1950–55	1955–60	1960–65	1965–70	1970–78	GDP/Capita Dollars (1970) 1950	1978
Costa Rica	8.3	6.0	6.5	7.0	6.1	322	758
El Salvador	4.6	4.7	6.8	4.5	5.2	203	347
Guatemala	2.2	5.3	5.2	5.8	5.6	255	450
Honduras	2.5	4.6	5.2	4.1	4.4	234	297
Nicaragua	8.3	2.3	10.2	4.2	4.0	223	409
Total Central America	4.7	4.6	6.0	5.1	5.4	242	428

Source: Rosenthal (1982, 20).

brokerages, the nation's largest brewery, and a vegetable oil processing facility.[19] Both of these groups were linked to a series of other financial agencies, including savings and loan associations, finance companies, and insurance agencies.[20]

The Somoza group was launched on a base of agricultural production in every major subsector and expanded into commerce and industry (airline, shipping, fishing, construction, cement, and real estate).[21] The financial component of this group rested on its own small bank, the Banco Centroamericano, and, more importantly, its ability to influence the distribution of resources in the state banking system. Labeled the "loaded dice" group (Wheelock Román 1980b, 163), this network of political and economic allies drew heavily on its political connections and effectively parried periodic jabs from other private sector elites.

The rise of these economic groups involved a new form of convergence across sectors. Unlike other sectors of the Nicaraguan bourgeoisie, the economic groups and various other "grupitos" that emerged in the 1950s linked disparate economic activities. Private investments made before the evolution of these groups in the 1950s tended to be narrowly sectoral; in contrast, investment by the emerging economic groups in the 1950s and 1960s crossed categories to fuse agriculture, industry, and trade. These groups used their respective components of the emerging banking system as a mechanism to transfer resources from waning but profitable activities toward rising sectors that promised increased future return. The banks were the linchpin in the system, providing credit and investment opportunities for group members on terms that were widely perceived as concessionary (Strachen 1976, 70). The banks also developed connections to foreign banks, such as the link between BANAMER and Wells Fargo Bank, helping group insiders to get access to foreign credit (Wheelock Román 1980b, 162).

Theoretically, the development of economic groups could have led to greater class cohesion within top bourgeoisie, and to their increased hegemony over the society. In Nicaragua, however, these groups failed to play that role. They remained sharply competitive among themselves and generally eschewed political action. Although the Nicaraguan elite was interlinked through kinship bonds (much like Zeitlin and Ratcliff [1988] found in the Chilean case), those family bonds did not automatically produce economic collaboration. Competition among the groups remained intense. Strachen's (1976, 17) close study of the composition of these groups in the 1970s found little overlap in the top membership.[22]

Not only did the competition among groups impede the fusion of this elite, but so did the group leaders' unwillingness to assume political roles. Unlike the Chilean elite, which figured prominently in Liberal and Conservative party politics (Zeitlin and Ratcliff 1988, 186–214), Nicaragua's top elite adopted a low political profile. Instead of stepping into leadership positions or welding together private sector organizations, group leaders avoided these commitments. More like top elites in contemporary Peru (Durand 1991) and Brazil (Weyland 1992), the largest Nicaraguan capitalists preferred the politics of individual bargaining in which they could trade on their economic prominence to secure special concessions or bureaucratic exemptions. This particularistic negotiation process undercut the Nicaraguan bourgeoisie's ability to serve as a hegemonic force. The economic groups evaded confrontation with the regime even as they faced rising competition from the Somoza family group.

State Control over the Economic Elite

Three mechanisms fostered state control over the local elite: (1) quasi-corporatist linkages with the bourgeoisie, (2) "sultanistic" dominance of private sector organizations, and (3) clientelistic politics that encouraged individual petitions and class segmentation.

Quasi-corporatist Controls

Even before the creation of the Somoza dynasty, during the period of U.S. occupation, the Nicaraguan government was already sponsoring private sector associations by granting them representational monopolies and providing state subsidies for their operations. This process created a series of quasi-corporatist mechanisms that the state could use to control private sector organizations.[23] As early as 1923 the government granted legal recognition and subsidies to handpicked organizations. The Asociación Nacional de Ganaderos, with the prominent participation of several military generals, was recognized in that turbulent year. Labeled an "enterprise of public usefulness" (*empresa de utilidad pública*), this organization was given tax exemptions and discounts on tariffs (*La Gaceta*, August 13, 1923).[24]

Chambers of commerce began to organize autonomously in cities like Managua and León as early as 1928 (CADIN 1975; Cámara de Comercio de León n.d., 3), but these organizations soon fell under state sponsorship. When the chambers of commerce, agriculture, and industry were given legal recognition in 1934, they were designated as the legal intermediary organizations between businesses and the regime (*La Gaceta*, September 3, 1934). As in Mexico and Ecuador during this era, the state mandated participation in these organizations. In Nicaragua, all businesspeople, agricultural producers, industrialists, and intermediaries were legally required to join these chambers; those who did not were denied the right to bring judicial proceedings or petitions before the state. This legal privilege secured the status of these associations but also created a bond of dependency between these fledgling organizations and the regime.

The Somoza regime incorporated carefully selected private sector organizations into government boards and was often directly involved in naming their representatives. For example, a small number of private sector organizations were given representation on the board of directors of the BNN when it was reestablished in Nicaragua in 1940.[25] Representatives of the private sector were also named to the board of the national development bank INFONAC when it was created in 1953 (*La Gaceta*, March 13, 1953).[26] Trying to shore up the national economy and build elite support,[27] Somoza García created the Consejo Nacional de Economía in 1949 as an advisory board for the Ministry of Economy (Walter 1993, 186–88). Representatives of several private sector organizations, including the Cámara de Comercio de Managua, the Sociedad Anónima de Cafetaleros, the Cooperativa Nacional de Agricultores, and the Asociación Agrícola de Nicaragua, were appointed to this council.

Private sector representatives were also named to sectoral agencies and commissions. The creation of CONAL in 1965 by newly installed President René Schick solidified the relationship between the state and the cotton bourgeoisie. The legislation creating CONAL gave five of its eleven permanent seats to the regional cotton cooperatives that had emerged in the 1960s (*La Gaceta*, Decree #1078, April 24, 1965). This assured the medium- and large-scale producers who dominated these cooperatives that they would have monthly meetings with political luminaries like the minister of agriculture and livestock or the presidents of the BCN and the BNN. Similarly, the rice growers' association (Asociación de Productores de Arroz de Nicaragua) was given representation on the board of the state grains marketing agency (the Instituto Nacional de Comercio de Exportación e Importación), and a coffee growers' association (the Sociedad Cooperativa Anónima de Cafeteros) was given a position on the board of the Instituto Nicaragüense del Cafe.

The regime also moved to channel private sector activity in the emerging industrial sector. Selected business associations, like the newly formed Asociación de Industriales de Nicaragua, were allowed to name members to the Comisión Consultiva de Desarrollo Industrial created by Luis Somoza in 1958.[28] The Cámara de Comercio and the Asociación de Industriales (renamed the Cámara de Industrias de Nicaragua or CADIN in 1965) enjoyed substantial state support. Import licenses, for example, were granted only to those who could demonstrate membership in these business chambers, and the concessions granted in the 1958 industrial development law were available only to affiliates of CADIN. These restrictions compelled the emerging urban bourgeoisie to join these organizations. These associations gained in size and resources, and the state developed a generally cooperative private sector affiliate.

Sultanistic Participation and Control

In some sectors, where relations with the state were complicated by the extensive, direct participation of the Somoza family in production and marketing, a "sultanistic" political arrangement emerged.[29] The political clan that ran the country used its public power to advance its own economic interests and those of its wealthy allies, currying favor and winning support in these quarters. Bolstered by the family's business interests, the state provided loans, infrastructure, and international connections that were essential to the success of the sector. In the most extreme cases, Somoza family members even served as top officials in private sector organizations for economic sectors where family resources were concentrated.

Livestock provided an important terrain for investment and accumulation by the Somozas beginning in the 1950s.[30] To promote this activity, Luis Somoza founded a new ranchers' association, ASGANIC, in 1955 and actively served as its president even after he became president of the country. Membership was confined to a small number of elite cattle producers and carried substantial privileges. Among other benefits, membership enabled this elite to meet regularly with the top ministers, bank presidents, and directors of development projects. It provided a regular forum in which these producers could coordinate activities and press their case for additional resources.[31] Unlike cotton growers, who suffered from the regional fragmentation of their organizations, the cattle elite was shaped by Somoza family powerholders into a forceful association from the mid-1950s on.

The state development bank INFONAC joined with ASGANIC to found a holding company, IFAGAN & Cia. Ltda., and establish the Matadero Modelo, Nicaragua's first modern beef slaughterhouse. Controlling 50–60 percent of export slaughter (Ballard 1985, 30), IFAGAN became in effect the state-sponsored beef commercialization agency, overseeing prices paid to both producers and consumers and coordinating the export of Nicaraguan beef.[32] In 1973 IFAGAN opened a new facility, the Fondo Ifagán de Desarrollo Ganadero, providing members with low interest, subsidized, long-term loans. These loans offered borrowers up to three grace years before any payment was due and eliminated all bank commissions (ASGANIC 1975, 4–5). Using profits from the Matadero Modelo, a fund of US$10 million was set up, providing these prominent cattle ranchers with an attractive alternative to the regular banking system.

The penetration by the Somoza family brought certain benefits to their allies. The increased state support for cattle production in the 1960s attracted loans and investment into the sector, and the regime helped to secure steady access to the U.S. beef quota. Those affiliated with the regime reaped ample rewards. Through ASGANIC the established cattle elites had access to government resources, and their co-ownership of IFAGAN generated additional profits and loans. As affiliates became indebted to the regime, their capacity for autonomous action was stifled. Nor was this effect limited to members. Although elites who were excluded from these private associations were less compromised, many of them aspired to membership. Those aspirants became supplicants whose ability to oppose the regime was undercut by their hope for admission into the regime's privileged circles.

Clientelism

To extract concessions from the regime, business elites typically resorted to informal, individual communication with well-placed bureaucrats. Discussing bureaucratic solicitation of that era, one prominent
cattle rancher described how he would court the regional state bank official, taking him to lunch and metaphorically "stroking his hair" in order
to get long-term credit (interview, August 6, 1991). Others recalled the era
more fondly. "If we needed something," one former leader in the construction sector observed, "we would just call the right minister. The ministers
were mostly our friends, anyway" (interview, August 7, 1991).

The Somoza regime limited the power of formal state economic agencies and concentrated decision making in the hands of family members.
The paper-thin legal and regulatory structure in Nicaragua was routinely
circumvented through skillful bargaining and deal making. Personal contacts and bonds were widely used by elites to secure special privileges.
Interaction between regime elites and leaders of the domestic bourgeoisie, consequently, had an unpredictable, ad hoc quality. Even prominent
figures in the elite had to deal with a highly personalistic authority structure. Power was discretionary, not governed by formal rules. Without rou-
tinized channels of communication and a more fully institutionalized
bureaucracy, private sector leaders faced recurring uncertainty.

Since regime functionaries were susceptible to individual appeals, there
was little need to work through private sector organizations. Indeed, pushing for a collective response invited a harsh response.[33] When collective
efforts were made, the results were often disappointing; they did not provide the individual capitalist with any special advantage or privilege. The
bargaining process that prevailed bound the elite to the state in the role
of individual supplicant and set up conditions that fostered intra-elite
rivalry and competition.

As a result, Nicaraguan capitalists scattered into a series of sectoral
and regional clusters. Without strong or autonomous national associations, producers retreated into regionalism and infighting. Producers often
formed local "societies" or "cooperatives,"[34] which were only regional
groupings without a strong national counterpart. Conflict developed between and among subsectors (cotton growers battled vegetable oil processors; small livestock producers competed with beef processors)[35] over how
the profits generated by a sector would be divided up. Intrabourgeois conflicts also flared over access to bank credit. Agricultural producers were

alarmed when agricultural loans dropped from 40 percent of the total in
1960 to 30 percent in 1965, and the portion of loans allocated to industry
and livestock tended to rise. (See Table 2.1.) In the absence of autonomous
national organizations that might mediate these disputes, and in a setting
that favored particularistic bargaining, intra-elite conflict was routine.

Movement toward Private Sector Opposition

In a system where fluctuating resources are seen as the product of a neutral market responding to the laws of supply and demand, the impact of
political decisions on rising or declining profits may not be clear. Under
those circumstances, producers often adjust to their shifting fates without raising the issue in the political arena. When "political capitalism"
(Schneider 1988–89, 91) prevails, however, economic performance is regularly and visibly tied to political decisions. Bank credit, trade options, and
labor costs are all the product of political negotiations, and those elites
favored by the regime receive substantial benefits. Groups not favored by
economic policy understand this as unfair treatment and may become
politically alienated.

Political capitalism had long prevailed in Nicaragua. By the mid-1970s
those elites who were relatively disadvantaged turned increasingly against
the regime. Old cooptive mechanisms were failing to function as effectively as they had in prior decades. Expectations rose, needs changed, and
performance deteriorated. Important sectors of the bourgeoisie were beginning to take aim at the regime. One indicator was the 1972 formation
of COSIP, Nicaragua's first business "peak association."[36]

Comparative literature on private sector organization in Latin America
points to a series of factors that contribute to or impede the formation
of peak associations (Durand 1991; Acuña 1991; Weyland 1992). Key factors analyzed have included (1) the size, heterogeneity, and regionalistic
tendencies of the bourgeoisie (Acuña 1991; Weyland 1992); (2) the degree
of corporatist control over private sector organization (Weyland 1992);
and (3) the degree of threat that private elites face from popular groups,
especially labor (Durand 1991; Conaghan 1991).

According to this body of literature, peak associations are more likely
to form when the private sector is relatively small, homogeneous, and free
of regional fissures. This kind of national association may also be encouraged by the absence of corporatist controls that bind the private sector
to the state. The mobilization of mass organizations that are perceived as

threatening to the collective interests of private sector elites can trigger the formation of peak associations. The recent democratization/redemocratization process in Latin America has also been seen as a galvanizing force behind more cohesive private sector organization, since it fosters mass mobilizations that can challenge business interests (Durand 1991). Conversely, business peak associations are less likely to emerge when the bourgeoisie is heterogeneous, fractured, and regionally divided; heavily shaped by corporatist controls; and free from major threats by labor or popular organizations.

In the Nicaraguan case, the absence of a dominant economic sector and the persistence of regional divisions contributed to delays in the formation of cohesive private sector organizations. Yet a peak organization was finally formed in Nicaragua in the early 1970s, in spite of the rising heterogeneity of the national economy in the 1950s and 1960s. The coincidence of this organizational development and increasing economic heterogeneity supports the argument that the socioeconomic characteristics of the bourgeoisie may be less important in determining their political organization than other political and organizational considerations.[37]

The Nicaraguan bourgeoisie began to converge organizationally when two developments coincided. First, as the Nicaraguan bourgeoisie developed and became better linked to a competitive international economy, it needed a state apparatus that was developmentally competent. Second, the quasi-corporatist and clientelistic mechanisms developed by the state to channel private sector participation deteriorated over time. The state dipped deeper into avarice at the same time as the aspirations of producers and their expectations regarding supportive state actions gradually rose. As the political elite concentrated on private accumulation, its ability to continue stoking the system was undermined.

The Somoza regime had, of course, long used public power to pursue private gain. Dynasty founder Somoza García was notorious for his use of kickbacks, "presidential commissions," extraction of bribes, demands to be included in lucrative enterprises, and seizure of properties held by politically vulnerable groups (Walter 1993, 109–10; Booth 1985a, 66–68). Over time, however, these practices became increasingly objectionable to other economic elites, who were adversely affected by the partial diversion of their surpluses and the considerable uncertainty this introduced into the economic environment. Instead of gradually curtailing these abuses, the regime became yet more corrupt in the 1970s during the reign of Anastasio Somoza Debayle. Particularly in the wake of the 1972 earthquake that devastated Managua, as international assistance poured into the country, the regime proved visibly corrupt. Moving into new business sectors (land development, construction supplies, housing), the Somoza family jostled broader sectors of the Nicaraguan elite and violated an unwritten assumption that economic gains would be more widely shared. As the informal boundaries that had delimited the sphere of public corruption widened and the sweep of the Somoza family's economic empire expanded, elite opposition sharpened.

The regime's approach to economic policy, with its emphasis on personalistic connections and its tendency toward erratic decisions, was no longer acceptable to an increasing number of economic elites. Instead, they began to push for a more neutral, regularized state apparatus that would better serve the needs of modern business. Economic elites needed wider access to improved technology, a more skilled and better-trained labor force, a more fully developed transportation and communication infrastructure, and social peace. What they got was an uneven and erratic distribution of these resources accompanied by widespread popular repression. As the regime became more acquisitive, rewards and resources were increasingly absorbed by its close political allies. The corporatist and clientelistic features of the regime were gradually overwhelmed by its sultanistic tendencies.

The political performance of the regime became more repressive and, simultaneously, less authoritative. Private sector leaders began to develop new points of reference, drawing on international connections that bypassed the regime. International business associates and USAID programs designed to support civic action may have unwittingly undermined the Somoza regime's bonds with its business class by providing an alternative vision of state-business linkages and by supplying the financial resources with which to buy greater independence.

In contrast to other cases in Latin America such as Peru or Mexico, in which business peak associations developed in response to a threat from the left, Nicaraguan private elites converged before any leftist threat had materialized. The FSLN in the early 1970s was still a tiny organization that had been largely defeated during the counterinsurgency campaign of the 1960s. Organized labor in Nicaragua barely existed, and the prospects for a successful insurrection seemed remote. Yet business did feel increasingly threatened. The threat to the collective interests of business was not posed by labor or popular groups, which were only weakly organized in authoritarian Nicaragua, but by the regime itself. The heavy-handed use of public power for private gain and the fundamental corruption of the judicial and legal systems undermined the predictability of the economic system and cut into the resources of the private sector. Episodic forays into different economic activities by members of the Somoza family or close allies meant that the terrain open to private competitors was reduced and uncertain. No business sector seemed immune to this threat, since even those not currently menaced could become tomorrow's victims.

The simultaneous deterioration of the quasi-corporatist and clientelistic mechanisms that had linked the private sector to the state, and the rising threat posed by a cleptocratic state elite, therefore, created circumstances favorable for the consolidation of a business peak association. COSIP moved timidly and uncertainly toward an increasingly oppositional stance to the regime.

This peak association was the brainchild of INDE, a business-civic organization that had been created in 1964. Reflecting the changes under way in the economy and society, this association drew primarily from the emerging urban bourgeoisie.[38] Unlike so many private sector organizations that developed at the behest of and under the protection of the state, INDE was relatively separate from the regime. Instead of focusing exclusively on local issues, this organization was closely tied to international organizations and foreign donors like USAID and the Inter-American Foundation. This financial tie allowed it to obtain an element of independence from the state (although not necessarily from its foreign donors) that had eluded other private sector organizations.[39]

INDE acted as a political lobbyist for a reform sector of the bourgeoisie. In contrast with the elite organizations established before it, INDE promoted a broader vision of private sector responsibilities and aspirations. Inspired by the concept of noblesse oblige, INDE called the "most responsible citizens" to preserve the values of the free world while promoting national development and social justice (INDE 1965, n.p.). This organization was particularly active in promoting educational projects and a self-help cooperative movement.[40] It recruited a professional staff to support its development projects and produced annual publications complete with detailed financial accounting.

The creation of INDE and its efforts to influence the direction of national development represented an important departure in the evolution of the private sector in Nicaragua. Through this organization, a segment of the country's small bourgeoisie was shifting from narrow sectoral activity toward broader class-based organization. Instead of focusing on particularistic interests of clusters of producers reacting to problems with taxes or bank credit, this organization pushed producers toward greater collective class awareness and broader concern about social and economic development. Instead of fragmenting into regional groupings, INDE functioned as the missing agglutinative, bringing economic elites together across sectoral and regional lines. These characteristics allowed INDE to inject an element of class coherence into the Nicaraguan political system.[41]

The Uncertain Evolution of COSIP/COSEP

At the end of the 1960s, INDE headquarters began serving as an informal gathering place in which leaders of private sector organizations could discuss their collective political concerns. By 1972 the INDE leadership moved to bring this array of sectoral leaders together in COSIP. This new umbrella organization linked twelve established associations, including most of the significant groups that had emerged in the previous twenty years.[42] Although the capacity of the organization to challenge the regime was muted by the inclusion of several associations closely tied to the Somozas, such as ASGANIC, the Asociación de Productores de Arroz de Nicaragua, and the Cámara Nicaragüense de la Industria Pesquera, the most important affiliates, like INDE, were relatively independent from the regime.[43] Although functionally distinct from INDE, COSIP operated under INDE's tutelage and direction.[44]

COSIP's capacity to mobilize business opposition deepened appreciably during its first year of operation. In the aftermath of the December 1972 earthquake in Managua, the Somoza regime's capacity for self-indulgence and indifference to national needs was starkly revealed. The imposition of a series of new emergency taxes, combined with the unrelieved suffering resulting from the earthquake, the accelerated theft of relief assistance by officials, and open profiteering by Somoza family members, led private sector leaders to adopt a more critical attitude toward regime mismanagement and corruption. The rebuilding process triggered the expansion of Somoza family businesses into growth industries—construction, real estate, and banking—that had traditionally been the province of the dominant economic groups. Direct economic threat merged with a smoldering sense of moral disdain to prompt elite intervention.

INDE/COSIP leaders decided to organize a national conference to air a series of their concerns. The Primera Convención Nacional del Sector Privado, held on March 1, 1974, in the Teatro Nacional Rubén Darío, was organized and led by some of COSIP's most prominent and articulate affiliates. The keystone of the meeting was the session entitled "Socio-Economic Development Strategy in the 1970s" (INDE 1975), which culminated with a series of critical observations about the regime and recommendations for change (Cruz 1974).

The convention's final resolution called for a political housecleaning (COSIP 1974). This statement conceded the need for public order and recognized the Somoza regime's efforts to maintain stability. It concluded, however, that the "preservation of order" was not enough; state responsibilities extended beyond this. Private sector representatives proposed "new joint efforts" (*esfuerzos mancomunados*) with the state to achieve these broader objectives. They agreed to accept a new tax system that would provide the state with increased resources if the state in turn would undertake internal reform. The government was called on to apply the law neutrally and use its revenues correctly (i.e., conduct public bidding on state projects, adopt an auditing system, and document spending in government accounts). Furthermore, the state would be required to cultivate a spirit of public service among its employees and eliminate the expectation of bribery. The private sector further demanded the participation of "genuinely designated" private sector representatives in state decision making instead of representatives who were handpicked by Somoza. Finally, the recommendations called for a program of effective economic planning to address national needs in housing, public transportation, and food and energy production. This state planning was to complement but not interfere with private sector initiatives.

These demands were hardly visionary. As Vilas (1986, 132) argues, "The kind of state demanded by the Nicaraguan bourgeoisie was thus a modern capitalist state that would efficiently fulfill its political-economic functions." In many ways, the COSIP meeting called for little more than the rule of law and elite participation in decision making. Given the nature of the Nicaraguan state, however, these demands would have required a profound change in the regime.

COSIP's first conference was an unexpected public success. Initially, organizers expected 500 people to attend, but attendance swelled to around 2,000 (Ramírez Arango 1985, 253–54; *La Prensa*, March 1, 1974). Observers came from the broader religious, academic, and political community to listen to this unique discussion. Somoza, attending the final session, left abruptly before the meeting concluded, signaling his distaste for the proceedings. No longer did the private sector present its position wrapped in the unctuous courtesy and recurring honorifics that characterized its earlier communication with government officials. It was now more direct, sharply critical, and increasingly insistent.

The formation of a national peak association, however, does not ensure its durability or power. Durand (1991) found in the Peruvian case that the first two business peak associations formed in the 1970s dissolved quickly as a result of internal policy disputes. The process in which the bourgeoisie consolidates politically in spite of its divergent priorities and a history of competition is often a gradual one that proceeds through several phases. In the Nicaraguan case, after its initial success, COSIP faded into the political background. INDE, which had been the prime mover behind the formation of COSIP, stepped forward again as the direct negotiator for the private sector. With an established institutional structure, a professional staff, and a budget that was relatively independent of the regime, INDE became the stalwart of private sector opposition during the escalating conflicts of the 1970s. Public confrontation with the regime only served to strengthen this organization. INDE's membership rose rapidly from 89 in 1974 to 523 in 1976 (INDE 1975, 1977).

For its part, the Somoza regime grew increasingly intransigent. Losing the political agility that had enabled Somoza García to survive several earlier challenges, the descendent regime now ignored public pressures or responded with violence. Elections in 1974 renewed the presidency of Anastasio Somoza Debayle, this time for a long, seven-year term. The fledgling FSLN, then about 150 members strong, surprised the country in December 1974 with an attack on a farewell party given by former minister of agriculture José María "Chema" Castillo Quant for departing U.S. Ambassador Turner Shelton. To get those taken hostage freed, Somoza paid a $1 million ransom, published an FSLN communiqué, and released Daniel Ortega and thirteen Sandinista supporters (Wheelock Román 1980a). Although initially giving the Sandinistas visibility and new credibility, this incident led to the imposition of another round of martial law. The dynasty's grip on the Nicaraguan state tightened, and the prospects for institutional or structural reform dimmed further.

Conflicts between economic elites and the regime recurred through the early 1970s. Cotton growers denounced the regime's alliance with foreign buyers instead of Nicaraguan producers during conflicts over contract compliance.[45] The cattle bourgeoisie challenged the exclusiveness of ASGANIC and the prices paid by the slaughterhouses dominated by the Somoza family. Although marginal adjustments were made by the regime,[46] elite dissatisfaction persisted.

Questions were increasingly raised about the basic political competence of the regime as it proved unable to stem or deactivate the growing mass insurgency. Repression was targeted at students and lower-income groups, but relations with private sector elites also deteriorated. Rising violence drew international attention to the repressive character of the state, feeding a negative image of the regime and further undermining private sector confidence. Following Somoza's heart attack in July 1977, momentum built again for regime change. Martial law was suspended in September upon Somoza's return to the country after a stay in a Miami hospital, raising hopes for some political opening. Using that moment, INDE leaders launched a public critique of the regime over the dramatic increase in the foreign debt, continued delays in the reconstruction of Managua, the inadequacies of the state energy agency ENALUF, the poor service provided by the state-run telephone company, corruption in the Instituto Nicaragüense de Seguro Social, and the continued lack of representation of the private sector in many state agencies (IHCA 1978, 1:31).

Still relying on traditional opposition tactics, INDE leaders turned again in the fall of 1977 to the perennial notion of a dialogue. In the hope of forming a new political accord, INDE called on Archbishop Miguel Obando y Bravo to convene and direct a new Diálogo Nacional. At this stage, the private sector lacked the skills and vision required for fuller innovation. As Somoza stalled discussions, INDE was outflanked from the left by the rise of the alternative elite group, Los Doce.[47]

This latter group was composed of twelve business, religious, and intellectual leaders who commanded considerable prestige both within Nicaragua and internationally.[48] Organized by Sergio Ramírez, a novelist and intellectual leader who had secretly joined the FSLN, this group represented a more confrontational elite. Los Doce publicly expressed opposition to another dialogue, noting that previous pacts had only served to consolidate the dictatorship. With this opposition, momentum for a dialogue dissipated by the year's end. The private sector became more confrontational. The regime became increasingly isolated.

This isolation deepened profoundly with the assassination of Pedro Joaquín Chamorro Cardenal. Chamorro came from an old elite family that had placed four of its members in the Nicaraguan presidency before the Somoza family took over Nicaraguan politics. The family was one of the foremost representatives of the Conservative party in the country, and young Pedro Joaquín had inherited the role of opposition leader. In that capacity he had endured periods of imprisonment, torture, and banishment under Somoza. Chamorro's family legacy, plus his position as editor of the opposition daily *La Prensa* and leadership of UDEL, a multiparty opposition movement, made him one of the most visible and intractable opponents to the Somoza regime.[49] His murder outraged many in the business elite who regarded him as one of their own.

Private sector leaders moved now to make a forceful statement of protest and directly confront the regime. Workers in several establishments had gone on strike after word of the assassination spread; the strike momentum built when business leaders endorsed a walkout. On January 26, sixteen days after Chamorro's death, seven major private sector organizations formally endorsed a general strike and called on their members to close down (INDE 1980).

This action received broad support from employers and workers alike. Although *La Prensa*'s January 30, 1978, report of 80 percent participation in the work stoppage (*paro*) may be influenced by the paper's position on the issue, widespread participation is generally acknowledged. Business activities in the Centro Comercial de Managua with its 200 shops came to a standstill, and many factories on the industrial strip on the Carretera Norte closed their doors. Most private banks closed, the workers at the San Antonio sugar mill supported the strike, several cotton gins ceased activity, a number of livestock and dairy producers in Boaco stopped delivering their goods, and some members of the rice growers' Cooperativa del Oriente slowed production (IHCA 1978, 1:44–48).

When the government announced that employers supporting the bosses' strike would have to pay their workers for missed days, the main business associations issued communiqués accepting this obligation and insisting that the stoppage would last until Somoza left the presidency (*La Prensa*, January 25, 1978). The government then threatened retaliation. The customs agency announced that it would suspend the import licenses of all striking businesses. A few days later, in an effort to break the cohesion of the Cámara de Comercio and the Cámara de Industrias, the minister of economy declared that businesses no longer needed to be members of these organizations in order to obtain import licenses. Permission to import would now be granted on a case-by-case basis following a careful scrutiny of the activities of the firm (*Novedades*, January 26, 1978).

The minister of labor reported that any workers striking voluntarily would be dismissed. The BCN mandated that all banks, public and private, must stay open. State employees who honored the strike were to be summarily fired (*Novedades*, January 26, 1978). In spite of these pressures, the stoppage continued. Finally breaking their historical pattern of negotiation with the state, the Cámara de Comercio representatives refused Somoza's invitation to meet with him at his retreat in Montelimar (*La Prensa*, January 24, 1978).

The number of private sector organizations endorsing the closedown grew steadily to sixteen at the beginning of February. The strike helped to sift out and reorganize the private sector, clarifying the lines of political cleavage. In spite of the defection of several private sector groups that were too closely tied to the regime or too detached from the political arena to accept the risks, a series of other, small associations now joined with the major groups in a deepening expression of private sector opposition to the regime.[50]

The strike was not an immediate success. Somoza reportedly responded: "As my father said, 'I'm not leaving, nor can they make me go'" (*Ni me voy ni me van*) (*Novedades*, January 28, 1978). In the face of regime intransigence, the private sector strike slowly fizzled. Leaders of the private sector then shifted gears. Former INDE president and agroindustrialist Alfonso Robelo shepherded business affiliates into a new business-led political party, the MDN. This organization was founded in March 1978 to unite Nicaragua's fractious traditional political parties behind private sector leadership.

In their years of interaction with the regime, the private sector organizations had never developed a political organ of their own. Nor had they much affinity for established political parties. In times of crisis they had used their sectoral associations to represent their case before the regime; more typically, they had simply drawn on personal contacts with regime leaders. This absence of a business-backed political party gave the private sector leaders an appearance of political detachment and neutrality. In some ways this appearance served their interests, immunizing them against retaliation by the regime. In other ways, the absence of a representative party made it difficult for them to present a sustained and coordinated response to regime initiatives. By 1978 these limitations were increasingly clear.

By the time private sector leaders realized this need, however, the leadership of the opposition was shifting away from them. Spontaneous uprisings in places like Monimbó, military skirmishes, and mass-based movements were gaining political ground. These mass movements took even the FSLN by surprise, and it rushed to organize the growing insurgency. Repression by the national guard and populist promises by Somoza restored a veneer of order by March 1978, but opposition groups operating at the community level were beginning to gain momentum.

Encouraged by the popular uprising, the Sandinistas attempted to gain leadership of the rebellion by boldly attacking the presidential palace in August 1978, and another round of mass insurgency began. Five days after this attack, a second general strike was called. This time the strike was sponsored by the emerging political wing of the bourgeoisie, the FAO.[51] The FAO had been created in May as a broad coalition of UDEL, Los Doce, and the newly formed MDN. Seventy-five percent of Managua's business establishments were reported to have joined the August strike (Booth 1985a, 165).

Again, the government responded with its own forms of pressure. On the economic front, Roberto Incer Barquero, president of the BCN, issued an advisory statement to the Consejo Nacional de Planificación denouncing the private sector for "surrendering itself unconditionally" to political groups that repudiated private property, for eroding the financial base of the country, and for undermining the country's economic capacity. He recommended that both foreign and domestic bank loans be made available only to those firms that ignored the strike call and remained open; those that closed were to be denied new credit and their old loans were to be called in (memo, August 28, 1978, published in Ogliastri-Uribe 1986, 19–22). On the political front, hundreds of opposition leaders were arrested, including leaders of the FAO.

In spite of this, the strike continued for almost a month. Business leaders were increasingly inclined to make use of their economic powers in opposing the regime. When a series of new taxes was passed in August to increase the revenues for the war, both INDE and the Cámara de Comercio urged a policy of nonpayment by their members (Booth 1985a, 165). Business leaders also attempted to destabilize the regime by urging international lenders to suspend further credits for the Somoza government (INDE 1980).

This hostility spilled over into the bourgeoisie's investment and production decisions. After years of overall growth broken only by the 1972 earthquake, the Nicaraguan economy contracted by 7.2 percent in 1978 (CEPAL 1984). Among the numerous forces leading to this sharp decline was the increasing economic withdrawal of the private sector. Production in the urban areas declined even more quickly than the national average; in the secondary and tertiary sectors, output dropped by 12 percent in 1978 (Spoor 1987, 3). The growing destruction unleashed by the war caused business confidence to decline. Capital flight soared, reaching by one account US$1.5 billion, at least $600 million of which was withdrawn by private elites (Vilas 1986, 137).

Somoza finally agreed to OAS mediation of the conflict in the fall of 1978. Predictably, OAS-sponsored mediation by the United States, Guatemala, and the Dominican Republic of the talks between the government and the FAO soon faltered and collapsed. Acting on cues from the FSLN, Los Doce representative Sergio Ramírez withdrew from the FAO on October 25 and sought asylum in the Mexican embassy. Somoza's subsequent rejection of a plebiscite ground the proceedings to a halt, and by the end of the year, the mediation had completely broken down (Pastor 1987, 101–21). Several Latin American governments moved publicly into opposition to Somoza, and even Carter administration officials cut back support (Schoultz 1981, 62–63, 344–45; Pastor 1987, 120–24).

By this point, however, the FSLN had taken clear leadership of the opposition movement. Internal divisions among the Sandinistas, which had fractured the FSLN into three hostile camps, were overcome in March 1979, and a coordinated military campaign to defeat the dictator advanced. Having been tainted by their prolonged participation in the doomed mediation efforts, established elites lost their claim to moral or political leadership of the opposition. The private sector's role in the final phases of the insurrection, while still important, became secondary to the main action of the war.

Nonetheless, the last six months of the dictatorship were a time of tremendous growth and political development for private sector organizations. Confrontations with the dictatorship deepened, and new organizations emerged. Cotton growers, who threatened not to plant in the coming agricultural cycle when credit shortfalls at the banks disrupted their work, were threatened with confiscation by the president of the BCN. Pressed to address this problem, Somoza threatened to take over their land and "rent it to the peasants" if the current producers left it idle (Navas Mendoza et al. n.d.[b], 65–66.) Neither profits nor property were fully secure, and the war continued to escalate.

Independent organizing among producers culminated in the creation of UPANIC in March 1979. At the outset, this organization drew together three core sectors: the cotton bourgeoisie, livestock sector dissidents, and coffee producers. Representatives of these three groups formed the first governing council of UPANIC. Marcos Antonio Castillo Ortíz, a young cotton producer from one of León's wealthier families, was elected to the presidency (Minutes of the founding meetings, March 22, 1979 and March 28, 1979). In the next several months, UPANIC gradually incorporated more associations and became an umbrella organization that united a growing segment of the country's large- and medium-sized agricultural producers. Affiliates came from the cotton, coffee, cattle, dairy products, rice, sorghum, banana, and sugarcane subsectors.[52] In May 1979 the brooding division in ASGANIC came to a head, and the Somoza regime's last major private sector affiliate split in two.[53] In addition to the broad opposition from industry and commerce, Somoza now faced a wall of opposition in the crucial agricultural bourgeoisie.

By 1979 dozens of associations and their regional affiliates were moving into the opposition, and the peak association formed in 1972 was reactivated. To facilitate coordination, COSIP leaders organized all participating associations into one of seven sectoral chambers: INDE, CADIN, Cámara Nicaragüense de la Construcción, CONAPRO, Confederación de Cámaras de Comercio de Nicaragua, UPANIC, and Asociación de Banqueros (which was dissolved following bank nationalization in July 1979). COSIP, now renamed the Consejo Superior de la Empresa Privada (COSEP), was streamlined and centralized. When the regime revoked the legal status of INDE and the Cámara de Comercio, COSEP, which had never sought legal status, continued to function. It now rejected Somoza's requests for dialogue and joined the FSLN's call for a national strike. The third and final strike began on June 4, 1979, and lasted until the dynasty was overthrown.

On June 6, COSEP issued a communiqué calling for the immediate resignation of Somoza and the creation of a new government of national unity. Eleven days after the JGRN was formed in Costa Rica, COSEP issued a statement formally recognizing it as the new government. Two representatives were sent to Costa Rica to make contact with the junta and discuss its plan for governing (INDE 1979). After years of battles and confrontations, organized economic elites finally broke with the regime and, at the last hour, formally threw their support behind the new government.

Conclusions

By the end of the 1970s the relationship that the Somoza regime had fashioned with the Nicaraguan bourgeoisie was no longer acceptable to growing portions of the elite. A policy of promoting growth, fragmenting the private sector, and parceling out favors failed to satisfy an economic elite that wanted a more predictable and efficient government. The economic model of the prerevolutionary era was out of sync with the needs not only of the poor but even of relatively prosperous sectors. Increasingly, emerging middle elites aspired to rule directly.

After five years of recurring confrontations with the regime, the private sector in Nicaragua had gradually become more politically competent. COSEP was resuscitated and invigorated by the proliferation of new private sector affiliates. In July 1979 private elites papered over their segmentation with shared political purpose to endorse the ouster of the old regime. With a hubris born of wealth, an exaggerated faith in the power and attentiveness of the United States, and failed imagination, these elites viewed themselves as the natural heirs of the dynasty. As one business leader of that era concluded, "The businessmen thought of the Sandinistas as their peons. They thought they could put [the Sandinistas] in the field to take care of the guard. Then they would step in and take over when Somoza fell. If there was a problem, the United States would stop the Sandinistas from taking power" (interview, August 6, 1991).

Drawing on their new organizational strength, private sector leaders began the task of developing a relationship with the incoming revolutionary government. The Nicaraguan private sector entered the revolutionary period better organized and more politically capable than it had ever been. The years of private sector division and individualistic bargaining, however, had a lingering effect. Fissures still lurked beneath the surface, and the revolutionary regime drew on them. Some private elites, such as UPANIC's first president, threw their lot with the Sandinistas. After the ouster of Somoza, these businesspeople took positions in the Sandinista government. Other private elites took a contingent position, aligning with the government at the beginning but soon moving to the opposition. Private sector representatives in the governing junta—Alfonso Robelo, former president of INDE, COSIP, and the MDN, and Violeta Barrios de Chamorro, widow of slain *La Prensa* editor Pedro Joaquín Chamorro, for example—joined the government but resigned after only nine months.

Finally, many private elites viewed the new regime with suspicion. Several of the most prominent elites emigrated, following their capital to the United States. Those who stayed soon secured the leadership of COSEP and its attendant associations and turned those organizations into the leading opponents of the revolutionary government.

chapter **3**

Revolutionary Transition and the Bourgeoisie (1979–1986)

One has to raise theoretically the question of whether the bourgeoisie could just simply produce, without power; if it can limit itself as a class to a productive role. That is, can the bourgeoisie limit itself to making use of the means of production and using these in order to live, not as instruments of power, not to impose itself on others. I believe that this is possible in Nicaragua.
—Jaime Wheelock Román, *El gran desafío*

The Sandinistas needed private enterprise like a zoo needs a gorilla.
—Large cattle rancher, August 6, 1991

The Nicaraguan bourgeoisie, like all bourgeoisies, are pigs. They are interested only in their own well-being. All they want is to take money out of the country, change it into dollars, send their sons and daughters abroad. They are rootless. They have no ties to the country.
—Former MIDINRA vice-minister, November 2, 1990

Vision, Views, and Deeds

In the years after the FSLN came to power, the relationship between the revolutionary government and most of the traditional economic elite was punctuated with hostility. Expropriations undercut the elite's hold on resources. Those producers who avoided expropriation faced a maze of bureaucratic controls that, many claimed, turned them into an "administrative bourgeoisie." Private investment plummeted, and production levels followed suit. COSEP became the regime's prime domestic adversary.

Yet during the same period, many private producers started new economic ventures. Throughout the country, businesspeople benefited from heavily subsidized credit from the state-owned banks. The state provided agricultural inputs ranging from fertilizer to tractors at prices that were only a fraction of their international costs. Staples producers sharply increased output in response to state subsidies for domestic consumption. The Sandinista-sponsored UNAG launched a membership drive that recruited even medium- and large-sized producers. An array of joint ventures and service contracts were negotiated between the state and more audacious private elites.

Competing images of the Nicaraguan bourgeoisie—as a beleaguered class on the threshold of extinction at the hands of orthodox Marxist-Leninists, and as a protected class that benefited disproportionately from state development initiatives—continue to complicate the interpretation of the Nicaraguan revolution. For analysts like Nolan (1984) and Bugajski (1990), the FSLN's early links with Marxism profoundly shaped the ideology and practice of the revolution. Says Bugajski (1990, 1), "Sandinista domestic policies provide a valuable laboratory and a largely accessible case study of how a Marxist-Leninist system is imposed and adapted in a developing country." Careful analysis by country specialists (Vilas 1986; Booth 1985a; T. Walker 1985; Conroy and Pastor 1988), on the other hand, casts doubt on the appropriateness of the Marxist-Leninist label. Arguing that the Nicaraguan revolution was "more anti-oligarchic than anticapitalist," Vilas (1986, 265, 268) defines the experience as a *"popular, agrarian, and national liberation revolution,* more than a proletarian or socialist one."

Close observation of the revolution reveals an array of concessions for the bourgeoisie interspersed with punitive batterings that defy simplistic interpretation. One productive way to integrate different threads of the experience is to unpack the concepts of ideology and behavior and to approach both in dynamic terms. Andrés Pérez (1992) suggests a useful analytical framework by differentiating between "pure ideology," which emphasizes a coherent worldview, and "ideology in use," which serves as a more direct guide to action. We might pursue the distinction by further differentiating between the ontology or broad philosophical moorings of revolutionary ideologues (vision), the more specific views and predilections of the leadership rooted in their concrete experiences (views), and the actual behavior of state elites in which such factors as resource restraints, established alliances, and habits play a role (deeds).

This chapter explores the interplay between the vision, views, and deeds of Sandinista leaders during the revolutionary transition in the opening years of the revolution (1979–86). It charts the rise of a statist model that centered the economy in the state sector, the inroads made into the resources of the traditional economic elite, and the regime's efforts to differentiate among sectors of the capitalist class in its quest for intersectoral allies and control.

Revolutionary Transition and State Expansion

The FSLN came to power in 1979 committed to the development of a mixed economy in which a private sector would continue to play a role. What that role would be was a matter of sustained dispute. For much of the FSLN leadership, the private sector's role was initially conceived as a limited one that would become less important over time. Yet several forces pushed the regime to retain a substantial private elite in spite of its reservations. Grudging recognition of the role some economic elites had played in the ouster of Somoza slowed the new regime's opposition. The extensive economic losses associated with the insurrection and concern about further erosion of national production also contributed to the decision to leave much of the bourgeoisie in place. The desire to avoid and, subsequently, blunt U.S. opposition, and to maintain political and material support from Western Europe, Canada, and Japan, served as a deterrent to precipitous antibourgeoisie action. The class extraction and family ties of some FSLN leaders may have also made them reluctant to move against the bourgeoisie.[1] A whole series of historical and political factors that were closely tied to the Nicaraguan context contributed to the Sandinista revolution's curious and fluctuating economic amalgam.

Although unwilling to move definitively against private sector elites, the FSLN leadership was ideologically committed to blunting their economic and social power. In the emerging revolutionary vision, the state-owned Area of People's Property displaced the private sector as the centerpiece of the national economy. The new government's first economic plan concluded: "The new State which is being constructed will be converted into the axis of the reactivation process and the transition toward the New Economy that our Fatherland needs" (MIPLAN 1980, 22). FSLN leader and minister of planning Henry Ruiz concluded that the APP "is the central axis, the most dynamic mechanism in the revolution's economic and social transformations" (Ruiz 1980, 15). In the emerging economic model, the state now became the "centre of accumulation" (Irvin 1983).

The newly formed state enterprises would not only absorb a growing proportion of the nation's workforce but would generate the surplus with which to finance the transformation of the country. The private sector, on the other hand, would play a subordinate role. As junta member and sub-

sequent FSLN vice-president Sergio Ramírez Mercado (1982, 83) explained:
"The mixed economy should take as its starting point the harmonious
and delimited insertion of the private economy within the great strategic
flow of the Area of People's Property."

The initial expropriations allowed the government to begin pursuing
this set of goals. The day after the JGRN assembled to replace the collapsing dynasty, all of the property of the Somoza family, military officers, and
high-ranking functionaries who had left the country was confiscated (Decree #3, July 20, 1979).[2] The result was a distinctive nationalization process. Unlike the Mexican case, in which the revolutionary regime slowly
constructed a parastate sector over several decades and transferred expropriated land to *ejidos*, the Sandinistas moved quickly to develop a large
public sector under direct state control. Unlike the Chilean case, where
the state sector expanded rapidly but each nationalization was the subject of intense contestation, the Sandinistas began their revolution with
consensual support for sweeping expropriations. As a result, the Sandinista state quickly acquired a considerable chunk of the economy without
extreme polarization, as least at the outset.

Confiscations in the first years provided the state with 1.6 million mz.
of farmland, roughly 20 percent of the nation's total, 78 percent of which
was in estates larger than 500 mz. (CIERA 1989, 1:293). In addition to the
roughly 1,200 estates that were acquired, the regime also took over five of
the nation's six sugar mills, three of its four slaughterhouses, the whole
tobacco industry, dairy plants, rice mills, cotton gins, coffee processing
facilities, and a host of other agroindustrial activities owned by former
Somoza affiliates (Mayorga 1990, 8). Foreign-owned mines were appropriated, as were a welter of other businesses and industries owned by Somoza
allies. Following the transfer of these and other resources to the state, public sector production expanded from around 15 percent of GDP in 1978 to
36 percent in 1980 (Ruccio 1987, 64–65).

The Sandinista state also gained control of the nation's financial apparatus (Enríquez and Spalding 1987). The large private banks that had
evolved since the 1950s had been bankrupted during the insurrection.
Bank managers and major depositors had spirited their capital out of the
country as the fighting heated up; borrowers who had taken out loans in
the relative calm of early 1979 were either unable or unwilling to repay
them. Only a handful of the smaller financial institutions in the country
had avoided complete collapse. When the state took over the devastated
financial system and assumed responsibility for its operations, there were
few initial complaints.

The most controversial of the early reforms was the establishment of a string of state trading monopolies.[3] These operations were designed to replace the open trading system that had roused controversy in the late Somoza era. In the cotton sector, for example, the local and international export houses that had bought and sold Nicaraguan cotton in the pre-1979 period were replaced by a new state monopoly, ENAL (Núñez Soto 1981, 47; Biondi-Morra 1990, 329). Although this new restraint on free trade was controversial, especially with larger private producers, it garnered support from some producers who welcomed its price stabilization aspects (Sequeira 1981, 124–33). The commitment of these firms to use surpluses that were generated when export prices were high in order to bolster payments when export prices dropped made some producers who had been battered by wild price fluctuations in the 1970s initially sympathetic to this project.

These first steps delivered a heavy blow to the traditional bastions of economic power in Nicaragua. The disarticulation of the top economic groups through the takeover of the financial and export sectors left the remnant of the bourgeoisie yet more dispersed and directionless. The leadership of the bourgeoisie was initially seized by the sector of the economic elite that had been most steadfastly anti-Somoza and had forged tenuous ties to the FSLN. Several prominent business elites who had endorsed the insurrection were given highly visible positions in the revolutionary government. Not only was Alfonso Robelo, the young manager of a foreign-owned cooking oil company and former COSEP president, named to the first JGRN, but COSEP was given a quota of seats (five of the original thirty-three) in the newly formed legislative body, the Consejo de Estado (Booth 1985a, 191–93). At all levels, prominent members of the business community were inserted into the government, from corporate lawyers in the cabinet to major landholders in the municipal councils. Business leaders also took on jobs in the rapidly expanding bureaucracy, working side-by-side with both Sandinista militants and lower- to mid-level officials from the Somoza government who remained in the country.

This visible presence of local and national economic elites in the government was a source of consolation to fearful producers. Assurances by people like Robelo that the Sandinistas were not communists held down the exodus of elites after the revolution. Some business leaders who had fled the country during the fighting even returned to sniff the air.

Soon, however, tensions began to rise. A scant nine months after the ouster of Somoza, Robelo and Violeta Barrios de Chamorro resigned from the junta. As the locus of political power shifted increasingly toward the nine-man national directorate of the FSLN and away from the more broadly based JGRN, these representatives of the bourgeoisie were steadily marginalized. Sectors of the elite, who had expected to direct the revolutionary government, now saw the regime taking a decidedly more radical direction than they had anticipated, and they were powerless to stop it. Chamorro resigned first, in April 1980, ostensibly for health reasons; her subsequent criticisms of the regime revealed an underlying political opposition. Robelo, who had weathered several skirmishes with the FSLN over the political content of the literacy campaign and the electoral calendar, resigned four days later, denouncing the planned expansion of the Consejo de Estado to include additional Sandinista-sponsored organizations. These defections signaled the fraying of the relationship with the reform bourgeoisie as they began to recognize the subordinate position they had been assigned in the revolution.

Seven months later, UPANIC president Jorge Salazar, who had entered into a counterrevolutionary conspiracy to divide the military and topple the regime, was killed by Sandinista state security amid allegations of gun running. Salazar became a martyr for the business elite, and the relationship deteriorated further. The alliance between the private sector and the government did not unravel completely at this time, however, due in part to the intervention of U.S. Ambassador Lawrence Pezullo. U.S. officials still hoped to moderate the revolution by keeping some of the bourgeoisie on board (Pastor 1987, 211–12).

Tightening the Vise: The Critique of the Bourgeoisie

Revolutions are commonly shaped by internal conflicts between feuding camps. Radicals are suspicious of moderates, and both wrangle with the revolution's conservative wing.[4] These divisions may be held in check through the efforts of a strong, dominant leader or an ideologically grounded and cohesive revolutionary political party. At the outset both were missing in Nicaragua.

Since at least the mid-1970s the FSLN has been an internally variegated, factionalized organization (Hodges 1986, 218–55).[5] Although reunification agreements and military victory in 1979 helped the organization to congeal, internal tensions remained. Furthermore, the FSLN did not have a monopoly over the Nicaraguan government; it governed in coalition with non-Sandinista reformers. The government papered over these differences in typical Nicaraguan style with agreements that gave something to all sides. The presence in the FSLN leadership of people who had differing priorities, combined with the vagueness of the principles endorsed by the revolution and the inclusion of non-Sandinista reformers in high-level positions, undermined the cohesiveness of the revolutionary government.

Pushing for greater coherence, the Sandinista government moved during the first year to replace conciliation figures in the cabinet with members of the FSLN national directorate and to fill the Consejo de Estado with representatives of the newly formed, pro-Sandinista mass organizations.[6] Tensions, however, remained, both within the FSLN and within the government apparatus. Top and mid-level Sandinistas understood the revolution in different ways, as did many of those in government who were not Sandinistas. Most of the lower-level positions in the government were occupied by holdovers from the Somoza period who could not be replaced because of the scarcity of trained professionals in the country.

In spite of these obfuscating features, the dominant trends in the emerging ideology soon became clear. Analysis of internal documents, speeches, and policies indicates that, from the beginning, the FSLN leadership regarded the bourgeoisie as an adversary. In the first national meeting of the national directorate and the Assembly of the Cadre on September 21–25, 1979, only two months after the new government was formed, the "sell-out bourgeoisie" (burguesía vendepatria) was at the top of the list of groups that threatened the revolution.[7] Not all members of the economic elite were included under this rubric, but the concept had a broad sweep. From the standpoint of the FSLN, threats were posed not only by the residue of the Somoza dynasty or the traditional financial oligarchy of the BANAMER and BANIC groups but by "the reactionary commercial and industrial sector which has not entered the financial oligarchy but which has played a leadership role in the private sector" and "the layer of the agricultural bourgeoisie that tries to establish alliances with the peasantry intending to create a counterrevolutioary social base" (FSLN 1990b, 91).

The election of Ronald Reagan to the U.S. presidency in November 1980, followed less than two weeks later by the Salazar incident, exacerbated the growing tensions. The steady hostility that Reagan displayed toward the Sandinistas in his campaign rhetoric, and the historical lessons learned from observing how the United States undermined revolution in Guatemala and Chile, fueled the fear of an impending military intervention. Whatever tendency the FSLN leaders had toward "verticalism" or centralization of power[8] left over from their experience as guerrilla leaders or their political training in socialist countries was quickly reinforced by the threat of a U.S.-backed counterrevolution. The results were tightened internal controls, even in the midst of gestures of moderation.

In spite of the Forum for Dialogue held with private sector leaders in early 1981, the relationship with the economic elite generally deteriorated (Winson 1985; Sholk 1984; Gilbert 1985). A series of developments attested to the rift. First, recruitment efforts by UPANIC, the newly formed organization of agricultural producers, were undermined with the formation of an FSLN-backed competitor. The establishment of UNAG in April 1981, under the leadership of FSLN militants, usurped the position of UPANIC as the sole national producer organization in the countryside. Affiliates in cooperatives and small-scale producers, who had been incorporated into UPANIC associations through the organizational work of leaders like Jorge Salazar, were now drawn into a competitor organization closely linked to the FSLN.[9]

Second, the government began a series of urban and rural confiscations that went beyond the original Somoza holdings. On the second anniversary of the revolution, junta leader Daniel Ortega announced the confiscation of fifteen major urban enterprises on the charge of "decapitalization."[10] After months of tightening up on sharecropping and land rental by large landowners, the government also decreed an agrarian reform law (Decreto #782, July 19, 1981). This new measure gave the government legal authorization to expropriate idle, underutilized, or rented land on estates larger than 500 mz. in the Pacific region of the country and 1,000 mz. elsewhere.[11]

Finally, a testy Sandinista leadership, put on edge by deepening U.S. involvement in the contra war and growing private sector hostility, escalated a war of words with bourgeois leaders. Defense Minister Humberto Ortega, from the moderate Tercerista wing of the FSLN, bristled: "If they [those who consciously or unconsciously assist the plans of imperialism] do not mature, if they do not join the defense effort, when aggression comes they will be the first to be hanged along the roads and highways of the nation" (*Nuevo Diario*, October 10, 1981). Taking this as a personal threat against dissenters like themselves, COSEP leaders issued a communiqué distributed to the international press. They warned of the preparation of a "new genocide" in Nicaragua targeted against those who exercise the "right to dissent" and concluded, "We identify an unmistakable ideological line of a Marxist-Leninist tendency [corte] that is confirmed in the discourse of members of the national directorate" (COSEP letter to Daniel

Ortega Saavedra, October 19, 1981). Charged with threatening national security, signatories to the document were arrested and imprisoned, and COSEP became the political archrival of the Sandinista revolution.[12] By the end of 1981 the bourgeoisie's role in the revolution was widely understood to be limited. The campaign against the bourgeoisie was not narrowly targeted against specific opponents but broadened to raise tough questions about the class as a whole.

In capitalist countries, business elites are often accorded a certain ideological or even moral authority. This occurs because economic elites have been successful in promulgating the belief that the general prosperity of the society results from their entrepreneurial activities. The perceived ability of the private sector to create jobs, growth, and prosperity affords it considerable political authority and ideological clout. In the Nicaraguan case, however, the bourgeoisie had failed historically to provide for generalized prosperity or even a clear future promise of it. Pervasive poverty made it difficult for the local elite to claim that they had played a socially constructive role or that their economic freedom was a prerequisite for rapid national development. From the standpoint of the FSLN leadership, the bourgeoisie had been given the opportunity to develop the country under the Somoza regime, and they had failed in this historic mission. Speaking at the second anniversary celebration, FSLN national directorate member Tomás Borge (1982, 134) pursued the point with rhetorical flare: "What have [the unpatriotic businessmen] done for Nicaragua? They made it into a rubbish heap, into a lake of blood, into a valley of tears. Because they didn't teach the people to read and write. Because they did nothing for the health of the people. Because they took this country, which because of its natural resources should have been a paradise, and kept it backward and miserably poor."

The FSLN's concept of national unity, which had initially embraced the local bourgeoisie, underwent gradual modification. The 1981 strategic planning document of CIERA, MIDINRA's research arm, describes the narrowing of this concept over three stages (CIERA 1989, 1:45–154). During the insurrection (1977–79), national unity was defined broadly to include all except that sliver of the bourgeoisie that was directly linked to Somoza or the nation's key financial institutions. Agricultural and industrial elites, including even large landowners (*terratenientes*), were cultivated by the FSLN in order to isolate and defeat the dictatorship (CIERA 1989, 1:47). In the second phase (1979–81), an effort was still made to win over the local bourgeoisie in order to reconstruct the country and have

Table 3.1

Projected Participation of Property Sectors in Agricultural Production (Percent)

Property Sector	Total Agricultural Area			Irrigated Area			Production Value		
	1981–82	1990	2000	1982	1990	2000	1980–82	1990	2000
APP	18.30	22.29	27.40	40.60	54.90	57.70	16.00	23.00	30.00
CAS	1.30	11.75	25.10	—	10.30	10.90	2.60	11.00	20.00
CCS	13.60	17.85	23.30	—	9.00	9.90	18.00	16.00	20.00
Large estates	12.00	9.36	6.00	54.00	24.00	18.50	14.00	10.00	5.00
Small and medium estates	54.80	37.75	18.20	5.40	1.80	3.00	49.40	40.00	25.00
Total	100.00	99.00	100.00	100.00	100.00	100.00	100.00	100.00	100.00
Area (mzs.)	7,953,861	9,124,280	10,777,856	76,492	262,461	409,774			

Source: MEDA (1983), from CIERA (1989, 1:157, 161).

the time to build up key revolutionary institutions like the armed forces and the state farm sector (CIERA 1989, 1:50–51).

The third phase, which was to begin in 1982, would introduce a "new policy of national unity" that would "neutralize the bourgeoisie." "Neutralize," according to the new strategy, "does not mean eliminating the bourgeoisie but to differentiate it, divide it and weaken it as a class." Five strata of the bourgeoisie were now identified, ranging from the "decapitalizing" and "counterrevolutionary" sectors to a sector that "invests and risks its own capital" (CIERA 1989, 1:75,76). If private elites could accommodate themselves to the new logic of revolution, those who continued producing without draining state resources or increasing their profit margins could fit into the scheme as subordinate partners; the others, presumably, would not.

Perhaps the most important policy planning statement issued in the early years was MIDINRA's Marco Estratégico del Desarrollo Agropecuario or MEDA, which was completed in 1983 (MIDINRA 1989, 155–230). After years of debate and ideological tussling, the members of MIDINRA's fractious directing team (Equipo de Conducción) came together and drafted a program of strategies and priorities that, it was envisioned, would guide policy development to the year 2000. This document was embraced by MIDINRA Minister Jaime Wheelock, who lobbied for and secured its endorsement by the FSLN's national directorate. In the absence of any competing, long-term national development plan, this MIDINRA document served as the main expression of the regime's economic vision.

According to this plan, the large landowners were destined to play an increasingly marginal role in the national economy. The portion of agricultural land held in private estates larger than 500 mz. was projected to drop from 12 percent in 1981–82 to only 6 percent in the year 2000; this sector's contribution to the value of agricultural production would drop still more, from an average of 14 percent in 1980–82 to only 5 percent at the end of the century. (See Table 3.1.) Even small- and medium-sized individual producers would experience an erosion as they were nudged into cooperatives. The landholdings of small- and medium-sized producers were projected to decline from an estimated 55 percent of the farmland in 1981–82 to 18 percent in the year 2000, with their contribution to national production falling by almost half.

Private owners were to be gradually replaced by new sectors nurtured by the revolutionary regime. Determining who, exactly, would replace the declining private elite was a matter of some controversy.

The New Economic Model: APPistas versus *Campesinistas*

To design the new economic approach, models of other socialist states were scrutinized to see how the land and ownership questions had been variously resolved (see, for example, CIERA 1989, 1:110–22). The two competing models were those that emphasized either the centrality of state farms, favored by the APPistas, or the preeminence of agricultural cooperatives, pushed by early *campesinistas*.[13] Sandinista planning documents reviewed cases in each camp, and the internal debate within Nicaragua mirrored the debate that had taken place more broadly in the socialist world.

The line of argument that took an early and sustained lead emphasized the centrality of state enterprises. The pro-statist camp passed through two phases in the first years of the revolution. Initially, emphasis was placed on reactivating and increasing production in the factories, firms, and farms that had been confiscated from the Somozas and their allies. By 1983, attention shifted from building on extant infrastructure to constructing new state agricultural and agroindustrial projects using long-term planning and sophisticated technologies.

Ironically, three normally divergent groups (socialist technocrats, ardent fans of advanced capitalist technology, and nationalist developmentalists of the ECLA school) converged in their support for a centralized, high-tech state model. For some policymakers, the experience and apparent success of the economic model in revolutionary Cuba argued for an emphasis on modern, state-run farms. As a former MIDINRA vice-minister explained, "Cuba was our closest reference point" (interview, August 17, 1991). Through a powerful demonstration effect and direct planning support, the Cuban model had a significant influence on the economic vision that emerged in Nicaragua. Cuba's impressive accomplishments in both the development of advanced technologies and the eradication of grinding poverty made a forceful impact on Sandinista policymakers. At the invitation of the Sandinistas, Cuban planners played important advisory roles in the development of pivotal agroindustrial projects like the TIMAL sugar mill/energy project and the Chiltepe dairy project.[14]

The inspiration for large state enterprises was not, however, purely socialist. Managerial centralism and large-scale operations were forceful trends in capitalist economies as well. Several Sandinista policymakers were heavily influenced by their experience with advanced Western technology and their role in managing sophisticated, large-scale private busi-

nesses in Nicaragua. At the vice-ministerial level of MIDINRA, for example, several Sandinista functionaries had cut their administrative teeth
at ISA in the prerevolutionary period.[15] ISA was not only, at that time, the
largest sugar mill in Central America, but it was also at the center of a network of related industrial and commercial operations.[16] Convinced that
the weak entrepreneurial impulse in much of the Nicaraguan bourgeoisie
made it a poor candidate for major development initiatives, these high-
level functionaries moved to fill the gap with state entrepreneurs who
would oversee the development of a vast network of state firms. Intense
lobbying efforts for this kind of state capitalist model found sympathetic
support within both MIDINRA and, eventually, other ministries involved
in making economic policy.

Not only in Nicaragua but throughout much of Latin America the
image of the state firm as the centerpiece in the industrialization process
was well established through the dissemination of the ECLA model in the
1960s and 1970s (ECLA 1951; Furtado 1976). The intervention of an activist
state that fosters increased production and rapid industrialization through
various policies, including, in some circumstances, the creation of state
enterprises, was generally consistent with ECLA prescriptions. Variants
of this model were employed in the Latin American countries, such as
Mexico and Brazil, that had grown rapidly in the 1960s and 1970s, accounting for much of the appeal of the model. According to some analysts,
therefore, the ECLA model, rather than Cuban socialism or managerial
capitalism, provided the central conceptual inspiration for the Sandinista
transformation (Conroy 1984; Conroy and Pastor 1988). The Nicaraguan
model in this early period differed from other structuralist programs in its
more emphatic hostility to pure market forces and its deeper ambivalence
toward its own private sector. For some analysts and policymakers, however, this difference was largely one of degree. The parallels between the
state-centered approach being developed in Nicaragua and that endorsed
elsewhere in the region lent further intellectual and theoretical support
to the experience.

To summarize, the development of large-scale state enterprises, at first
justified by the infrastructure and technological integration of the properties inherited from the Somoza family, was subsequently supported with
an array of economic rationales. Although not entirely in agreement about
the role of the private sector, most economic policymakers endorsed an
economic model that centered on high-tech, state-owned corporations.

This vision of the state emerged clearly from program statements of the era. According to the 1983 MEDA, where the long-range structural vision of the revolution was most clearly sketched, the state sector was to continue expanding through the year 2000, when it was projected to control 27 percent of the farmland in Nicaragua, up from 18 percent in 1981–82. (See Table 3.1.) Furthermore, the state sector was projected to dominate the country's most productive land, with its control over the country's irrigated land rising from 41 percent of the total in 1982 to 58 percent in the year 2000 (MIDINRA 1989, 161). Its contribution to agricultural production was expected to almost double, rising from 16 percent in 1980–82 to 30 percent of the production value at the end of the century.

Indeed, in the first two years after the revolution, the APP property did continue to expand, even without the benefit of new agrarian reform legislation, through continued land invasions and a program of *compactación* or land takeovers to smooth the geographical boundaries of state farms. Following the agrarian reform decree in 1981, the portion of agricultural land under APP control increased from an estimated 20 percent of the total farmland in 1980 to 24 percent in 1981 (Deere et al. 1985, 79). Land expropriated under this law was initially retained by the state sector, as MIDINRA waited for evidence that the emerging cooperatives would consolidate into stable organizations.[17]

The state's financial and organizational resources were funneled heavily into the APP enterprises. Agricultural credit, for example, went disproportionately to this sector. Whereas it held only 20 percent of the farmland in 1983 (Deere et al. 1985, 79), the APP received 43 percent of all agricultural credit that year (CIERA 1989, 1:318). Agricultural machinery was also heavily concentrated in the state sector. Data for 1984, for example, indicate that the state sector had acquired 62 percent of the country's tractors and 71 percent of the harvesters (CIERA 1989, 1:353).

Some of the initial enthusiasm for the state farms was dampened as evidence mounted of their weak economic performance. By 1982 the state farms were experiencing clear difficulties; 47 percent of their bank obligations were already more than ninety days overdue. This delinquency prompted the first debt clearing (*saneamiento*) for the APP in 1983, in which around one-third of the debt was forgiven and the rest was restructured as long-term loans (Biondi-Morra 1990, 282, 283). According to Biondi-Morra (1990, 103, 136–41), between 1982 and 1985, two-thirds of the APP enterprises had losses, with deficits continuing in most plants even after the 1983 *saneamiento*.

Multiple factors contributed to the inability of the state enterprises to generate surpluses, ranging from the "historic vacation" taken by workers who reduced their workday to as little as three hours a day,[18] to the overvalued córdoba that, in spite of low-cost imports and subsidized credit, ultimately eroded the profitability of the agroexport products that most state farms were cultivating (Biondi-Morra 1990, 136–41), to the extreme pressures placed on the state farms to raise production and participate in state development projects, regardless of the costs involved (Biondi-Morra 1990, 295–304), to the priority given to the political objectives of the state farm sector over the objectives of production and profitability (Colburn 1990, 130). These problems helped Sandinista activists in the opposing camp to push for a shift from the state farm emphasis toward more attention for the peasantry.

Campesinistas, located primarily in CIERA, MIDINRA's agrarian reform research arm, advocated more accelerated land redistribution and the more equitable parceling out of state resources. Initially, the *campesinista* camp was most enthused about the development of the fully collectivized cooperatives (CAS). The formation of credit and service cooperatives (CCS) among current small- and medium-sized landowners was envisioned primarily as an interim step in the development of collectivized holdings. By 1983 the pro-peasant camp was able to secure a planning commitment for the allocation of 25 percent of the farmland to the CAS and 23 percent to the CCS by the year 2000. (See Table 3.1.) Nor was this simply a planning projection; the area organized into cooperatives actually did increase over time. The CAS sprang from nothing to occupy almost 9 percent of the agricultural land, and the CCS reorganized private holdings into cooperatives on over 11 percent of the land by 1988. (See Table 3.2.) MIDINRA pushed its regional directors hard to locate land for redistribution and sent teams into each region to sustain the pressure on regional officials. The number of cooperatives rose, reportedly reaching 3,160 with 71,539 members in 1988, up from 2,849 with 65,820 members in 1982 (Mayorga 1990, 15).

These cooperatives were extremely fragile, however, and tended to disintegrate quickly. As the contra war heated up, pressure for increased allocation of credit to these cooperatives, in order to make participation more attractive and bolster these frail institutions, resulted in some shift of bank credit. By 1986, 44 percent of agricultural credit was channeled to the coops and small producers affiliated with the *crédito rural* program (CIERA 1989, 1:318).

This relative increase in attention to the peasant sector, however, failed to dislodge the state sector from its preeminent position. The land held

Table 3.2

Land Distribution by Strata and Tenancy (Mz. and Percent)

Sector		1978		1984		1988	
		Area	%	Area	%	Area	%
Private		8,073.0	100.0	5,929.5	73.4	6,419.8	79.5
Farms	>500 mz.	2,920.0	36.2	1,025.7	12.7	604.8	7.5
	200–500 mz.	1,311.0	16.2	1,021.0	12.6	1,090.2	13.5
	50–200 mz.	2,431.0	30.1	2,391.0	29.6	2,295.6	28.4
	10–50 mz.	1,241.0	15.4	560.5	6.9	1,323.1	16.4
	<10 mz.	170.0	2.1	127.0	1.6	188.6	2.3
Credit and service coops (CCS)		0.0	0.0	804.3	10.0	917.5	11.4
Production coops (CAS)		0.0	0.0	626.6	7.8	705.0	8.7
State farms (APP)		0.0	0.0	1,516.9	18.8	948.2	11.7
Total		8,073.0	100.0	8,073.0	100.0	8,073.0	99.9

Source: Wheelock Román (1990, 115, table 7).

in the APP sector did decline after 1983 when the state began to pare down the size of the state sector and reallocate some APP properties to cooperatives and small producers. As Table 3.2 indicates, the portion of the nation's farmland in the APP sector declined from 18.8 percent in 1984 to 11.7 percent in 1988. In spite of these trends, the state sector remained central and, in some ways, was enhanced during this phase of the revolution.

Care was exercised to retain the core of the state farm system. A MIDINRA study of the area ceded between 1984 and 1986 concluded that 71 percent of the land divested by state farms had not been under cultivation.[19] According to one former MIDINRA director who had been in charge of MIDINRA operations in three different regions, the state farms generally trimmed off land that was less valuable due to its distance from the road system or its lack of infrastructure (interview, October 30, 1990).[20] Commenting on the APP divestment process, one mid-level MIDINRA employee concluded that regional directors were "giving the coops land around the periphery of the APP farms in order to have a readily available labor force for the APP harvest" (interview, August 6, 1991).[21] Not only did the APP retain the best of its lands, but it also tended to siphon off many of the best-trained ministry personnel, complicating the development and implementation of programs for the peasantry.

APP and the *Grandes Proyectos*

In addition to giving continued attention to the existing state farms, the regime launched a whole new series of state investment projects.[22] The initial plan in the MEDA for the *grandes proyectos*[23] envisioned the creation of thirteen large-scale agroindustrial projects (MIDINRA 1989, 227). Included were projects like lumber mills, a sugar mill, a cotton gin, and milk and fruit processing facilities. This agroindustrial development scheme was projected to cost, in the heady days of the early 1980s, US$1.5 billion by the year 2000, with two-fifths of the funding coming from abroad (MIDINRA 1989, 226). As this program was developed and refined, it grew to encompass thirty-eight agricultural and agroindustrial projects (Wheelock Román 1985, 128–29).

Because of its aggressive developmentalism, MIDINRA became the center of investment planning in Nicaragua. This ministry was the only sector to produce a long-term development plan, and it quickly assumed center stage.[24] In a 1985 study of state investment activities by the FNI, an affiliate of the BCN, 71 percent of investment spending in the forty authorized projects then under way was targeted to the agricultural and agroindustrial sector (Argüello Huper and Kleiterp 1985, 85). MIDINRA's goals were ambitious: to meet national nutritional needs and make the country self-sufficient in food production while also increasing and diversifying export crop production.

The biggest projects were major agroindustrial schemes designed to dramatically increase exports. According to the FNI study, the new export-oriented sugar mill TIMAL (subsequently renamed Victoria de Julio) was to absorb 24 percent of the state's investments in the agricultural projects, and the export-oriented burley tobacco project another 14 percent (Argüello Huper and Kleiterp 1985, 83). Even in production for the domestic market, investment focused on the introduction of advanced technology on state farms. The cattle industry was to be dramatically transformed with the introduction of new breeding and dairy production techniques in the Muy-Muy Matiguas, Chiltepe, and León Viejo–La Paz projects. Most remarkably, even maize production was to be shifted from the traditional low technology, peasant sector into high-tech production. The government planned to transfer food production out of the mountainous interior where it was found to exacerbate soil erosion and relocate it in the fertile flatlands of the Pacific (Wheelock Román 1985, 42–43).

This heavy emphasis on large-scale, modern production technologies was designed to overcome the social and economic problems that had traditionally plagued the Nicaraguan economy. Production fluctuations that are the bane of agricultural economies, for example, were to be attenuated with the introduction of irrigation. Seasonal unemployment, a major liability of agroexport economies, would be addressed through a system of double cropping, in which cotton and maize would be produced in alternate cycles (see Wheelock Román 1984, 12–14; M. Coronel Kautz 1984, 12–13). This new grains production program in the Pacific region, called the Plan Contingente, would also protect the country against the loss of staples production as the contra war heated up in the interior. A new vision, which emphasized the "development of production forces through the application of science and technology" (M. Coronel Kautz 1984, 12), was expected to raise the skills and productivity of the workforce, allowing them to command better and more stable incomes.

The general policy of conserving the best of the APP operations and investing heavily in building new production and processing facilities was defended as laying the foundation for the long-run development of the country. The standard Latin American practice of import-substituting industrialization and the newer injunctions about using "appropriate technology" were both rejected in favor of a state-of-the-art industrialization strategy that would allow Nicaragua not only to fill its own consumer needs but also to export competitively. As Wheelock Román (1984, 14) concluded, "We're not a country of 'appropriate technology', which has as its philosophy the institutionalization of underdevelopment. Even though we do sympathize with the appropriate technology approach, we don't regard it as the fundamental solution for the country, but as a complementary effort that must also be made. We still have, as a major goal, the task of producing fertilizers, for example, and agricultural machinery. . . . We are already doing the studies in order to move in this direction." To transcend dependency and underdevelopment and become competitors in the world market, highly sophisticated technology was required. Long-run schemes envisioned energy self-sufficiency through the development of alternative energy sources such as hydroelectric and geothermal power. Eventually Nicaragua would even produce its own inputs and machinery for agricultural and industrial use.

In spite of growing economic difficulties, state investment continued to rise in real terms, reaching a peak in 1986 when investments equaled a remarkable 24 percent of the GDP. The investment rate in the agricultural sector was particularly high and equaled 58 percent of the value of agricultural production in 1987 (CIERA 1989, 1:341). Although the portion of long-term bank credit allocated to APP declined after 1983, project development continued through the PIP, a program of direct state investment. According to plans for the 1983–90 period, 71 percent of projected investment was to go to APP enterprises, whereas only 25 percent was targeted to the coops; the medium- and large-sized private producers were projected to receive only 4 percent of the total (CIERA 1989, 1:350).[25]

The Bourgeoisie at the Margins: Adversarial Confrontation and Neglect

In the internal debate about sectoral priorities, the big loser was the local bourgeoisie. For much of this long first phase of the revolution, private economic elites were squeezed between the state sector, which sucked up many of the available financial and human resources of the society, and the peasantry, which pressed for increased attention and occasionally received it. The large- and medium-sized private producers experienced an erosion of land, credit, and political voice as state farms grew and monopolized resources.

The government's early approach to the private sector was generally one of adversarial neglect. Traditional economic elites were regarded with suspicion and disdain, and the official rhetoric about the bourgeoisie was often tinged with implicit threat. In terms of the government's medium- and long-range plans, the private sector's role was that of a minor adjunct. Evidence of the decline of the bourgeoisie is found in the patterns of land expropriation, land sales, credit allocation, and the distribution of agricultural technology.

Land Expropriation

To consolidate the state sector and respond to peasant land demands, private estates were taken over. Whereas the first phase of the land reform program (1979–80) concentrated on the Somoza properties, the second (1981–84) and third (1985–88) targeted non-somocista landowners, particularly the terratenientes or latifundistas who owned more than 500 mz. of land. Marxist theoreticians and developmentalists converged in their intention to remove valuable national resources from the hands of a lackluster, nondevelopmental private elite. Large landowners, estimated to number around 1,700 in 1978 (Deere et al. 1985,78), experienced a major erosion. The portion of agricultural land in large estates declined from 36.2 percent in 1978 to 12.7 percent in 1984 and dropped still further to

Table 3.3

Number of Properties and Area (in mz.) Affected in Agrarian Reform, 1981–1988

Region	1981 No.	1981 Area	1982 No.	1982 Area	1983 No.	1983 Area	1984 No.	1984 Area	1985 No.	1985 Area	1986 No.	1986 Area	1987 No.	1987 Area	1988 No.	1988 Area	Total No.	Total Area
I			84	24,231	70	43,202	17	4,937	29	7,047	41	51,275	28	7,483	3	1,870	272	140,045
II			73	72,582	44	35,271	36	39,941	70	58,451	114	47,084	30	4,872	18	1,262[a]	385	259,463
III							2	440			2	205			1	379	5	1,024
IV	13	16,412	16	8,539	85	51,111	7	4,305	93	12,052	168	33,581	4	2,320	2	100	388	128,420
V			61	82,097	13	28,601	19	13,547	13	7,722	71	38,807	57	27,851	2	28,515	236	227,140
VI	20	11,369	29	26,744	32	18,780	25	13,687	30	5,570	52	19,324	23	12,142	3	1,447	214	109,063
VII			2	825													2	825
VIII											1	2,050					1	2,050
IX	1		1	1,948	4	11,116			2	2,555					1	6,000	8	21,619
Other[b]			2	163	3	817			2	58							7	1,038
Total	33	27,781	268	217,129	251	188,898	106	76,857	239	93,455	449	192,326	142	54,668	30	39,573	1,518	890,687

Source: CIERA (1989, 9:40, table 2).

[a]Does not include 28,500 mz. that were expropriated with the Ingenio San Antonio in June 1988.

[b]Includes properties that cross regional boundaries.

82

7.5 percent in 1988. (See Table 3.2.) Indeed, the contraction of these large estates proceeded even more rapidly than planned; the MEDA had projected that private estates over 500 mz. would still control 9.36 percent of the agricultural land in 1990 (see Table 3.1).[26]

The major instruments for the reduction of these estates were the 1981 and 1986 agrarian reform laws. Data on the land acquisition process presented in Table 3.3 reveal the patterns of expropriation during the second two phases.[27] (See Table 3.3.) In the 1981–84 period, reform began cautiously but soon accelerated. The pace of expropriation was particularly rapid in Region I, the area where Sandino's army had historically prospered and which remained a Sandinista stronghold. Over a quarter (171 of 658) of the 1981–84 expropriations were carried out in Region I alone. Nationally, the average size of the estates expropriated during this phase was 776 mz., although the size of the estates taken varied from region to region.

The pace of land reform slackened in 1984, as land demands were met by the state farms shedding their less productive territories. By 1985, however, land reform accelerated again, now pressured by the wartime need to secure a stronger peasant constituency for the regime. As the contra war heated up, the Sandinistas were faced with a double problem. Landless and small peasant producers in the interior of the country, who had been a low priority for the regime and had received few concrete benefits, were being increasingly drawn into the contra army, often through material rewards and promises (Bendaña 1991). At the same time, the FSLN was having increased difficulty recruiting for its own army as draft evasion became rampant. To undercut contra recruitment efforts and bolster its own, the FSLN moved to step up land reform and land titling programs. By signaling a deeper commitment to the redistribution of resources, the Sandinistas hoped to secure an elusive peasant base.[28]

Large- and medium-sized landowners bore the brunt of this campaign. Faced with increased land needs, and unwilling to give up the state-centered model, MIDINRA quickened the pace of private sector expropriations in 1985. After a year of controversial land seizures, particularly in the densely populated Region IV where traditional land pressures were now exacerbated by the influx of refugees from the war zone, the agrarian reform law was altered to give the regime more legal latitude. The 1986 version of the law allowed the government to expropriate idle lands regardless of the size of the property and legalized the practice of expropriating lands for use in "national development zones."

In 1986 the land reform movement exploded, particularly in Regions IV and II. In that year alone, 30 percent of all agrarian reform expropriations took place. Ironically, the contra war that was fought, from the Reagan administration's point of view, to stymie the expansion of communism now hastened the erosion of the Nicaraguan landed elite. Although the government claimed that "efficient" producers were still protected from expropriation, hundreds of private producers who had escaped the chopping block in the preceding seven years now fell to the war-induced land reform push.[29]

Land Sales: Voluntary and Involuntary

In addition to land that was expropriated, MIDINRA also acquired land through donations and purchases. Indeed, around 200,000 mz., or roughly 8 percent of all "reformed" land, was obtained through sales, negotiations, or donations (interview, Mireya Molina Torres, October 1, 1990). Sandinista partisans who were large landowners frequently donated family lands to the state, particularly after they were given positions in the government. Unable, because of constraints on their time, to attend to their private holdings, and uncomfortable about their status as large landowners, these officials commonly turned their lands over to the APP sector.

In other cases, the transfer was less voluntary. The line between a property sale and an expropriation was often fuzzy. Although some owners were willing to part with properties and reached a satisfactory agreement about the terms of the sale with the local MIDINRA representative, many agreed to a sale only to forestall an expropriation that was already under way. Faced with a land invasion or an expropriation notice, some producers moved quickly to negotiate a sale in order to secure a cash payment rather than receive the "worthless" agrarian bonds that accompanied many expropriations.

In the early years, when the state still had some financial resources and could offer quick cash payments, these arrangements were often acceptable to the owners. Eighty percent of the land acquired in this fashion was obtained in the 1984–85 period, however, when the state's financial resources were becoming seriously strained (interview, Mireya Molina Torres, October 1, 1990).[30] With the deepening of the war and the slide in production, land sales to the state became more problematic. Sellers received payments only after long delays during which inflation ate up most of their earnings. In some cases, the sellers then refused to accept the payment and attempted to reopen the negotiation, alleging that they had, in effect, been expropriated without cause.[31]

By 1986 the state's financial disarray made it increasingly difficult to make credible purchase offers to landowners or to have those offers accepted. The government reverted back to expropriations in order to acquire land needed for redistribution.

Control over Credit

Land loss was accompanied by other reductions that attested to the eroding position of the agricultural bourgeoisie. One important area of decline was in control over bank credit. Following the nationalization of the banking system in 1979, there was an explosion of bank credit.[32] Most of the credit increase was absorbed by the expanding APP sector and, secondarily, by the growing cooperative and small peasant sector. The portion of bank credit received by medium- and large-sized producers declined from 96 percent of the total in 1978 to only 43 percent after the dust had cleared in 1981 (CIERA 1989, 1:318).

In part, this reduction resulted from the shift of the *somocista* properties out of the *crédito bancario* program over to the APP sector. Furthermore, the rapid expansion of credit meant that even a declining percent of the total could adequately cover most of the private sector's credit needs. The decline in the regular private sector credit continued until 1984, however, when medium- and large-sized private producers held 55 percent of the farmland[33] but received only 24 percent of the bank credit (CIERA 1989, 1:318). This gap suggests the marginalization and mutual withdrawal taking place between the state and the private sector.

More of an issue was the limited access to long-term credit. The mushrooming state sector absorbed almost half of this credit in 1983, leaving only a quarter of it apiece for the still-considerable medium- and large-sized producers, on the one hand, and coops and small producers on the other. After 1983 the shift of APP investment financing from the bank credit system to the PIP reduced the state stranglehold on long-term credit. The state farms, however, were immediately replaced by the small producers and coops, who came to absorb 63 percent of the long-term credit in 1986. In contrast, the medium- and large-sized private producers were allocated only 24–27 percent of this credit in the 1983–86 period (CIERA 1989, 1:319). Long-term credit was still available to private producers, but it was highly competitive and relatively difficult to secure.[34]

Bank credit was heavily subsidized. In this sense the private producers who got bank funding received considerable benefits from the new regime along with other producers.[35] Nonetheless, the credit patterns reflect the lower priority given to the eroding private sector as the regime consolidated its new development scheme. This declining access occurred in spite of the fact that this sector's repayment rates were higher than those of the others.[36] Indeed, the backlog of unpaid debts in both the peasant sector and the APP was such that the bank system resorted to periodic *saneamientos* to reduce and restructure their outstanding debts. As the nationalized bank system shifted away from the profit logic and began to emphasize new developmental and social objectives, the traditional link between finance capital and economic elites unraveled.

Agricultural Technology

As with the credit system, the priority given to other sectors also reduced the agricultural bourgeoisie's access to new technologies. Even by regional standards, Nicaragua had acquired little modern agricultural technology at the time of the revolution. A readily available labor supply and very low wages led the country to import only modest levels of advanced agricultural machinery. In 1979, for example, Nicaragua had only 2,850 tractors (CIERA 1989, 1:352). The Sandinistas' commitment to rapid development led to the quick expansion of this paltry fleet. An additional 997 tractors were imported in 1983–84.

Most of the new agricultural machinery went directly to the state sector, again reflecting the regime's commitment to a state-centered model of accumulation. In 1984, 62 percent of the nation's 4,051 tractors were located in the state sector; only 30 percent were owned by private individual producers (CIERA 1989, 1:353). The coops were least favored in terms of access to advanced technologies, receiving only 8 percent of the tractors in 1984.

Constraints to Ideology: Elite Fragments and Strategic Alliances

Shaped by vaguely socialist aspirations and a forceful commitment to rapid national development, the Sandinista regime pushed for a state-centered economy that alternately confronted and neglected the local bourgeoisie. But its ability to realize a social transformation was constrained by a range of domestic and international forces. In spite of the new statist model, the regime remained economically dependent on the private elite. Not only was the presence of a stable bourgeoisie necessary to hold down Cold War aggression, but the production of both consumer staples and essential export income still depended heavily upon this sector. One study of sectoral production patterns found that as late as 1986–87, large- and medium-sized producers generated 41 percent of total agricultural production. Their contribution to export production was a slightly more pronounced 45 percent of the total (Baumeister 1988, 30).[37] Furthermore, much of the labor force still depended on employment in the private sector.

The Sandinista leadership recognized that many of the particular characteristics of Nicaraguan society impeded full centralization. Wheelock (1983, 101–2), noting the importance of small producers in the Nicaraguan economy, concluded, "We cannot resolve the transformation of our society via the expropriation of all the means of production. This would not lead us to socialism; on the contrary, this could even lead to the destruction and disarticulation of society." For both pragmatic and tactical reasons, the Sandinistas attempted to accommodate more variation in their model than was common in socialist states.

Instead of adopting a rigid, ideological opposition to the bourgeoisie as a whole, the Sandinista regime ultimately opted for an approach in which the "rules of the game would be defined in the process itself, to identify, not theoretically but historically an original role that private enterprise can play in the construction of the new Nicaraguan economy" (MIPLAN 1980, 14). Sectors that played a useful role or made a contribution would receive rewards; those that did not would not. Although the bourgeoisie as a whole eroded in Nicaragua during this period, some sectors survived and even flourished. In spite of the generally adversarial relationship that emerged between the Sandinista state and the bourgeoisie, the complexity of both the state and the local elite impeded the impulse to unwavering opposition. The result was an often sharp differentiation between the vision and views of state leaders, on one hand, and their behavior or deeds on the other. Although a pattern of adversarial neglect characterized the overall relationship with the elite, more positive linkages emerged with specific subcategories, reflecting practical political and economic considerations.

In practice, the Sandinista model identified several axes along which the economic elite could be divided during the first years of the revolution. An effort was made to differentiate between the productive and the unproductive economic elites, to favor medium-sized over large producers, to provide special support for those who produced essential prod-

ucts for the domestic market over the traditionally dominant agroexporters, and to build alliances with the "homegrown" bourgeoisie instead
of its more cosmopolitan counterpart. Producers who employed efficient
production practices, who refrained from egregious forms of decapitalization, who had strong links in their local communities, who produced in
priority sectors, and who were not conspicuously wealthy or hostile to
the regime were identified as patriotic and generally given a protected
position within the revolution. Large capitalists, with sharply declining
production levels or in low priority areas, who were denounced locally
for decapitalization or abuse of their workers and who had extensive ties
abroad, on the other hand, were viewed negatively and became targets for
expropriation.

Productive/Unproductive

The first cut made in the economic elite divided those who were productive from those who were not. As CIERA's 1981 planning document
indicated, the bourgeoisie was first differentiated by dividing those who
could produce without draining the nation's resources from those who
produced little or did so only by drawing heavily on the state's coffers
(CIERA 1989, 1:73–79). Using this criterion, the commercial sector and
"non-priority urban services" fell into disfavor relative to the agricultural
sector (CIERA 1989, 1:85). The industrial sector, which was quite import
dependent and tied to the collapsing Central American market, also became a lower priority for the government. The agricultural sector, which
not only supplied most of the country's food needs but also generated
needed foreign exchange, quickly became the national priority.

Within the agricultural sector, further differentiation took place. Unlike many Latin American agrarian reform programs, including those in
Mexico and pre-1973 Chile, the Nicaraguan variant did not use size as
the primary criterion for determining which properties would be expropriated. Productive use of the land by its owners was the key legal factor
employed in Nicaragua. Although this provision was not always honored,
in most cases where productivity was high and maintained, the land was
not expropriated.

Middle- versus Large-sized Producers

Like the revolutionary regimes in Mexico and Chile, the Sandinista
regime sought to build an alliance with small- and medium-sized producers. Producers with extensive holdings were expected to be closely tied

to the traditional regional oligarchies. In contrast, small- and medium-sized producers were thought to be less wedded to the status quo and more open to economic and political change; these producers could serve as a battering ram to challenge traditional rural social structures. Further, promotion of the middle sector was consistent with a growth model that dispersed wealth more widely through the population.

Middle-sized producers had long been economically significant in Nicaragua. As Baumeister's (1984b) work on the stratification of production in the 1952–76 period indicated, middle-sized producers were generally responsible for a larger percentage of national production of key exports than were large producers. In 1971, for example, middle-sized producers generated 53 percent of the cotton crop (vs. 42 percent for large producers), 44 percent of the coffee (vs. 30 percent for large producers) and owned 29 percent of the cattle (vs. 19 percent for large ranchers) (Baumeister 1984b, 12).[38] Polarization of production and landholding in Nicaragua was much less acute than that found in regional neighbors like El Salvador and Guatemala.

The prominence of this middle-sized sector encouraged the Sandinista regime to assume that the contraction of large private estates would not seriously damage the economy, and that a development model which allowed private ownership for small- and medium-sized producers could be viable in Nicaragua. Initially, the middle-sized producers were not legally subject to expropriation, and property held in medium-sized estates remained relatively stable over time.[39] Whereas the portion of farmland held in large estates had declined from 36 percent of the total in 1978 to 7.5 percent in 1988, the portion in medium-sized estates dropped only from 46 percent to 42 percent. (See Table 3.2.) Private farms of 200–500 mz. held 16.2 percent of the farmland in 1978; this sector retained 13.5 percent of the farmland in 1988, and had actually expanded modestly in the 1984–88 period. The 50–200 mz. sector, which had 30.1 percent of the farmland in 1978, eroded only modestly, dropping to 28.4 percent in 1988.

The fact that this interim stratum remained roughly the same size in the 1978–88 period does not mean that medium-sized producers were completely untouched by the agrarian reform. Indeed, following the passage of the 1986 agrarian reform law, which allowed the expropriation of idle, inefficiently used, or abandoned land regardless of the size of the estate, hundreds of medium-sized properties were also expropriated. According to case-by-case data compiled by the Dirección de Tenencia de la

Tierra of MIDINRA (1987), properties expropriated in 1986 ranged in size from 1.5 to 7,159 mz. Seventy-nine percent of the 357 expropriated properties analyzed in that document were smaller than 500 mz. In that year, for example, 37 percent of the properties expropriated were smaller than 100 mz. and 55 percent were smaller than 200 mz.[40] As data in Table 3.3 demonstrate, the average size of the properties expropriated in the 1985–88 period was 442 mz., down from 776 mz. in the 1982–84 phase.

The agricultural elites in Nicaragua often owned several properties; these properties were sometimes in different parts of the country. Expropriation of one property generally left others intact. Some of the large property owners, therefore, dropped into the middle-sized bracket following an expropriation but continued to live and work in Nicaragua on the reduced properties that they retained. One large coffee producer, for example, lost a mountainous, underdeveloped woodland but held on to all of the land he had planted in coffee trees. Another lost the plots he and his family had historically allocated to peasants who participated in his cotton harvest but retained the larger portion that he managed directly. The relatively stable percent of the nation's farmland found in the middle strata is due, therefore, not simply to the infrequency of expropriations in that category but also to the shifting of some large property owners into the middle-sized category following land sales or expropriations.

Nonetheless, a much smaller portion of medium-sized property owners underwent expropriation than those who held more extensive properties. According to Baumeister (1988, 29), even after size restrictions were eliminated in the 1986 agrarian reform law, only 8 percent of the land redistributed in the 1986–87 period came from private estates that were smaller than 500 mz.[41] This suggests that the regime tried to avoid undermining the middle-sized producers that it wanted to include as part of its base.

Domestic Market versus Agroexport Producers

The government also pursued a less confrontational relationship with sectors of the bourgeoisie who produced basic staples for domestic consumption (Spoor and Mendoza 1988; Utting 1991). The Sandinistas' commitment to improve the urban diet by subsidizing prices for staples had quickly led to increased food demands. As the per capita consumption of rice, vegetable oil, chicken, pork, and eggs rose sharply following the revolution (Utting 1991, 45), pressure built for increased domestic production. Unable, at least in the short run, to fulfill this increased demand on state farms, the regime was forced to rely on private producers, including even large-scale capitalist producers of these strategic products. To secure increased production of basic products, the government developed a series of supports and incentives targeted toward producers in the Pacific region, particularly rice and sorghum producers, but benefiting large-scale maize and even cotton producers (who provided raw ingredients for cottonseed oil) as well.

After the revolution, almost half of domestic rice production was supplied by a small number of large-scale private rice producers (CIERA 1989, 9:92). Developmental support from the Somoza regime had allowed these large producers to install irrigation systems and achieve relatively high levels of production. With the national rice consumption now substantially dependent on the continued production of this sector, private rice producers were able to acquire a series of special concessions from the state. The guaranteed price paid to rice producers, for example, rose rapidly in the 1979–80 to 1981–82 period, more than tripling in two years.[42] More importantly, the regime used international financing from Western European governments in 1982 to purchase harvesters and other essential agricultural machinery, which it allocated to large rice growers on highly concessionary terms (interview, Mario Hanón, president of ANAR, August 23, 1986).

Nor was this sector targeted for expropriation, even though most of the private rice growers held large properties. According to the president of ANAR for this whole period, not a single ANAR member was expropriated (interview, Mario Hanón, May 3, 1990).[43] Although this sector faced numerous problems (erratic electricity disrupted the irrigation systems and burned out pumps, inadequate storage systems caused spoilage, etc.), private producers were able to increase their production through 1982–83. According to official government statistics, even as late as 1987–88 private rice producers had production levels that were as good as or only slightly below the levels that they had obtained in 1980–81 (CIERA 1989, 9:92). This output stability in large-scale private rice production was achieved at a time when private production levels of many other crops had plummeted. It facilitated major increases in total rice production in the 1979–80 to 1983–84 period.[44] (See Appendix 2, Table A.1.)

Other large growers producing for the domestic market also received favorable treatment. The animal feed industry grew rapidly as the Sandinista government attempted to increase consumption of protein-rich foods like eggs and chicken. This feed expansion boosted sorghum production and favored the generally large- and medium-sized producers who cultivated this crop. As with other crops, the government's price-fixing policy guaranteed producers a price that would cover costs plus provide a profit margin that was negotiated annually. MIDINRA's cost assessments generally assumed that producers used an intermediate level of technology. For producers who had access to modern technology and whose yields were higher than average, as was the case for most larger sorghum producers, costs were lower than those used in MIDINRA calculations, and the return was substantially higher (Spoor and Mendoza 1988, 30–31).[45] For this stratum, the government's guaranteed price and guaranteed market eliminated two of the chronic problems that had traditionally plagued the animal feed sector.

The same was true for many large-scale, modernized maize producers. For peasant producers, prices of manufactured goods rose more rapidly in the first half of the decade than guaranteed maize prices, leading to production disincentives and a decline in marketed output. For larger, better-capitalized producers, however, production costs were much lower and the guaranteed prices provided a substantial return. Utting's (1991, 28) index of maize production costs for 1983–84 found that for highly mechanized maize producers, the production costs per qt. were only 57 percent of the producer price. For peasant producers using traditional technologies, on the other hand, production costs surpassed producer prices by 18 percent, leading to net losses.

Large-scale staples producers benefited from subsidized credit, cheap electricity for irrigation and energy supplies, low cost inputs, and in some cases, access to inexpensive agricultural machinery. Perhaps even more than peasant producers, agrarian capitalists producing for the domestic market were able to take advantage of the supports provided for staples production.[46]

Chapiolla versus Comprador Bourgeoisie

The categories used to differentiate among sectors of the bourgeoisie were not all economic. A final distinction made by the regime focused on political and cultural differences found within the elite. In an effort to make inroads into the medium- and large-sized producers' strata, UNAG, the Sandinista-sponsored producer association, attempted to differentiate between a homegrown and an urban-based, internationally linked bourgeoisie. UNAG leaders posited the existence of a distinctively Nicaraguan, newly emergent bourgeoisie that could accommodate itself to the revolution. This sector, colloquially labeled the *burguesía chapiolla*, was defended as a legitimate participant in the revolutionary process and was actively courted by the regime.[47]

UNAG was initially designed in 1981 as an organization of prorevolutionary peasant producers who had already formed, or could be shepherded into, cooperatives. In 1984 this association began to undergo a transformation and gradual reorganization, signaled by the selection of new UNAG national president Daniel Núñez.[48] At the UNAG national assembly meeting in which Núñez was selected, a number of large- and medium-sized private producers were highly visible participants and drew praise from the new leadership.[49] Under Núñez's direction, larger-scale producers were actively recruited through the recognition of preexisting local producer associations and the creation of new specialized commissions. By 1986–87, for example, UNAG reported that 151 organizations of private producers had been incorporated into its network (Luciak forthcoming, 62; see also Luciak 1988, 9–10). In 1987 the number of these associate members claimed by UNAG climbed to 2,807, and members who had joined as individuals totaled 26,618. (See Appendix 2, Table A.2.) These figures represented 24 percent of the total UNAG membership. Looser forms of affiliation that allowed local autonomy, along with UNAG's growing commitment to the protection of property rights, made UNAG more attractive to agrarian elites.

In the search for large- and medium-sized members, UNAG leaders differentiated between "unpatriotic producers affiliated with COSEP," who for political and cultural reasons were outside the pale, and "patriotic producers," who were actively courted. The former were not just politically objectionable; they also were characterized by a style of life that separated them from the UNAG mainstream. These included large producers who "run their farms from afar. They are people who live in the cities. They have managers on the farms, but they only go on weekends or every two weeks." These producers had little direct involvement in the production process. From the standpoint of UNAG organizers, these producers functioned much like absentee landowners whose social and economic contribution to society was suspect. According to Núñez, "These people who live in Managua had more access to culture, to society, to the clubs, to all the comforts or deformations that life carries with it" (Núñez 1985a, 367–68).

In addition to their objectionable lifestyle, these sectors were more closely tied to the international market. They were more fully involved in the processing and marketing activities where exorbitant profits were concentrated. In Núñez's words, "They used to own slaughterhouses; they had everything. They used to buy coffee. They used to buy cattle. They used to buy everything to export. They themselves were the exporters of what the peasantry produced in this country." This cosmopolitan bourgeoisie, "who traveled outside the country and who received a different education" (Núñez 1985a, 369, 368) formed the core of the COSEP organizations and was seen as closely tied to the U.S. Embassy and the counterrevolutionary war. To effectively challenge the old power structure and batter down the forces of imperialism, this elite had to be displaced.

"Patriotic producers," on the other hand, were more fully rooted in rural life and were more directly involved in the productive process. According to Núñez, even though some of these producers were large landowners, "their dynamic of work in the countryside makes them rich peasants. That is to say, they have not become declassed [sic], separated from production, by moving to the cities" (Núñez 1985a, 367). This *chapiollo* sector was composed of medium- and large-sized producers who were of "peasant origin" (Baumeister 1988, 31). They were "normally a first generation bourgeoisie that opened space for itself by challenging the power of the large landowners" (Ortega and Marchetti 1986, 26).

The UNAG strategy of courting these medium- and large-sized producers who might be more susceptible to the appeals of the revolution was difficult and controversial. Ortega and Marchetti (1986, 38–39), for example, equated this sector with a "kulak" class and argued that the UNAG's efforts on its behalf reaffirmed the old power structure of the hamlet (*comarca*) and "weakened the poorest of the poor." Concerns about this new direction led to conflict with segments of the FSLN (Haugaard 1991, 22), as some revolutionaries decried the *enbourgeoisment* of their rural affiliate. Nonetheless, UNAG continued its recruitment campaign and found many of its most active regional and national leaders within this sector of the bourgeoisie.

Conclusions

The relationship between the Sandinista regime and the national bourgeoisie during the first seven years of the revolution was fraught with tension. Departing from pro-statist assumptions that rippled between populist and socialist poles, the Sandinista leadership adopted an attitude toward the private producers that generally shifted between hostility and neglect. Not only was the bourgeoisie's behavior in the early years of the revolution found to be counterproductive to economic recovery and the political consolidation of the new regime, but its activities in the decades prior to 1979 were judged to be nondevelopmental and contrary to national interests. Its claim to resources and legitimacy, consequently, was found to be feeble. In the new development model embraced by the revolutionary government, traditional economic elites were displaced from the economic center; the state assumed direct responsibility for the transformation of the Nicaraguan social and economic order.

In practice, however, the regime moved quickly to pragmatic adaptations. An ever-shifting concept of national unity pushed the government to identify sectors and subsectors of the traditional elite with which to seek an accommodation. Even under the most optimistic projections, the state could hardly hope to replace the extensive private sector that remained after 1979, and speedy reactivation of production required the participation of a wide swath of producers. The inclusion of private elites in the new model was also a response to geopolitical objectives; charges of Marxist-Leninism and communism could be held at bay and the Cold War rhetoric more successfully challenged if a substantial private sector was retained. Finally, the personal linkages between revolutionaries and local capitalists, forged by family ties, school experiences, or shared risk during the insurrection made mutual vilification more difficult. In this small, fractured society, class-based labels did not stick.

The regime began to differentiate among strata and sectors within the traditional elite. Those who were able to maintain or even increase their production were to be preferred over those whose production eroded rapidly; the middle-sized bourgeoisie was to be protected even as the large-scale elite was targeted for extinction; those who contributed to increased domestic consumption and improvements in the national diet were to be favored over the traditional agroexport elite; the homegrown, provincial bourgeoisie that was rooted in the land was to be preferred over denationalized, cosmopolitan capitalists who had suspiciously warm ties to the United States.

These distinctions gave shape to the Sandinista variant of the mixed economy. Each of these divisions gave rise to some controversy within the FSLN, and commitments made to favored groups were not always honored. Further complicating the debate about alliances was the fact that sectors that were favored according to one criterion were sometimes out of favor according to another. Some very large landowners, for example, were also highly productive; some important staples producers were also those cosmopolitan elites that UNAG derided. On the other hand, some mid-sized grains producers experienced declining productivity and decapitalized briskly, hardly meriting their privileged status. Complications arising from this intricate categorization scheme made the development of consistent policies very difficult. As a result, conflicting signals were sent even to potential allies. The consolidation of a new relationship was elusive, even as tactical understandings emerged between individual political and economic elites.

The Recrudescence of the Economic Elite (1987–1990)

> I take off my hat to the private producers who stayed in Nicaragua. In spite of all the problems, they continued to produce. . . . The bourgeoisie that stayed was the most progressive in Central America.
>
> —Former Sandinista secretary of programming and the budget, August 1991

> The Revolution ended some time ago.
>
> —Economic adviser to the Sandinista government, August 1989

B ROKE, battered, and under pressure from foreign enemies and allies alike, the Sandinistas moved, toward the end of the decade, to promote a fuller economic alliance with the local bourgeoisie. Leadership of the government's economic team changed, and U.S.-trained economist Alejandro Martínez Cuenca was named to head the SPP. According to Martínez Cuenca (1990, 137), the new economic program "was not a program to realize some economic doctrine, but simply a practical response to a no-win situation (*situación sin salida*)."

Situación sin Salida

Revolutionary regimes often follow an established economic pattern. After an initial downturn when the regime comes to power, the new government consolidates itself and some economic reactivation occurs. This surge is followed by an economic falloff as the regime attempts to push through structural changes. Economic contraction strains the cohesion of the revolution, erodes its base of political support, and contributes to further polarization. Internal and external pressures mount. The revolutionary regime then typically either moderates its course, as in the case of Peru, or is ousted, as in the Chilean case. Nicaragua was no exception to this general pattern.

In Nicaragua, the economic nosedive associated with the insurrection was followed in 1980 and 1981 by a brief period of economic reactivation. (See Appendix 2, Table A.3.) Sustained economic recovery proved elusive, however, and by 1984 a long economic slide began. According to CEPAL data, Nicaragua's GDP declined 9.6 percent in the 1981–89 period, compared with the regional total for that time period, which rose 11.7 percent. On a per capita basis, the contraction was even worse: whereas the regional GDP per capita dropped 8.3 percent between 1981 and 1989, that for Nicaragua plummeted 33 percent (CEPAL 1989, 18, 19). Nicaragua's GDP per capita, which had fallen to 1950s levels during the 1978–79 insurrection (Gibson 1987, 24), continued its descent under the Sandinistas to levels of the 1940s. By 1990, the GDP per capita was only 42 percent of what it had been in the 1975–1979 period (Gibson 1991, 25).

Because the revolutionary transition in Nicaragua involved the military defeat of Somoza's national guard and the creation of a new, guerrilla-based military, economic decline did not immediately threaten the survival of the regime. Unlike the Chilean experience, or even the plight of the Christian Democratic government in El Salvador, the reforms introduced by the Sandinista regime were forcefully defended by its armed forces.

The ensuing contra war, however, took a tremendous economic toll and set in motion forces that would later lead to electoral defeat. According to calculations by the Sandinista government, the war costs for the 1980–88 period totaled $17.8 billion (Wheelock Román 1990, 126). Economic costs included losses associated with the direct destruction of infrastructure and production, the loss of international credits, the costs linked to the U.S. economic embargo launched in 1985, and the budgetary distortions caused by increased defense spending. By 1987 the costs of the war soared to 62 percent of the government's budget, or 30 percent of GDP (Conroy 1990, 16).

The state-led development model the Sandinistas had adopted was slow to generate production increases and probably contributed, at least in the short run, to the production decline. The twenty investment projects in the agricultural sector that had been approved and launched by 1985 had an average lead time of four years before they were expected to be completed, and some, such as the Victoria de Julio sugar mill and the African palm development projects were expected to take yet longer (six and nine years, respectively) (Argüello Huper and Kleiterp 1985, 83). Poor planning, financing shortages, and an inadequate supply of trained administrators,

skilled workers, and construction materials meant continual cost over-
runs and operational delays. Furthermore, the emphasis placed on the
rapid expansion of these agroindustrial projects robbed other sectors of
needed resources. As Argüello Huper and Kleiterp (1985, 60) concluded,
"This form of investment supports a structural change in the Nicaraguan
economy, but the rhythm of its implementation, in view of the scarce
resources that the country has, is detrimental to the productive sectors
(state, private and cooperative that have installed capacity and maintenance and modernization needs), draining them of the minimal resources
needed for their on-going production."[1]

The resulting economic slowdown generated two major deficits in the
national economy. The first gap was in the internal government accounts.
Initially, tax pressure was increased by the Sandinista government to help
provide resources needed to finance the transformations it envisioned.[2]
Even when the tax pressure was rising, however, the fiscal deficit reached
destabilizing levels. In 1983 the fiscal deficit equaled 49 percent of government expenditures and 30 percent of GDP. (See Appendix 2, Table A.3.)
The rising costs of defense, combined with the political inability of the
government to cut social and economic projects deemed integral to the
revolution, triggered a growing gap in the government accounts. This gap
was covered by inorganic emissions from the central bank that generated
inflationary pressures.

Other government policies also contributed to a soaring inflation rate.
The use of multiple exchange rates to make essential imports available
at low cost led to massive exchange rate losses that were covered by the
central bank.[3] According to Arana Sevilla (1990, 46), exchange rate losses
equaled 9.5 percent of GDP in 1986. Bank losses from heavily subsidized
credit were also monetized by the central bank. These losses became even
more significant after inflation accelerated and the government failed to
index interest rates. According to calculations by Spoor (1989, 11–12),
the banks recovered only 8 percent of the real value of the loans they
issued in 1987, given the low, fixed interest rate and the soaring inflation levels. The combination of a large fiscal deficit, extensive exchange
rate losses, and massive credit subsidies, all of which were covered by
inorganic emissions, fueled an inflationary spiral (Taylor et al. 1989, 17;
Gutiérrez 1989, 167). The inflation rate became a major problem by 1985
and then skyrocketed, reaching record levels of over 33,000 percent in
1988. (See Appendix 2, Table A.3.)

These economic imbalances contributed to the second gap, that in the external sector. Throughout the period of the revolution, Nicaragua ran a negative trade balance. International prices declined for several of the country's traditional exports, and production levels tended to sag. Harvested area for agroexport products, which had averaged 455,000 mz. in the 1974–78 period, declined to an average of 361,000 mz. in the 1980–84 period and fell further to 268,000 mz. in the 1985–88 period (CIERA 1989, 9:73). In 1987–88, cotton production was only 27 percent what it had been in 1974–78, having fallen off sharply following a brief recovery. (See Appendix 2, Table A.1.) Coffee production also began to fall after 1982–83, reaching only 75 percent of its 1974–78 average in 1987–88. The drop in agroexport production contributed to a collapse in export earnings. The value of exported goods, which totaled $646 million in 1978, had fallen to only $290 million in 1989. (See Appendix 2, Table A.3.)

The overvalued córdoba and restrictions on foreign exchange created an "anti-export bias" (Mayorga 1991, 35) in economic policy that deterred private investments in agroexport production. Ad hoc efforts to stimulate increased export production through the proliferation of multiple exchange rates for different categories of exports and through the use of subsidies were "too little, too late, and unevenly applied" (Gibson 1991, 29). Even when producers wanted to increase production, other problems emerged, such as an inadequate harvest labor supply or delays in the delivery of fertilizers and pesticides (Enríquez 1991b). For some coffee producers and cattle ranchers, the spread of the contra war into their zones further impeded production. These difficulties led to an erosion of export earnings.

Import levels, on the other hand, rose rapidly after the revolution and continued to be high throughout the decade. For most years, the value of imports was more than double export earnings. Nicaragua was able to continue acquiring essential imports even as its economy ground down.[4] It did so through foreign borrowing, with loans increasingly coming from socialist countries responding to appeals for socialist solidarity or to the Cold War overtones of the U.S.-backed attack.[5] Nicaragua's foreign debt rose from US$1.6 billion in 1980 to an extraordinary $9.7 billion in 1989. (See Appendix 2, Table A.3.)

As export earnings declined and foreign borrowing increased, Nicaragua's ability to meet its external obligations diminished. In a region and an era afflicted with debt crisis, Nicaragua's situation was unparalleled. By 1990 the total foreign debt was five times the nation's GDP (Gibson 1991, 28). Whereas the interest payment on the foreign debt as a percent of exports for Latin America as a region was 29 percent in 1989, the ratio for Nicaragua was 61 percent. As a consequence of this extraordinary indebtedness, Nicaraguan external debt paper traded on the secondary market at 1 percent of face value by the end of 1989 (CEPAL 1990a, 34, 35).

By 1988, economic contraction, now in its fifth year, deepened sharply, and the economy spun out of control. Although the revolutionary government, in a military sense, had turned the corner in the contra war, it was losing the economic war. Uncontrollable budgets, rampaging inflation, soaring foreign debt, and declining production created an untenable situation. On almost every economic indicator, Nicaragua's problems were unparalleled in Latin America. No other revolutionary regime had survived as long in the face of such sweeping economic collapse.

The Push for Economic Reform

As economic imbalances became apparent in the mid-1980s, some sectors within the government began pushing to reorient economic policy. A tense competition to define the national economic direction flared. Moderates like Martínez Cuenca conflicted with those whose views were more fully Marxist, like Minister of Planning Henry Ruiz.[6] Others, loosely labeled as monetarists, clashed with ambitious developmentalists in MIDINRA (Biondi-Morra 1990, 299–306). The result was a series of faltering economic adjustment programs. The first, in early 1985, included a devaluation, new production incentives, and an effort to trim the fiscal deficit. It was a halfhearted measure, however, and it produced minimal results. Economic imbalances worsened.[7]

As the economic crisis deepened and the contra war waned, a policy shuffle in the government again focused on these problems. Between February 1988 and January 1989 the government lurched through three economic adjustment programs that were designed to stabilize the economy. Though the initial reforms had several "heterodox" features (Conroy 1990, 20), the adjustments became progressively more "orthodox" over time (Gibson 1991; Stahler-Sholk, 1990). By the end, the Sandinista government had moved forcefully toward a more conventional economic approach.

The first round of attack, announced February 14, 1988, included a complete remonetization. The government introduced a new córdoba equal to 1,000 of the old units, unified the exchange rates, and executed a major devaluation, with the official value of the córdoba relative to the U.S. dollar dropping from 70 to 10,000 in the old currency. These financial adjustments were accompanied with a downsizing (*compactación*) of the state through the reorganization of more than forty government agencies, a 10 percent cut in the government budget, and a layoff of more than 8,000 state workers (CIERA 1988; Gibson 1991; Conroy 1990).

To offset the burden these reforms would place on the low-income groups, two unorthodox provisions were included in the first round of adjustments. Minimum wages were to be increased an average of 225 percent, and price controls were to be retained on forty-six basic products.[8] Four months later, however, most of these palliatives were removed. In spite of price increases associated with a new round of devaluations, most of the remaining subsidies were eliminated, and price controls were lifted.[9] Galloping inflation eroded wage increases; wages continued their precipitous descent.

Recognizing problems with the political palatability of the new program, government officials pointed to the features that would boost the earnings of low-income groups (Martínez Cuenca 1988, 19–23; Conroy 1990, 22). The removal of price controls on basic food products, for example, was expected to benefit peasant producers who, because they used traditional technologies, were not expected to be negatively affected by the reintroduction of "real" prices for capital goods, electricity, petroleum, fertilizer, and other commodities.[10] Deregulation of wages was also expected to produce wage increases among more productive workers.[11] Most wage workers suffered a continual, catastrophic erosion in their earnings, however, making on average in 1988 only 3.7 percent what they had in 1980 (Arana Sevilla 1990, 48).

Natural disaster, so common in Nicaragua, compounded the problem. The cleanup and rebuilding efforts after hurricane Joan imposed an unexpected financial burden on the government at the end of 1988. In spite of the 1988 reforms, the fiscal deficit soared again to 26.6 percent of GDP. (See Appendix 2, Table A.3.) Inflation now reached astronomical proportions; even sharper adjustment was attempted. The third round of adjustments, launched in January 1989, included more drastic budget cuts and massive layoffs of state workers, now affecting even troops. This *compactación* resulted in the dismissal of 8,314 civil servants and a reduction of 13,000 army troops (BCN 1990, 5). Even though the government failed to raise the tax pressure, the fiscal deficit was now slashed to 6.7 percent of GDP in 1989, suggesting the depth of the spending cuts.

These measures were presented and defended by the newly named minister of the SPP, Martínez Cuenca. A moderate insider who, as minister of foreign trade, had criticized the statist direction in economic planning, Martínez Cuenca now became the government's economic point man.

Models and Alternatives Reconsidered

In attempting to restructure its development model, the Sandinista state had three basic options. It could push ahead with the emphasis on state-centered development, expanding the scope of state control. Alternatively, it could abandon the statist model and make a fuller commitment to the radical redistribution of resources, including those held by the state, with the creation of a new form of grassroots socialism. Finally, it could mend the fences with the private sector elite and attempt to restart the national economy by triggering private entrepreneurial investment.

The first of these approaches continued to have defenders, even through the end of the revolutionary period. According to Martínez Cuenca (1990, 139), the debate within the FSLN national directorate about the 1989 round of adjustments lasted for a full month, including weekends. One proposal still on the table was to abandon the mixed economy model and assume direct state control of the economy.

In the end, that route was not taken. Critics charged that many carefully forged external alliances would be lost if the regime were to move against the private sector. The government would forfeit not only crucial assistance from Western Europe but even support from the socialist states that were struggling through their own identity crises. The changing character of world politics ran counter to a state socialism option. Nicaragua's small, poor, and trade dependent economy made regime leaders reluctant to ponder the acute isolation that would result. Instead of embracing fuller state control, investment in state enterprises was finally slowed, and the state sector began a grinding shift toward stricter financial accountability. The 1988 reorganization of the state sector into a series of corporations attempted to put APP operations on a profit footing. Market forces were making headway.

The second argument, which favored a more radical redistribution of resources, including resources of the state, had been forcefully made by *campesinistas* since the early years of the revolution. Represented by CIERA and the IHCA, this group criticized the state-centered model. Some *campesinista* arguments implied that the MIDINRA development model and the methods used to advance it in the countryside were philosophically and economically akin to the Stalinist forced collectivization experience (Marchetti 1989, 35–45). This group called for more attention to the peasantry, initially emphasizing those who were organized into collective cooperatives, but coming over time to a more sweeping pro-peasant position. *Campesinistas* favored not only a more extensive agrarian reform program that would incorporate the perhaps 50,000 peasants who still remained landless at the end of the revolution, but also give more attention to the needs of small-scale producers and land reform beneficiaries. Instead of channeling millions of dollars into large-scale investments and assigning the best-prepared technicians to the APP sector, the government was called to invest in the development and dissemination of small-scale technologies that would raise peasant production.[12]

After 1985, as the contra war heated up and the evidence of economic difficulties began to mount, the *campesinistas* did win some ground. The pace of land reform accelerated, individual peasant land claimants were responded to more favorably,[13] and agroindustrial development projects were modified to integrate cooperatives more fully into their production process.[14] Still, although the government attempted to redress the imbalances that had resulted in few gains for the peasantry, it was unwilling to pursue a radically pro-peasant course. The historically low levels of productivity of the Nicaraguan peasantry and the recurring need to pardon its unpaid bank loans, combined with the modernizing, high-tech predilections of much of the MIDINRA leadership, militated against any such departure. Instead, the government began to reconsider its relationship with the bourgeoisie.

With the state sector being slow to take off and the peasant sector plagued by low production levels, the bourgeoisie was regarded as the last remaining option. The economic behavior of this sector was also problematic, but its performance in the first years of the revolution made some analysts optimistic that its productivity levels could be restored at relatively low cost. Furthermore, strengthening this sector would address the concerns and perhaps win the approval of foreign donors in capitalist countries.

The redefinition of the role of the bourgeoisie in the revolution involved a conceptual sleight of hand. Whereas in the previous period the government had taken pains to differentiate between sectors and strata of the bourgeoisie, these distinctions now became muted. The old distinctions between the "sellout" and "patriotic" bourgeoisie or the medium- and large-sized producers, for example, became less acute. Prominent economic policymakers like SPP head Martínez Cuenca began to insist that the producers who had stayed in the country during these long years of war and decline all deserved to be participants in the new economy (interview, Martínez Cuenca, August 16, 1991). The *terratenientes* and financial speculators were gone now; those who remained were the patriots.

This transition was based in part on real changes in the capitalist class. Many of the leading economic elites who were most opposed to the revolution had indeed left the country; others who stayed had gone through a hard process of learning to accept the revolution and even embracing some of its objectives. Yet some of those now being courted by the regime had been the objects of its scorn during the opening years of the revolution. To pursue an alliance with this group, the FSLN had to reconceptualize its development model.

After years of continuing economic crisis, and almost a decade of political control, the Sandinista leadership began to actively court the bourgeoisie. This transition did not materialize out of the blue. As we have seen in Chapter 3, the Sandinista government had already moved to identify specific fragments of the elite as potential alliance partners. Building on relationships established with those elite fragments previously identified as patriotic, and on interpersonal connections with strategically located businesspeople developed before or during the revolution, the Sandinistas now pursued a fuller rapprochement with the bourgeoisie. Although laboring under the burden of the economic adjustment, the traditional bourgeoisie generally regarded these overtures with approval.[15]

State-Elite Rapprochement

By 1988 the government had moved to give higher priority to private producers. In addition to the reestablishment of most market forces, realistic prices, very low wages, and reduced regulations, the regime responded to private sector complaints about the lack of security and the poor investment climate. It began to channel more resources to this sector and to reopen the formal communication channels with this group.

Rechanneling Economic Resources

Perhaps the most sensitive issue dividing the bourgeoisie and the government was the question of land ownership. The vulnerability of producers to expropriation on any of a series of often ill-defined charges led even those who had been favored by the regime to be wary of its leaders. At the end of the 1980s, however, the pace of expropriation dropped sharply.

Table 4.1
　　Sectoral Distribution of Long-Term Agricultural Credit, 1983–1988
　　(Percent)

Sector	1983	1984	1985	1986	1987	1988
Medium and large producers	26	24	27	26	31	70
State farms	48	38	27	11	16	10
Small individual producers and cooperatives	26	38	46	63	53	20

Source: CIERA (1989, 1:319).

In 1988 only 30 properties were expropriated, down from 449 in 1986.[16] (See Table 3.3.) Only three cases occurred in 1989.[17]

The general pattern of declining expropriations suggests the increased willingness of the regime to accept established land tenure arrangements, which favored current owners over the landless and the state farm sector. The changing patterns of credit allocation reinforce this assessment. After years of playing the third and last role in the credit system, the medium- and large-sized private producers now moved center stage. Whereas from 1981 to 1984 the portion of agricultural bank credit for these producers declined from 43 percent to 26 percent, by 1985 the pattern began to reverse slowly. In 1988 economic elites received 47 percent of all agricultural bank credit, compared with 26 percent for the state sector and 27 percent for coops and small producers (CIERA 1989, 1:318).

The new ascendance was even more marked in long-term agricultural investment credits. After declining in 1984 to the point where it received only 24 percent of long-term credit, compared with 38 percent for the state farms and 38 percent for the peasant sector, the private enterprise sector suddenly regained much of its historic control over investment credit. (See Table 4.1.) According to CIERA data, in 1988 a remarkable 70 percent of all long-term agricultural credit went to medium- and large-sized producers, up from 31 percent the year before. The APP now absorbed only 10 percent of this credit, and the rural credit program for coops and small producers received only 20 percent of the total, falling from 63 percent two years before. The bank system was undergoing a full restructuring along more conventional, less revolutionary, lines.

The shift in credit clients was the product of a new emphasis on bank solvency adopted in 1988. As the bank sought clients with demonstrated ability to repay their loans, it also inaugurated a new program that would index the cost of that credit, pegging it to the rate of inflation. In fact, however, the monthly increases in the interest rates still fell behind the galloping inflation rate, and even the revised program continued to provide subsidies to borrowers (Spoor 1989). Now those borrowers were heavily concentrated in the private elite.

New Organizational Openings

One way in which economic elites gain power is by having easy access to political leaders. The existence of regular channels of formal and informal communication allows business leaders to keep their needs and wants highly visible to policymakers and to monitor closely the state response. When business elites themselves rotate in and out of public office or when close family ties link the political and economic leaderships, this kind of access is most complete. Even without that personal or familial identification, however, friendship and school networks can still facilitate the development of communication channels that enhance the political position of the wealthy class.

In Nicaragua, as the expropriations decreased, the number of formal and informal contacts between top government officials and private producers increased. The government initiated a new round of consultations that culminated in the creation of new policymaking boards. It also launched a *concertación* process that blunted private sector opposition to the regime and heightened the internal political division of the bourgeoisie.

The Breakdown of Communication: 1979–1986.   In the early years of the revolution, the private sector's access to the political power centers was restricted. Communication between traditional elites and the Sandinista state became erratic and highly charged. The government wanted private producers to learn to produce without making demands about "extraneous" matters like the content of the national ideology, the educational system, press freedom, or election procedures.

In its effort to redefine the political roles of the private sector and avoid confrontations, the government adopted a series of strategies. One was to divide the private sector by level, deflecting attention from the top umbrella organizations like COSEP and UPANIC and focusing instead on *gremio* or sectoral organizations. Instead of meeting with UPANIC leaders, who focused on the need for systemic change, for example, the government representatives met with rice or cotton growers about technical issues such as access to inputs or marginal price increases.

During this phase, the main channel of communication with the bourgeoisie was a network of consultative commissions. These commissions had been created by decree in February 1980 and placed under the auspices of the then Ministerio de Desarrollo Agropecuario.[18] They brought together producers and labor representatives with officials from government ministries involved in production and distribution. Their work focused on technical production issues including labor rates, technological packages, bank credit, costs of inputs, and final prices.[19] The creation of these committees allowed government agencies to work with actual producers on a narrow, predefined agenda rather than meet with the politically ambitious leaders of the national private sector organizations.

Even for these production-oriented groups, however, the top FSLN leadership was inaccessible. Requests for meetings with key ministers were often denied or, more routinely, not answered. Representatives of the sorghum producers, for example, reported waiting for over a year during this period for an audience with MIDINRA minister Jaime Wheelock (interview, ANPROSOR, August 22, 1986). One leader of CADIN reported that friends in the government would meet him now only as a private citizen and requested that he not use official CADIN stationary in his correspondence with them (interview, CADIN, August 11, 1987). The FSLN, to one prominent cattle breeder, was a "masonic group . . . like the mafia. Those who didn't belong to it were outside" (interview, ACBN, June 28, 1990).

This separation was particularly important in the Nicaraguan context. As we saw in Chapter 2, the personalism of the Somoza dictatorship and the weakness of the legal system had produced a process in which business leaders were required to negotiate arrangements with political leaders on almost a case-by-case basis. These clientelistic negotiations were routinely done through face-to-face communication in which personal bonds carried great weight. Key business and public policy discussions took place in the homes of the elite, over drinks, in a convivial atmosphere. Friendships, often laced around extended family ties, sealed deals. Little information was publicly available about such matters as trade negotiations, investment opportunities, contracts, and bids. The country had no stock market, nor did it require public reporting of corporate earnings. The few corporations that issued stock generally sold it to a handful of insiders, often of an extended family. The system revolved around personal contacts.

After 1979 the old system was collapsing, and the new institutions were relatively inaccessible to the bourgeoisie. Comparing the Somoza and Sandinista eras, one large sorghum producer explained, "Somoza and his ministers would at least talk to us. They might tell us 'no' but at least they would talk" (interview, ANPROSOR, August 22, 1986). Although some economic elites had family ties to Sandinista leaders, particularly Luis Carrión Cruz and Jaime Wheelock, personal connections at that level were infrequent and often strained.[20]

This distance from the bourgeoisie buffered Sandinista leaders from private sector demands and allowed them to focus on their priority constituencies. But it had a political and, ultimately, economic cost. The sudden ostracism, combined with several spates of antibourgeois rhetoric, pushed many of these producers further into the opposition. Even *gremio* leaders began to suspend their attendance at consultative commission meetings. Arguing that they were only tokens at meetings otherwise stacked by pro-Sandinista representatives, these *gremio* representatives boycotted meetings or were suddenly unavailable for appointments with state bureaucrats.[21] Following the 1985 expropriation of SAIMSA, the large corporation managed and largely owned by COSEP president Enrique Bolaños, UPANIC affiliates formally renounced any further participation in these or any other gatherings called by the government (UPANIC 1985).

Renewal of Communication: 1987–1988.   Beginning in 1987 a new phase in state-capital relations got under way.[22] After two years of very limited contact with private producers, MIDINRA minister Jaime Wheelock moved to break the ice. MIDINRA now called a series of direct, large-scale meetings that Wheelock himself presided over. An acrimonious meeting with cattle ranchers, in which government programs were roundly criticized by representatives of both FAGANIC and UNAG, was followed by meetings with dairy farmers in FONDILAC and rice growers in ANAR (COSEP 1987a). As continuing complaints were lodged by cotton and coffee producers, the government moved to formalize high-level communication with those producers as well.

In April 1988 four national agricultural commissions were created.[23] These organizations became high-profile policy boards that replaced the defunct consultative commissions. The presidents of the new commissions approached their task as "ambassadors," representing the government but with greater attention to the views and beliefs of those private producers in whose terrain they tread.[24] The attendance of UPANIC representatives at meetings soon normalized. Ironically, after years of verbal sparring, UPANIC leaders now found common cause with UNAG representatives who took an increasingly entrepreneurial line on issues of property and prices.

Concertación: 1989.   Throughout much of Latin America the economic crisis of the 1980s prompted governments to seek a new social pact with business and labor. A search began for new forms of agreement about how the economic costs of recovery would be allocated and what the future rules governing economic negotiations would be. This search typically brought together an array of established adversaries for tough negotiations about the economic model that would be adopted. Concertación, or the process of striking a new social contract, required competing parties to make a series of calculations estimating short-term losses and long-term gains under different scenarios (O'Donnell and Schmitter 1986, 45–47).[25] Knotty topics that had often divided business and labor, including ownership, wages, profits, strikes, subsidies, taxes, trade priorities, and regulation, were back on the agenda.

Drawing on imperfect information, areas of mutual benefit or inverse gain had to be reassessed throughout the region, now under the pall of economic decline. Workers, themselves often stratified and disorganized, struggled to determine how best to reduce their losses and increase their opportunities in the face of economic collapse. Labor representatives weighed the costs of accepting current wage reductions or job loss against the uncertain prospects of future benefit following from a round of increased investments. Employers, often torn between their desire for state support and the appeal of the market, maneuvered to maximize their access to resources. They faced complex pressures for the return of flight capital and increased investment in a risky environment in return for the prospect of enhanced social legitimacy and possible future gain. The state, now shorn of the financial resources that fueled state activism in prior decades, struggled to retain essential powers even as it underwent deep retrenchment. The political leadership was forced to search for new methods to secure growth and promote national development. For all parties, the way in which the society's resources were to be divided was at stake.

Plagued by deeper economic crisis and social division than most, the Nicaraguan government opened a highly publicized economic concertación process in 1989. The Nicaraguan variant of concertación focused on the relationship between the state and private producers. Representatives of labor either did not participate in Sandinista *concertación* consultations or had only a minor presence. Consequently, *concertación* under this kind of government had a lopsided quality due to the absorption of much of organized labor under the Sandinista banner. Unionization had been extremely limited under the Somoza government; most labor organizations in Nicaragua emerged under the protection of the revolutionary regime.[26] The political and ideological dependence of organized labor on the Sandinista regime made it difficult for unions to exercise an independent voice.

Beginning in January 1989 intense meetings were held by top government officials with a small group of the country's most important cotton producers and processors to discuss the needs of that crucial sector.[27] In the weeks that followed, various UPANIC leaders were consulted about the 1989 economic adjustment plan before the measures were announced.[28] In April 1989 the government called for a fuller, open consultation with private producers in a two-day meeting. This Proceso de Concertación Nacional brought together Daniel Ortega, all of the leading economic ministers, and over 600 private producers in an event monitored by the diplomatic community.[29]

Including representatives from both UNAG and UPANIC, this session formally committed the regime to providing more resources for private producers. In a desperate move to restart the production process, multiple concessions were made.[30] The government agreed to reduce and fix the interest rates (at no more than 20 percent monthly rates for regular agricultural loans); reduce import taxes and port charges; lower other taxes by 50 percent for producers making investments to benefit their workers (better housing, potable water, etc.); extend the grace period for loan repayment for coffee producers and cattle ranchers; offer special price incentives for coffee producers who exceeded by 25 percent their production levels for the last three years; reduce long-term interest rates for the cattle sector; and forgive 50 percent of unpaid loans of irrigated rice, sorghum, basic grains, perishables, and sesame growers and restructure the remaining 50 percent. A special subsidy program was created for cotton producers, reducing costs, increasing the price, and suspending/renegotiating past debts on soft terms (five-year repayment period, one year of grace, 5 percent monthly interest) for those who agreed to plant again in the coming year.[31]

Perhaps most important was the government's renewed affirmation of established property rights. When Daniel Ortega presented the 1989 economic plan to the national assembly and called for a beginning of the *concertación*, he noted that there were still landless peasants in Nicaragua whose demands for land were just. Their demands would be met, however, by reassigning land held in those cooperatives with large, unused tracts of land. Private sector participants in the *concertación* process need not fear further expropriations (*Barricada*, January 31, 1989). Five weeks later, Wheelock announced that the government was preparing draft legislation to halt any future land expropriations (*Chicago Tribune*, March 6, 1989).

Respect for property rights was again affirmed in the April *concertación* meeting.[32] Concerning past expropriations, the government responded to producers' hostility to the highly politicized Tribunal Agrario, which decided legal appeals of expropriation decisions. Ortega proposed that the tribunal be placed under the jurisdiction of the Nicaraguan Supreme Court, which had, in previous years, periodically reviewed expropriation cases and found against the government (*Nuevo Diario*, April 21, 1989). In the words of UPANIC leader Ramiro Gurdián, the government was now using a "new language" in its conversations with the private sector (*Nuevo Diario*, April 22, 1989).

The following month, Ortega invited prominent private sector representatives to accompany government officials on their approaching sojourn to Stockholm, Sweden. The May 1989 Stockholm meeting was to allow the new economic officials in Nicaragua to meet with representatives of sixteen countries and three international organizations that were potential foreign donors. The government representatives, supported, it was hoped, by private producers, would describe the economic adjustments already under way and seek new foreign loans with which to finance economic reactivation and stabilization of the economy. Although most private sector leaders declined, several accepted the invitation, including two who held leadership positions in UPANIC.[33]

Deepening Fragmentation: A Cunning Invitation to Division

The *concertación* process was denounced in the opposition newspaper, *La Prensa*, as a "cunning invitation to division."[34] For private sector elites, the regime's newfound support for local capitalists muddied the political waters. Entrenched opponents remained skeptical, fearing a cynical plot. More moderate elements, however, moved to seize the opportunities opened by the negotiation process and to abandon the confrontational COSEP stance. A handful of private sector leaders were even drawn into the

FSLN camp and came to serve as its close allies. The fragmentation process initiated in the 1979–86 period now intensified as both the government and the private sector wearied of prolonged conflict.

Entrenched Opposition

For those who continued their strident opposition to the regime, the reforms of 1988–89 fell short of the mark. Although some of their economic concerns were being addressed, their behavior was never based solely on calculations of profits and growth. The bourgeoisie was not just an economic class; it was also a social elite. As Conaghan (1988) argues in her study of the Ecuadorean elite, interpretations of the behavior of the bourgeoisie that fail to consider the "moral culture" of the class may produce seriously misguided analysis. Just as Scott (1976) advanced the understanding of peasant behavior with an inquiry into their moral vision, so too must the analysis of the bourgeoisie be alert to the conception of a morally correct social order that pervades this class.

From the standpoint of economic elites, the Sandinista revolution had not only reduced their ability to accumulate but also undercut their social status and the respect with which they were viewed in their community. The trappings of wealth and bourgeois tastes, such as luxury cars or suits and ties, were now regarded with derision in the state-controlled mass media. Throughout the country, the private clubs, which had anchored the bourgeoisie as a social class, had been turned into public "cultural centers" and meeting places for the revolutionary government. Newspapers no longer carried a society section. Not only did formal titles like *Licenciado* and *Ingeniero* cease to be used, but even honorifics such as *Don* and *Doña* became less common. Workers sent former *patrones* into fits of apoplexy by using the informal form of address with them. The respectful, even affectionate attitude employers had taken for granted in their employees was replaced with detachment and hostility. Many employers now feared their workers. Several younger producers I interviewed in 1990 described the outrage and indignation these changing social relations had sparked in their fathers' generation. Some who had come of age in the prerevolutionary period now hesitated to visit their own farms and firms because of concern about a possible confrontation; many of them turned direct management of their enterprises over to their offspring.

Opponents also blamed the government for the dissolution of their families. Fearful of the regime's ideological appeals to their children and the impact of revolutionary propaganda on the beliefs their children would adopt, many of those with economic resources sent their children to live abroad.[35] The military draft provided another reason for sending their sons out of the country.[36] The diaspora of the new generation contributed to the further denationalization of the Nicaraguan elite as well as its brooding resentment against a government that would make family dislocations necessary. These and other objections to the Sandinista revolution were hardly dissolved by a few economic guarantees. Even if the Sandinistas responded positively to the bourgeoisie's economic demands for market prices and property assurances, the hostility of many was unwavering.

Furthermore, the emerging political aspirations of the economic elite were frustrated by the sweeping dominance of the FSLN. Elections were initially postponed until 1984 and then were won overwhelmingly by the FSLN. For private producers from the old Conservative party aristocracy in Granada, whose grandfathers and great-grandfathers had been presidents and ministers in the pre-Somoza era, or from the PLI, the oppositional offshoot of the Somoza family's party whose members viewed themselves as Somoza's rightful heirs, the prospects of realizing established political ambitions were made more remote by the consolidation of the Sandinista revolution in 1984. For other producers, who had not previously had political ambitions, the experiences of the revolution and their roles as leaders of the private sector organizations created aspirations that were steadily frustrated. COSEP and UPANIC leaders who carried the banners of the opposition for almost a decade and who became the political counterpoint to the government began to see themselves as natural successors to the Sandinista regime.

Inconsistency in actual government behavior only deepened this group's skepticism. Although the number of expropriations declined in 1988 and 1989, those that occurred were among the most highly publicized and politically controversial of the decade. In 1988, for example, the Sandinistas expropriated the ISA, historically Central America's largest sugar mill, from the powerful Pellas family.[37] The three expropriations that took place in 1989 involved the takeover of properties of some of the regime's most vociferous critics. These three producers were not only prominent figures in UPANIC and leaders of their respective coffee producer associations; they were also prominent members of the right-wing opposition party, the PLC.[38]

The regime made hurried efforts to control the damage done by these expropriations. For example, it succeeded in converting the ISA expropriation into a purchase after some months of negotiations.[39] It also attempted to return the three coffee estates expropriated in 1989 and offered compensation for the owners' losses.[40] This pattern of inconsistent signaling, however, undermined the Sandinista government's coalition-building efforts. The inability of the government to develop consistent policy hinted at the internal tensions at play within the regime. Disbelief and skepticism on the part of bourgeois opponents about the depth and durability of the new line were a natural result.

Private Sector Conciliators

For some private sector leaders, however, the general package of reforms and concessions made by the regime suggested that it was pursuing a new direction. This sense of possibility appealed to these entrepreneurs, and two new cleavages emerged. The first was a deepening fissure within COSEP itself. The second was the creation of a new organization that offered an alternative to COSEP-style confrontation.

First, schismatic tendencies erupted in UPANIC. COSEP had ruled against the participation of its members in the private sector delegation to the May 1989 Donors' Conference in Stockholm. COSEP leaders argued that this delegation would serve the partisan purposes of the Sandinista regime by helping it secure foreign financing. When one of the members of UPANIC's directorate, Juan Diego López, president of FONDILAC, decided to join the delegation in spite of this admonition, UPANIC president Ramiro Gurdián publicly urged his ouster. FONDILAC's officers rejected the move and reaffirmed their leader's status as president (*Barricada*, May 12, 1989; *Nuevo Diario*, May 13, 1989).[41] This episode highlighted the division within the organization between the central core and its affiliate associations. Whereas the COSEP/UPANIC leadership emphasized confrontational tactics and a desire to centralize decision making, some of the affiliate associations preferred to negotiate.

UPANIC affiliates also split over continued participation in the national agricultural commissions after the expropriation of the three coffee leaders. In spite of the national coffee leadership's call for producers to withdraw from the commissions, regional leaders in the affiliate in Jinotega, the country's most important coffee growing region, refused to cooperate.[42] UPANIC representatives on other commissions also rejected the boycott.[43] Again, UPANIC representatives and affiliates were unwilling to follow the lead of their more confrontational leaders when they judged their group interests to be better furthered through cooperation.

At the same time, COSEP's ideological and tactical leadership was being

challenged by the creation of a new private sector think tank. As part of
the process of dialogue, eight of Nicaragua's top business leaders and academics formed a new organization, CORDENIC. CORDENIC was the brainchild of two of the Nicaraguan representatives on the Comisión Internacional para la Recuperación y el Desarrollo de Centroamérica, colloquially
known as the Sanford Commission after commission founder U.S. Sena-
tor Terry Sanford. Five months after the Sanford Commission initiated its
operations, former COSEP president Enrique Dreyfus and INCAE economist Francisco Mayorga brought together six other moderate leaders of
the Nicaraguan business community to form a local spinoff.

The Sanford Commission was an international, privately funded task
force established in the wake of the Esquipulas II peace accords to promote
reconciliation and development in Central America.[44] It was composed
of forty-seven members from twenty different countries, including four
from Nicaragua.[45] This commission sponsored twenty-five meetings between 1987 and 1989 to promote dialogue among key representatives in
different camps. Emphasis was placed on addressing the urgent problems
of those displaced by war and suffering extreme poverty, but the long-term
analysis focused on development needs and democratization processes.[46]

Inspired by the Sanford Commission model, Dreyfus and Mayorga
pulled together a committee of private sector leaders to break through the
polarization that had characterized political and economic discussion in
Nicaragua.[47] CORDENIC emphasized the need for open dialogue and negotiation instead of isolation and confrontation and called for a change of
style in state–private sector communication. New "attitudes of cooperation" had to be cultivated "in all sectors of the community" (CORDENIC
1988). To this end, it organized a series of dialogues in which previously
antagonistic groups, such as competing unions or the wide spectrum of
political party leaders, were brought together to discuss common problems (CORDENIC 1990). Although CORDENIC seminars were wryly criticized by the newly established weekly newspaper La Crónica (August 24–
30, 1989) as a "dialogue of the deaf," they did foster the first of a series of
exchanges among divergent, antagonistic groups.

Since it was not a mass-based organization, CORDENIC did not compete
directly with COSEP. Many COSEP leaders, however, saw it as an implicit
critic and rival.[48] Instead of the stale condemnations laced with Cold War
rhetoric that characterized much of COSEP's communication, CORDENIC
used a reformist rhetoric that even included positive references to the
revolution. "The task is not to find who is guilty," concluded CORDENIC

member Antonio Lacayo at a fractious session in December 1988. Instead, he urged the country to "relaunch the Revolution" (*Barricada*, December 14, 1988).

CORDENIC represented a stratum of Nicaragua's urban-based, managerial bourgeoisie. This group of entrepreneurs was distinctly non-Sandinista. Two had been jailed by the Sandinistas, and one member's firm had been expropriated. They did, however, have various complex links to the revolution. Among them were two entrepreneurs who had participated in joint business ventures with the Sandinista state, one who had been given a lucrative import monopoly by the government, and one who had been a consultant in the Ministry of Planning for three years during the revolution. Another member had even held a leadership position in the FSLN during the 1970s. Generally young, with strong academic preparation, continued links to Nicaraguan universities, and diversified entrepreneurial investments that extended to other Central American nations, these private producers responded less personally to the government's attack on the bourgeoisie.[49] Their pattern of interaction with the Sandinistas separated this moderate, entrepreneurial cluster from the mainstream of COSEP leadership. Unlike COSEP leaders, CORDENIC members accepted the Sandinista revolution as an established fact.

CORDENIC's development in 1988 began to fill a gap in the spectrum of views and tactics that had polarized during the 1979–85 period. As the Esquipulas peace process brought Sandinista and contra leaders to the conference table and the prospects for peace increased, a new round of discussions about the definition and future of the revolution became possible. Some segments of the bourgeoisie, less inclined to ideological purity and more willing to accept the social goals of the revolution, now began to enter into that discussion. Weary of war and economic erosion and backed by the reform initiatives of the Sanford Commission, this group looked for compromise.

As a result of these developments, new forms of communication were opened between sectors of the elite and the regime. Social networks, underdeveloped and brittle during the earlier phase of the revolution, were now cultivated by some participants on both sides. Pivotal figures, like FONDILAC president López, worked to bridge the gap, bringing together some intrepid business colleagues and top FSLN leaders for social engagements. A handful of family or school connections between economic elites and government officials, most of which had ruptured during previous years, were now tentatively reestablished. Given the traditional

importance, in a small society, of face-to-face interactions and social contact to sediment relationships, these developments were symbolically and
psychologically important.[50]

The 1990 Elections and the Search for New Allies

The 1990 elections would determine the fate of the revolution. Under
the terms of the 1987 constitution, officials at all levels of government
were to be selected simultaneously. The presidency and vice-presidency,
all national assembly seats, and all municipal/regional council slots were
to be contested on February 25, 1990.

The elections of 1984 had given the FSLN sweeping control over the
government, in spite of COSEP-led opposition efforts.[51] Against six party
competitors from the left and the right, the Sandinistas won handily in
what were generally judged by observers to be relatively fair elections.[52]
With 67 percent of the valid vote, Daniel Ortega was chosen to be president, and the Sandinista legislative bench (composed of Sandinista party
members along with a number of close sympathizers) won sixty-one of
the ninety-six seats in the national assembly.

As the 1990 election approached, the Sandinistas worked hard to convey the electoral message that they had won the war and were now ready,
with the help of the private sector and foreign allies, to rebuild the economy. With parts of the country still an armed camp and the economy badly
tattered, however, it was difficult in 1990 for the Sandinistas to convince
the war-torn nation. Furthermore, unlike in the elections in 1984, the
opposition to the Sandinistas was now both committed to participating in
the election and largely united in its effort. The Group of 14, composed of
fourteen political parties that opposed the FSLN, successfully negotiated
a series of agreements with the government over campaign rules, media
access, advertising, financing, and international observation. This group
formed a coalition called UNO to challenge the regime.

Ranging from parties generally associated with the left, like the Partido
Socialista Nicaragüense, and parties on the right, like the PLC, this coalition was fraught with tensions. The weak miniparties that made up the
bulk of the coalition could not produce strong contenders for the executive positions; the business leadership again stepped in. In the first major
decision made by the UNO coalition, the selection of presidential and
vice-presidential candidates, the two leading factions of the bourgeoisie
battled for ascendance.

On one hand, Enrique Bolaños, former president of COSEP who had led the charge against the Sandinistas for years and whose property had been expropriated in 1985, was supported by conservative elements who wanted a full confrontation with the regime. On the other, Violeta Barrios de Chamorro, as the widow of Pedro Joaquín Chamorro and former member of the JGRN in its first year of operation, was regarded as less antagonistic to the reform process and more committed to national reconciliation. After two days of repeated balloting, Chamorro narrowly defeated Bolaños in the closed selection process through which the candidate was chosen. She headed a ticket that included Virgilio Godoy, longtime leader of the PLI, as the vice-presidential nominee.[53]

Although she was relatively inexperienced politically, Chamorro had a series of assets that made her an attractive candidate. The sentimental appeal of her late husband, her commitment to the revolution in the early years when it was most widely supported, her prominent opposition afterward through La Prensa, and the inclusion in her family of members who were in opposing political camps made her appear less objectionable to those who had earlier supported the revolution but now wanted a change. Bolaños, on other hand, suffered both the stigma of wealth and the reputation of uncompromising hostility to the revolution. Chamorro seemed more electable; her relative lack of experience may have made her seem more malleable to others who hoped to influence her future development. Once nominated, she named her son-in-law, CORDENIC member Antonio Lacayo, to head her campaign.[54]

The FSLN labored hard to win, using sophisticated campaign tactics, massive campaign spending, and the powers of incumbency to appeal to voters. Recognizing that the economy was its Achilles' heel, the government held down prices for basic public services, such as gas and water, and tried to convey the image that they had now won the confidence of business leaders and local producers. The idea that the Sandinistas were rebuilding their relationship with the private sector was conveyed in three ways. First, producers were included prominently as candidates on the FSLN slate. Second, the government offered a blizzard of new concessions to traditional elites. Third, the government staged a series of last-minute meetings with producers to demonstrate the access and ongoing dialogue that now marked their interactions.

The FSLN as a political party began to undergo a redefinition during the campaign. As the Central American peace process produced results and the contra war abated, the FSLN began to shift away from the "vanguard" structure to seek broader representativeness. Apparently recognizing that their core support group had thinned over the years, the leadership sought to build linkages with outside groups by including the leaders of those groups on the FSLN slate of candidates. According to then vice-president Sergio Ramírez, the FSLN consciously adopted the strategy of recruiting representatives of an array of large social groups, even if those representatives were not closely aligned with or ideologically linked to the FSLN.[55] The FSLN leaders decided to accept wide diversity within the party bench in order to maximize their chance to win the election.

One group courted by the party, somewhat incongruously, was the business sector. Several prominent business leaders and agricultural producers were included on the slate of candidates to be ratified at the party convention, and others were added from the convention floor.[56] The FSLN publicized prominently, in full-page newspaper ads, a list of twenty-four producers who were legislative candidates on the FSLN slate.[57] It built on the division that had emerged in the UPANIC leadership and successfully recruited the president of FONDILAC to run on the FSLN ticket. Other prominent business leaders, like Andrés Franceries, owner of Sandy's, a popular fast-food restaurant, joined the Managua municipal-level ticket and became outspoken campaigners.

At the same time, the regime announced a series of policy changes that further responded to private sector demands. Private non-*somocista* stockholders in companies that had been partially owned by Somoza allies and, therefore, confiscated under Decrees #3 and #38 had, in most cases, continued to hold their stock in these companies but were unable to exercise voting rights and received no dividends. Beginning in 1988 the reorganization of COIP, the state holding company that administered more than eighty of these industrial firms, allowed private stockholders to resume participation in the administration of these companies (Pasos 1990; *Barricada*, February 7, 1990; see also Fonseca 1989). The government expressed a willingness to take on private sector partners in selected state firms, and some state enterprises were reportedly offered for privatization.[58] The government attempted to rescind selected expropriations, including those of the three coffee-producing political leaders who lost their property in June 1989.[59] The unpopular reliquidation program, under which coffee producers were paid for their crops in a series of installments spread over the year instead of receiving the full amount at the time of the sale, was suspended (*Barricada*, August 10, 1989).[60] In meetings with private producers in December 1989, Wheelock reportedly proclaimed the failure of the Sandinista economic model and asked these elites to help the Sandinistas formulate a new economic strategy (interviews, ANAR, June 23, July 14, 1990). Just weeks before the election, Wheelock again proclaimed an end to expropriations, announcing, "As of 1990, there will no longer be confiscations or expropriations" (*Barricada*, February 14, 1990).

Finally, Sandinista leaders had a series of public and private meetings with agricultural producers in the final weeks of the campaign. New concessions were offered and public pledges made, including the prospect of producer participation in the administration of state trade monopolies (*Barricada*, February 16, 1990). Long interviews with national and regional leaders of COSEP and its affiliates were a staple of Sandinista media coverage in the days before the vote. UPANIC president Ramiro Gurdián was now quoted in *Barricada* (February 19, 1990) as saying, "There's space for us to work together." *Barricada* headlines blazed: "Mutual Confidence between Government and Producers" (February 16, 1990).

The FSLN strategists probably did not expect to win over many private elites with these tactics. Indeed, according to one study, only 10 percent of those who classified themselves as owners and proprietors voted in favor of the FSLN in 1990 (Oquist 1992, 14). The FSLN's goals were more vital. Rather than persuading the small number of private elites in the country to vote for the FSLN, the government hoped to persuade the large numbers of peasants, workers, and unemployed Nicaraguans that the economy could be reactivated under their leadership through a renewal of private sector investment. Demonstrating the private elite's willingness to cooperate with the FSLN, it was hoped, would restore the confidence of the larger population.

In fact, for a series of different reasons, this approach failed. The heavy emphasis on an alliance with private producers may have even undercut support from the FSLN's social base. The FSLN's newfound affinity for the bourgeoisie surely perplexed and antagonized some former supporters.[61] The Sandinistas lost the election, gaining only 41 percent of the presidential vote to UNO's 55 percent. They lost not only the executive branch but at every level of the election. At the assembly level, UNO received 54 percent of the vote and won 51 seats, whereas the FSLN got 41 percent of the vote and won 39 seats.[62] UNO also swept the municipal council races, winning a majority of the seats in 99 of 131 municipalities (see LASA 1990, 34–39). The Sandinista era had now passed.

Conclusions

Like revolutions elsewhere, the Nicaraguan revolution went first through an ambitious phase, in which important structural transformations were attempted, and then followed with a more difficult phase of retrenchment, as international pressure and domestic problems mounted. In the Nicaraguan case, this second phase entailed repeated overtures to local business elites. The early economic model, which incorporated selected, strategic sectors of the bourgeoisie, was now revised to admit business as a whole. Jinotega coffee growers and FONDILAC officers now being approached by the regime were hardly the medium-sized or *chapiollo* producers identified as potential allies in the earlier phase. Indeed, CORDENIC members were among the most wealthy and prominent business leaders in the country. Convinced that the bourgeoisie that remained in Nicaragua was the most progressive in Central America, and caught in a no-win situation, the regime reconceptualized the role of private elites in the revolution, now in a more favorable light.

As foreign loans dried up and state development projects continued to absorb rather than generate resources, local capital from the private sector was thought to provide the only remaining hope for economic revitalization, both as a source of investment and a force that could mobilize new foreign support. Some in the elite, convinced that the Sandinistas had permanently altered the nature of their society, accepted negotiations with the regime. This approach succeeded in further fragmenting the Nicaraguan private sector into entrenched opponents and those who were open to dialogue. It failed, however, to renew economic growth or persuade the Nicaraguan population that the country was on the road to economic recovery. Ultimately, the Sandinistas were expelled from office.

Debate continues about the wisdom of this strategy. For some, this shift to the right undermined the Sandinistas' popular base (IHCA 1988c, 1989). For others, the overtures to the bourgeoisie revealed a fundamental, long-term interpenetration of the Sandinista leadership and old-line economic elites, particularly from the Granadan oligarchical families (Vilas 1992). Certainly the return to market principles during the economic restructuring and the indiscriminate courtship of the bourgeoisie challenged the Sandinistas' alliance with the Nicaraguan poor.

But the range of options available to the FSLN leadership contracted sharply with the economic crisis. Unwilling, because of geopolitical reasons and their own understanding of Nicaragua's needs, to tread new ground and radically redistribute the nation's wealth, the FSLN went a more conventional route. This strategy, in turn, helped FSLN leaders build a relationship with the segment of the reform bourgeoisie that succeeded them, laying the groundwork for a postrevolution negotiation process in which they could preserve some of their interests and some of their reforms.

chapter **5**

A Profile of the Elite Leadership

The Sandinistas were enriching themselves. They were not Marxist-Leninists; they were just grabbing up things. They were giving Marx a bad name. They never had a firm ideology.

—UNCAFENIC leader, July 23, 1990

The Sandinistas did an important thing teaching workers their rights, teaching people how to read. . . . The Sandinistas were able to raise, in a way that could be felt, the people's sense of worth. In this sense, Nicaragua has a better future than Guatemala, which has a very high level of inequality.

—ANAR leader, June 23, 1990

The Political Segmentation of the Economic Elite

To go beyond structural analysis and glimpse the inner workings of the economic elite, we must consult the bourgeoisie itself. This chapter draws on almost two hundred interviews conducted with leaders of the Nicaraguan private sector between 1982 and 1991. It focuses on 143 semistructured interviews with 91 private sector leaders that were conducted between January 1990 and August 1991. These respondents were chosen from a targeted group of business elites who played leadership roles during the FSLN era. Participants in this study were selected using a positional/reputational methodology. (See the discussion of methodology in Appendix 1.) Interviews were conducted with top-ranking officials of the major private sector organizations, private sector representatives on national boards and commissions, and others that respondents in the first two groups specifically recommended for inclusion in the study based on their informal leadership roles.

Politically, these respondents can be divided into five groups: (1) the moral-political opponents who waged ideological warfare against the Sandinistas; (2) the technical opponents who focused more narrowly and less rancorously on the pragmatic failings of the Sandinista government; (3) those in the middle, for whom the accomplishments and gains of the period were balanced against the problems and losses; (4) advocates of the

Sandinista reforms who tempered their support for the revolution with a critical assessment of specific policies or leaders; and (5) enthusiasts who took on the role of regime defenders.[1]

The first sector, composed of the moral-political opposition, was locked in a fundamental conflict with the Sandinista government. Actions of the regime that purportedly served the national interest or the concerns of the poor were interpreted as a cynical ruse designed to cover up the self-serving ambitions of the political leaders. For example, agrarian reform was understood not as an effort to empower the landless or increase resources available for national development but simply as a device to extend the dominance of the FSLN in the countryside and to centralize power and wealth in the hands of Sandinista leaders.

Although some of those most opposed to the FSLN saw the Sandinistas as diehard, orthodox Marxist-Leninists who were out to eliminate any vestige of private ownership, others did not credit them with any ideological convictions. "They weren't ideologues, they were bandits," said one adversary. "They didn't have consciences; they were prepared to kill," said another. Moral-ideological opponents frequently drew comparisons between the Sandinistas and the Somoza government. For this group, the Sandinistas represented a deteriorated variant of *somocismo*. "Both were dictatorships," said one interviewee, "but the Sandinistas were more repressive." Another alleged, "Somoza never robbed like the Sandinistas."

For this group, the losses of the era were not narrowly economic but also social and moral. Several respondents focused on the destruction of basic social institutions, like the family, and on the loss of traditional religious and cultural values. "Sandinista policy was bad in all senses. It divided the family, delinked the society," said one man who had moved his whole family to Guatemala in 1986. Traditional respect for older people, religious leaders, and employers was said to be gone, replaced by "shamelessness," "militarism," and "admiration for those who could steal the most." One leader of the UPANIC sorghum growers association concluded, "Sandinista policy was not bad, it was nefarious." Bitterness about this assault on the traditional social order gave this group's denunciations a strong emotional twist. In several cases, this hostility was deepened by the grueling experience of having been detained or imprisoned on various security charges by the Sandinista regime.

For this group, the policy shifts that took place at the end of the decade did not reflect any substantive adjustment on the part of the regime. As one large coffee producer said, "If you think that the Sandinistas moderated their course after 1988, you are mistaken. Any apparent change they made was just a tactic to get Western aid." The Sandinistas' belated commitment to end land expropriation also lacked credibility for this group. Several Masatepe coffee producers claimed in 1990, for example, that the Sandinista government had simply suspended these takeovers for electoral purposes and had targeted their lands for immediate expropriation right after the February 1990 election. A Matagalpan coffee producer echoed the charge: "If they had won in February [1990], they would have eliminated the rest of the bourgeoisie. The Sandinistas became the new bourgeoisie, and they wanted to take what remained from the old bourgeoisie."

There was a strong tendency in this group to assign responsibility for all of Nicaragua's problems, even those that predated the revolution, to the Sandinista government. The contra war as well was regarded purely as the product of Sandinista aggression. Some of these opponents concluded that the Sandinistas actively sought the conflict. As one sorghum producer put it, "The Sandinistas wanted the *contra* rebels, the war. They were begging on their knees for the U.S. to invade. That was the way to get more foreign assistance."

While the moral-political opponents had a prominent place in the opposition, a second voice was also heard. Leaders of the private sector who opposed the regime did not all concur on the nature of the problem or the best approach to take in interactions with the government. A second group, composed of technical-policy opponents, offered a more moderate critique. They too opposed the government but did not argue that the revolution was fundamentally corrupt, socially deviant, or driven by malicious intent. Rather, this group emphasized that the Sandinistas' vision was "impractical" and their programs "badly run" and "mismanaged." The emphasis here was on concrete policies, particularly those directed toward the business sector. For example, technical-policy opponents objected to land expropriations, not by arguing that private property was sacred, but by claiming that many of those expropriated were productive and that their expropriation was a violation of the Sandinistas' own agrarian reform policies. When asked to describe the main problems they had during the Sandinista era, these respondents focused on technical issues like prices, the poor quality of inputs, delays in the dispersal of credit and supplies, an insufficient or poorly trained labor force, and excessive bureaucracy. These critics argued that prices paid by the regime were too low to cover production costs. Producers were surviving, one coffee grower claimed, "by eating up their capital."

As with the first group, these producers were also unwilling to read Sandinista policy in a positive way. Even policies that favored private producers, like subsidized interest rates, were interpreted as miscalculations made by incompetent government officials rather than conscious efforts to stimulate production. Price supports and other nonmarket features adopted by the government to stabilize production and woo producer endorsement were not well regarded by this group, which favored a market-based approach. One of the nation's largest cotton growers, for example, derided the "artificial economy" and "fictitious currency" of the era. "Everything here was subsidized. That's the reason for the economic failure," said a former supporter turned opponent. A leader of ANAR concluded, "In the Sandinista period, we didn't have to work very hard. We knew we'd always get by. But I was pulled down by gravity. I've been deteriorating."

Accustomed to market forces, and skeptical of any other model, these private sector leaders viewed the unorthodox features of the Sandinista model with disdain. The government was viewed by these opponents as a "nine-headed monster" whose collective leadership style under the nine-member national directorate was found to create inconsistent or constantly changing policy. A medium-sized rice grower concluded, "Everything was the reverse of what an economy should be. Expensive things were cheap. Plans changed every day. . . . [The Sandinistas] said there would be no more confiscations, then they did it again the next day. Things that were 'good' one day were prohibited the next. . . . This showed the immaturity of the system, the lack of seriousness. You could only work for today, never make plans for tomorrow."

Unlike their more extreme counterparts, the second group did not regard the government as a diabolical force with which they refused to consort. Members of this group were relatively open to dialogue with government officials. For them, these interactions at least provided the opportunity to continually put forward an alternative program and "make some noise" (*hacer la bulla*). One large Jinotega coffee producer explained: "I'm one of those who believes that the fight is made within, that if you stay on the outside, you don't have any influence." This group generally responded more favorably to the post-1987 reforms, seeing them as a genuine move in the right direction.

Nicaraguan society became highly polarized during the revolution, and few private producers took the middle ground. A third group of mixed mediators did, however, detach themselves somewhat from the political debate and pointedly pursue a careful balancing act. One cotton grower concluded, "It's like you're standing in a rocking boat. Not too much to this side; not too much to that. . . . We must be moderate. There are two sides in the country. Neither can do away with the other." When asked about their opinion of the Sandinista government, favored descriptions in this small group included "I'm of the intermediate line, without politics" and "I'm of the center, unaligned." One prominent producer, whose family included both Sandinistas and their opponents, concluded that "in politics, one must be ambiguous. . . . Ideology makes everything fail. You have to be pragmatic."

Weary of acrimony and war, those in this middle group sometimes tried to function as mediators. They would describe achievements or positive aspirations of the revolution, such as agrarian reform or labor union negotiation, but they followed quickly with criticisms of the expropriations of non-*somocistas* or misuse of government power. Several members of this group saw the FSLN both as a victim of an aggressive U.S. foreign policy and as a provocateur, actively baiting the Reagan-Bush administration in self-defeating ways.

Perhaps most intriguing were those in the fourth and fifth groups: private sector leaders who supported the revolution. These leaders were anomalous, since they acted in ways that were not consistent with most standard theories of elite behavior. New approaches to social theory, however, sketch a conceptual model that may be of use here. Traditional explanations of economic and, indeed, even political behavior generally draw on a "rational actor" model that assumes that behavior is a calculated response to perceptions of self-interest, narrowly construed.[2] Some recent theory, however, rejects these assumptions and argues that "pro-social motivations" such as duty, love, and malevolence (Mansbridge 1990, ix) or sympathy and commitment (Sen 1990, 31) also shape political and economic choices. Decisions of economic elites to refrain from opposition to a revolutionary movement and, indeed, even provide political support, may respond to more complex motivations than those conventionally employed.[3]

Most members of the elite who came to support the revolution linked up with the FSLN during the period of the insurrection, when they were deeply frustrated by the abuses associated with the Somoza dynasty. Several of those who stayed with the revolution had been *colaboradores históricos*, directly involved in supporting the military effort of the FSLN in 1978–79. Unlike other private sector leaders, their opposition to Somoza included a fuller critique of the prerevolutionary social order and its underlying development model. They focused on the resources siphoned off not only by Somoza but by the "collateral economic structures—cotton gins, pesticide manufacturers, export houses," the "big ranchers who owned the slaughterhouses," or the animal feed industry.

This resentment was not limited to those who monopolized economic power; arrogant denizens of the Somoza-era social hierarchy also drew criticism. Those who were not admitted into social clubs dominated by the upper elite were sometimes embittered by their exclusion. Even some members of the elite who were admitted into these chambers responded negatively to the social arrogance of their peers. The concentration of wealth and social power in the hands of agroindustrialists or local oligarchs was a source of dissatisfaction for many producers who looked to the revolution for an alternative.

A range of forces served as catalysts to link these producers to the Sandinista cause, including religious conviction, intellectual persuasion, and family tragedy. Several mentioned the powerful pull of liberation theology espoused by radical teachers at prestigious prep schools, like the Colegio Centroamérica, that were favored by this class. The humiliating taunt by classmates at a U.S. university that his nation was a banana republic under Somoza led another into the protest movement. Age-old feuds going back generations between their families and that of Somoza propelled some into the opposition. In several cases, the loss of a beloved child to a rampaging national guard led elite leaders to repudiate the regime. The profound failures of the Somoza regime drew even economic elites into the making of the revolution.[4] Some subsequently dropped away, but those who took on leadership roles in the insurrection generally developed a long-term commitment to the cause.

Support for the Sandinista government required more than just a repudiation of Somoza-era institutions. Regime supporters shared a belief that "an active state role in the economy was necessary in developing countries." One supporter concluded, "The mixed economy is valid. State enterprises *should* exist in order to promote development, as an axis of development to generate resources that can be used for the whole society. They can help provide technical assistance to private producers and improve social conditions for workers." A common view in this segment of the bourgeoisie was that production, in the long run, must be built on a corporatist-style acceptance of the rights of workers. "Workers," said one former UPANIC leader, "are an integral part of production." Marginalized, illiterate, and abused workers would impede the collective development of the nation; literate and well-cared-for workers would advance its long-term development.

A few of the regime supporters entered the movement only after the Sandinistas came to power. For them, the contra war and the prominent role played in it by the United States often served as a catalyst. Said one, "My sympathy for the Sandinistas accelerated with the war. I am proud of Nicaragua; I didn't want it pressured from the outside." Ironically, a war that the Reagan administration defended as necessary to impede the advance of communism led some Nicaraguan business leaders to befriend the Sandinista regime.

Although the bourgeoisie as a class experienced a sharp economic erosion during the revolution, two considerations weighed against uniform elite opposition. First, ideology is not purely a reflection of objective material calculations. Even among elites, ideology is a refraction of various forces, including social ideals, a sense of historical junctures, and previous political frustrations. Second, although the bourgeoisie as a class lost resources under the Sandinistas, not all lost equally. Some lost massively; others actually gained. Interclass hostilities and the prospect of personal economic gain also helped to elicit the support of some prorevolution elites.

Not all of those who supported the regime were equally enthusiastic about the government, however; many had reservations. Supporters tended to divide into two groups: one that endorsed the regime, but with significant reservations, and another that identified more completely with the FSLN. The moderate reformers who had some reservations constitute the fourth group in this study; regime apologists were the fifth and final segment.

Several developments prompted most moderate reformers to retain a certain critical independence from the regime. In spite of the regime's affirmation of the "patriotic" producers, the Sandinista leadership's discourse against the bourgeoisie as a class and the waves of expropriation that occurred presented a major challenge to private sector supporters. As a result, many producers who endorsed the revolution had reservations about some of its central programs. One coffee producer who became an FSLN assembly candidate explained: "I am a private producer, and I represent private producers. I can't go along with the expropriation of other private producers." A dairy and rice producer explained his decision to run on the FSLN ticket as an effort to "moderate the FSLN" and weigh in against the "extremists."

Some large producers who supported the revolution noted that they were viewed with suspicion by regime leaders because of their "white skin" or "style of dress" and were often not consulted even in their areas of expertise. This contributed to mistaken economic measures. One problem described by many elites was what they called *yoquepierdismo* ("Me, what-do-I-lose-ism"), that is, a loss of personal incentive among producers.

Unlike regime apologists, moderate reformers included FSLN policy mistakes and excessive state control in their explanations of the crisis that engulfed their country. The support these producers gave to the FSLN in spite of these reservations was linked both to their ability to interpret their interests in a way that was consistent with a rising standard of living for the majority and to the revolution's own porousness and policy vacillation. The increasing pluralism of the FSLN, especially toward the end of the decade, allowed the regime to pull in and retain reformist elements of the bourgeoisie who found enough similarity between their own views and the diffuse goals of the revolution to warrant their participation. For those in this group, their relative position in society was less central than the prospect of collective advancement.

The fifth and final group of private sector leaders was composed of those who remained unambiguous regime apologists to the end. For members of this group, the problems faced by the Sandinista government were wholly rooted in the U.S.-backed contra war. When asked to list the factors that caused the economic crisis in Nicaragua, these leaders focused solely on "the war," "the economic blockade," and "North American imperialism." Much like the Sandinista leadership during this period, these private sector defenders were slow to reflect on any responsibility the government itself might have for the problems it faced. They took a fundamentally uncritical position on FSLN government decisions, including even those that were widely unpopular and contributed in 1990 to the electoral defeat. Arguing, for example, that the military draft policy was necessary, one coffee producer concluded, "If the government had done away with the draft, the president of Nicaragua in 1990 would not have been Violeta Barrios [de Chamorro] but [the former national guard colonel and general commander of the Nicaraguan resistance] Enrique Bermúdez." The decisions and policies of the government were presented as uniformly correct in the context of the times. One defining trait of this group was its failure to identify any negative characteristics of the Sandinista government.

As with the moral-political opponents to the regime, the regime apologists were often disconnected from their roots as producers. Although occupying positions as leaders of private sector organizations, many of those respondents in the first and fifth categories were defined primarily by their political roles and less by their activities in direct agricultural production. In some cases, those in the last group had left production and spent years working in high-level government positions, only returning to agricultural production in the final years of the Sandinista government. Although still serving as spokespersons for private producers in their associations and in the press, their direct connection with the production process had been weakened.

Most of those interviewed in this study were opponents of the regime. It is not possible to say with precision how representative they are of the bourgeoisie as a whole since no comparable study of a random sample of private producers has been done. As leaders of organizations, they are likely to be more politicized than those who have not been placed in leadership positions; this study may also contain a larger percent of supporters than was found generally in this class.[5] These respondents did, however, represent the bourgeoisie in the sense that they were the primary elected, appointed, or nominated spokespeople for the main private sector organizations during the Sandinista decade. The purposive nature of the selection process used here resulted in the inclusion of most of the top private sector leaders at the national level and those who were most prominent in the five regions included in this study (Regions II, III, IV, V, and VI). Respondents included, for example, seventeen (61 percent) members of UPANIC's twenty-eight-person *directorio* from the 1988–89 period. In all, a considerable portion of the universe of private sector leaders participated in this study, particularly at the national level, making the issue of the randomness of the sample less relevant.[6]

When given the opportunity to provide their own evaluation and assessment of the Sandinistas, 38 percent of the participants in this particular study were moral-political opponents whose statements will be categorized in the following tables as reflecting strong opposition. Thirty-three percent of the respondents were technical-policy opponents who gave a more muted critique of the FSLN and are classified here as expressing moderate opposition. A third, small group, composed of 8 percent of the respondents, offered a mixed assessment of the FSLN government. Balancing criticism of the regime against positive observations, these producers have been placed in the mixed category. A fourth group composed of moderate reformers, representing 11 percent of the respondents, provided what will be labeled moderate support for the Sandinista government. Finally, regime apologists who, when asked about the failures of the government, found none, composed 10 percent of the respondents. Their responses will fall under the label of strong support in this study.

If private sector leaders were not uniform in their condemnation of the Sandinista government, how might we explain the range of variation in their views? In particular, two patterns of attitudinal variation are relevant. The first is the differences in degrees of opposition between those registering strong opposition to the regime and those expressing moderate opposition. Why did some producers adopt an adamantly ideological position that admitted no negotiations or compromise with the regime, whereas others who opposed the regime adopted a more flexible approach that was more attuned to shifts in the behavior of the government? The latter group is especially interesting in a political sense because of its capacity to enter negotiation about the reform process instead of simply rejecting dialogue out of hand.

The second pattern focuses more generally on the differentiation between those who opposed the regime and those who supported it. Why, when most of the bourgeoisie was opposed to the Sandinistas, did some come to support the regime and even, in some cases, to become candidates for political office on the Sandinista ticket?[7] What sectors of elite society were most likely to lend support to a revolutionary regime? Which were its most likely opponents?

To explain these variations, several factors are worth exploring, including (1) differences in the economic and social characteristics of these elites, (2) the kind of organizational nexus in which they were embedded, and (3) the type of concrete experiences that they had with the reforms of the revolution. These issues will be analyzed in turn in the next three sections of this chapter. The final section explores the implications of this attitudinal variation for the elite's production behavior.

Wealth, Social Authority, and Politics

As the opening chapter of this book demonstrates, the bourgeoisie is not a uniform, homogeneous entity. It is often riven by subclass tensions and rivalries as elites compete fiercely among themselves. Some of the prop-

ertied are more prosperous than others and may be highly protective of
their privileged position. Some enjoy tremendous social prestige among
their peers and use this power to check the social advance of potential
challengers. Some have wealth that was inherited and may be in decline;
others have only recently obtained these resources and are in economic
ascent. These variations in economic and social characteristics may contribute to differences in political orientation and behavior within the elite.

In an attempt to understand the political segmentation of the bourgeoisie, several hypotheses about the impact of economic and social variations
might be offered. One might expect the most privileged members of the
society, who have the most to lose from redistributive social policy, for example, to be most resistant to revolutionary change. This study explores
the political consequences of two dimensions of class: access to economic
resources, like land, and access to prestigious social goods, like advanced
education.

Economic Resources and Political Views

In the agricultural sector, capitalists who are large landowners might be
expected to be more hostile to revolution than their medium- and small-
sized counterparts, particularly a revolution that is centered on agrarian
reform. Members of the economic elite who have access to scarce social
goods such as prestige educations obtained in institutions that confer
social status on their graduates might also be expected to resent the level-
ing, or at least reshuffling, impact of revolution. We might hypothesize,
therefore, that land size and educational attainments would be related to
bourgeois leaders' views on the Sandinista government.

In the Nicaraguan case, views on the government did vary modestly
with property size. The agricultural leaders with the largest landholdings
and production levels at the end of the 1970s were indeed among the
most vociferous opponents to the regime. In this study, 42 percent of the
leaders who were large producers in their activity in the period before
1979 were among the most intense, ideological critics of the revolution
and were classified as registering strong opposition.[8] (See Table 5.1.) A
slightly smaller proportion of the leaders with medium-sized holdings (37
percent) were in this extreme category. A sharper difference yet was found
with the few leaders who had been small producers before the revolution.
Among this handful of private sector leaders, only 20 percent registered
strong opposition to the Sandinistas at the end.

The Sandinistas' thesis that small- and medium-sized producers had

Table 5.1

Views on FSLN Government by Producer Strata (Percent)

	Strata			
	Small (n=5)	Medium (n=19)	Large (n=60)	All (n=84)
Strong opposition	20	37	42	39
Moderate opposition	40	32	32	32
Mixed	—	10	7	7
Moderate support	20	16	10	12
Strong support	20	5	10	10

a protected place within the revolution was designed to drive a wedge between those groups and the large producers. This study suggests that this strategy had a modest effect, most visibly with leaders who had been small producers. Overall, the more privileged among the private sector leaders *were* the more adamant in their opposition to the regime. This superelite's opposition may have deepened, both to protect its extensive resources and as a response to Sandinista hostility. If they were not opponents of the regime at the outset, years of hostile Sandinista discourse against the *terratenientes* and an agrarian reform program that targeted large landowners tended to elicit that opposition over time. Conversely, among the handful of private sector leaders who had been small producers in the late 1970s, 40 percent endorsed the revolution, either moderately or strongly. (See Table 5.1.) Not targeted for special repudiation, the latter were less fully drawn into the opposition.

The relationship between prior landholdings and subsequent political views was, however, far from absolute.[9] Even those leaders who had been small producers tended overall to oppose the regime. A full 60 percent registered some degree of opposition, suggesting that this group shared the general disgruntlement of its class. Moreover, 20 percent of those who had been large producers before the revolution actually offered a positive evaluation of the FSLN government. These large landowners were equally divided between those who expressed moderate support for the regime (10 percent) and unmitigated enthusiasts who expressed strong support (10 percent). Most of those in the latter category had taken positions in the Sandinista government, in some cases as vice-ministers, and became fully identified with the regime. The ambiguous character of the revolution allowed for the incorporation of a sector of even highly privileged members of the society into its ranks; the participation of these elites in the revolution in turn muted its class content and, over time, moderated its course. The failure of the revolution to crystallize its class base contributed to the somewhat amorphous relationships found in Table 5.1.

Social Class and Political Views

Class is not just an economic category. This concept also has a social dimension involving issues like status, influence, and authority. Although there is obviously an interrelationship between the economic and social aspects of the concept, each has its own distinctive features. Access to property or high production levels provides elites with wealth and economic clout as employers or generators of growth; social status confers respectability and authority, allowing elites to exercise influence over others and assert a form of cultural hegemony.

Social status in Nicaragua was not just the product of individual holdings but was also linked to the kind of familial and social networks in which elites were enmeshed. For example, a small subset of the elite from prominent families, like the Chamorros and Cuadras, whose ancestors had held or vied for political power in the previous century, was the bedrock of the vaunted aristocracy of Granada, Nicaragua's premier social class (Stone 1990; Vilas 1992). Living in prescribed neighborhoods or even on certain streets, like Calle Atravesada in Granada, gave their residents a social patina much cherished by the elite. A network of society heavyweights controlled admission to prestigious clubs that anchored elite social life in Nicaragua's larger cities.

The social hierarchy in Nicaragua was not, however, entirely static. The elite structure had been particularly receptive to entrepreneurial foreigners during the Somoza years. Among the private sector leaders in this study, for example, 22 percent mentioned having either parents or grandparents who were immigrants. Some immigrants had scampered quickly up the economic and social ladders. Beginning typically in some commercial activity, these entrepreneurs soon joined other elites in the acquisition of land and became agricultural producers and ranchers. Those respondents with immigrant backgrounds were even more likely than those from nonimmigrant families to be strongly opposed to the Sandinista regime.[10] This increased opposition may be linked to their relatively greater prosperity before the revolution or to the greater importance they gave to the social prominence that their families had only recently achieved.

Table 5.2

Views on FSLN Government by Educational Attainment (Percent)

	Level of Education			
	Secondary School or Less (n=11)	Post-Secondary Technical School or Some University (n=25)	University Graduate or More (n=53)	All (n=89)
Strong opposition	27	36	41	38
Moderate opposition	18	28	38	33
Mixed	9	8	7	8
Moderate support	18	16	7	11
Strong support	27	12	6	10

Mobility within the elite was influenced by education, and Nicaragua's economic leadership had acquired considerable educational credentials. Eighty-eight percent of the respondents in this study had gone beyond the secondary school level, and 77 percent had at least begun university training. A full 60 percent of the respondents had completed their university degrees or gone beyond.

In general, those who had the privilege of pursuing an education tended to be more opposed to the Sandinista regime than their less privileged counterparts in this study. Forty-one percent of those who had completed their university degrees were strongly opposed to the regime, serving as moral-political opponents. (See Table 5.2.) On the other hand, only 27 percent of those who had completed secondary school or less were so forcefully opposed to the regime. Indeed, the strongest support levels for the Sandinista government were found among those in this elite who had lower educational attainments. Whereas only 6 percent of those with university degrees offered strong support for the regime, a full 27 percent of those who completed only high school or less were in this category.

The greater opposition to the regime on the part of the more highly educated private sector leaders may be partly the result of the more rigorous intellectual training they received. A university education may bolster mainstream (nonrevolutionary) ideologies and provide the intellectual self-confidence needed to resist popular pressure. At the same time, the preexisting social class characteristics of better-educated individuals almost certainly had an impact on their views. In a society in which over

Table 5.3

Views on FSLN Government by Where Educated
(University Graduates, Percent)

	Nicaragua (n=27)	Foreign (n=26)	All (n=53)
Strong opposition	30	54	41
Moderate opposition	48	27	38
Mixed	11	4	7
Moderate support	7	8	7
Strong support	4	8	6

half of the adult population was illiterate, this credential conferred considerable social status on the graduates. Having farther to fall and less to receive from the revolution, this privileged sector tended to move forcefully into the opposition.

Social prestige in Nicaragua was enhanced by receiving an education abroad.[11] For many Nicaraguan elites, local universities did not offer either the technical sophistication or the social prominence that accompanied a foreign degree. As one social analyst who moved in and out of elite circles wryly observed, "If you were educated abroad, spoke another language fluently, and knew how to dress and eat well, then the elite families would accept you." One suggestion of the allure of a foreign education is found in the educational experiences of the elite. A full forty percent of the participants in this study completed their educations outside Nicaragua; half of them did so in the United States.[12]

The experience of living abroad, and particularly being educated there, apparently had political repercussions.[13] Among the respondents in this study, those who received a prestigious, foreign education were more likely to oppose the Sandinista regime virulently. If we control for variation in educational levels and look just at those who completed a university degree, 54 percent of respondents educated abroad registered strong opposition to the regime. (See Table 5.3.) Only 30 percent of the university graduates who were educated in Nicaragua were so profoundly opposed to the regime. For the latter group, the most common position was one of moderate opposition, a response that permitted ongoing negotiation with the Sandinista government.

The reasons for the association between a foreign education and increased political opposition are probably complex. Acquiring a university degree in a foreign country had several implications. Producers educated in the United States, for example, were among the larger landowners, and their opposition to the Sandinistas was probably influenced by their relatively privileged economic status.[14] In addition, the formal and informal content of a university education in the United States or in Franco's Spain may also have had an independent impact through the transmission of an anticommunist, promarket ideology that clashed sharply with the Sandinista model.[15] Certainly one of the lobbying strategies used to support U.S. educational exchange programs during the Cold War era was to emphasize how foreign participants would then come to affirm the American way of life. Evidence from this study suggests that this connection may have been made.

Conversely, the formal and informal content of a Nicaraguan education may also have played a role in reducing the extent of opposition to the revolution among those who remained at home. The argument that the Sandinistas were controlled by the Soviets, for example, may have held less sway among those who attended the Jesuit-run Universidad Centroamérica or the public university in UNAN-León. These Nicaraguan universities were hotbeds of student radicalism and FSLN organizational activities in the 1970s. Attendance at these institutions gave their alumni a relatively fuller familiarity with the actors and issues that shaped the FSLN. This exposure probably helped to clarify the domestic roots of the revolution for this subset of the elite and may have reduced their propensity to adopt the most extreme forms of opposition.

The relationship between educational privilege and regime opposition should not, however, be overstated.[16] Regardless of where they were educated, most university graduates in this study were opposed to the regime. Although there were differences in the level of opposition, 78 percent of private sector leaders who graduated from Nicaraguan universities registered some degree of opposition, compared to a very similar 81 percent of those who were foreign graduates. (See Table 5.3.) Furthermore, graduates of Nicaraguan universities were no more likely than those who graduated abroad to register support for the revolution. Indeed, among the small number of university graduates who supported the regime, the percent educated in universities abroad was slightly higher than the percent who graduated from Nicaraguan universities. The small number of respondents in this category makes it impossible to generalize, but these data again illustrate the ambiguities in the subclass base for regime support.

In all, data in this study suggest a modest relationship between the economic and social class characteristics of these private sector leaders and their views of the revolution. The association, however, between large landholdings or university education and extreme political opposition, on the one hand, or between small landholdings or high school education and strong political support, on the other, was far from uniform. The presence of subclass mavericks in the opposing camps weakened the statistical relationship between these variables and hinted at the often complex class alliances that characterized the Nicaraguan revolution.

The Organizational Nexus and Politics

In contrast to the measures of class, the relationship between organizational affiliation and political attitudes in the Nicaraguan private sector leadership was quite sharp. The findings in this section suggest the utility of separating the analysis of organizational characteristics from the discussion of class background. Class and subclass tendencies get filtered through organizations, which may then add their own distinctive influence to the formation of political ideology.

The two major private sector organizations in Nicaragua, COSEP and UNAG, supported markedly different political orientations and were embroiled in tense rivalry.[17] The political views of private sector leaders varied sharply depending on the association with which they were affiliated. In this case, the differences in views were absolute, not simply relative variations. In all, 91 percent of those who were affiliated with COSEP's agricultural branch, UPANIC, registered either strong or moderate opposition to the regime. In contrast, 75 percent of those who were UNAG affiliates expressed either strong or moderate support for the Sandinista government. Those who were independent divided roughly in the middle, with a total of 37.5 percent expressing some degree of opposition and an equal percent indicating some degree of support. (See Table 5.4.)[18]

The highly politicized and polarized orientations of both organizations reduced the possibility for free-ranging pluralism within their leadership. UPANIC had made an effort in the early years of the revolution to expand its base, recognizing the limitations confronting an elite organization in a society undergoing social revolution. UPANIC's attempt to recruit small producers, particularly among *cafetaleros* in the Matagalpa region, however, disintegrated when UPANIC leader Jorge Salazar was killed in 1980. The effort of ADACH, the UPANIC-affiliated cotton growers' association in Chinandega, to recruit a large number of small- and medium-

Table 5.4

Views on FSLN Government by Private Sector Organization
(Percent)

	UPANIC (n=65)	Independent (n=8)	UNAG (n=16)	All (n=89)
Strong opposition	49	25	—	38
Moderate opposition	42	12.5	6	33
Mixed	3	25	19	8
Moderate support	5	25	31	11
Strong support	2	12.5	44	10

sized members also ended disastrously, from its leaders' point of view. The newcomers soon denounced the UPANIC orientation, and a reform leadership took control, splitting ADACH in two in 1984. This division dissuaded UPANIC leaders from further recruitment of political unknowns and potential defectors (interview, former president of ADACH-UNAG, July 4, 1990; interview, former president of ADACH-UPANIC, May 28, 1990; "Algodoneros de Chinandega censuran actitud de UPANIC," *Barricada*, July 16, 1984). By 1984 the traditional elite circled in and abandoned its expansion effort.[19]

The few UPANIC leaders who were not anti-Sandinista, such as UPANIC's first president, soon withdrew from the association. Growing tensions between the government and COSEP after 1980–81 made it difficult for producer-revolutionaries to comfortably remain active in that association. Furthermore, several of these leaders took positions in the government and turned their properties over to the state. Since they were no longer actively involved in production, their participation in these associations ceased. Purged of their participation, UPANIC became vociferously anti-Sandinista.

UNAG, meanwhile, recruited vigorously. Following a major reorganization in 1984, this association "widened what had been up to then a small opening" and began to recruit even large producers (Núñez 1985a, 369). As UNAG moved into the organizational terrain traditionally held by UPANIC groups, middle-sized producers especially were pulled between the two. Even some prominent producers with elite family backgrounds left UPANIC affiliates and came to serve as UNAG leaders and spokespeople.[20]

UNAG's history as an FSLN-sponsored mass organization and its leadership by FSLN militants, even under its new president, Daniel Núñez, bound it closely to the cause of the revolution. Until the organization's dramatic embrace of demobilized contras in the post-1990 period, the range of views reflected by its leadership was also limited. UNAG leaders did become more independent of the FSLN over time (Haugaard 1991; Luciak forthcoming), but always remained prorevolution.

To some degree, the differences in the political orientations of UPANIC and UNAG reflect variations in the class fragment from which these leaders were derived. Although both organizations had leaders who were quite prosperous, large landowners were more likely to affiliate with UPANIC. Among those interviewed in this study, 76 percent of the UPANIC leaders who were landowners in the late 1970s were large producers during that era; in contrast, only 43 percent of the UNAG leaders fell into this category. The bulk of the UNAG leaders interviewed (57 percent) who owned property during that time were medium or small producers in the 1970s; only 24 percent of the UPANIC leaders were from these strata.

Not only did UNAG leaders tend to own less property, they were also less likely to be among the social elite of the country. Unlike their UPANIC counterparts, 47 percent of whom had lived in the United States at some point, only 25 percent of the UNAG leaders had this kind of experience.[21] The UNAG leaders were also less likely to have completed a college education (25 percent vs. 70 percent for UPANIC leaders), and only 12.5 percent of the UNAG leaders had been educated abroad (vs. 45 percent for UPANIC leaders).

Among private sector leaders, therefore, those in UNAG were substantially less prosperous and socially prominent than those of UPANIC. UNAG leaders matched more closely the *chapiolla* bourgeoisie concept developed by CIERA's theoreticians to differentiate the locally grounded producers from those with strong international connections (Núñez 1985a, 367–69; Baumeister and Neira Cuadra 1986, 181–82). Lacking the social cachet to, in some cases, even be admitted to elitist producer associations in their hometowns, these highly motivated leaders rose quickly within the ranks of UNAG soon after the new organization was founded.[22]

These organizations did not just reflect differences in the perspectives that their members brought into the associations. Both COSEP and UNAG made a concerted effort to disseminate a political viewpoint within the organization's circle of influence. For the COSEP national organization, oppositional politics was its raison d'être. Using periodic speaking tours, generous access to the pages of the anti-Sandinista daily *La Prensa* and, when *La Prensa* was closed by Sandinista censors, its own *Memorandum de la Presidencia,* COSEP leaders conveyed their views and positions to their constituents. UNAG leaders also attempted to forge a certain mentality among their affiliates, using inserts in the Sandinista newspaper *Barricada* and their own magazine, *Productores,* for these purposes. These efforts did not always succeed.[23] This practice suggests, however, that the organizational affiliation of bourgeois leaders may have had its own, additional impact on their views, reinforcing or deepening the political tendencies that they and other members already had.

National versus Regional Leaders

Of course, not all leaders of these associations were equally committed to their organization's political line. As Table 5.4 indicates, there was some range of variation in the leaders' perspectives in both organizations. Differences between national leaders and those at the sectoral or regional level of their organizations, for example, were striking. Among UPANIC affiliates, 63 percent of the respondents at the national level expressed strong opposition to the FSLN government, denouncing it on moral and ideological grounds. (See Table 5.5.) In contrast, only 41 percent of the regional level leaders registered this kind of strong opposition. The latter group was somewhat more inclined to express moderate opposition, criticizing the regime on more narrow, technical grounds (46 percent vs. 33 percent for national leaders).

These differences in outlook penetrated to the level of economic philosophy. When asked to describe the economic model they most preferred for their country, 50 percent of UPANIC's national-level leaders affirmed a commitment to pure market capitalism, whereas only 29 percent of those at the regional level took that position. The majority (53 percent) of the regional leaders preferred moderate capitalism, with some regulation of the market, whereas only 31 percent of UPANIC national leaders preferred that model. Indeed, some regional UPANIC affiliates actually came to support the Sandinista regime, even running as FSLN candidates in the 1990 election.[24]

To some degree, differences in political behavior among COSEP leaders reflect a tactical decision to recruit strong, ideological opponents into the national leadership, where they would repeatedly confront the FSLN on political grounds, and to leave the sectoral and local leadership in a relatively protected position, where the emphasis in the discussion would be more technical. UPANIC national leaders, then, would routinely denounce

Table 5.5

Views on FSLN Government by Leadership Level (Percent)

	UPANIC		UNAG	
	National (n=27)	Regional/ Sectoral (n=37)	National (n=7)	Regional/ Sectoral (n=10)
Strong opposition	63	41	—	—
Moderate opposition	33	46	—	10
Mixed	—	5	14	30
Moderate support	—	8	29	30
Strong support	4	—	57	30

FSLN transgressions and reject any attempt at dialogue, while leaders of sectoral associations like that for rice growers (ANAR) or regional organizations like that for León cotton growers (ADAL) would continue to meet with MIDINRA personnel to press for improved prices or easier access to productive inputs.

These differences were not, however, simply tactical. They also reflected variations in the social backgrounds that prevailed at these two levels. Regional and sectoral leaders of UPANIC tended to be drawn from a more modest background than their national counterparts. For example, 78 percent of the UPANIC national leaders had completed a university education; only 60 percent of the regional and sectoral leaders had done so. National leaders were almost twice as likely to have been educated abroad (59 percent vs. 32 percent for regional leaders) and had more commonly been large producers in the 1970s (81 percent vs. 72 percent).

Parallel divisions were found among UNAG leaders, although the smaller number of respondents involved makes it more difficult to draw clear conclusions. In this study, 57 percent of the national-level leaders in UNAG expressed strong support for the Sandinista government, whereas only 30 percent of the regional leaders were as enthusiastic. (See Table 5.5.) In contrast, 40 percent of the regional leaders offered either a mixed appraisal or indicated moderate opposition to the regime. None of the national leaders indicated opposition to the regime, and only 14 percent offered a mixed evaluation.[25]

Whereas the top leadership of UNAG was composed of members of the FSLN or those who were very closely identified with the cause, the regional UNAG leaders were more diverse. Most UNAG regional leaders were not overtly partisan, and several were quite critical of the Sandinista government. One was even a party activist in the opposition PLI and a close relative of a Somoza-era puppet president. These regional leaders endorsed social change in Nicaragua, but they were less willing to serve as political mobilizers for the FSLN. They explained their association with UNAG in a variety of other ways: as a rejection of the hyperpoliticized hostility of the UPANIC associations, a response to the insularity and snootiness of a closed local elite, a nationalistic response to the contra war, or a response to economic opportunities that UNAG offered agricultural producers.

Often operating in regions where the contra forces were strong and the FSLN's popularity was low (Boaco, Chontales, Matagalpa, Jinotega), these local leaders generally played down their links with the Sandinista government. As the president of the Boaco UNAG association explained, "Producers here won't even talk to you if they think you're from the Frente Sandinista. Leaders of producers here can't have political lives." These leaders attempted to build their organizations by emphasizing the openness of meetings to anyone who wanted to participate; their ability to bring in technical assistance and financing, particularly from Scandinavian countries; and their effectiveness in navigating a complex and sometimes menacing government bureaucracy. Recognizing that many UNAG members joined for instrumental reasons rather than from revolutionary conviction, these local leaders attempted to respond to concrete needs.[26]

As with UPANIC, the political differentiation within UNAG was associated with subclass variation among its leaders. In contrast with UPANIC, UNAG's national leaders tended to have less extensive landholdings and lower educational attainments. Whereas only 33 percent of UNAG's national leadership was among the large producers in the 1970s, 56 percent of the regional leaders interviewed were in this category. The percent of regional UNAG private sector leaders with university degrees was 30 percent, more than twice the 14 percent found among the national leadership. For both UPANIC and UNAG, therefore, the positions taken by the national leadership differed measurably from the preferences and views of mid-level leaders. These differences suggest both the polarizing quality of the national debate, which divided its participants more emphatically than did deliberations at the regional and sectoral level, and the variation in subclass composition of the leadership in different levels of these powerful organizations.

Experiential Factors and Political Views

The Sandinista government expected that the concrete experiences different producers had with government policies would also influence the ways in which those producers responded to the regime. Although some benefits and burdens were generalized, many government actions and policies tended to favor one set of producers over others. As we saw in Chapter 3, the FSLN government initially adopted a segmented view of the bourgeoisie. During the period in which this model prevailed, the government attempted to devise policy that favored those who fit into the revolutionary model while draining resources from those who did not.

Two kinds of experiences with the regime might be expected to have a pronounced impact. The first is whether or not the producer underwent land expropriation by the Sandinista government. The second experience concerns the principal crop the producer cultivated and the priority it was given in the national economic policy. Being allowed to retain ownership rights and being given subsidies and financial supports should logically encourage producers to adopt a less oppositional view of the state; producers in low priority areas who underwent expropriation, on the other hand, should be good candidates for the opposition.

Expropriation and Political Views

Agrarian reform legislation under the Sandinistas authorized the expropriation of land that was not being used productively. This framework gave MIDINRA officials considerable latitude for action. Stipulations against decapitalization, for example, could refer to a wide range of common practices, in a country where wartime dislocations and generalized economic decline led to low investment levels and deterioration of infrastructure. Regulations governing expropriations were not applied uniformly throughout the country. A deteriorated farm in one part of the country might be expropriated, while a similar property in another part might be passed over. Much depended on the land pressure in the region, development projects on nearby state farms, the status of the war, and the convictions of local authorities. This variation, along with the much-publicized expropriations of top COSEP officials, led to the perception among producers that expropriation was a political tool used by the Sandinistas against their enemies. To a degree, this view was accurate.

Over one-third (36 percent) of the private sector leaders interviewed had experienced one or more expropriations. (See Table 5.6.) As expected, the

Table 5.6

Views on FSLN Government by Expropriation Experience (Percent)

	Hard Expropriation (n=17)	Soft Expropriation (n=15)	Never Expropriated (n=57)	All (n=89)
Strong opposition	47	47	33	38
Moderate opposition	41	27	32	33
Mixed	6	—	10.5	8
Moderate support	—	13	14	11
Strong support	6	13	10.5	10

experience of being expropriated was associated with a negative evaluation of the regime. The link was particularly pronounced for those who underwent a "hard expropriation," in which they received little or no compensation. For that group, 47 percent of the respondents provided a strongly opposed assessment of the regime, and another 41 percent of that group was moderately opposed. In all, 88 percent of those who underwent a full-scale expropriation wound up the decade with a negative view of the regime.

Almost half of those who were expropriated experienced what might be labeled a soft expropriation, in which they were subsequently able to recover some property.[27] Some of those in this group eventually had the most valuable part of their property returned; others received comparable property in a land or machinery swap (*permuta*). Those who underwent a soft expropriation also registered substantial opposition to the regime (also 47 percent strongly opposed), suggesting that expropriation triggered moral outrage and fierce hostility, even when it was subsequently softened by retraction or compensation. Overall, however, those who underwent a soft expropriation were slightly less hostile than those in the first category (74 percent expressing some form of opposition, vs. 88 percent). Indeed, over a quarter (26 percent) of those in this group offered a positive evaluation of the regime.

Most of those whose holdings were not expropriated were opposed to the regime as well. Almost two-thirds (65 percent) of those who had escaped expropriation were nonetheless opponents of the regime. This finding suggests that personal experiences with expropriation may have had less impact on the political views of private sector leaders than the Sandinista government expected. Indeed, in discussing expropriation, many private sector leaders noted that although they had not been expropriated themselves, close relatives or neighbors had been. One popular refrain in these interviews ran, "Every pig has its Saturday [market day]." Many of those not expropriated labored under the expectation that their turn would come, sooner or later. The fact that they had not yet undergone this experience provided little sense of permanent security or protection for this group. Their opposition may be explained, therefore, as an anticipatory or affiliational response.

The level of opposition for this third group was, however, somewhat lower than that for those who were personally expropriated. Sixty-five percent of those in this group registered some degree of opposition, for example, versus 88 percent for those who underwent a hard expropriation. Again, and less surprisingly, a segment (25 percent) of those in this group expressed some degree of support for the Sandinista government. The fact that they themselves did not lose land in this fashion probably contributed to their lessened hostility to the regime. Although the government's expectation that those who were not expropriated would respond positively was naive, some modest differences in the degree of opposition may be associated with this experience.[28] The breadth of the opposition regardless of personal expropriation, however, suggests that this particular experience was generally not a crucial determinant of the political views of private sector elites.[29]

Sectoral Favoritism and Political Views

For some producers, Sandinista production and price policy actually brought economic benefits. Not only did they escape expropriation, they received hefty subsidies and ready access to production inputs. Theoretically, as was demonstrated in Chapter 3, Sandinista production policy in the early years was designed to favor those producing for the domestic market and to extract the surplus from the previously favored agroexport elite. This approach was roughly analogous to the strategy adopted elsewhere in Latin America by populist regimes (Cardoso 1972; Conaghan 1988). Those strategies emphasized the formation of an alliance between the state and the segment of the bourgeoisie that produced for the local market and would benefit from an improvement in the purchasing power of labor. Elsewhere in Latin America, this approach had elicited the support of local industrialists in the state's confrontation with traditional agrarian oligarchs or export-oriented industrialists whose prosperity was dependent on low labor costs and foreign sales.

In theory, the early redistribution of resources in Nicaragua and the increase in food consumption, combined with staples subsidies, could have consolidated a link between staples producers and the revolutionary state. In practice, although these producers did respond by decreasing production less than others, their leaders did not typically become political allies of the regime. In fact, of the private sector leaders interviewed in this study, staples producers overwhelmingly registered strong opposition to the regime, more so than any other single sector. Fifty-four percent of private sector leaders whose primary activity was staples production (rice, sorghum, and maize) were strongly opposed to the Sandinista regime. In contrast, only 18 percent of cotton growers, 29 percent of those in livestock (cattle and dairy), and 46 percent of coffee producers registered such extreme opposition. Unlike what the theory would predict, government policy did not succeed in generating a show of support among staples sector leaders in Nicaragua. This may be because policy was so inconsistently applied and signals were so confused, or because other policies at the end of the era were so counterproductive that early positive results were undermined.[30]

On the other hand, some government programs probably did elicit elite support. Perhaps the clearest example of government favoritism that may have diluted opposition was found in the cotton sector. As a major export crop, cotton should not have been particularly benefited by a pro-food policy. Since cottonseed oil was a staple in the Nicaraguan diet, however, this crop crossed the boundaries between export and domestic market, suggesting the porousness of these conceptual categories. Cotton production also dominated the regional economy of northwestern Nicaragua and was the main source of employment for that region. For several reasons, therefore, the Sandinista government worked to salvage cotton production, at least on the most productive lands. One independent study of the Nicaraguan cotton sector indicated that both the profits and the costs of production were financed by a transfer of resources from the state through inorganic emissions from the BCN (Evans 1987, 19). Although international prices were tumbling and cotton producers elsewhere in Central America were shifting out of production during the 1980s, cotton production fell less sharply in Nicaragua.

Cotton growers did not always perceive that they were being subsidized by the state. The welter of controls and artificial prices set by the government made such calculations extremely difficult. But many *algodoneros* did observe that cotton production in neighboring Guatemala had declined sharply due to falling international prices, while the decline in Nicaragua had been arrested by government production policy. Recognition that the Sandinistas' cotton policy had preserved the cotton sector in Nicaragua led several cotton association leaders to offer positive assessments of Sandinista production policy. Indeed, 30 percent of the cotton producers expressed some level of support for the regime, surpassing the support levels in any other sector.[31] Cotton growers were, therefore, much less likely to join the moral-political opposition to the regime than were those whose livelihoods centered on livestock, coffee, or basic grains.

These observations suggest that the Sandinista government was able, to some degree, to adjust the level and location of bourgeois opposition through its own sectoral development programs. Elite opposition was not simply a given, uniformly preordained by the revolution. Private sector perspectives were probably influenced by at least some concrete state actions. To the extent that the revolution could identify and cushion producers in strategic subsectors, like cotton producers, it could blunt elite opposition. Lower priority sectors or those that were dealt with in an inconsistent manner, in contrast, were more likely to become centers of opposition politics.

The government's power to orchestrate elite responses was limited, however, because private elites were not just affected by their particular production experiences. They also responded to the general social and economic climate and to the experiences of others in their class. Even if they were not personally targeted for hostile action or unfavorable policies, they often responded as if they had been. Furthermore, one response of producers to the uncertainties of the 1980s was to diversify production. Policies that favored them in one area might have negative consequences for them in their other activities. These considerations made the impact of government policy on elite perspectives less straightforward than it might have been. Finally, as state resources dried up, the regime's ability to provide selected supports to favored fragments of the elite was steadily reduced. By the end of the era, it had little room in which to maneuver for political favor.

So What? Politics, Production, and Investment

It is not theoretically adventurous to note that political perceptions affect economic behavior. Political views, of course, are not the sole determinant of economic decisions. Projections of probable costs, potential markets, expected competition, and, ultimately, future returns are obviously crucial variables. In bad economic times, such as those prevailing in Nicaragua (and indeed much of Latin America) during the 1980s, one would expect production and investment to decline generally, regardless of political perceptions. But acrimonious interactions and hostile political evaluations might logically be expected to provoke further economic withdrawal on the part of the economic elite.

When producers are convinced that the government under which they operate is corrupt or led by moral degenerates and ideological fanatics who intend to destroy them, this perception obviously takes a toll on their willingness to engage in entrepreneurial activities. On the other hand, if producers believe that the government is visionary, committed to national development, and principled, then this belief may inspire them to participate in the emerging economy in spite of the risks.

In the Nicaraguan case, the interview data suggest a clear, statistically significant association between the political views of private sector leaders and their economic behaviors. The concluding section of this chapter looks at two ways in which political views and economic behavior were connected. The first explores the link between political appraisals and investment behavior. The second focuses on the relationship between assessments of the regime and production outcomes.

Political Views and Investment

Private sector leaders in this study who evaluated the regime positively were much more likely than opponents to have made major investments in their operations during the decade. Whereas 58 percent of supporters indicated that they had made major investments,[32] only 29 percent of the opponents had done so. (See Table 5.7.) More telling, 43 percent of those opposed to the regime indicated that they had made no new investments in production during this period. In contrast, only 16 percent of those who supported the regime reported no new investments, and those were producers whose political and bureaucratic workload had drawn them away from their agricultural activities.[33]

Of various kinds of major investments, the most significant was the acquisition of land. Surprisingly, in an era of large-scale land expropriation, some elites did buy land. Since land purchases in Nicaragua were not financed by the bank (either before or after the revolution), these investments required the buyer to risk his or her own capital—in spite of the possibility of subsequent expropriation.[34] Offsetting this risk was the

Table 5.7

Investment Level by Views on FSLN Government
(Percent)

	Oppose (n=63)	Mixed (n=7)	Support (n=19)	All (n=89)
Major investment	29	29	58	35
Minor investment	29	57	26	30
No investment	43	14	16	35

lure of very low land prices. The price of land was severely depressed due to expropriations and general economic conditions. Many landowners were willing to sell cheaply as they prepared to emigrate.[35] For those who were bold enough to take the risk of acquiring new land, the Sandinista era provided a golden opportunity. One large cattle rancher affiliated with FAGANIC reported buying seven farms during this period, acquiring land biannually between 1982 and 1986 and annually between 1987 and 1990. His landholdings swelled from 8,000 mz. in 1977 to 18,000 mz. in 1990, making him one of the country's larger landowners.

Although a handful of producers who were adamantly opposed to the regime took the risk of buying land, supporters were more likely to engage in this behavior, particularly in the turbulent 1982–88 period. Overall, 37 percent of supporters bought land during this period, and a full 50 percent of the moderate supporters did so.[36] Of opponents, only 17 percent took that risk.[37]

Some producers went beyond land purchases to make investments in agroindustrial operations. GRACSA, Nicaragua's largest oilseed production facility, provides a notable example. At the recommendation of General Manager Antonio Lacayo, the majority shareholding group of GRACSA established a series of spinoff corporations (Spalding 1991). Most remarkably, this group's investment rose briskly even during a long period (1982–88) when GRACSA was "intervened" by the Sandinista government. To bolster its legal appeal challenging this takeover and to take advantage of investment opportunities, this group founded seven new corporations during the six year period when the company was intervened. As its stockholders awaited the (successful) outcome of their appeal to the Nicaraguan Supreme Court, this group linked both forward and backward from GRACSA's initial operations.[38] GRACSA's owners continued making investments in the years that followed, founding three new enterprises in 1989 alone. One of the most entrepreneurial investment groups in the country, the GRACSA group not only launched spinoff corporations; it also entered into joint ventures with the government for the development of nontraditional products and the introduction of new technologies.[39]

Business leaders who bought land, took on new investments, participated in government development projects, or joined joint ventures were generally less vehemently opposed to the regime than those who did not. They were not necessarily supporters of the revolution; as we have seen, even opponents undertook major investments in some cases. However, a less oppositional perspective facilitated negotiations in the complex political and economic environment that prevailed during the Sandinista period.

Political Views and Production

Like investment decisions, production levels depend on many factors, including the expansion or contraction of the market, the availability of inexpensive inputs, the labor supply, climate, and expropriation experiences. In addition to these economic variables, however, producers' perceptions of the regime can also have an impact. Political support can animate the production process by encouraging producers to take bold initiatives, make long-term investments, and plan for the future. A negative assessment, on the other hand, makes long-range thinking more difficult and can undermine the producers' contribution to national growth. In a revolutionary setting, in which the economy is highly politicized, political attitudes may have a particularly important impact on production.

Evidence from this study suggests a close relationship between political views and production levels in the Nicaraguan case. Overall production levels during the revolution fell disastrously, but the pattern again varied across producers. Over two-thirds (69 percent) of those opposed to the regime reported a decrease in production between the late 1970s and the late 1980s.[40] (See Table 5.8.) In contrast, a relatively modest 37 percent of the supporters had this experience, and many in this group reduced production voluntarily as the result of donating properties to the state or devoting attention to their government jobs instead of their estates.[41] Among private sector leaders interviewed in this study, those who viewed the regime positively reported more success in maintaining or even increasing their production levels. Thirty-seven percent of those who favored the regime reported an increase in production. In contrast, only 10 percent of those registering opposition expanded at that rate.

Table 5.8

Level of Production Change by Views on FSLN
Government (Percent)

	Oppose (n=61)	Mixed (n=7)	Support (n=19)	All (n=87)
Decrease	69	43	37	60
Stable	21	43	26	24
Increase	10	14	37	16

Assessing the link between politics and production is particularly difficult, however, because of the complex interrelationships among these variables. Political attitudes may shape production behavior, but the causal relationship may also operate in the opposite direction: changing production outcomes may influence political views. A sharp decrease in production, for example, could trigger political opposition if the decline was attributed to unfavorable regime decisions (price policy, expropriation, supply breakdowns) rather than neutral or uncontrollable forces. Political opposition could then in turn feed further economic withdrawal. Without more detailed information on production and attitude shifts broken down over time, the exact sequence of these connections cannot be clearly unraveled.

Conclusions

In this chapter, various factors shaping the political views of Nicaraguan economic elites come into focus. The bourgeoisie, which had been historically fragmented and lacking in political authority in the prerevolutionary period, continued to suffer from these characteristics under the Sandinistas. Although this factionalism was reduced when the Somoza dynasty collapsed and the Sandinista revolution presented a broad threat to the economic elite, divisions remained. The increasing amorphousness of the Sandinista model, the regime's policy inconsistency, and the Sandinistas' own "divide and rule" strategy all helped to further fragment the bourgeoisie.

Interview data suggest that the views of leaders of producer associations in the agricultural sector were divided by subclass strata. Those who were large producers in the period before the revolution were disproportionately among the virulent opponents to the regime. Furthermore, those with greater access to education, particularly prestige educations obtained abroad, were also more likely to strongly oppose the Sandinistas than were those less privileged. Opposition among leaders who were medium- and small-sized producers, less well educated, and educated at home was generally less pronounced.

This link, however, was weakened by the presence of some large-sized, foreign-educated business leaders among the regime supporters and by the fierce opposition to the regime manifested by some private sector leaders who were less privileged (small- and medium-sized producers, those who completed only high school). As a result of these anomalous cases, the association between subclass characteristics of elite leaders and their political views was not strong enough to demonstrate a clear, consistent relationship. This information points, instead, to the somewhat amorphous class alliances of the Nicaraguan revolution.

Other factors, such as the organizational affiliations of these leaders, were more closely linked with their political views. Divisions within the elite were reinforced by the organizational segmentation of the Nicaraguan private sector. Involvement in competing associations tended to further polarize these producers, particularly those who operated at the national level. UPANIC functioned as a rallying point for those agricultural producers who launched a moral-political critique of the regime. UNAG, on the other hand, clustered together private sector defenders of the revolution. Even within these organizations, however, some variation in political ideology was found, particularly between those leaders at the national and the sectoral/regional levels. National leaders tended to adopt more extreme positions (either strong opposition or strong support) whereas those at the sectoral or regional level had more moderate views.

The producers' concrete experiences and interactions with government officials during the revolution probably also had some impact on their views, though less than the Sandinista leadership expected. The experience of having land expropriated did prove politically alienating. But opposition was generalized even among those leaders whose landholdings were not expropriated, suggesting that individual experiences may have been . less important in forming elite views than their assessments of overall class relations.

On the other hand, opposition was apparently blunted when the regime buffered producers in particular subsectors, such as cotton, from international downturns. In some instances, the regime may have been able to elicit an element of elite support through particularly favorable treatment. In general, however, private sector opposition was not closely tied to government actions.

Interview data compiled for this study indicate that the elites' political views had marked consequences for their economic behavior. Investment and production patterns varied sharply with the level of political opposition or support expressed by these leaders. Regime supporters were more inclined to take on new investments, buy land and machinery, expand housing for their workers, and try out new technologies. They were also more likely to keep their production levels stable or even increase their output during this period. Opponents, on the other hand, were more reluctant to buy new land, even though prices were rock-bottom, or to undertake extensive new investments, even when credit was available. Over time, their production levels dropped, in many cases by over half.

In conclusion, information from these interviews suggests considerable variation among the private sector leaders in Nicaragua on a series of issues. This kind of fragmentation prevented the Nicaraguan bourgeoisie from functioning as a united bloc or pursuing a clear, common agenda. For many reasons, including its own internal cleavages, the bourgeoisie continued to have difficulty asserting political authority. It did not, as in the Chilean case under the Allende government, convoke a series of general strikes that ground the economy to a halt. Nor did it, as in the Salvadoran case, mobilize a paramilitary force to terrorize opponents. It could not form a strong political party of its own or orchestrate a mass movement that could divide the Sandinista military and drive the FSLN from power.

On the other hand, this elite did tilt heavily into the opposition. The Sandinistas failed to restructure the private producers into a patriotic bourgeoisie. Even after the regime's multiple concessions in the post-1987 era, its toehold in the bourgeoisie remained modest. The regime never won enough support to counter the economic impact of the contra war and its own problematic policy choices. Having concentrated too heavily on the development of state enterprises, failed to win a large enough segment of the bourgeoisie to the cause of moderate reform, and given too little attention to the sustained organization and training of small producers and cooperatives, the regime was unable to create a solid economic base on which to consolidate the revolution.

chapter 6

From Revolution to Neoliberalism

Private Sector Ambivalence in
Postrevolutionary Nicaragua
(1990–1993)

We will give back to the producer what he should have: the right to
make the decisions and take the risks.
> —Silvio de Franco, minister of economy
> and development, May 19, 1990

Neoliberalism? Fine, let it come. We accept neoliberalism as long as the
economy is democratized.
> —Jaime Wheelock Román, National
> Directorate, FSLN, June 27, 1992

Last year [1991], we prepared the terrain to wage economic battle. . . .
We confronted the traditional bourgeoisie in [agroindustry, commerce,
and banking], as well as the Sandinistas. They're definitely the same
thing but with different ideological colors.
> —Sinforiano Cáceres, vice-president
> of FENACOOP-UNAG

IN APRIL 1990 Violeta Barrios de Chamorro was inaugurated as president of Nicaragua, and the FSLN leadership relinquished official power.
Given the close ties between Chamorro's electoral coalition and the
United States, it was widely assumed that the new government would attempt to undo the revolution and move the country in a classically liberal
direction.[1]

The dynamics of economic change are complex, however, and the configuration of political forces weighs heavily in this process. The intricacies
of political negotiation are even more delicate for a government coming
out of a revolutionary experience than for one attempting economic transition in less turbulent times. A revolution, if it merits the name, should
reweave the nation's social fabric in a way that leaves a long-term trace.

It should restructure options, forge durable new alliances, mobilize previously powerless groups, and create a new political panorama. Social revolution should build strong buffers against the neoliberal tide.

The next three sections of this chapter explore (1) the configuration of forces that generally supports the adoption of a neoliberal economic model, (2) the actors and processes that emerged in the postrevolutionary period in Nicaragua, and (3) the brisk move toward neoliberalism that ensued in Nicaragua in 1990–92. The Nicaraguan transition, however, varied in notable respects from the more classical shift toward neoliberalism. These crucial differences are described in section four. The fifth section analyzes the reaction to this amalgam by four different sectors of the Nicaraguan bourgeoisie. As it had in prior periods, the Nicaraguan elite responded in varied ways, ranging from sharp rejection to eager participation.

The Politics of Neoliberal Economics

Comparative research on structural adjustment and the transition toward a neoliberal economic model suggests that the successful implementation of the model depends on a series of propitious conditions (Haggard and Kaufman 1992a; Nelson 1990). Key elements include (1) strong backing from international financial actors, (2) the development of a technocratic policy team to oversee the program, (3) forceful executive support, (4) the debility and/or cooptation of popular sectors, and (5) the active cooperation of an influential sector of the local elite.

Although an analysis that presents neoliberal reform solely as the product of IMF or U.S. government intrusion ignores the complex dynamics of economic change, international financial actors typically play a pivotal role in the process. The IMF and the World Bank facilitate the movement toward economic reform both by disseminating the classical liberal ideology and by providing partial financing of the structural adjustment process (Stallings 1992). The U.S. government directly supports this transition through USAID programs and the zealous promotion of free trade.[2] Using billions of dollars' worth of targeted assistance, the IMF stabilization and adjustment programs and the Bush administration's Enterprise for the Americas had an unprecedented impact on regional economic policy in the 1980s and early 1990s.

But the U.S. government and international financial institutions cannot simply dictate policy reform. A crucial mechanism through which external actors wield influence is the training of a domestic technocratic elite that links local and international economic actors (Nelson 1990, 330–31; Kahler 1992, 124–27). This insular elite, labeled the "reformist cadre" by Haggard and Kaufman (1992a, 13) and the "change team" by Waterbury (1992, 191), mediates the transfer of the economic ideology and associated policy prescriptions as it oversees the local initiation and implementation of the policy reform.

To implement its neoliberal program, for example, the Belaúnde government in Peru reabsorbed Peruvian technocrats who had been dispersed abroad in international lending institutions and who had few ties to local politics (Conaghan et al. 1990, 15). The infamous "Chicago boys" who developed Chile's new economic program during the military dictatorship (Foxley 1986), and officials from the SPP and the Banco de México who led the move toward a free trade regime in Mexico in the 1980s (Heredia 1991), were foreign-trained technocrats distinctly separated from the bargaining process of party politics. International linkages and local detachment allowed them to pursue a radically new economic model that redefined the role of the state in the economic order.

To succeed in this effort, the economic team needs firm support from the president and a political system weighted heavily toward executive control. If the executive branch is too weak, the dispersal of power through a series of institutions that compete for control can give opponents of the neoliberal project an instrument through which to block the reform. When the legislature serves as an effective check on presidential dominance, powerful groups may succeed in diverting the economic program by riddling it with exemptions and loopholes, if not derailing the project altogether. Centralization of political authority in the hands of the executive, on the other hand, allows a president committed to the new agenda to pursue it with fewer impediments. The ability of the president to rule in effect by decree, in spite of any formal divisions of power or constitutional constraints, fosters the implementation of economic restructuring. Neoliberal reform is also promoted when executive power extends deep into the bureaucracy, which otherwise could undermine the effort.[3]

Various groups in civil society, including both popular sectors and privileged elites, will have reason to object to the new economic model. The immediate, and often longer-term, impact of the neoliberal project is the withdrawal of economic supports that have buffered important segments of the popular classes. Subsidies on basic goods and services are terminated, causing price hikes; wage indexation is eliminated, allowing real wages to tumble; agrarian reform land may be returned to former owners or made available for sale, fostering reconcentration of the land; public sector employment is cut, leading to a ripple of job loss in adjacent sectors; and import competition increases, resulting in a loss of industrial jobs. There is a strong tendency for popular groups to resist paying the high social costs of the transition to free market capitalism.[4]

Neoliberal reform can be implemented in spite of these social costs if mass organizations are weak and the antistatist ideology is successfully disseminated. For much of the region, the long experience of authoritarian rule followed by a decade of debt-induced economic crisis left unions and mass organizations weakened and unable to challenge the new economic orientation effectively (Buchanan and Putnam 1992). The repression of politics in Chile and its circumscription in Mexico, for example, allowed these governments to proceed with the neoliberal approach without sustained popular upheaval.[5]

In the long run, however, the consolidation of the new model requires the construction of a support network that endorses the reform. Antistatism triggered by many years of authoritarian government, combined with a rejection of the ECLA development model following a decade of economic crisis, may create an environment in which the neoliberal ideology can take root. But the cultivation of durable support, particularly in the strategic sectors of the business elite who must back the new project with their own investments, poses a challenge.

Not only the popular sectors but important segments of the local economic elite are negatively affected by the neoliberal reform. When much of the local elite is "historically wedded to an intricate scheme of rent-seeking behavior" (Glade 1991, 8), the transition from a development model in which the state plays a central role to one in which its involvement is relatively modest can undercut the position of traditional powerholders. Evidence from the Chilean case suggests that small- and medium-sized business operations, which were not bolstered by ties to international capital or the major financial groups, were disproportionately injured by the withdrawal of state supports after 1973.[6] In Peru, industrialists, shaken by the infusion of foreign imports when tariff barriers were reduced, and nontraditional exporters, who lost export subsidies, became major opponents of the Belaúnde reforms (Conaghan et al. 1990, 19). Credit restrictions and increased foreign competition drew industrialists, agroindustrialists, and exporters into the opposition in Bolivia during the economic shock treatment of the Víctor Paz Estenssoro administration (Conaghan et al. 1990, 20).

When the "change team" is effectively insulated from even business pressure, neoliberal reforms may be imposed in spite of business opposition. Effective consolidation of the new model, however, requires the construction of a new state-capital alliance around the emerging accumulation pattern. Efforts by the Pinochet regime to reinforce linkages with the reconstituted agroexport elite, for example, helped to stabilize the Chilean transition to neoliberalism in the 1980s (Stallings 1989, 190–93). Without the cooperation of strategic producers, the regime will be unable to generate the investment needed to refound the national economy.

Many elements supporting neoliberal reform were present in Nicaragua following the electoral defeat of the Sandinistas. Extensive support for transition was provided by the Bush administration and international financial institutions. U.S.-trained technocrats were prominent in the economic team, and political power was concentrated in the executive branch. There were, however, several important obstacles to reform. Prominent among them was the counterforce of relatively mobilized popular sectors. The factionalized politics of the bourgeoisie also made it difficult to line up private sector support for the neoliberal package, although pockets of support emerged (ironically including even Sandinistas-cum-entrepreneurs). The result was a modification in the model that reflected the political conjuncture of the postrevolutionary moment.

The Framework for Neoliberal Politics in Postrevolutionary Nicaragua

Years of economic crisis had already prompted the Sandinista government to begin the shift away from a state-centered development strategy; electoral defeat of the FSLN now catapulted Nicaragua into the neoliberal camp. International financial organizations and the U.S. government responded heartily to the new government. For the Bush administration, the election of Violeta Chamorro represented the successful conclusion of the divisive contra aid policy and a hallmark of the U.S. commitment to democratization of the region. The White House maneuvered a foreign aid package through Congress that supported neoliberal reform, restoring trade and the sugar quota that had been terminated by the Reagan administration and forgiving bilateral loans lingering from the Somoza era.[7]

The USAID mission in Nicaragua was a central agent in this process (Saldomando 1992). Of the $614 million in the USAID program for Nicaragua in the 1990–92 period, two-thirds was assigned for balance of payments support to maintain the flow of imports like petroleum and food staples. The local currency generated by the sale of this foreign exchange provided the Nicaraguan government with funds to cover its deficits and support its programs. USAID funds allowed the government to cover bank losses associated with the March 1991 devaluation of the currency, the deficits of state enterprises such as the sugar trade monopoly CONAZUCAR that was being prepared for privatization, severance pay for state workers taking early retirement, the government's failed plan to resuscitate the cotton sector, and the clearing of the arrears with the World Bank and the IDB. Smaller amounts of USAID support covered the costs of setting up the new superintendency of banks, which monitored the state bank system and oversaw the creation of private banks; of designing a privatization program; of creating an export promotion center; and of covering the operating expenses of private sector organizations like COSEP, UPANIC, and the newly formed association of producers of nontraditional exports, APENN (USAID 1992; interview, Janet Ballantyne, director, USAID-Nicaragua, July 1, 1992).

With U.S. backing, the Chamorro government was able to swing foreign loans and donations amounting to a total of US$356 million in 1990, $1.3 billion in 1991, and another $800 million programmed for 1992 (Ministerio de Cooperación Externa 1992; Larson with Nitlapán-UCA 1993, 7, 9).[8] By 1991 crucial support for economic reform was being provided by the multilateral lenders. Reforms launched in March 1991, which eliminated domestic financing of the government deficit, were designed with staff support from the IMF, the World Bank and the IDB (Stahler-Sholk 1992, 26). The World Bank subsequently approved a structural adjustment loan, and in September 1991 the IMF issued its first standby loan for Nicaragua since 1979. By 1992 the Nicaraguan government had normalized its relationship with these multilateral lenders and had secured new loans from the IMF, World Bank, and IDB totaling US$450 million through 1994 (U.S. GAO 1992, 3). Multilateral sources were expected to provide a growing portion of Nicaragua's foreign loans.[9]

External support, however, was both politically and economically conditioned, most visibly on the part of the U.S. government. The pace of the Chamorro government's land devolution and its refusal to remove Sandinista leaders from key posts raised eyebrows in conservative quarters of the U.S. Congress. In June 1992, U.S. aid flows of $104 million were temporarily halted by Congress when Republican Senator Jesse Helms, member of the Senate Foreign Relations Committee, and Democratic Representative David Obey, chair of the House Appropriations subcommittee on foreign operations, requested the suspension pending a review of aid policy.[10] After several months of negotiation, the Nicaraguan government responded with a shake-up in the police force and a series of presidential decrees renewing the regime's policy on property claims and establishing indemnization procedures.[11] Aid was eventually released following the electoral defeat of President Bush, but was temporarily suspended again in mid-1993 pending investigation of Nicaraguan linkages with international "terrorist" groups.[12]

Powerful as these external forces were, they would have been unable to reconstruct the Nicaraguan economy without the active cooperation of local actors. In Nicaragua the team of advisers brought in to guide the economic policy of the rookie politician who formally headed the UNO government was drawn heavily from three sectors: CORDENIC, a business-academic coordinating body; INCAE, the Harvard-affiliated business school; and returning expatriates who had acquired technical training abroad. Most significant were the members of CORDENIC, the moderate economic think tank inspired by the Sanford Commission. Four members of the new cabinet were drawn from its ranks. Foremost among them was Antonio Lacayo, the president's son-in-law and campaign director, who became the minister of the presidency.[13]

CORDENIC members were joined by a network of academics from INCAE, the Central American business school on the outskirts of Managua.[14] The initial ministers of finance and of economy and development hailed from INCAE, as did a series of vice-ministers, program directors, and consultants. According to a U.S. GAO report (1991, 21) 16 top technical advisers in the BCN, the newly formed Ministry of Economy and Development (MEDE), and other economic agencies were drawn from this institute. With $3.3 million in contracts from USAID, INCAE provided 28 consultants for government and private sector groups and organized 80 seminars for 3,000 public and private sector participants by April 1993 (USAID 1993, 2).

Finally, these two sectors were joined by a network of "Miami boys," as they were colloquially known. These former expatriates, some of whom had worked in the FSLN government during the early, more optimistic years, had subsequently left the country and taken up residence in the United States, where they continued their educations and began new careers. A handful of these returnees had affiliated themselves with various contra organizations during the 1980s.[15] Others held business or academic positions. Miami boys now returned to staff the Chamorro government's major economic ministries.

These three groups formed the core advisory network that represented the Chamorro administration. Notable for their absence in administrative positions were the leaders of the political parties that made up the UNO coalition and COSEP leaders. The transition teams appointed immediately after the February election by Chamorro to suggest nominees for cabinet positions systematically included figures from both the political parties and COSEP. When final appointments were made, however, few were extended beyond the inner circle of Chamorro advisers. What effort there was to include prominent COSEP leaders ultimately backfired. Two COSEP leaders, the organization's President Gilberto Cuadra and Matagalpan coffee association leader Jaime Cuadra, were named to the first cabinet but resigned immediately when Chamorro announced that Sandinista defense minister General Humberto Ortega would be retained as the head of the armed forces.[16]

Compared with other top political actors, the economic team that took over from the Sandinistas was relatively removed from the local political context and had a strong commitment to market criteria. The economic cabinet members were trained, with few exceptions, in the United States and in technical fields like economics and engineering. Several had spent much of the Sandinista era outside Nicaragua removed from the debates and daily conflicts of the period. Supported intellectually by the business program at INCAE, these professionals moved quickly toward a neoliberal formula.[17]

At the outset, the commitment of the new president and her coalition to an orthodox, neoliberal program was not entirely clear. In selecting Chamorro over COSEP leader Enrique Bolaños and incorporating only a modified version of Bolaños's plan of action into the UNO platform, the UNO coalition eschewed a clear embrace of classical liberalism.[18] The platform's commitment to a "social market" economy, for example, split the difference between those who favored the restoration of the market and those who endorsed a model that was attentive to the needs of the poor.

Land policy was also contradictory, embracing, on one hand, the norm of returning expropriated properties and, on the other, the consolidation of the cooperatives and land grants issued under the Sandinista regime (UNO 1989). Recognizing the broad-based popularity of the revolution in its early days, and sharing some of its social goals, the Chamorro government was unwilling to discard all aspects of the Sandinista economic model.

On the other hand, the years of expropriations, press censorship, war, and state controls fed an antistatist sentiment that was quite widespread in the society. The move toward the market was in part a rebellion against the expanded state controls of the 1980s and a bid to close the breach that had been opened between Nicaragua and its traditional regional allies in the United States and Central America. These considerations, combined with the general enthusiasm for private enterprise in the economic "change team" members like BCN president Francisco Mayorga,[19] drew the new government toward a neoliberal formula.

In addition to foreign economic support and the backing of a technocratic elite, structural characteristics of the executive branch also bolstered economic reform in Nicaragua. As a legacy of both the Somoza and the Sandinista eras, political power in Nicaragua was quite concentrated in the presidency. The legislature, which had been fully dominated by Somoza and his allies in the prerevolutionary era, was generally compliant in the Sandinista era as well.[20] The Chamorro government inherited a strong executive branch and a weak legislative tradition.

Initially, Chamorro's administration secured a foothold in the legislature by having erstwhile ally Alfredo César elected president of the national assembly through a path-breaking coalition of moderates in the UNO ranks and FSLN supporters. When César later defected from the ranks of the moderates and threw his weight behind the more conservative sectors, Chamorro maneuvered around him, often by securing FSLN votes to get her proposals approved. When necessary, she used veto powers to prevent the legislature from circumventing executive initiatives. Faced over time with a deepening schism in the UNO ranks and boycotts of the legislature by both the FSLN and UNO groups, Chamorro used executive powers to bypass the assembly and governed frequently by decree.[21]

The extensive centralization of political authority in Nicaragua allowed the president considerable institutional leeway in charting the nation's economic course. But she faced a notable challenge from the popular sectors that had been mobilized by the FSLN during the insurrection and early

Sandinista period. Organizations like the CST and the ATC were poised to impede the restoration of the status quo ante.

These organizations had not, historically, been highly autonomous entities or been forcefully directed from their base. Instead, they had been closely tied to the institutional interests of the FSLN and often served to advance the cause of the revolution over their particular sectoral interests.[22] Once the FSLN was defeated and forced to hand over government power, however, the relationship became much more complex. When the FSLN leadership attempted to restrain labor activism as part of ongoing negotiations with the Chamorro government, Sandinista mass organizations began to resist control and assert a growing degree of autonomy. To prevent the full erosion of their base and collapse of their organizations, union and mass organization leaders now had to commit themselves m[...] [...]lly to protecting the specific material interests of their mem[...] [...] still linked ideologically to the FSLN and attentive to its [...] [...]anizations emerged as an increasingly independent [...]ent [...] [...]plementation of a neoliberal model (Stahler-[...]lk[...] [...] Sand[...] [...]aders now awkwardly scrambled to position [...]emsel[...] [...] the [...] f wildcat labor movements or, in some cases, to [...]eal to w[...] ke[...] ist in confrontational mobilizations. Unlike many [...] [...]es in [...] merica, where the neoliberal model was imposed in [...] [...]thoritarian period in which unions were suppressed or co[...] [...] oduction of neoliberalism in the Nicaraguan case occurred wh[...] s organizations were still relatively mobilized and as they were beginning to free themselves from the constraints imposed by the revolutionary government.

The Chamorro government faced not just political opposition from FSLN organizations but from local business elites as well. The government was unable to secure the endorsement of traditional elites, in spite of the personal and organizational connections that existed between key ministers and the major private sector associations.[23] Nicaragua's factionalized, fragmented bourgeoisie was incapable of rallying behind any program. Most economic elites backed the UNO coalition during the election, but many were simultaneously wary of the new government that they themselves had promoted.[24] This issue will be discussed more fully below, but in general both COSEP leaders and many individual producers who were negatively affected by neoliberal policies quickly moved into the opposition. The government did have important allies in the bourgeoisie, including both entrepreneurial producers who had weathered the Sandinista era and some prominent business leaders who had returned from exile. But the Chamorro government failed to win the full backing of the private sector in spite of the generally antistatist, promarket thrust of its economic policy.

Implementing the Model

Between 1990 and 1992 the Chamorro government gradually introduced a series of changes that dramatically altered the economic course of the nation. According to the Government of Nicaragua's (1992, 1) 1992–96 development plan,

> The Government's medium-term development strategy . . . implies moving away from dependence on a paternalistic, all-powerful State to self-reliance and spontaneous forms of solidarity; from pervasive Government control and intervention in economic activity to a free market economy; from rent-seeking behaviour at all levels of society to productive hard work; from a high degree of conflict and militarization to a peaceful civil society; from large, inefficient public sector bureaucracies to smaller, more efficient organizations focused on those few areas where the role of Government is indispensable; and from inflationary monetary and credit policies to a solid monetary stability that encourages long-term saving and financial planning.

The government moved quickly to begin (1) the return of expropriated property held by the state, leading to a large-scale privatization process; (2) a reduction in the numbers of both military and civilian personnel; (3) deregulation of the economy, ceding control of foreign trade and banking to the private sector; (4) trade liberalization; and (5) fiscal and monetary reform.

One of the government's first acts (Decree #11-90) was to set up a formal appeal and review process under which expropriated land would be legally returned to former owners. In theory, land that had been titled to cooperatives would not be returned; claimants would instead receive some other form of compensation. In practice, however, the new land policy put pressure on cooperatives as well, since the Sandinista government had been slow to provide final legal title to many of the cooperatives it established.[25] Without legal, registered titles, or with titles handed out under controversial circumstances during the sixty-day lame duck period at the end of the FSLN era,[26] these cooperatives were vulnerable to having the land they occupied classified as state lands and returned to former owners.

In all, 5,384 claimants reportedly filed for the return of over 15,000 expropriated urban and rural properties (Roberto Larios, "Devuelven 50 propiedades a confiscados," *Barricada*, February 12, 1993, interview with Uriel Soto, Procurador de la Propiedad). Approximately 1,000 certificates of devolution were issued in the first year by the five-person review commission chaired by the *procurador general* before the review process was suspended amid charges of mismanagement and corruption (*La Prensa*, April 30, 1991).[27] A new Comisión Nacional de Revisión de Confiscaciones was named in October 1992 to renew the property return/compensation process. Although problems continued for economic elites when workers occupied enterprises that had legally been returned to former owners, the UNO regime's commitment to privatization was clear. "We've made a 100 percent shift away from statism," proclaimed Antonio Lacayo to an assembled group of private producers (*Barricada*, June 27, 1991).

Not only were former owners regaining their properties but the remaining state enterprises that had been confiscated from Somoza allies or built by the Sandinista regime were also being privatized. State sector operations were reorganized under CORNAP, which pulled together an array of farms, agroindustries, factories, and commercial, transportation, and tourist facilities that had become state property during the FSLN era. When it was formed in May 1990, CORNAP controlled 351 companies that were responsible for 31 percent of national production and employed 78,000 workers, or 9 percent of the workforce (CORNAP 1991, 6). The new regime moved quickly to divest itself of these operations, returning sugar mills like the ISA to the Pellas family, slaughterhouses like San Martín to former stockholders, and SAIMSA to former COSEP president Enrique Bolaños. By March 1993 CORNAP had released 237 of these companies (68 percent of the total) with 158 of them either being returned to former owners or sold (or, in a few cases, rented) to new private owners.[28] (See Table 6.1.) Procedures initiating the privatization of the remainder were to have begun by the end of 1993. Even operations that had often escaped the privatization ax elsewhere, such as gold mines, were put up for sale. Although some of the firms transferred out of CORNAP's control were handed on to other state agencies, the total participation of state enterprises in the economy was targeted to fall to less than 10 percent of GDP when the privatization process was completed (U.S. GAO 1992, 22).

Table 6.1

Privatization of State Enterprises, May 1990–March 1993

Total number of state enterprises		351
State enterprises privatized		
State farm enterprises returned/sold	43	
Other enterprises returned	66	
Other enterprises sold/rented	49	
Enterprises transferred to other state agency	28	
Enterprises liquidated	51	
Total privatized		237
Remaining state enterprises		114

Source: CORNAP.

Unlike the Mexican case, where the antinationalist sting of privatization could be assuaged by the promise that new revenues coming in would support social programs (Dresser 1991), the Nicaraguan government did not expect to generate much revenue from privatization. Deteriorated machinery and antiquated technologies made most of these operations unattractive, as did their sometimes truculent workforce and the weak internal market. According to Minister of Finance Emilio Pereira, the government hoped only to recover enough from their sale to pay off their past bank debts and cover unpaid taxes (interview published in IHCA 1991d, 23). The gain in privatization, from the state's point of view, would be that the facility would be in the hands of private entrepreneurs, who would then be responsible for reactivating production. The rapid pace of privatization would also, presumably, persuade foreign creditors and investors of the seriousness of the government's commitment to a market-based economic model and encourage new investment.

To restart the economy on a neoliberal foundation, the size and realm of the state needed to be reduced. Of particular concern to the Chamorro government was the size of the public sector workforce. The armed forces, already reduced following the approval of the Esquipulas accords from 96,000 in July 1989 to 40,000 at the time of the 1990 election, were targeted for further reductions. By the end of 1990 only 28,000 troops and officers remained. This number was lowered further to 15,250 by early 1993.[29]

In addition to the reduction in the size and budget of the armed forces, the government cut the number of its civilian employees. State workers were offered a series of financial inducements to leave public service. According to USAID, 28,000 state workers left the public sector under this agreement, including both those directly employed in the central government and workers in the state enterprises undergoing privatization (USAID 1993, 1).[30] This represented approximately 19 percent of the civilian, public sector workforce.[31]

Those state workers who remained were put on a more market-based footing. Key government services, such as education and health programs, which had been free during the Sandinista era, now began to employ user's fees. Other services, such as water, light, electricity, public transportation, and telephones, which had been heavily subsidized, now began to charge market rates.

At the same time, the government deregulated whole sectors of the national economy and eliminated the government monopoly over key economic activities. In 1991, for example, new banking legislation allowed the return of private banks; by 1993 seven private banks had been authorized. These banks opened with limited capital and few branch offices, but they had captured approximately 32 percent of all bank deposits by September 1992 (USAID 1993, 2; UNAG n.d., 4).[32]

Private firms also returned in the export sector. Initially there were delays in allowing the reestablishment of private intermediaries due to competing interpretations of constitutional provisions designating exports as a state monopoly and as a result of prior contracts signed by state firms for the advance sale of the 1990–91 harvest (Pryor 1991, 105–6). These constraints slowly dissolved. By the end of 1991 105 export firms had received five-year licenses from the government (E. Pérez 1992, 4). Old distributors like Calley Dagnall and CISA renewed their operations, and new marketing links were started by organizations like ECODEPA, the farmer's store affiliate of UNAG. The state export firms retreated, becoming purchasing agents for marginal producers (IHCA 1992d, 33).

In foreign trade, the government moved forcefully toward liberalization. Maximum import duties, which had been 350 percent for some low-priority items at the end of the Sandinista period (BCN, *Nicaragua Economic Report*, November–December 1991, 7), were reduced to 10–60 percent in November 1991 and dropped further to 10–40 percent in April 1992. The government's goal was to reduce the maximum import duty to 10–20 percent by 1993, at which time all import tariffs within the newly established Central America Free Trade Area would be eliminated (Government of Nicaragua 1992, 10–11). Under the terms of the

Export Promotion Law, exports were to be promoted through a series of incentives, including a 100 percent exemption on import tariffs for export producers and an initial 80 percent income tax reduction for exporters of nontraditional products.[33] The return of flight capital and an increase in foreign investment were to be promoted under a new foreign investment law that allowed 100 percent profit remittances, capital remittances after three years, and a three- to five-year tax holiday.[34]

Finally, after years of battling inflation, monetary stability was achieved. The elimination of multiple exchange rates and the establishment of free convertibility of the new córdoba, followed by a 400 percent devaluation in March 1991, did away with exchange rate losses that had plagued the Sandinista financial system. The BCN also cut off the credit valve to the state banking system and issued a requirement that new credit authorizations be based on deposits and the recovery of past loans. The result was a credit squeeze that dramatically curtailed state bank activities.

The 1991–92 transition was marked by a sharp reduction in government spending. The fiscal deficit, which had widened to 19.7 percent of GDP in 1990 as a result of the electoral campaign and the public sector strikes following the transition, began to close in 1991, when it declined to 8.0 percent of GDP. (See Appendix 2, Table A.3.) Under the new monetary policy, the deficit could no longer be covered by central bank emissions. The relatively modest deficit that remained was covered by U.S. donations, and the inflation rate fell sharply in 1991, with almost all of the increase coming in the first three months of the year. In the twelve months between October 1991 and October 1992 the inflation rate fell to 2.2 percent, a level not seen in Nicaragua since before 1978. The fiscal deficit was reduced in spite of the introduction of a tax reform package in February 1992 that continued the general downward trend in tax rates.[35] The government's revenues were now drawn heavily from indirect taxes (76 percent of the total in 1992), particularly from excise taxes on the "fiscal industries"—beer, rum, soft drinks, and cigarettes—that tend to have a regressive impact.[36]

In all, there was a notable shift away from the development model of the Sandinista era, even the modified one of the 1988–90 era, and an emphatic commitment to the neoliberal guidelines. The shift, however, was not absolute; the revolutionary era had a continuing influence.

Postrevolutionary Political Bargaining

Polarized politics and unstable governing coalitions are significant obstacles to the consolidation of neoliberalism, tending instead to support the adoption of populism (Kaufman and Stallings 1991; Haggard and Kaufman 1992b). Sharp divisions in Nicaraguan society and government, therefore, served to undermine the neoliberal shift. The Chamorro government, in spite of its impressive political victory, had a weak political base. It had no strong links to a powerful political party or to mass organizations; even its ties to elite associations were weak. Only a thin thread connected the new government to the social order it presided over. The FSLN, still reeling over its electoral defeat, mobilized for multiple confrontations with the regime in the early months of the transition.

Repeated batterings in the May–August 1990 period, complete with two major national strikes, lockouts of top ministers, land and industry takeovers, and episodes of spontaneous civilian violence, pushed the government to search for new forms of dialogue and consultation. The Chamorro administration, which had campaigned on a platform of national reconciliation, looked for ways to avoid a showdown with the still-powerful FSLN and to restart an economy anchored on a new national consensus.

Twice in 1990–91 the government called the warring parties to the table for a socioeconomic *concertación* process. The locus of economic deliberation was shifted from the weak, fractious legislature and handed to direct economic actors. The assembly, filled with erstwhile allies and intractable foes often representing newborn miniparties, lacked the political authority to legislate definitively in the area of economic policy. To put together a meaningful accord, the government needed to get the principal actors themselves to agree about the rules of the game. Tough discussions were opened about fundamental economic and social issues, including property rights, resource distribution, and investment and economic priorities.

Building on the *concertación* process the Sandinista government had initiated in 1989, but now with a fuller range of issues in play, the Chamorro government opened the first round of negotiations from September 20 to October 26, 1990. The government called together the representatives of thirty-five organizations divided between employers and workers. Eighteen producer associations, including affiliates of both COSEP and UNAG, met with representatives of seventeen employee associations that included both organizations like the CST and the ATC, which had been linked historically to the FSLN, and unions like the Confederación de Unión Sindical and Central de Acción de Unidad Sindical, which were allied with the UNO coalition.[37] After fifteen full days of discussions that were broadcast almost nonstop on the nation's one major TV channel, and periodic walkouts on both sides, an accord was finalized (República de Nicaragua, 1990a).

The agreement gave something to everyone and extracted some concessions all around. After initially encountering forceful opposition, employers got Sandinista unions on record accepting the return of or compensation for expropriated properties.[38] Workers also were persuaded to accept the return of private enterprises in the banking and export sectors. In turn, labor succeeded in inserting statements calling on employers to increase investment, moderate profit levels, generate new employment, and maintain labor protections established under the FSLN government. Employee representatives also got the government to agree to establish reduced tariffs on basic services for low-income groups and maintain at least the prevailing spending levels for health and education.

The government, in turn, got an agreement that the fiscal deficit had to be reduced through a decrease in military spending and the rationalization of public expenditures. Making a case for a reduction in the size of the state apparatus, the government presented its early retirement program for state workers. Although at the final moment the representatives of COSEP-affiliated organizations refused to sign the document, this pact initiated an unprecedented form of dialogue between political and economic adversaries.

Formal acceptance of general principles did not, however, translate into agreement about specific cases. Whereas Sandinista labor organizations signed off on provisions for the return of expropriated land, for example, ATC leaders often organized standoffs and lockouts of former owners attempting to enter their properties. The ATC not only took over properties of those attempting to reclaim their estates, it also launched invasions of the properties of unrelated private producers. This new form of triangularized bargaining attempted to pressure powerful private producers, who presumably had privileged access to the new government, to use their influence with the government to avert the full privatization of state-owned farms.

The *concertación* efforts might have gone further toward reestablishing a social agreement if the economic crisis had been less severe. In periods of growth, when all parties can simultaneously receive some benefits, the costs of adjustment are easier to bear. In a zero-sum context, on the other hand, increased resources for capitalists mean reduced resources for their workers. After a long, lagging decade of decline, the continued economic erosion of labor's resources in Nicaragua triggered combustible confrontations.

In a postrevolutionary setting, where consensus on fundamental issues was missing and the society's resources were up for grabs, parties on all sides insisted, along with Hobbes, that clubs were trumps. The renewed fall in the standard of living of the majority after the March 1991 devaluation fed deepening unrest and periodic outbursts of violence. Terms of the initial pacts were not fulfilled; crucial issues like worker ownership had not been addressed precisely. Obfuscation had allowed all parties to claim victory at first, but tensions soon flared. In the hope of building a new social consensus, the government called for a second round of *concertación* discussions.

Concertación II ran intermittently from May to August 1991, bringing together much the same lineup of employer and labor groups in a more sluggish consultation. Discussion again focused on the pivotal question of property ownership and how the resources of the society would be divvied up. Workers in state enterprises wanted to protect their quota of state resources, arguing that it was their labor that kept these operations afloat during the hard days of economic embargo and war. COSEP representatives, on the other hand, wanted to minimize worker ownership in order to give maximum latitude to prospective buyers. In the end, *Concertación II* concluded with an agreement that workers in state firms would be allowed to acquire 25 percent of the stock in the operations being transferred to the private sector.[39]

This combination of agreements, while failing to provide workers with other supports such as job protection, guarantees about retraining, or any minority veto power in managerial decisions, did parcel out some of the resources of the state to workers. The government was able to come to this decision in part because there had been no rush of private investors willing to snatch up these state resources. State properties, therefore, were available for use in responding to popular pressures. The weak response of capital to the first phase of transition fostered further deviations from the neoliberal model.

The *concertación* process reduced, but did not eliminate, social tension.[40] Strikes continued throughout 1991 and reached significant proportions in the banking, health, education, sugar processing, port, airport, customs, hotel, and mining sectors.[41] With the active support of top FSLN leaders, however, there were no major uprisings, even in the face of ongoing economic restructuring. This relative political containment suggests a certain success in the *concertación* process.

The Nicaraguan economic reform was not, however, simply a conventional neoliberal package. Although much of the public rhetoric on the left would characterize it in these terms, the economic program that emerged contained several unconventional features. Compared with neoliberal experiences elsewhere in the region, the Nicaraguan variant differed in several notable respects.

Neoliberalism with a Twist

The neoliberal model entails more than just a checklist of discreet economic policy reforms. It also involves a restructuring of the sociopolitical arena. Although central economic policies were altered in postrevolutionary Nicaragua, the social and political configuration proved more resistant to change. The broader contours of the neoliberal shift were subject to tough negotiation. As a result of this complex and ongoing political bargaining, the neoliberal formula was modified in the Nicaraguan case in four interrelated areas.[42] These areas were (1) worker ownership, (2) restraints on the forces of repression, (3) eased contraction of the public sector workforce, and (4) ongoing consultation and conciliation with the political opposition.

Worker Ownership

The Nicaraguan version of privatization had several distinctive features. Soon after the first *concertación* accord, the government set up a special commission to oversee the privatization of the state farm system. This commission finished its work quickly. By mid-1991, the Chamorro government had disposed of most of its agricultural property, divesting itself of HATONIC, the state cattle corporation that owned almost one-third of the state farmland, as well as the cotton corporation AGROEXCO and the coffee corporation CAFENIC, which together administered the most valuable state-owned land and most advanced processing facilities.

In privatizing these properties, the state attempted to respond to multiple demands, including those of workers. Pulling together the claims filed by former owners, the demands made by the ATC, and the promises

Table 6.2

State Farm Land Distribution Program, 1991

	Area	
	Mz.	%
Cattle Sector (HATONIC)		
Returned to former owners	80,455	26
Cattle sector farmworkers	99,319	32
Discharged from armed forces	59,034	19
Demobilized resistance	70,619	23
Total	309,427	100
Cotton Sector (AGROEXCO)		
Returned to former owners	17,221	49
Cotton sector farmworkers	11,396	32
Discharged from armed forces	4,482	13
Demobilized resistance	2,299	6
Total	35,398	100
Coffee Sector (CAFENIC)		
Returned to former owners	26,890	35
Coffee sector farmworkers	24,942	33
Discharged from armed forces	10,250	13
Demobilized resistance	14,542	19
Total	76,624	100
Total state farm land distribution		
Returned to former owners	124,566	30
State farmworkers	135,657	32
Discharged from armed forces	73,766	17
Demobilized resistance	87,460	21
Total	421,449	100

Source: CORNAP.

the government made to demobilized contra and EPS forces, the government divided up resources among these four competitors. The former owners reacquired 49 percent of the state cotton land, 26 percent of the state ranch land, and 35 percent of the state coffee territory. (See Table 6.2.) But the group receiving the largest portion of this land was made up of former state farmworkers, which secured the right to acquire 32–33 percent of the area of each of these corporations. Once the properties to be returned to former owners were identified, agricultural workers were consulted by the ATC leadership about which of the remaining properties should be claimed for the workers. By December 1992, 17,148 workers became stockholders (*socios*) in 131 agricultural enterprises (FIDEG 1993, 23).

The remainder of this land was divided between discharged soldiers and demobilized contra troops. Contra soldiers received somewhat more of the ranch and coffee land in the mountainous interior, where these forces had been concentrated. On the other hand, the EPS soldiers received somewhat more of the cotton land on the Pacific side of the country than their resistance counterparts. Overall, discharged soldiers received 17 percent of the divested land, and demobilized rebels received 21 percent.

This agrarian privatization process was followed by divestment in the industrial sector. According to the terms of the second *concertación* agreement, state workers in the industrial sector were to receive 25 percent participation in these better-capitalized and technologically complex operations. Negotiations about how the allocation of these shares was to proceed were more difficult and time consuming than negotiations about agricultural properties. In some cases, the enterprise was not financially viable, and workers did not want to assume responsibility for its debts. In others, the former owners insisted on complete control and refused to sell partial ownership to the workers. So complex was the situation that negotiations proceeded sector by sector and even company by company. In February 1993 the government announced an agreement with CST under which nine state enterprises were to be sold in their entirety to workers, partial control was accepted in another eighteen, and three were to be returned in their entirety to former owners (Gobierno de Nicaragua-CST, *Acuerdo*, February 2, 1993).[43]

The redistributive impact of this privatization process had several limitations. The workers' ability to acquire these resources was reduced by the requirement that they purchase their shares rather than receiving them outright. CORNAP's policy of giving concessionary terms (access to credit, low interest rates, grace periods) to "social groups" that acquired state property was expected to allow workers to participate in the process.[44] In all probability, however, at least some of these new owners will be unable to complete these payments, and the whole negotiation process will enter another phase after the grace period elapses. If the power configuration in Nicaragua shifts, workers and former combatants could wind up losing the properties they obtained during the opening phase of the privatization process.

Furthermore, formal ownership does not automatically mean worker empowerment and administrative control. In order to preserve as much of the APP framework as possible and to reduce divisive tendencies among the workers, former state farmworkers were encouraged by Sandinista leaders to form holding companies run by professional administrators, some of whom had played similar roles during the Sandinista government. If the old patterns of top-down management continue unabated, the workers' formal ownership of these enterprises may not, therefore, give them meaningful control over their property. Finally, these new property arrangements divide the working class by differentiating those state workers who can buy into their firms from those who do not have this opportunity.

On the other hand, these kinds of privatization arrangements, which fostered worker participation and decentralized ownership, highlight the sustained political capacity of groups mobilized by the FSLN and the inclusionary efforts of the postrevolutionary government. In this sense, privatization in Nicaragua represents a third alternative to privatization efforts in Czechoslovakia or Poland, where the process was linked to a decentralized "citizen capitalism," and such efforts in Mexico or Argentina, where the divestiture process catered to a relatively small number of elite economic groups.

Restraints on Repression

The regime also differentiated itself from other neoliberal regimes in Latin America, particularly the military version in Chile and Argentina in the 1970s, by forgoing an extensive capability for mass repression. By allowing the leadership of the military and police force to remain in the hands of those who held these posts during the FSLN era, the Chamorro government obtained the cooperation and even loyalty of these organizations. But it did so by accepting a policy of exceptional restraint in the face of mass mobilizations.

In the July 1990 general strike, for example, soldiers and police did not take forceful action against protesters who closed the capital for over a week by breaking up the streets to build barricades. Recurring strikes in the public sector in 1990 and 1991 were rarely confronted by the police or armed forces. The periodic takeover of private farms during crucial moments in the agricultural cycles in 1990 and 1991 was not effectively challenged by the authorities. In these kinds of events, strikers and protesters would typically disperse when the police or soldiers approached but return as soon as the police departed. Both protesters and troops shared a mutual commitment to avoiding outright confrontation. This relative softening of the forces of repression in the Nicaraguan case gave freer reign to regime opponents. It also reduced the gap between the Chamorro government and the FSLN, facilitating more extensive consultation and agreement.

The September 1992 replacement of Sandinista police chief René Vivas following the suspension of U.S. aid, and Chamorro's announcement in September 1993, following another aid suspension, that Humberto Ortega would be retired in 1994, could begin to alter this pattern. Since this shake-up was presumably insisted upon with an eye to reducing FSLN power and increasing protection of property claims, the remodeled military forces may become more confrontational with strikers or those involved in land invasions. They are unlikely to undergo a full metamorphosis, however, since Sandinista stalwarts in the leadership of both the police and the military are several layers thick. Replacement at the top only leads to the promotion of other Sandinista affiliates who move up from the lower ranks. The kind of repression that accompanied the neoliberal transformation in Chile is unlikely to be replayed in Nicaragua, at least during this phase of the transition.

Eased Public Sector Contraction

Recognizing the political and economic difficulty of laying off thousands of public sector employees, many of whom were diehard FSLN supporters, the government devised an "occupational conversion" plan that cushioned this process. Voluntary retirement from the government payrolls would earn state workers a bonus of up to 10,000 *córdobas oro* ($2,000), with which they could make the transition to the private sector. The initial program, designed for those employed directly by the central government, was expanded to include workers laid off due to liquidations or transfers of parastate companies. Financed by the USAID mission, this early retirement program reportedly cost $47.5 million by mid-1992 (USAID 1992, 1).

The payments failed by much to cover the costs of moving into the private sector, and with the enduring economic crisis the program has worsened the glut of unemployed professionals. However, the vast majority of state workers were retained, leaving much of the public sector with proreform sentiments, however tinged they may be by weariness and disillusion. Unlike in other postrevolutionary settings, where state cutbacks were accompanied with political purges or abrupt amputations of ministries, Nicaraguan functionaries were generally allowed to choose between retirement with a substantial severance allowance or remaining in public employ. This approach buffered the transition of public employees into the private sector and allowed the regime to avoid a fierce political backlash.

Consultation with the Opposition

President Chamorro noted repeatedly in 1990, "We won an election, not a war." Her political adversaries were not required to sign an unconditional surrender. Quite to the contrary, the new regime was willing to extend protections and resources to the FSLN. Beginning with the Protocol of Transition prior to the inauguration of the Chamorro government, the new regime made a series of agreements with the FSLN in the name of stability and reconciliation. Because of its own precarious political position presiding over a fractious and quickly disintegrating coalition, the Chamorro government made repeated overtures to the FSLN in the 1990–93 period. The regime resisted recurring internal pressures to divest FSLN leaders of the residential properties they had acquired during the era of their control; it was desultory in reviewing the land and property titles that had been extended during the *piñata*, preferring that the FSLN police itself and sanction members who had illicitly grabbed state resources; it allowed the military high command to use its own criteria in reducing the size of the officer corp instead of forcing a political purge; and except in top positions, it did not force FSLN party members to surrender their government offices.

The regime participated in regular consultations with top FSLN leaders, informing them of pending economic moves and involving them in international campaigns for foreign financing (interviews, Luis Carrión Cruz, March 20, 1991; Daniel Ortega, June 29, 1992).[45] This process both dampened the neoliberal character of the regime's economic policy and co-opted key elements of the FSLN's leadership. Unable to devise a clear economic alternative, and having moved, in the 1988–90 period, down the road toward the restoration of the market principles, the FSLN was hard-pressed to resist the Chamorro government's overtures. FSLN leaders and the Chamorro government officials now collectively and publicly embraced a modified version of the neoliberal model that buffered key constituents of the FSLN. In early 1993 this cooperation even brought several prominent Sandinista party members back into government in second tier ministerial positions, raising the charge of *co-gobierno* (cogovernment) between the Chamorro administration and the FSLN.

The Bourgeoisie's Responses to the New Economic Direction

As had been the case, to a greater or lesser degree, throughout the revolutionary period, the Nicaraguan private elite remained divided. To the established fissures were added new divisions, as emerging and returning elites took their place in the bourgeoisie. Within two years of the postrevolutionary transition, the economic elite arguably was arrayed in four clusters. Although there was some overlap among these groups, they differed from each other in the way they combined their political styles, investment strategies, and alliance tendencies. At the apex of the economic elite stood two groups: the antirevolutionary politicos, who forcefully criticized the Chamorro government, and the hegemonic returnees, who generally preferred quiet negotiation and tacit support. Beneath these leading groups were two other business sectors: the disoriented agricultural elites, who foundered economically during the economic reform and became politically disaffected, and the new entrepreneurs, who moved quickly to identify emerging opportunities.

Antirevolutionary Politicos

Antirevolutionary politicos continued to dominate the COSEP and UPANIC national leadership in the postrevolutionary period. By this point, the political orientation of COSEP had taken on a life of its own. The primary goal of these leaders had never been to determine what views and opinions prevailed among private producers and to reflect those views. Instead, leaders were chosen by a small group of insiders who elevated to power the most articulate defenders of the organization's preestablished position.[46] Those who were most drawn to COSEP and who tended to rise within the organization were those who found its strident hostility to the Sandinistas to be most congenial. As Chapter 5 demonstrated, national-level leaders of COSEP and UPANIC were drawn heavily from the moral-political opponents of the regime.

After 1990 the ranks of these organizations were resupplied by a network of new volunteers who were perhaps even more stridently anti-Sandinista than those they replaced. To the old core of leaders were now added several expatriates who returned to Nicaragua to reclaim their expropriated properties. The inability or unwillingness of the Chamorro government to dispose quickly of their claims, to halt ongoing land invasions, and to restore the traditional social relations to the countryside led many COSEP and UPANIC leaders to sharply criticize the new government.[47]

The resignations of two COSEP leaders from the Chamorro government on the day it was inaugurated, the refusal of COSEP representatives to sign either of the two *concertación* agreements, COSEP's support for the new Association of the Expropriateds (Asociaciones de Confiscados), and the links between the UPANIC leadership and the right-wing PLC reflected the enduring alienation of this elite sector from the government, in spite of the adoption of the neoliberal reforms by the Chamorro government.[48] The stridency of the COSEP opposition, in view of the adoption of these reforms, suggests that the political culture of the organization had been frozen in place. Organizations have stylistic propensities that are forged during defining periods and subsequently become difficult to change. COSEP's formative experiences during the hard, early years of the Sandinista government had inclined it toward confrontational politics. That style, which had, in some ways, served the broad political interests of COSEP leaders, became an organizational trademark that it could not surrender.

Hegemonic Returnees

Because of its long history leading the opposition to the FSLN government, COSEP was widely regarded as the primary political agent of the bourgeoisie. Its preeminence, however, was not universally accepted. One important challenger was drawn from the elite families that historically headed the major economic groups in the prerevolutionary period. Many members of the hegemonic families of the pre-1979 era fled the country in 1978 as the insurrection heated up. They generally took up residence abroad, typically in the United States. A handful of these elites had accumulated extensive additional resources during the period of their self-exile; others had survived and prospered after making a tough adjustment. Drawn back to Nicaragua once the Sandinistas were ousted, members of this group and their descendants now began to reestablish their dominance over core activities like banking and export trade.

Unlike COSEP leaders, members of these prerevolutionary elite families were more likely to make investments and start new projects during this transition period. Three of the new banks were established by old, elite families, who could draw on foreign financing and international connections. Eduardo Montealegre, son of the founder and long-term presi-

dent of BANIC, returned as cofounder and manager of the Banco de Crédito Centroamericano in 1991; his cousin Haroldo Montealegre became
a founder and the general manager of the Banco Mercantil; Carlos Pellas,
son of Alfredo Pellas of the BANAMER group, negotiated both the return of
the ISA and the creation of the Banco de América Central, a third private
bank.[49] Unlike COSEP, which was locked into a confrontational stance,
several members of this group of hegemonic returnees tended to adopt a
low political profile, in some ways similar to the one their families employed during the Somoza regime. When they did surface politically, they
generally adopted a conciliatory approach toward the government.[50] Less
overtly ideological and more concerned about practical consequences, less
inclined to scrappy political infighting and more skilled at negotiation,
less mired in old battles and more willing to start afresh, this prime elite
differentiated itself from the COSEP leadership.

COSEP leaders, many of whom had logged years in hard political
struggle and had experienced tremendous economic decline during the
Sandinista period, resented the return of a relatively unscathed traditional
elite. These competitors came back with extensive international connections and investment skills that those who remained in Nicaragua "fighting the good fight" had not acquired. Those who stayed were dependent
on antiquated and deteriorated technologies in an era of FAXes and conference calls. As returning elites reasserted their positions in banking and
export trade, those who had remained behind found their own ambitions
frustrated. The unwillingness of prerevolutionary leaders to toe the COSEP
political line challenged the latter's political prominence and deepened
the elite divide.

Disoriented Agricultural Elite

Producers at the local and regional level who had risen to prominence
in the prerevolutionary period as agroexporters and large-scale staples
producers, and who had generally stayed in Nicaragua during the Sandinista era, emerged in the neoliberal economy as victims of economic
displacement. Cotton producers who expected a return to the heady days
of the 1970s were confronted with tremendously increased costs and declining real prices for cotton. Stimulated by temporary access to state
bank credit in 1990 and generous restructuring arrangements for the unpaid loans in 1991, cotton production in 1991 increased 21 percent over
1990 (CEPAL 1992b, 28). But Nicaraguan cotton, heavily dependent on
multiple pesticide applications, had ceased being profitable at world mar-

ket prices (CARANA Corporation and Sparks Companies 1991, 79–84). By 1992, production plummeted and the value of cotton exports declined a reported 41 percent between 1991 and 1992 (FIDEG, *Observador económico* 12 [December 1992]: 14). Although cotton growers particularly had been favored in the first years, ultimately their loss of competitiveness and the pesticide contamination of their soils spelled disaster.

Other producers of traditional crops had similar problems. Coffee producers faced a return to the market just as the international coffee organization collapsed; prices in 1992 for Central America's mild Arabica coffee were at their lowest point in 17 years.[51] Sorghum producers, accustomed to price supports from the Empresa Nicaragüense de Alimentos Básicos (ENABAS), were now hit with reduced internal demand and heavy competition from more efficient regional competitors. Cotton and coffee producers faced financial ruin; cattle breeders resisted the importation of competing breeds; industrialists feared the onslaught of cheap imports (author's observation of meetings of Asociación de Caficultores de Managua, May 16, 1990, and ACBN, August 6, 1991; *La Prensa*, August 8, 1991; IHCA 1992d, 36; interview, CADIN, June 26, 1992).

The combined loss of subsidies and increased international competition spelled rising economic difficulties and political disaffection for much of the business elite. The traditional vagaries, such as drought, merged with new policy constraints, like more restrictive bank credit, to make economic life difficult for this sector. The new government's efforts to cut taxes, stabilize the currency, and provide moral support did not replace the guaranteed profits and hefty subsidies that many traditional producers had become accustomed to during the FSLN period. Low prices, a credit squeeze, and production problems meant declining export earnings; average earnings for traditional agricultural exports fell 23 percent between 1990 and 1991. The drop was most acute for coffee and beef producers, whose export earnings declined 47.9 percent and 52.7 percent, respectively, during that period (CEPAL 1992b, 36).

As in other Latin American countries that had undertaken neoliberal reforms, substantial sectors of the local bourgeoisie were actually hurt by the policy, even when they had been adamant proponents of market reforms. They became disoriented by the changes, unsure of how to proceed, averse to new beginnings, and disillusioned with political outcomes they themselves had supported. Surveys completed by 413 producers during five daylong seminars organized by COSEP, MEDE, and INCAE in May and June 1992 suggested the pessimism and disaffection that prevailed among those respondents. Fifty-eight percent of these producers classified the government's treatment of producers as negative; 42 percent indicated that they were pessimistic about the future (COSEP et al. 1992, 78, 125).[52] Although some policies were evaluated more positively than others,[53] only 7 percent indicated that they would vote for either Violeta Chamorro or Antonio Lacayo for president.[54]

Given the stresses of economic and political transition, some even remembered the Sandinista era with nostalgia. As a former president of the sorghum association ANPROSOR explained,

> [Then BCN president] Mayorga says that Nicaraguan producers are going to be paid the price prevailing in Central America. But I say back to him, when I'm watching him on TV, the prices may be Central American prices but the costs here are higher than they are [elsewhere] in Central America. . . . Under the Sandinistas, we had a guaranteed profit margin. We would propose to them that the profit margin be 50 percent and they gave us that. We earned much more then than now. . . . We should have a guaranteed price, not supply and demand. (Interview, October 18, 1990)

New Entrepreneurs

In the period following the Sandinista defeat, a small but important segment of producers continued the search for new economic opportunities. Less preoccupied with the political debate or more satisfied with the postrevolutionary outcomes, and more agile in their response to economic crisis, these elites emerged as the new entrepreneurs. They included sectors as varied as irrigated rice producers interested in nontraditional exports, large-scale industrialists exploring new capital ventures, UNAG leaders attempting to link forward from the production process, and former state functionaries from the Sandinista government eager to prosper under the new rules.

One key area for development was nontraditional agricultural exports. Most of the Central American countries had moved forcefully in this direction in the 1980s. Nicaragua, under the Sandinistas, had been the regional laggard. As U.S.-Nicaraguan relations normalized, the opportunities provided by the Caribbean Basin Initiative were now available to Nicaraguan producers and served as a stimulus to production changes. Only weeks after the Chamorro government was elected, a group of agricultural producers who had begun to experiment on a small scale with nontraditional crops met to discuss new opportunities for export to the

United States. At the close of this session, the group formed a new organization, APENN.[55] Not affiliated formally with any other private sector
organization, the association pulled together a small group of relatively
elite producers, primarily from UPANIC, who were willing to undertake
some state-supported experimentation. APENN cultivated linkages with
U.S. suppliers and distributors. Financial support from USAID, which
covered APENN's operating expenses, allowed the organization to develop
technical and informational services and increase its membership.[56] Funds
channeled through the state investment fund, FNI, provided start-up capital at low interest rates, and the Export Promotion Law provided massive
tax reductions on nontraditional export earnings.

With this kind of institutional support, nontraditional exports like
honeydew melons began to compete for entry into the U.S. market. Melon
production more than doubled between 1990–91 and 1991–92, and export
earnings rose from $1.6 to $7.4 million (interview, James Johnson, APENN,
Departamento de Transferencia de Tecnología, June 24, 1992). Although
far behind the other Central American countries, and faced with massive
problems (erratic electricity, a deteriorated and war-damaged transportation system, clogged international telecommunications), a small network
of Nicaraguan entrepreneurs now moved to catch up.

A second group that displayed a willingness to take on new investments was found among UNAG leaders. Unlike some business elites who
seemed immobilized as they awaited the return of the prerevolutionary
era, UNAG leaders were eager to work within the social and political
framework that emerged from the revolution. Building on their relatively
positive relations with labor, their funding ties to past benefactors like the
Scandinavian countries, and their easy access to the consultants among
unemployed Sandinista technocrats,[57] these producers sought new opportunities.

Evaluations were made of investments in processing facilities, export
trade, and banking. Taking advantage of the new opening for private exporters, UNAG's supply and distribution affiliate, ECODEPA, set up its own
coffee-processing and marketing facilities in Regions IV and VI. Building
on a solidarity network that sold Nicaraguan coffee in European markets
during the economic embargo imposed by the Reagan administration,
ECODEPA marketed 15 percent of Nicaragua's coffee exports in 1991–92.[58]
UNAG leaders also figured prominently in the plan to privatize CARNIC,
a Managua slaughterhouse that had been confiscated from the Somoza
family. Under the CARNIC privatization agreement, the slaughterhouse

was to be jointly acquired by its workers and a group of cattle ranchers, with UNAG leader Juan Tijerino serving as president of the newly re-organized corporation (interviews, Iván Saballos, CORNAP, June 24, 1992; Bayardo Matamoros, Secretaria de Finanzas, Cooperativa Nuevo CARNIC, R.L., June 24, 1992; UNAG 1993, 18). Finally, UNAG moved gradually toward the creation of its own bank, the Banco del Campo, to circumvent the credit crunch that emerged in the postrevolutionary period.[59]

A third group of new entrepreneurs was composed of Sandinistas-cum-businesspeople. This sector included ex-officials in the Sandinista government who now directly entered the economic competition as private producers. Some of these Sandinista entrepreneurs had been wealthy prior to the revolution and now reclaimed old properties that they had neglected or tendered to the state during the 1980s. Others acquired properties in the final stages of the revolution in the period of the *piñata*. Some drew on professional and managerial skills acquired in government to set up new business operations. Unlike much of the traditional economic elite, the Sandinista bourgeoisie moved rapidly to launch new ventures and expand their activities. The presence of these elites in private businesses deepened the confusion about what businesses were owned and operated by the FSLN as a party and what operations were owned and managed by individuals who had been prominent government officials during the FSLN era.[60]

The high profile of many of these new enterprises, in an economy that was badly depressed, also exacerbated tensions within the FSLN. Party members and supporters who were slipping into deeper economic decline resented more prosperous members (derisively labeled the *nueva burguesía sandinista* or NBS) who were expanding their economic activities; Sandinistas who now managed their own business operations ran into conflict with workers who threatened strikes or land invasions. Defenders of the "revolutionary bourgeoisie," however, argued that Sandinista business leaders were becoming the "patriotic producers" that the revolution had so long mythologized. This revolutionary elite, it was hoped, would continue the breakup of an anachronistic social order in the fields and factories, contribute to the modernization of production, and exert pressure on the Chamorro government to moderate the neoliberal formula. Indeed, the participation of the Sandinista elite in the private sector even won approval in some corners of the government and the business elite. One CADIN leader observed, "It is better to have them on the inside, dealing with the problems that we face in business, than to have them on the outside causing trouble" (interview, CADIN, June 26, 1992).

In sum, not all producers were equally cautious about the new economic and political configuration.[61] During the 1990–93 transition, a diverse collection of private sector elites began to explore new activities. Investment in nontraditional production, export marketing, and the financial sector suggested various areas for economic expansion. This investment trend was modest. It fell far short of providing a foundation for a new economic strategy; it could not even generate short-term economic growth. The "new entrepreneurs" did, however, begin to hint at some of the possible features of postrevolutionary development.

Conclusions

In spite of some positive trends, the obstacles to economic reactivation and restructuring in Nicaragua remained massive. An unfavorable international market for traditional products, entrenched local hostilities, and the elusiveness of a new social and economic consensus all impeded economic renewal. Even after three years only a small portion of the capital flight of the 1970s and 1980s had been reversed, and a large portion of the new investment going on was centered around short-term commercial activities. The pervasiveness of grinding poverty and a brutally low standard of living for the majority provided a weak foundation on which to restart the economy.[62] The push for nontraditional exports brought its own set of problems and seemed unlikely to offer any quick or clear remedy.[63] The inability of the postrevolutionary state to play a catalytic role impeded corrective action. Even the FSLN, which had directed a decade-long social revolution, was unable to articulate any alternative. Nicaragua became mired in the economic quagmire, with economic production continuing to decline in the period following the revolution.

But the Sandinista period had introduced notable changes in the Nicaraguan social order. First, the revolution deeply politicized the bourgeoisie. Economic elites who, for decades, had remained politically passive and had consigned the political world to the Somoza family were drawn into the political wranglings of the times. Business leaders emerged as central political figures in the 1980s and 1990s. Among COSEP leaders, a common refrain ran, "As the Sandinistas put the government into the economy, so the private producers were pushed to enter into politics." One result has been a hyperpoliticized business leadership dominating the major national business association.

Second, the Sandinista era reshuffled the Nicaraguan bourgeoisie. The traditional economic groups that had been so prominent in the prerevolutionary period were broken apart during the revolution. The departure of central figures in the old elite families created space for the rise of a new set of economic heavyweights. The experience of revolution, then, set the groundwork for even more decentralization of the economic elite than had prevailed in the Somoza era. Instead of the three economic groups that predominated in the prerevolutionary era, five or six may emerge in the postrevolutionary period, including some involving UNAG leaders or Sandinista producers, who were not previously part of these networks.

The decentralization of elite resources is, of course, quite different from a full redistribution of national wealth or the significant inclusion of the peasantry in an integrated development model—the purported goals of the revolution. The rise of some and the fall of others does, however, reflect a certain democratization of the bourgeoisie.

Third, the revolution dispersed the economic elite internationally, as private producers sent their children abroad, attempting to shield them from the violence and ideological shake-up that was taking place in their country. Whereas many of the parents had gone abroad for a few years as young adults to complete their educations, their children were dispersed through the United States and Latin America at younger ages and for much longer periods of time. Even after the FSLN's electoral defeat, many did not return. Those who did return had extensive linkages to other regions, setting the groundwork for a less distinctively Nicaraguan, more internationalized elite culture.

Finally, some elements of the Nicaraguan elite became less antagonistic to discussions of workers' rights and the needs of the nation's poor. Not only did a significant group of elites come to align itself with the revolution, but others who remained opposed came to accept some of the revolution's social goals. After decades under the Somoza dynasty, in which unions and mass organizations hardly existed, many Nicaraguan producers were forced to the bargaining table with their workers. In the process, many elites became accustomed to this form of interaction; some came to regard it as constructive. After years of agrarian reform and debate about property rights, many economic elites began to accept the idea of worker ownership of state properties and shareholding in privately owned businesses. These transformations would not have come easily out of Somoza's Nicaragua. For many Nicaraguan elites who lived through the Sandinista era, an improved capacity for dialogue with workers and peasants may constitute part of the lingering legacy of revolution.

chapter 7

The Nicaraguan Revolution in Comparative Perspective

WHEN revolutionary regimes leave the local economic elite in place, they run inevitable risks. If the regime pushes forcefully for structural change, the business sector can use its considerable resources to retaliate. Broadly disseminated denunciations, brisk capital flight, and coup plotting can undercut the revolution and lead to its reversal. On the other hand, if the regime attempts to assuage business fears by responding favorably to their concerns and incorporating their leaders, the revolution can be coopted. Unable to push for structural transformation, the revolution loses momentum and fails. The bourgeoisie question—that is, how to negotiate capital's accommodation to change—is one of the central dilemmas of social revolution.

In Latin America, regimes committed to structural change have not been highly successful at achieving their goals. Various forces impede transition; the resistance of the local bourgeoisie is a crucial element. Not all business elites are identical, however, and some revolutionary regimes have maneuvered for their cooperation more successfully than others. This book explores that variation by analyzing four historical cases and the recent Nicaraguan experience. These cases point to five factors that shape state-capital relations. (See Table 7.1.)

The first component focuses on inherited oligarchical tendencies in the bourgeoisie. If the elite evolved from an oligarchical family network without a fundamental rupture in the general historical pattern of dominance, then it is more likely to maintain its unity and be propelled forcefully into combat. Conversely, a more fragmented bourgeoisie is likely to emerge when there is no segment that, for reasons of tradition and economic domination, can exercise a hegemonic function and provide political leadership for the class as a whole. A weak oligarchical profile is more probable when the economy is diversified, with multiple, competing eco-

Table 7.1

Configuration of State-Capital Characteristics and Bargaining Tendencies

	Confrontation	Accommodation
Hegemonic force of traditional oligarchy	high	low
Business organizational autonomy	high	low
Perception of class threat	high	low
Institutionalized political capacity of the regime	low	high
Economic viability of the regime	low	high

nomic groups vying for resources and crisscrossed with strong regional traditions and hostilities. Conversely, oligarchical control is more likely when the economy is centered on agroexport production and economic diversification is less pronounced.

The unity or the fragmentation of the elite is further conditioned by its organizational characteristics. The capacity to organize autonomously without extensive control on the part of the state facilitates the coordination of a common elite strategy. If business organizations expand laterally, to absorb much of the private sector, and vertically, to create a powerful peak association, then they can become formidable opponents of a reform regime. On the other hand, if private sector organizations are sparse and frail, leaving much of the elite unorganized, or if they depend heavily on the state for financing and legal recognition, then they may be more susceptible to control by the regime.

The third factor that shapes the interaction is the degree to which the elite perceives the regime as a threat to its fundamental interests. When capitalists of all sizes come to believe that private accumulation and social stratification themselves are in jeopardy and that the risks of loss are ubiquitous, elite fusion and confrontation with the regime are highly likely. Conversely, if these elites regard the risks as problematic for only a discrete subset of the capitalist class, and particularly an issue for foreign as opposed to domestic firms, then highly divergent responses, including strategic accommodation, may follow.

Fourth, the degree to which the revolution achieves political institutionalization is also critical. If the state is too fragile, internally divided, or fails to mobilize a broad popular base, then economic elites will have little incentive to enter a bargaining process with political leaders. They may instead, often in coalition with powerful external actors, push to have the regime ousted, clearing the way for counterrevolution. However, if the regime succeeds in institutionalizing the reform by consolidating its political resources and embedding these changes in a new legal order, then it becomes a worthy foe. Without the easy option of eliminating the regime, private elites may be drawn into negotiations.

Finally, the state must not only display notable political capabilities but it must also resolve the complex problem of constructing an alternative economic model. If the state lacks the economic resources to carry out reform, or depends exclusively on the private sector for their generation, then private elites are empowered to collectively undermine the revolution. Sharp patterns of economic decline coupled with hyperinflation are particularly likely to elicit private sector hostility, in turn accelerating economic deterioration. In contrast, if the regime can design an economic model that carries the promise of future return and general growth, then the elites may succumb to the inevitability of the transition and begin looking for their niche in the new order.

In sum, certain combinations of characteristics (weak oligarchical control, an organizational void in the private sector, relatively low threat perceptions among local propertied classes, firm political consolidation of the regime, and sustained economic growth) make it easier for the regime to negotiate with economic elites, even as it pursues redistributive reform. On the other hand, the converse conditions (continued oligarchical hegemony, broad and autonomous private sector organization, a relatively acute perception of threat to local property owners, weak political institutionalization, and marked economic instability) foster a harsh and unified elite response that can produce a forceful counterrevolutionary backlash.

This chapter focuses on these five issues in terms of the four historical cases analyzed in Chapter 1 and the more recent Nicaraguan case. Each section first explores the conditions that favor elite unity and confrontation with the revolutionary state, and then turns to an analysis of those that foster business fragmentation and accommodation with the regime. The concluding part of each section places the Nicaraguan case into this general framework.

Oligarchichal Tendencies

The Persistence of Oligarchy and the Habit of Command

If a relatively small cluster of notable families traditionally dominated the central core of the economy and key institutions of government, and its dominance was not broken by the rise of competing working- or middle-class actors, then the bourgeoisie may still be characterized by what Conaghan (1991, 37) calls a "seignorial cultural style," or what I have called here the "habit of command." This tradition may give the dominant core of the elite both the perceived moral authority and the predilection to speak on behalf of the whole private sector. To the extent that this tradition is historically and culturally sanctified, political power may be heavily concentrated in the oligarchical segment of the private sector.

Historically, this elite's authority was related to its considerable control over land. To survive deep into the twentieth century, however, a traditional elite must fan out from its original core activities. The extension of the coffee elite of El Salvador from coffee production into coffee processing, banking, cotton production, and, finally, industry illustrates the process. An overlapping, interpenetrated ownership pattern tended to bind different sectors of the traditional elite together and produce a common bargaining strategy within the Salvadoran bourgeoisie. Thus land reform or bank nationalizations that affected large landowners or bank stockholders triggered broader elite opposition, even among commercial leaders and industrialists who were not specifically affected by the reforms.

Because of the extensive resources dominated by this land-based elite, private producers that emerge subsequently tend to develop as subordinate actors. They depend on the dominant group for financing, subcontracts, or political protection, and they too benefit from a system that the oligarchs can take responsibility for creating. These characteristics serve to forestall the development of an alternative, independent perspective in the nonhegemonic elite. Again, the Salvadoran case is instructive. Not only were ANEP leaders successful in preventing any subsector of their association from sustaining serious negotiations with the Christian Democratic government; they were also successful in organizing a sweeping bourgeois coalition against the reform. The Alianza Productiva included even small business associations and professional/managerial organizations; it became an important electoral force opposing the reform regime.

The power of a traditional economic elite is generally diminished by political emancipation and mass mobilization. In several Latin American cases, however, the process of democratization did not extend very far. The franchise was effectively denied to a significant portion of the population (such as illiterates in Ecuador); unions and other mass organizations remained small and weak; political parties functioned only intermittently or only in the urban areas; and electoral results that threatened the established order were nullified or altered (Malloy and Seligson 1987; Booth and Seligson 1989).

Under these circumstances an oligarchical elite has fewer problems preserving a relatively high level of unity. It need not seek out nonelite coalition partners or accept extensive compromises. The cultural style and views of the traditional elite continue to frame the discourse of the political leadership. Issues like land reform can be kept off the political agenda in spite of the continued importance of the land question to the bulk of the population.

In these cases, even relatively mild or carefully delimited reform proposals can be met with harsh resistance. Processes that are commonly associated with modern capitalism, such as unionization, profit sharing, or income taxes, may be viewed with extreme alarm by elites for whom these ideas are an unthinkable violation of a long-established social order. Moderate reformers from center or center-left political parties or even officials from conservative U.S. administrations like the Reagan administration may, as in El Salvador, be regarded by prominent sectors of the local elite as harboring secret sympathies for socialism or local revolutionaries because they support agrarian reform.

Where the traditional elite's assumptions about its rights and privileges have never been seriously challenged, the bourgeoisie will tend to respond in a forceful, unified way, even to relatively modest efforts to alter the social order. It may even, as in Salvador in 1988, retain enough resources (social authority, control over the media, economic leverage, capacity for violence) to reaffirm its political prominence through electoral politics.

The Absence of Hegemony and Elite Porousness

In contrast, sectors of the bourgeoisie are more likely to pursue conciliation with the revolutionary state when traditional oligarchical networks have been fractured. The bourgeoisie is then more readily divided into disconnected, even competing, segments that may be played against each other by revolutionary leaders.

Various processes have undermined oligarchical power in Latin

America. In both Mexico and Peru, revolutions led to a disintegration and displacement of the traditional oligarchy. In neither case were landed elites and their descendants entirely stripped of their assets; these elites did, however, experience a major erosion in their wealth, a collapse of their social status, and a revocation of their political authority. Industrialization, particularly that promoted by recent immigrants, may also increase the complexity and sectoral differentiation of the bourgeoisie and further undermine the preeminence of any one group, making oligarchical hegemony more difficult.

When the oligarchy disintegrates, other business elites, who are less accustomed to playing a direct political role, may not be prepared to unite into a cohesive front. Without a clear internal leadership norm, the bourgeoisie more readily fragments into a series of competing groups and sectors. Even family ties or shared class interests may not be sufficiently strong to forge full unity during periods of transition and change. The factionalization of the elite makes it possible for sectors to emerge who weigh their interests differently and make divergent strategic choices.

The particular sectors that were most likely to negotiate with state reformers varied from country to country. In Velasco's Peru as well as Jamaica during the first Manley government, exporters who were just emerging depended heavily on the state for financial support and assistance in opening markets and establishing trade connections. In these two cases, the exporters' associations ADEX and JEA tended to have more positive relations with the Velasco and Manley governments, respectively, than did most other associations of private producers.

In some countries, small industrialists became regime allies; in others, stronger ties were forged with larger industrialists. In Mexico, for example, small industrialists were singled out for special support during the Cárdenas era; their state-sponsored association, CANACINTRA, became a progovernment stalwart in the years that followed. In other countries, like Peru, larger industrialists, many of whom were also interested in export promotion, had more cordial ties with the government, and small- and medium-sized industrialists were more antagonistic to the Velasco regime. Under the latter's leadership, the industrialists' association SNI became the leading private sector critic of the Velasco government—a stance for which the organization paid dearly. In Chile as well, small- and medium-sized business owners became vociferous critics of the Allende regime and provided the public leadership of the bourgeois opposition. This occurred in spite of the government's official commitment to a supportive alliance with this nonhegemonic elite.

In contrast to theories suggesting that smaller industrialists producing for domestic consumption might be more supportive of a developmentalist and redistributive state, the case studies analyzed here demonstrate more varied alliance patterns. Much depends on the particular dynamics of the case, such as the previous experiences of various sectors with state intervention, the particular programs and policies adopted by the revolutionary state, the foreign exchange and financial constraints faced by the government, and the skill of state leaders in cultivating connections with different groups. This variation suggests that the characteristics and decisions of the state leadership play a crucial role in determining the degree to which an alliance with the bourgeoisie is formed, a point to which we will return below.

The Failure of Ontological Givens: Class Division in Nicaragua

Nicaragua lacked a national oligarchy capable of providing hegemonic leadership for the bourgeoisie. The country was strewn with deep regional divisions; oligarchs, such as they were, tended to be local in nature and fiercely competitive among themselves. No one production sector or social group emerged to dominate the nation. Elites in Granada hewing to the Conservative banner vied with elites from León who endorsed the Liberal cause. Nineteenth-century wars between these groups spilled over into the twentieth century. Enmity was suppressed but not eradicated by the long dictatorship of the Somoza family. With the banking system and much of foreign trade under the control of foreigners or the Somoza dynasty, no one sector of the Nicaraguan bourgeoisie was able to consolidate economic power by diversifying into these strategic enterprises. With the political system controlled first by the U.S. occupation and later by the Somoza family, economic elites also had little opportunity to experience direct political control.

Although the Nicaraguan business sector began to move into banking and foreign trade and to coalesce into economic groups in the 1950s, this process was quite limited. The key economic groups remained competitive among themselves; none provided a political challenge to the Somoza regime. Lacking a hegemonic center, the Nicaraguan private sector in the prerevolutionary period tended to be known for its regionalism, fragmentation, and, aside from the political escapades of a handful of Young Turks, political passivity. The small size of the country and of the wealthy class in Nicaragua meant that many in the elite knew each other personally; important segments were bound by friendship and marriage ties. In spite of this, no sector of this group was capable of exercising class hegemony. Continued regional and economic competition, political acquiescence to the regime, and the inability to project broad social authority in the society spelled political debility for the elite.

With the insurrection, much of the top business elite fled the country. The takeover of the collapsed banking system and export trade by the FSLN government effectively decapitated the disintegrating Nicaraguan bourgeoisie; the remainder of the class was even less cohesive. Several leading business figures joined the revolution; others moved increasingly into the opposition. Without a long history of collective action and political convergence, the Nicaraguan elite was unable to construct and maintain a common front under the Sandinistas. Within UPANIC, for example, divisions soon surfaced. A harsh, ideological critique of the government was launched by larger producers from more prestigious social backgrounds who commanded the national COSEP/UPANIC front. Regional leaders, with generally less prestigious school ties and more modest holdings, on the other hand, offered a more modulated critique and were more willing to negotiate with the regime. Other producers, generally still lower on the social hierarchy, even joined the rival association, UNAG, and tied themselves organizationally to the revolution.

The Nicaraguan case differs significantly from that of its regional neighbor, El Salvador, where a much more moderate reform regime was confronted with a much more fully united and fiercely opposed national elite. In this area, the Nicaraguan bourgeoisie may have more in common with that found in the reformist era in Peru, where the elite failed to form a united front. As in that case, the absence of a powerful oligarchical elite after the revolution left a segmented private sector that responded in divergent ways to the regime.

Organizational Characteristics

Private Sector Organizational Autonomy from the State

The private sector is more likely to confront the regime if its organizations have emerged as authentic representatives responding to initiatives of the elite itself. If the juridical protections provided for these groups are strong enough so that the state cannot easily dissolve them, and their financial base is independent of the regime, then these organizations should be less vulnerable to state pressure. Generally these conditions prevail when the organizations are created through autonomous interactions rather than state decree and where participation is voluntary rather than mandated by the state.[1]

Business associations are likely to be stronger if they emerge in every major sector of the economy, thus filling the available space for elite organization and preempting state-sponsored competitors, rather than being spottily organized in a few sectors or regions of the country. The formation of a peak association that brings together business representatives from across the nation also fosters intra-elite cohesion and cooperation. Finally, organizational autonomy allows the elite to develop its own, independent means of communication, including newspapers and radio or television stations, that can extend the reach of the elite into other social sectors. This power, defended in the name of political pluralism, can help the elite to check the organizational efforts of nonelites and extend its power beyond its class base.

Of the cases we have explored, Chile had the most autonomous and durable form of private sector organization. Four powerful associations date back to the 1800s. The six most prominent associations had formed one of the region's oldest peak associations, COPROCO, in 1935. Even small- and medium-sized businesses had a firm set of associations established decades before the democratic socialist transition was attempted.[2] Business groups had privileged access to state policymaking boards, but their associations remained relatively free of government controls. Several of these organizations had thick links to right-wing political parties. Partisan connections intensified their resistance to government appeals when the government was in the hands of political opponents.

Whereas the more overtly authoritarian Velasco regime was able to simply dissolve, restructure, and rename private sector organizations, the reform regimes of Allende, Duarte, and Manley, which emerged in more pluralistic settings, could not. Leaders of SOFOFA, ANEP, and the Jamaican Chamber of Commerce proved skillful and adaptable opponents. In Chile, El Salvador, and Jamaica, where the media remained a branch of private enterprise and the government was obligated to give it free rein, the fiercely antirevolutionary major daily newspapers (El Mercurio, the Diario de Hoy, and the Daily Gleaner, respectively) led a steady, hyperbolic, and often hysterical attack on the regime. The norms of press freedom and political pluralism gave private sector leaders mouthpieces with which to exert broad influence over public political discussion, uniting opponents, persuading doubters, and subverting the revolution. If the revolutionary regime is not capable of circumscribing business's organizational power or stimulating the rapid growth of popular sector alternatives to counterbalance it, then the autonomy of elite organizations may lead to effective oppositional collaboration and the defeat of revolution.

Independence from the regime should not be equated with indifference to all external influence. Indeed, several private sector organizations that were institutionally autonomous vis-à-vis the state were openly influenced by their connections to foreign actors. CIA funding for the bosses' strike in Chile in 1972, for example, encouraged the consolidation of the Chilean bourgeoisie. IMF pressure for economic policy changes bolstered the internal critics who were hostile to the reformers in Peru and Jamaica. Powerful external actors like the U.S. government or the IMF, therefore, can serve as an alternative reference point, encouraging the local bourgeoisie to fuse and reject the options offered to it by state reformers.[3]

Controlled Organization and Muted Responses

It is difficult for the state to establish institutional and organizational controls over the business sector the way it sometimes has over labor and peasant associations. By definition, economic elites have resources (wealth, social status, influence over their workers, technical knowledge, control over investment, international connections) that make it hard for the state to control their activities. The state, however, can exercise influence and promote accommodation, particularly when private sector organizations are not fully developed. When there are few strong business groups, or their membership is very restricted, the state can sponsor the creation of new organizations that incorporate those elites who have been historically excluded.

This process was, of course, relatively easy for the Mexican government when it created the Confederations of the Chambers of Industry and of Commerce in 1917 in the wake of the revolution and before such organizations had emerged spontaneously from within the private sector. When a segment of the business elite later moved to create its own organization, COPARMEX, the Mexican regime responded by fusing its two confederations into one organization and mandating the participation of all (except very small firms) in the state-sponsored association. A few years later, the Mexican state divided the industrial and commercial chambers again, to prevent them from becoming too powerful, and created an additional organization, CANACINTRA, that steadily backed regime initiatives. State intervention in Mexico produced a controlled fragmentation of business organizations that delimited their bargaining capabilities.

The process was more complex in Peru, where the organizational terrain of the private sector was relatively full by the time of the revolution in the late 1960s. In that case as well, however, the regime was able to affect the setting by dissolving the agricultural association (SNA) and withdrawing legal recognition from the industrialists' association (SNI), while simultaneously approving legal status for the more accommodating exporters' association (ADEX). In this way the regime could fill the organizational landscape with less oppositional associations. A revolutionary regime may be more successful at deflecting bourgeois opposition if it mobilizes private producers who have not been previously organized and establishes quasi-corporatist links with business associations.

A similar logic applies to the media. In the Mexican case, the government had a series of tools with which to influence the media, including control over newsprint, advertising, and the ability to restrict access to political leaders and to periodically reshuffle owners and editors. In Peru, the 1974 press law expropriated daily newspapers and turned them over to selected social actors. As a result, in these two cases the private sector's ability to undercut the government through its control over the media was limited. Without a media mechanism to disseminate its views, the business elite finds it more difficult to enforce unanimity within the private sector and build a mass base for its position.

The Mix of Autonomy and Dependence in Revolutionary Nicaragua

The Nicaraguan private sector associations never achieved the extraordinary political autonomy found historically in Chile or El Salvador. They were, however, somewhat more independent of the regime than core business groups operating in Mexico in the 1930s and 1940s. The closest parallel for the Nicaraguan case may be found in Peru, where some established organizations had relatively autonomous histories but other organizations were more dependent on the regime.

Several factors contributed to the organizational weaknesses of the Nicaraguan elite. First, even in important economic sectors like coffee cultivation, Nicaraguan elite organizations tended to be both regional and ephemeral. Those that became a permanent part of the political landscape were generally heavily influenced by the government either through quasi-corporatist linkages with government boards, the direct participation of Somoza family members in their administration, or a dense network of clientelism. In their dealings with the Somoza regime, private elites resorted heavily to particularistic bargaining to advance their individual claims. As a result, they lacked a solid institutional legacy that might have strengthened their hand in dealing with the Sandinista regime.

Private sector organizations did, rather belatedly, gather momentum and turn hostile to the Somoza dynasty. Goaded by urban elites affiliated with a USAID-funded INDE, Nicaraguan business finally founded a peak association (COSIP, later COSEP) in 1972. This national organization pulled together business leaders from an array of sectors to challenge the corruption and weak developmentalism of the dynasty. However, compared with that in Chile or even regional rival El Salvador, private sector coalescence was late and frail in Nicaragua.

The 1970s mobilizations did provide the elite with some training in political confrontation and autonomy from the regime. The revolutionary era began with the lateral proliferation of private sector organizations and the vertical consolidation of the peak association. COSEP soon became a potent opposition force, complete with a media arm (*La Prensa*). For political reasons the Sandinista regime was unable to destroy COSEP, even though the government never granted it a legal charter and did censor and periodically close *La Prensa*. In some ways the existence of COSEP served the interests of the FSLN. COSEP's continued strident opposition demonstrated how the regime kept faith with its commitment to pluralism, even when provoked. A steady diet of vituperation from an organization of the wealthy also helped to validate the regime's credentials as a defender of the poor. Nonetheless, the internal denunciations and external lobbying of COSEP did pose a challenge to the regime. Instead of eliminating this opposition group, the Sandinistas attempted to curb its influence by periodic harassment and, later, cooptation.

Much like the Peruvian and Mexican cases, the Nicaraguan government also moved to create an alternative organizational pole for economic elites. By 1984 UNAG had metamorphosed into a broad producer association that welcomed even medium- and large-sized producers. This state-sponsored association was closely linked to and dependent on the regime. A full quarter of its budget came from the FSLN; one of its most effective recruiting ploys was the implicit pledge to intervene on behalf of members in the event of expropriation; and many of its top leaders were prominent members of the FSLN. Although UNAG became more critical of the Sandinista government performance over time, it remained a close ally and supporter of the revolution.

The Sandinista regime was unable to redesign the organizational infrastructure of business in Nicaragua. It did, however, alter this terrain by interposing an organization of its creation and cultivating regional and sectoral organizations that were less ideologically hostile to the revolution.[4] Political parallels may be drawn with Peru, where adversarial elite organizations from the prerevolutionary era were forced to make room for some newer, supportive organizations that emerged in the wake of that revolution. On the other hand, Nicaragua's peak association remained as stridently antiregime, as did the parallel organizations in Chile or Salvador. Like them, it drew on a powerful oppositional newspaper to challenge the revolution.

Perception of Threat

Classwide Threats and Elite Fusion

In none of the cases examined in this book was the existence of the private sector threatened. In each case, there was space, both in the general conceptual model that guided the restructuring and in actual practice, for continued private ownership and private accumulation, at least for the bulk of the private sector. But the perception of a classwide threat of annihilation became pervasive in several cases. The Chilean case is instructive.

Although some elements of the Chilean private sector panicked when Allende was elected and began organizing in opposition, others initially searched for some accommodation with the regime and expressed a tentative willingness to cooperate. The bourgeoisie swung en masse into the opposition only after the UP government began a campaign of expropriations and interventions that seemed ill defined and uncontrolled. The UP government provided no meaningful guarantees to private producers as it lurched from intervention to intervention. Perhaps most important, expropriation was directed against local capitalists as well as foreigners.

Although direct comparisons are difficult, expropriation of local capitalists was probably more extensive in Chile than in Mexico or Peru. The agrarian reform program affected approximately the same proportion of agricultural land in Chile as in Mexico and Peru (McClintock 1981, 61), but state expropriations in the urban, industrial sector were more extensive. Whereas state expansion in the Mexican and Peruvian cases tended to occur through the creation of new industries that would presumably benefit even private producers or through benign takeovers of bankrupt private firms, state expansion in the Allende period tended to rely on the forced transfer of existing resources from the private to the public sectors.

Family networks that extended across key sectors in the top stratum of the elite, such as those identified by Zeitlin and Ratcliff (1988) in Chile and by Colindres (1977) in El Salvador, facilitated a unified hostile response. The crucial blow came in the Chilean case, however, when even producers outside those top networks—the small- and medium-sized entrepreneurs, shopkeepers, the self-employed, and neighborhood businesses—moved forcefully into the opposition. Movements to expand the state-controlled "social area" on multiple fronts (banking, agriculture, extraction, manufacturing), to expropriate small and medium enterprises as well as large, and to take over local as well as foreign operations proved too sweeping and indiscriminate for the Chilean private sector.

From the perspective of the Chilean elites, two conclusions about the expropriation pattern were possible. Either the governing coalition had lost control of the state and state erosion of the private sector was proceeding according to some unofficial agenda controlled by extremist sectors outside the formal government, or the government remained in charge but was duplicitous about its actual intentions since it continued to violate its own commitments to protect the small- and medium-sized producers. In either case, formal guarantees provided by the government carried little weight for these groups. Even regulatory actions that were consistent with modern capitalism were seen as a prelude to further erosion of private ownership. Because the UP's efforts to restructure the economy were judged to follow a class logic, rather than a more inclusive national one, the private sector overcame its segmental tendencies, and a palpable class identity emerged.

The ideological ascendance of socialist theory in Chile was much sharper than in the other cases. Decades of intense ideological discussion within the parties of the left in Chile produced a clearer repudiation of capitalist principles there, and the forceful involvement of unions and popular organizations made it harder for the UP government to diverge from more radical prescriptions. The political base of the Chilean regime, therefore, pushed the state to expand the socialized sector more quickly by expropriating more heavily. Fears of full-scale state control, fanned by El Mercurio, affected even elites not specifically targeted.

Even in cases where the regime is not formed by theoretically sophisticated leftist parties and militant labor, the private sector can still panic. Reform moves in El Salvador, for example, triggered extreme fears in the Salvadoran bourgeoisie in spite of the reformers' moderate views and poor mobilizational skills. The simultaneous targeting of three key economic sectors (agriculture, banking, and export), the emphasis on expropriation of local rather than foreign firms, and the sharp discontinuity between the impunity enjoyed by the elite before and its circumscription after 1980 all fed a sweeping and intense elite opposition that seemed out of proportion with the objective threat that it faced.[5] As in the Chilean case, this factor deepened the state-capital divide and fueled sharp retaliation.

Moderate Threats and Class Division

If the state is seen as ultimately developmentalist and committed to national advancement rather than fundamentally anticapitalist, then class loyalties and fears will not be invoked as fully. Some elite sectors may be open to the idea of a tactical alliance. This pattern is more likely to occur when expropriation focuses on foreign-owned operations and local businesses are largely exempt. Selective expropriation of foreign firms can build a national consensus, whereas extensive and indiscriminate takeovers of local firms feed bourgeois panic and retaliation.

To avoid arousing generalized elite hostility, any expropriations of local capital should be carefully targeted with a clear set of rules guiding the process. Of course, discretionary expropriation, where takeovers are more random and individual bargaining occurs, may draw more producers into the negotiation process as each one individually attempts to bargain to retain property. This style of expropriation, however, breeds deeper resentment, since no business owner has an enduring protection from an arbitrary state. In the long run, overly discretionary expropriations seem likely to generate more hostility than accommodation.

In the Mexican and Peruvian cases, emphasis was placed on the expropriation of foreign rather than domestic capital; even foreign holdings were expropriated only selectively. In Mexico, Peru, Jamaica, and even Chile, the state takeover of foreign corporations did not alienate local business elites, and in several cases it was actually applauded. Outside the agricultural sector, expropriation of local capital in Mexico and Peru tended to be quite restricted. When it occurred, it was often prompted by the bankruptcy of a local firm rather than state targeting. The pace of state expansion was relatively slow, and small- and medium-sized firms were largely exempt. Indeed, in Mexico these enterprises became favored allies during the 1930s and 1940s.

In their study of democratic socialism, Stephens and Stephens (1986) suggest that the state sector should be formed essentially through the construction of new enterprises rather than through the expropriation of existing ones. Space should be carved out for those elements of the private sector that can contribute to the new model, and their medium- and

even long-term existence needs to be guaranteed. The state must demonstrate through its actions that important portions of the private sector
will be respected. This kind of carefully delimited revolutionary vision
may foster accommodation on the part of strategic economic elites.

Symbolic communication may also assuage elite fears. Like most political communication, the interaction between political and economic elites
draws on coded messages and signals. Cárdenas's decision to reenact the
confrontational speech to the Monterrey business elite three years later in
Saltillo, this time with an emphasis on the constructive role that business
can play, served as an important signal to the disaffected bourgeoisie.[6]The
use of interlocutors who elicit trust at both ends, such as Central Bank
president Montes de Oca during the revolutionary transition in Mexico
(Hamilton 1982, 130–31) or the former president of the Chamber of Commerce in Velasco's Peru (Bamat 1978, 216), also facilitates communication
and successful negotiation. The creation of privileged communication
channels for top business leaders or for leaders of priority economic sectors, such as CANACINTRA in Mexico or ADEX in Peru, conveys a capacity
for inclusiveness that could bring economic elites to vie for these opportunities. Such gestures lower the perception of generalized threat and tend
to divide entrepreneurs into competitive factions seeking access to these
resources.

Threat Perception and Expropriation Policy in Nicaragua

Although the FSLN was viewed with suspicion by some private elites
during the insurrection, those who stayed generally made common cause
with the revolutionaries to oust the Somoza regime. Business leaders
were wary, but most did not regard the FSLN as an intolerable menace
at that point. Nor were the initial expropriations cause for alarm. Early
confiscations in Nicaragua focused on the properties of *somocistas* and
the bankrupt banking system. These opening confiscations were clearly
circumscribed and directed against political outsiders. As such, they were
accepted consensually by the rest of the elite.

The Sandinistas did not target foreign enterprises for takeover. Indeed,
the Nicaraguan revolution was quite extraordinary in its careful avoid-
ance of the expropriation of multinational corporations. Coming to power
at the end of the 1970s, when the era of such expropriation had passed
and the belief that foreign investment was destructive had waned, and
unwilling to rouse further the hostility of foreign governments, the FSLN

left foreign holdings largely untouched. In any case, foreign ownership was modest in Nicaragua and would have provided limited resources. Not taking the route of foreign expropriation, the Sandinistas turned more toward their own domestic elite.

When new rounds of expropriation began in 1981 that affected the properties of non-*somocistas*, elite fears surged. Although initially targeting large estates that were underutilized or decapitalized, the agrarian reform process occasionally entailed the takeover of medium and small properties that bordered on state farms. Medium-sized farms lost any legal protection with the 1986 reform of the agrarian reform law. Even highly productive estates could be taken on the imprecisely defined grounds of social utility. Hundreds of influential producers lost properties between 1981 and 1989.

Although expropriation policy focused heavily on the agrarian sector, industries and commercial establishments like SAIMSA and ISA were also taken. During the period of most extreme control, even small producers and petty traders faced the loss of their inventory when they attempted to transport food across regional lines.

The Sandinista government tried to mute private sector opposition with a sectoralized approach that separated the "patriotic" from the "unpatriotic" bourgeoisie. They publicly favored productive elites over unproductive ones, small- and medium-sized producers over large producers, staples producers over agroexporters, and the *chapiolla* bourgeoisie over those who were more internationalized. These distinctions attempted to differentiate between those who would be incorporated into the revolutionary model and those who would not. Private elites had a number of mechanisms they could use to buffer themselves against expropriation, including downsizing, intensifying production, changing crops, manipulating family or friendship ties, joining UNAG, and improving relations with workers. But the generally negative image of the bourgeoisie that prevailed in the early years and the latitude for expropriation allowed in the law were sweeping enough to generate widespread fear in the Nicaraguan elite.

This concern was attenuated somewhat after the 1988 reforms. The big-splash introduction of a *concertación* process, the elevation of moderate Martínez Cuenca to the SPP, and the creation of a series of national agricultural commissions with the prominent participation of leading private producers all signaled a reorientation of the economic model. Informal

socializing between top *comandantes* like MIDINRA chief Jaime Wheelock and private sector leaders altered the nature of the communication
process, thereby reducing tensions.

In spite of these adjustments, the prior experience with expropriation
and extensive controls, combined with erratic takeovers even into 1989,
made much of the private sector distrustful of the regime. Egged on by
antirevolutionary media sources like *La Prensa* and Radio Católica, and
having dispersed their children abroad to prevent them from being converted to the cause or seized in the draft, many elites regarded the regime
as a threat to the survival of their way of life. In this sense, elite threat
perceptions in Nicaragua were probably more like those found in Chile or
El Salvador than those that prevailed in Mexico or Peru. Alarmed and on
guard, much of the elite rallied, implicitly or explicitly, to the opposition.

Political Institutionalization

Weak Political Capacity and the State-Capital Standoff

Two aspects of institutionalization are important for this analysis. The
first concerns the *political* capacity of the state, that is, the internal cohesion of the state itself and the consolidation of its mass base. The second
focuses on the *economic* capacity of the regime, that is, the ability of the
regime to generate a viable economic model through which growth can
be maintained.[7]

One key indicator of low political institutionalization is chronic division and infighting in the upper echelons of the state apparatus. The failure to consolidate the state leadership leaves the regime open to ready
challenge by economic elites. The division of the state into competing
camps makes it easy for business opponents to identify prospective government allies and to penetrate the sectors of the state under their control.

Linkages can then be struck between economic elites and internal
state dissidents. Two examples illustrate the point. In both Chile and
El Salvador, the reform regimes were unable to assert control over their
militaries. This dissonance in the state structure allowed conservative
business groups to cultivate an alliance with right-wing military officers
in opposition to the reform. Overtly, through a military coup in Chile,
or covertly, through violence and terror in Salvador, the military upended
the reform process. Another institution that may run counter to reform
is the court system, particularly those judicial appointees from a prior
era. The ability of coffee elites to get the constitutionality of INCAFE re-

jected by the Salvadoran courts, for example, shows how fissures in the state apparatus may encourage continued, multiple challenges by private elites.[8]

Institutionalization of the new order can also be limited if the revolutionary government is perched precariously on a slim plurality of support, if its alternative ideology fails to make inroads into a densely organized oppositional terrain, or if the revolutionary state fails to create a broad, durable mass base. Again, in both Chile and El Salvador, the electoral weakness of the reform regime invited continued business opposition. The Allende government was gaining momentum, with its electoral base expanding from 36.2 percent in the 1970 national election to 48.6 percent in the 1971 municipal elections (Valenzuela 1978, 40, 54). But even at its peak it still appealed to far less than the sweeping majorities that might have quieted elite opposition. Likewise in El Salvador, the reformers had great difficulty securing broad electoral support, losing the constituent assembly contest in 1982 and winning the presidency in 1984 only with massive financial backing and campaign support from the United States.

Curiously, revolutionary regimes can have problems establishing a solid political base even among beneficiaries. Land reform beneficiaries in Chile during the Allende period, for example, remained supportive of the oppositional Christian Democrats who had authored the agrarian reform law, even when they received land through the efforts of the UP government (de Vylder 1976, 204–6). The failure to consolidate a solid mass base and to mobilize a stable constituency for the revolution allows political opponents and economic elites to invade that terrain and attempt to recruit support. ARENA, for example, campaigned heavily among low-income groups, using electoral propaganda that blamed grinding poverty in El Salvador on the failures not of the traditional elite but of the short-lived Christian Democratic government. Since the Christian Democrats had not developed a solid political base among the low-income sectors, ARENA was able to make inroads into that population. Without electoral support from this sector of society, the right-wing would not have been able to win in the 1988–89 elections.

When the regime fails to institutionalize politically, it leaves itself vulnerable to electoral or military reversals. Recognizing their power under these conditions, private elites are less likely to enter into serious negotiation with the regime. In El Salvador, for example, the low level of institutionalization of the reform regime (the absence of hegemonic acceptance of the regime by either the left or the right, the executive's inability to control the military or the courts, weakness of electoral institutions and fragility of electoral victories) made it an unattractive ally. Any private sector organizations or leaders that aligned with it stood to gain very little and to lose heavily when the government collapsed. Under these circumstances, the state would have great difficulty building support anywhere, but particularly with the economic elite.

The Institutionalized State and Worthy Foes

Conversely, a state that has achieved a high degree of institutionalization through internal coherence and the consolidation of a strong mass base is more likely to secure compliance from the private sector. If economic elites do not emigrate, they will be pressured to cooperate.

To minimize infighting and internal cleavages, revolutionaries must develop a framework that brings them together while imposing order on their interactions. This involves tough decisions about how to dispose of disagreements within the political leadership without provoking defections, and how to solve the succession problem through a leadership selection system. The clockworklike change in the occupant of the Mexican presidency, for example, has contributed significantly to the coherence of the Mexican political elite (Smith 1979, 159–87).

Congruence between the military and the reformers, or at least institutional subordination, is necessary to undercut counterrevolutionary pressures from a military–private elite alliance. The Peruvian model, in which the military itself initiated the reform process, can assure at least some degree of institutional coherence. Even then, the divisions within the military between "bourgeois liberals," "progressives," and "the Mission" (McClintock 1981) undercut state unity and ultimately contributed to the Morales Bermúdez countercoup.

Successful negotiation with economic elites is promoted when the state is backed by a broad mass base. Positions proposed by the regime then seem less the whimsical propositions of today's officials and more an evolving social consensus about the new rules of the game. Ironically, economic elites may be more drawn to negotiation with a *powerful* adversary, where their success is not assured and serious negotiation is necessary, than with a weak, ephemeral one. Ideally, this mass support should not be overly effervescent; it should be channeled through some durable institutions and organizations. Again, the creation of a dominant party in Mexico and its successful incorporation of mass organizations during the Cárdenas era is instructive.

Mass mobilization and sweeping popular indulgence may be easier to obtain when the state leadership emerges from a national, revolutionary struggle against a repressive regime as in Mexico and, as we shall see, Nicaragua. Emerging victorious from a revolution confers immense legitimacy on the winners as well as providing a powerful set of symbols to use in appealing for continued support. This kind of durable popular base may be harder to extract from conventional politics, such as elections or military coups, where victory is tied to the electoral clock or the population is less mobilized.

Political Capacity in Revolutionary Nicaragua

The Sandinista government developed a high degree of political institutionalization during its decade in power. Although the original JGRN represented a compromise and included non-Sandinista members, a political shake-up in December 1979 gave the major cabinet positions to Sandinista stalwarts and consolidated FSLN control. Not only did the FSLN dominate the executive by controlling three of five junta positions and the cabinet, it controlled the military and the police, a clear majority in the Consejo de Estado, the banks, the courts, and a substantial part of the media. The remarkable internal cohesion of the FSLN national directorate and the institutional sweep of government positions by FSLN affiliates meant that this revolutionary government was able to govern without the division and infighting that plagued most transformation efforts.

The Nicaraguan regime was also successful in cultivating a broad mass following. Before the insurrection reached its final months, the FSLN was actively mobilizing mass organizations. Associations of workers, peasants, agricultural laborers, women, young people, and neighborhood groups gave the government a broad national support base (T. Walker 1985; Ruchwarger 1987). This wide support allowed the FSLN to go into the 1984 elections with strong backing and emerge with an impressive 67 percent endorsement of its presidential candidate (LASA 1984). The new national assembly, with 64 percent of the seats held by the Sandinista camp, drafted a constitution that further sedimented the institutions of the Sandinista era.

The major challenge to the regime's political authority during this era was the contra war. In the 1984–86 period, when the war heated up, the government felt the challenge and intensified controls (censorship, strategic relocations, expropriations, harassment) to counter this pressure. By 1987, however, the FSLN military victory seemed assured. Even contra-backers among the private elite now resigned themselves to the inevitable. This perception of inevitability drew the private sector leadership into increasing dialogue in 1988 and 1989.

There was, as we now know, a silent erosion of the FSLN's political strength during 1985–89 (Oquist 1992). Several mass organizations were crumbling, and the political base of the revolution was shrinking. By 1990, the Sandinistas won the endorsement of only 41 percent of the electorate and lost the election. Even if they had been elected with that plurality, that level of support would have encouraged elite opposition by raising the prospect of a political knockout in the 1996 elections. In spite of this erosion of their popular base, however, the FSLN still had a large and powerful constituency. Only the masterful incorporation of almost all opponents into the fourteen-party UNO coalition made the Sandinistas' electoral defeat possible.

Compared with several other revolutions considered here, therefore, the Sandinista variant was relatively successful in institutionalizing a political base. Unlike military reformers in Peru and Ecuador, where countercoups were soon followed by disabling elections, or Chile, where the electoral process that allowed a left-wing victory was quickly abolished and followed by long-term military rule, the Sandinista revolution persisted for a full decade and left a strong political party and several important mass organizations. Although not as durable as the Mexican regime, whose hold on political power is virtually unsurpassed in the modern world, the FSLN may prove to have a long-term presence in Nicaraguan politics.

Economic Viability

Economic Failure and Elite Hostility

In most reform efforts, the creation of a viable economic model is an elusive goal. The financial costs of building a new government apparatus, creating a state sector to supplant or complement the private sector, and promoting the social objectives of the revolution are generally high; sources of financial support are limited. To cover the costs of its programs, the regime typically runs up mounting deficits that are financed through internal and, increasingly, external borrowing. This gap deepens the economic crisis by fueling inflation, and the economic climate becomes increasingly unstable.

In anticipation of, or in response to, economic uncertainty, local and foreign capitalists typically begin to withhold investment and engage in capital flight. Disinvestment becomes a virtual rule of revolution. As the economy begins to contract, a zero-sum game begins. When scarce resources like foreign exchange or bank credit are channeled into the state's priority programs, the private sector often finds its access to resources declining. New taxes or mandated wage increases erode profits, raising fears about the long-run future of private accumulation. Even if property and profits are not affected, restrictions on access to imported luxuries or limits on access to hard currency for travel abroad may provoke sharp hostility from those who are accustomed to these privileges (Stephens and Stephens 1986, 118–24). Certainly the sharp, immediate economic downturn following the introduction of reform in El Salvador and the unleashing of hyperinflation in Chile undercut the new regimes' ability to present themselves as credible alternatives.

The precariousness of the economy increases the regime's vulnerability to pressure from local elites and outside creditors. This weakness allows external actors like the U.S. government or the IMF, with the endorsement of domestic business organizations, to move against the heterodox features of the revolutionary economic model.

Because of the revolutionary state's frequent failure to institutionalize a new economic order, the private sector is little drawn to negotiate with or make concessions to the new regime. Why enter negotiations with regime leaders if the fiscal viability of the state itself is in question? Why slug through tough transactions if state collapse may be imminent? If the state lacks the kind of durable structure that would make it a worthy bargaining partner, then economic elites will be less committed to serious consultation and alliances. Some will confront the regime directly on these issues; others may use the traditional tactics of weaker parties in negotiations—foot dragging, delays, attempts to circumvent new requirements—in the hope that the regime will soon collapse and the rules will be reversed.[9]

Economic Success and Durable Bargaining

To bargain effectively with the bourgeoisie, the revolutionary state needs to achieve some economic success, even in the face of declining private sector investment. A temporary bubble of growth triggered by state-decreed wage increases, as we found in the Chilean case, will probably not inspire private sector confidence. If profit increases are quickly offset by wage increases, that moment of growth will soon subside. However, when the revolutionary state can create a new source of growth and wealth, from which even segments of the local private sector can hope to derive some benefits, then the state may be able to secure grudging complicity from local capitalists.

One way for the state to stimulate growth is by rechaneling foreign-owned resources. In Mexico, the requirement that insurance companies invest their reserve within the country caused foreign agencies to retreat; this created ample space for the expansion of both state-owned and privately owned local firms. The "bonanza development" (Becker 1983) strategy of Peru and the petroleum boom in Ecuador allowed state leaders to envision no-cost development financed from abroad through export earnings. The unilateral increase in the bauxite levy in Jamaica also expanded state resources temporarily and eased access to foreign exchange for the local private sector.[10] In the end, of course, most of these bonanza schemes failed to stimulate long-term growth, for a variety of reasons. To the extent that a new development strategy succeeds, however, it can play an important role in drawing in private sector collaborators. If the state experiences some economic success in the first few years, then the ideas enshrined in its development plan may appear more viable to economic elites, and private sector withdrawal may be attenuated.

If the economy is stimulated and grows, then a positive-sum game can emerge. Gains for the state and its working class/peasant allies will not mean inevitable losses for the bourgeoisie. It will be possible also to provide credit, concessions, or exemptions to private producers involved in innovation and development. The inevitable tensions that emerge with expropriation can be assuaged through adequate compensation. As private producers in priority sectors sense that they too can win under the new rules, they may be less inclined to repudiate the process and instead begin searching for ways to insert themselves into the development model.

In the end, dialogue and negotiation may be enhanced when there is some rough balance in the resources held by the state and the bourgeoisie. If the state is too weak relative to the economic elite, due to a failure to institutionalize or to its feeble grip on the national economy, and depends too directly on the private sector to finance its reform agenda, the bourgeoisie will find it easy to withdraw resources and reverse the revolution. In this sense, it can be constructive if the state has some assets of its own through the control of profitable state enterprises and ready access to foreign financing. By acquiring its own resource base, the state reduces its dependence on local capitalists and improves its capacity to engage them in tough bargaining.

At the same time, the state should not be so strong relative to the local bourgeoisie that it devalues the capacity of the private sector to contribute to the nation's future. If the local bourgeoisie is too weak, incompetent, and inefficient, then the state will find little reason to provide it with resources. Revolutionaries may be tempted toward a statist model in which the private sector is marginalized or even, in the most extreme case, eliminated.

Economic Crisis and Elite Resistance in Nicaragua

In the area of economic consolidation, the Nicaraguan revolution failed. Although some economic reactivation was achieved in the three years following the ouster of Somoza, the economy never regained its prerevolutionary production levels and, after years of steady decline, had a GDP equivalent to that found in the 1940s at the end of the Sandinista era. With inflation rates that reached world records, the economic crisis in Nicaragua made setbacks in the rest of the region look minor. Even Allende's economic problems in 1973 appear modest by comparison.

The Sandinistas faced an exceptional obstacle: war. Only reformers in El Salvador shared this difficulty, and even there it was not accompanied with trade displacement, economic embargo, and foreign aid problems. The war took a major toll, estimated by Sandinista government sources at US$17.8 billion in an economy that produced at its peak only US$2 billion a year (Wheelock Román 1990, 126). The war distorted the government budget, caused shortages of supplies and labor, destroyed production and processing facilities, damaged transportation and communication infrastructure, and was responsible for output losses in much of the country. Compared with the credit freezes or low-level sabotage imposed by the United States on other revolutionary regimes, the costs of foreign pressure in Nicaragua were extraordinary.

Economic problems associated with war were exacerbated by the development model the Sandinistas endorsed. Fundamentally a state-centered approach, it depended heavily on the success of large-scale and long-term development projects like the TIMAL sugar mill or the Chiltepe livestock project. Focusing so strongly on long-term projects, the regime was unable to counter the economic downturn with measures that would stabilize production. In the end, the *grandes proyectos* proved so difficult to realize that most were suspended before completion, producing no economic boost.

Economic duress in the late 1980s made the regime look more warmly at its own private sector. Private producers who were ideologically suspect in the early years were redefined as patriots for remaining in Nicaragua in spite of the problems. But that same economic decline further undermined the tolerance of many business elites. Private producers, who were faced with bottlenecks in the distribution system and who had problems, at times, getting long-term credit for their own projects, were increasingly skeptical of a regime that could not deliver. Even those who did not oppose the regime on moral or ideological grounds often did so on technical grounds, concluding that the government officials were so incompetent and ill prepared that they could not effectively guide the nation. Elites who might have been willing to accommodate the regime had the economy not contracted so rapidly were hard pressed to accept a continuation of the regime in the midst of a full-blown collapse.

In this area, therefore, Nicaragua is more like El Salvador, where economic decline exacerbated elite opposition, than Mexico, where the economy continued to grow, creating opportunities for prioritized sectors. The ubiquitous deterioration in Nicaragua meant there were few who prospered. Even the Sandinistas concluded that the model they employed was not viable and began to reverse course by the end of the decade.

Conclusions

In moments of crisis and change, it may not be obvious to local entrepreneurs whether their interests are best served by accommodation to revolution or by headlong confrontation. Should elites take advantage of the moment of uncertainty to invest heavily in enterprises that can be unloaded for a profit in more normal times? Or should they exit and safeguard their capital abroad? Should they dig in their heels and place the private sector organizations in the front line of the onslaught against objectionable revolutionaries? Or should they proclaim themselves patriotic producers who can accommodate the new rules, even as they attempt to moderate them? Should they reject the revolution because it undermines their social position, even if they are prospering? Should they accept it in spite of their declining income because it fosters national development and the prospects for future gain? The answers are not always obvious.

In general, the Nicaraguan elite adopted a posture of opposition. Of the five factors considered in this chapter, two pulled the Nicaraguan state-elite relationship toward confrontation. (See Table 7.1.) The perception of a classwide threat was high, and the economic viability of the regime was low. An additional factor—business organizational autonomy—was mixed. Although some associations were closely linked to the regime, others were highly autonomous and became stridently adversarial.

Unlike several reformist regimes in the region, the Sandinista government did not target foreign corporations for expropriation. Instead, they concentrated on local estates and businesses, including large-, medium-, and in some cases small-sized producers who were deemed inefficient or obstreperous. This contributed to a wide perception of threat and undercut elite acquiescence.

Sustained economic decline also alienated business. The inability of the new government to stabilize the economy or generate new growth areas in which private elites might participate fed the generalized disaffection and encouraged capitalists' convictions that they, unhampered, could do much better. Unable, under the rules of political pluralism to which the Sandinistas had a public commitment, to dissolve opposition groups or effectively counter the opposition press, the regime had difficulty deflecting its opponents' attack.

The Sandinista regime did, however, secure cooperation from sectors of the private elite—more perhaps than might be expected looking at the sweep of the economic changes made and much of the political rhetoric about the revolution. Two of the five factors examined in this chapter pushed the state-elite relationship toward accommodation. (See Table 7.1.) The hegemonic force of a traditional oligarchy was low, and the institutionalized political capacity of the regime was high. Again, the organizational autonomy of the business sector was mixed, but several features favored accommodation. The regime proved adept at spinning off alternative private sector organizations and, in the end, constructing a political network that drew in strategic private sector allies.

Lacking a powerful traditional oligarchical leadership with the social authority to direct a coordinated elite response, the Nicaraguan elite began the revolutionary era with a fractured foundation. In contrast, the Sandinista regime moved quickly to consolidate its base. Building on the momentum provided by a popular insurrection to oust a despised dictatorship, the Sandinista leadership created a strong political organization that dominated the state, most mass groups, and the 1984 elections. Unable to effectively challenge this monolith, many economic elites sought a private accommodation. While not necessarily backing the regime, many rejected the role of public opponent.

The government developed a client organization for agricultural producers, UNAG, that recruited among sectors of the bourgeoisie. This organization-building effort succeeded in deepening some fissures in the elite and mobilizing some producers who had not been previously incorporated into the opposition. By providing resources and support for elites in strategic sectors, the regime cultivated private sector toleration of reform and even selective participation in development initiatives. By the end of the era, the symbolic communication between the regime and the elite fostered fuller interaction and cooperation as the revolution deradicalized and elites began coming to terms with reform.

The result of these competing dynamics was a mixed relationship between the state and the private elite in Nicaragua. Without either the stable accommodation and mutual understanding achieved in the Mexican case, or the unanimity of opposition achieved in the Chilean, a highly politicized and fragmented bourgeoisie entered the fray with the Sandinistas.

These complex interrelationships continue as Nicaragua enters the postrevolutionary era. Without enough elite cooperation to consolidate a new economic base and stabilize production until the war could be won, the Sandinistas lost power in 1990. But the patterns of dialogue and linkages with local capitalists established during the decade of revolution provided a foundation for continued interaction with the reform-oriented bourgeoisie in the postrevolutionary era. Sandinista reformers were never as isolated and overpowered after their fall as was, for example, Allende's coalition. The relatively complex patterns of confrontation and accommodation that characterized state-capitalist relations in Nicaragua contributed to both a deradicalization of the Sandinista revolution in its final stages and greater continuity of the Sandinista reforms in the postrevolutionary setting.

Much of the literature on social revolution assumes that the bourgeoisie must be definitively defeated in order for meaningful social change to occur. In my judgment, however, the elimination of this class is hardly a realistic or desirable objective. Not only would that transformation tend to concentrate too much power in the hands of the state, it would also deprive the society of the skills and resources of private elites and bring, at best, international isolation. What is needed are better ways to expand property ownership and provide the fuller inclusion of marginal sectors into the national economy. This complex and delicate work can be fostered by looking back at a range of cases to identify those circumstances that were most propitious. This study of elite political segmentation and state-elite bargaining suggests that variations in the inherited characteristics of the bourgeoisie and the dynamics of the bargaining process may produce markedly differing alliance patterns. Structuralist assumptions about elite opposition to reform require further refinement, as we work toward more complex models of revolutionary transition.

Methods

In 1990–91, as the Sandinista period came to a close, I conducted a series of semistructured interviews with 91 leading private agricultural producers. The agricultural sector was targeted because of its central role in the Nicaraguan economy. However, respondents were commonly involved in nonagricultural activities as well (professions, commerce, industry, etc.).

Interviewees were selected using the positional/reputational method. Initial interviews were arranged with the presidents of the major agricultural organizations at the national level and with their largest sectoral and regional affiliates. Association presidents were then asked to recommend others who had been particularly active and influential private sector leaders. Of the 91 producers interviewed, 72 were current or recent officers in their producer associations. Most of the remainder were or had been representatives of the producers on government commissions or boards.

Within the framework of the positional/reputational methodology, an effort was made to target respondents across organizations, products, and regions. Because of its relatively long, central role in organizing the medium- and large-sized producers, approximately three-fourths (74 percent) of those interviewed were affiliated with UPANIC. Most of the remainder (18 percent) were affiliated with the Sandinista-sponsored (though increasingly independent) organization, UNAG. A relatively small group (9 percent) were not affiliated with any organization or were leaders of associations that had chosen not to affiliate with any national organization. Interviews were also conducted with three members of the agrarian bourgeoisie who had been prominent private sector spokespeople before moving into high-level positions in the Sandinista government.

Respondents were distributed among four key sectors: 21 percent primarily in cotton production, 26 percent primarily in coffee, 31 percent primarily in livestock, and 14 percent primarily in basic grains (rice, sorghum, or maize). (The remaining 8 percent were primarily in banana or sugar production or had ceased production following expropriation.) With few exceptions, participants were medium- or large-sized landowners.

A total of 143 interviews was conducted with 91 producers. Sixty producers (66 percent) were interviewed only once, 24 (26 percent) were interviewed more than once, and 7 (8 percent) were interviewed three or more times. Those who were approached for and agreed to multiple interviews contributed more in-depth information about the social and political construction of the Nicaraguan elite.

Because of the political and economic dominance of Managua and the small size of the country, much of the economic elite maintains a residence in the capital. Forty-five percent of the interviews took place in Managua. In an effort to tap the experiences of those living outside Managua and operating exclusively at the regional level, interviews were conducted in ten other municipalities (Masaya, Masatepe, Jinotega, Granada, Juigalpa, Boaco, Matagalpa, Jinotega, Chinandega, and León). Five different regions of the country (Regions II, III, IV, V, and VI) were represented in this study.

Almost half (45 percent) of the interviews were conducted in the respondents' homes. Of the remainder, 34 percent were held in their association headquarters, 16 percent in private offices outside their homes, and the remaining 5 percent in other settings (restaurants, bank offices, etc.). On average, the interview time per producer was 2 hours and 45 minutes, but the total amount of time ranged at the extremes from 1 to 18 hours. In approximately 20 percent of the cases, prior interviews had been conducted with the producer between 1982 and 1987, so a basis for frank discussion was already well established, and interview data could be compared across time.

The respondents in this study cannot be taken as typical of the Nicaraguan bourgeoisie, since they were by definition those most actively involved in the organizational leadership of their class. Demographic surveys and censuses needed to draw a fuller picture of the Nicaraguan elite do not exist, so I cannot say exactly how these respondents compare with the rest of their social class. However, since these individuals have, in one form or another, been selected by their peers as leaders and representatives, their responses and positions should have special significance for the Nicaraguan private sector.

Respondents were asked a series of open- and close-ended questions concerning their demographic background, family economic history, personal production history, production resources, the problems and opportunities they encountered during the 1979–90 period, investment and expropriation experiences, political views and activities, organizational involvement, economic philosophy, and policy recommendations.

Findings presented in Chapter 5 should be regarded as exploratory. There is no well-established model of elite attitudes and behavior during revolutionary transitions, nor has there been much effort among social scientists to explore political divisions within the elite using individual-level data. This research represents a firm step in the direction of more rigorous analysis of these issues.

Statistics

Table A.1

Agricultural Production by Crop, 1974/75–1987/88

Year	Cotton[a]	Coffee[a]	Rice[a]	Sorghum[b]
1974–75	7,998,400	890,800	1,733,500	1,127,600
1975–76	7,282,800	1,068,200	1,268,900	1,336,400
1976–77	8,159,900	1,102,500	838,100	2,113,700
1977–78	9,152,500	1,251,200	1,030,600	930,000
1978–79	8,152,400	1,263,100	1,175,000	1,356,200
1979–80	1,244,700	1,228,100	1,359,000	1,379,500
1980–81	4,878,590	1,284,934	1,376,800	1,939,519
1981–82	4,080,999	1,327,969	1,947,000	1,951,400
1982–83	5,070,136	1,568,375	2,134,000	1,150,588
1983–84	5,690,739	1,069,694	2,233,033	2,224,200
1984–85	4,608,645	1,115,000	1,942,900	2,354,400
1985–86	3,349,900	768,700	1,773,700	3,346,300
1986–87	3,289,037	942,000	1,725,000	3,769,200
1987–88	2,200,000	839,667	1,502,400	2,408,046

Source: CIERA (1989, 9:74, 76, 92, 94).

[a]Qt. oro

[b]Qt.

Table A.2

UNAG Membership Data, 1987

Regions/ Zones	Members of Cooperatives[a]				Associate Members[b]	Individual Members[c]	Total
	CAS	CCS	CSM	CT			
Region I	8,070	11,856	330	333	—	2,834	23,423
Region II	4,293	9,789	396	1,013	96	3,310	18,897
Region III	2,250	2,272	—	800	—	943	6,265
Region IV	5,364	5,939	—	499	2,207	1,947	15,956
Region V	2,559	927	—	—	—	11,491	14,977
Region VI	4,114	22,251	1,489	—	504	4,768	33,126
Zone I	298	1,586	—	202	—	565	2,651
Zone II	1,082	1,109	—	515	—	—	2,706
Zone III	1,092	398	—	255	—	760	2,505
Nation	29,122	56,127	2,215	3,617	2,807	26,618	120,506

Source: Luciak (forthcoming).

Acronyms: CAS Sandinista Production Cooperative

CCS Credit and Service Cooperative

CSM Dead Fence Cooperative

CT Work Collective

[a]Members of the various cooperative organizations are affiliated with UNAG through their base structures and as individuals.

[b]Associate members are affiliated with UNAG as members of their coffee and cattle associations.

[c]Individual members affiliate with UNAG but do not belong to any base structure.

Table A.3

Nicaragua Economic Indicators, 1978–1992

	1978	1979	1980	1981	1982	1983
GDP growth rate (%)	−7.2	−26.4	4.6	5.4	−0.8	4.6
Per capita GDP growth rate (%)	−10.0	−28.4	1.6	1.9	−4.0	1.2
Tax revenues/GDP (%)	—	—	18.4	18.7	20.3	25.9
Fiscal deficit/ government expenditures (%)	50.7	36.5	30.3	36.0	34.8	49.1
Fiscal deficit/GDP (%)	—	13.5	9.2	12.4	13.6	30.0
Inflation rate[b] (%)	4.3	70.3	24.8	23.2	22.2	32.9
Exports (goods, FOB) (millions $)	646	616	451	500	408	429
Imports (goods, FOB) (millions $)	553	389	803	922	723	819
Trade balance (millions $)	+93	+227	−352	−422	−315	−390
Foreign debt (public) (millions $)	961	1,131	1,579	2,163	3,139	3,789
Interest due/exports (goods and services) (%)	14.3	8.9	24.3	37.4	41.8	43.5

[a]preliminary

[b]consumer prices, December–December variation 1978–91; October–October variation 1992.

Sources:

GDP and per cap. GDP growth rates	1978 (CEPAL 1984, 2); 1979–82 (CEPAL 1985, 2); 1983–84 (CEPAL 1990a, 25); 1985–92 (CEPAL 1992a, 42–43).
Tax revenues/GDP	1980–87 (Arana Sevilla 1990, 42–43); 1988–91 (CEPAL 1992b, 46).
Fiscal deficit/GDP and fiscal deficit/government expenditures	1978 (CEPAL 1984, 2); 1979–84 (CEPAL 1986, 2): 1986–87 (Neira Cuadra and Acevedo 1992, 107); 1988–92 (CEPAL 1992b, 25, 46; CEPAL 1992a, 48).
Inflation rate	1978–83 (CEPAL 1987, 17); 1984–92 (CEPAL 1992a, 45).
Exports, imports, balance	1978–82 (CEPAL 1984, 33); 1983–84 (CEPAL 1986, 26); 1985–86 (CEPAL 1987, 21); 1987 (CEPAL 1989, 24); 1988 (CEPAL 1990b); 1989 (CEPAL 1992b, 36, 38); 1990–92 (CEPAL 1992a, 55).
Foreign debt	1978–81 (CEPAL 1984, 2); 1982–84 (CEPAL 1987, 23); 1985 (CEPAL 1992b, 25); 1986–1992 (CEPAL 1992a, 59).
Interest due/exports	1978–79 (CEPAL 1984, 35); 1980–83 (CEPAL 1990a, 34); 1984–92 (CEPAL 1992a, 60).

Table A.3 (continued)

1984	1985	1986	1987	1988	1989	1990	1991	1992 [a]
−1.6	−4.1	−1.0	−0.7	−12.1	−1.9	−0.7	−0.5	0.5
−4.8	−6.7	−3.5	−3.0	−14.2	−4.5	−3.7	−4.0	−3.4
30.7	27.8	27.7	24.6	19.2	21.7	17.7	19.8	—
41.4	41.9	35.3	37.2	55.7	22.2	56.5	24.1	—
24.8	23.4	18.0	16.4	26.6	6.7	19.7	8.0	7.3
47.3	334.3	747.4	1,347.2	33,547.6	1,689.1	13,490.2	775.4	2.2
386	301	243	295	236	290	332	268	235
826	830	836	734	718	615	570	688	730
−440	−529	−593	−439	−482	−325	−238	−420	−495
4,362	4,936	5,760	6,270	7,220	9,741	10,616	10,454	11,200
57.9	78.3	88.5	75.6	96.7	62.1	58.3	110.4	122.4

Table A.4

Strata Definitions

	Small-sized	Medium-sized	Large-sized
Basic Grains	0–50 mz.	50–500 mz.	500+ mz.
Coffee	0–15 mz./	15–65 mz./	65+ mz./
	0–200 qt.[a]	200–1,000 qt.[a]	1,000+ qt.[a]
Cotton	0–50 mz.	50–200 mz.	200+ mz.
Cattle	0–200 mz.	200–1,000 mz.	1,000+ mz.

Source: CIERA (1981).

[a] as modified by Baumeister (1984b).

Table A.5

UPANIC Membership and Landholding Data, 1985

Organization	Number of Members	Mz. in Production
FAGANIC	3,578	582,000
FONDILAC	1,236	100,000
UNCAFENIC	820	47,000
CAAN	372	49,850
ASCANIC	180	30,000
ANPROSOR	136	29,846
ANAR	75	16,000
ANPROBA		1,550
Total	6,397	856,246

Source: Unpublished COSEP data, 1985.

notes

Preface

1. See Collier and Norden (1992) for an insightful discussion of the strategic choice model and a review of recent literature employing this approach. For an early illustration of strategic choice analysis developed in the 1960s to explore the possibilities for "reformmongering," see Hirschman (1973).

Chapter 1

1. See the discussion of the Chilean Popular Unity strategy below.

2. In a fulsome critique of Eurocommunist theory as developed by the French Communist party, Poulantzas concluded that the effort to define the non-monopoly sector as an "exploited bourgeoisie" under the heel of the monopoly sector was fundamentally flawed. The work of imperialism theorists was reviled for its fallacious assumption of "a supposed class solidarity between the popular masses of the dependent countries and their own bourgeoisies ('the exploited nations') against the imperialist bourgeoisies" (Poulantzas 1978, 151). Poulantzas argued that the monopoly and non-monopoly sectors are bound together in a relationship of "organic interdependence" (Poulantzas 1978, 149). Far from being a natural ally of the popular classes, the non-monopoly sector, because of its greater competitiveness and lower profit margins, may actually be more directly conflictual and exploitative in its relations with labor than its monopoly counterpart. Although Poulantzas delineates multiple contradictions within and between the monopoly and non-monopoly sectors of the bourgeoisie, he concludes emphatically that "the relationship of exploitation is that between the bourgeoisie as a whole and the working class and popular masses" (Poulantzas 1978, 151). Interpreting Latin American class dynamics, André Gunder Frank concluded that the internationalization of capital was "driving the entire Latin American bourgeois class—including its comprador, bureaucratic and national segments—into ever closer economic and political alliance with and dependence on the imperialist metropolis" (Frank 1969, 396).

3. Zeitlin and Ratcliff's work raises provocative questions; in attempting to explain the political behavior of the capitalist class, however, the family-network framework suffers from significant limitations. Analysis of only upper echelon elites in the largest economic operations neglects the fissure between the domi-

nant elite and the rest of the capitalist class, whose members do not occupy directorships of leading national banks or industrial conglomerates. Furthermore, the assumption that kinship is the central bond defining social relations may overstate the cohesiveness of family structures and obscure divisions within those units. This formulation may assume too much about the collective economic purposefulness of the extended family and the ability of family brokers to resolve competing interests. Divisions within the top elite may not, in Zeitlin and Ratcliff's words, be "ontologically real," but, in moments of crisis and social transformation, they may be politically quite real.

4. A third type of outcome, in which a revolutionary socialist regime of the Cuban type confronts and eliminates the bourgeoisie, was not included in this analysis. Because that type of regime effectively eliminates the bourgeoisie, it provides little information about the ongoing dynamics and complex negotiations in the relationship between a transformative state and the dominant class.

5. My original study of this issue also included an analysis of elite resistance in Ecuador during the period of military reform (1972–76) and complex negotiation in Jamaica during the first Manley era (1972–80). Those cases have been summarized in an abbreviated fashion in notes in this chapter and Chapter 7.

6. Evelyne Huber Stephens and John D. Stephens (1986, 333–36) differentiate democratic socialism from its more moderate cousin, social democracy, based on several criteria. Social democratic governments have tended to emerge in highly industrialized countries in Western Europe where local capital is relatively dynamic and foreign penetration is less intense. Because of these characteristics, income redistribution and economic growth can be achieved through tax and regulatory policy and social welfare programs, without extensive state control of the local economy. In Third World countries, on the other hand, where foreign participation in the economy is much deeper and aligns with local capital, they argue that more direct state ownership is required to achieve dynamic growth and lower foreign dependence. Thus while democratic socialism and social democracy share certain general objectives (increased social equality and promotion of political democracy), the role of the state and the economic logic of each is found to be distinct.

7. The industrial data are for 1969. According to de Vylder (1976, 136), there were an estimated 35,000 industrial firms in Chile at that time.

8. As early as 1940, over one-third of the industrial work force was unionized (Valenzuela 1978, 28). As the political contest deepened in the 1960s with the extension of the franchise and the election of Eduardo Frei, social organization intensified with the growth of unions, neighborhood groups, and rural organizations.

9. According to Drake (1973, 315), economic and political elites were closely linked. Forty percent of the leaders of the Conservative party and 34 percent of the Liberal party leaders belonged to the SNA in 1931–33.

10. The Association of Banks and Financial Institutions was established in 1943, and the Chamber of Construction was founded in 1951. The National Mining Society includes only Chilean mine owners and represents medium-sized mining rather than the largest mines, which were foreign-owned prior to 1971.

11. Bitar (1986, 208–9) notes that SOFOFA had a membership of only around 2,200 in the early 1960s. Genaro Arriagada's (1970, 116–71) study of Chilean employers' associations identified a series of features, such as the inclusion of non-elected officials on the executive councils and low leadership turnover, that tended to increase centralized control in these associations and limit internal democracy.

12. The 1967 law allowed landowners to retain a *reserva* of their choosing equivalent to eighty hectares of irrigated land in the Central Valley. Furthermore, reformed land was allocated only to those workers currently employed on the estate. These measures allowed the landholding elite to retain all capital and considerable land resources and did little to address the serious problems faced by landless migrants and *minifundistas* not employed on the large estates. The UP government did, however, accelerate the pace of implementation of that legislation. Between 1965 and 1973, 5,036 large estates (*fundos*) were expropriated, 70 percent of them after 1970. See de Vylder (1976, 176–98).

13. According to McClintock (1981, 61), the portion of agricultural land redistributed in Chile between 1967 and May 1973 was comparable (36 percent) to that distributed in Mexico and Peru (36 percent in Mexico as of 1960, and 35 percent in Peru through 1977), but the portion of rural families receiving land was much lower (9 percent in Chile versus 25 percent in Mexico and 24 percent in Peru).

14. It took the government almost a full year to specify a concrete expropriation plan for that sector. The bill it proposed in October 1971 targeted around 250 of the largest private stock companies for expropriation. Private stock companies with capital valued over 14 million escudos (then about US$1.4 million) in December 1969 would either be fully expropriated and transferred to the social property area or be partially expropriated and turned into mixed enterprises. Congressional resistance pushed the government to lower the target to around ninety enterprises a few months later. In a rare exception to the general pattern, the government was actually able to secure support for this proposal from the National Association of Small Manufacturers, whose constituents, of course, would not be affected by the bill (de Vylder 1976, 136–37).

15. Two hundred and forty-eight were under full or partial state ownership and 259 were intervened or requisitioned (CORFO 1989, 226–27, 244). In the final months of the Allende government, the number of firms taken over by their workers increased rapidly, with the addition of around 50 small- and medium-sized firms following an attempted coup in June 1973 (de Vylder 1976, 144–45).

16. In February 1972, congress passed an amendment to the constitution that in effect precluded further expropriations without congressional authorization. Allende vetoed the measure and argued that a congressional override required two-thirds approval, something that the opposition could not muster. The opposition countered that constitutional reforms passed in 1970 made it possible to amend the constitution with only a simple majority vote. Allende proceeded with expropriations as if the constitutional amendment were void, leading some of his challengers to allege that his regime operated outside the law and hence deserved to be removed by extralegal means. By the time Allende pushed a compromise

proposal through his fractious coalition (which would give the government legal authority to expropriate, with compensation, eighty enterprises, while requiring specific authorization from congress for any future nationalizations), the right wing of the Christian Democratic party had become dominant, and the Christian Democrats refused to back the measure (see Valenzuela 1978, 75–76).

17. Arturo Matte Larraín, head of the prominent Matte family and brother-in-law of defeated presidential candidate Jorge Alessandri, was involved in the International Telephone and Telegraph (ITT) conspiracy to prevent Allende's inauguration. His nephew Benjamín Matte Guzmán, who headed the SNA, vehemently opposed even the Christian Democratic agrarian reform program and became a clandestine leader of the far right-wing paramilitary organization Patria y Libertad. Agustín Edwards Eastman, whose family owned a controlling interest (42.75 percent) in the Bank of Edwards and 69 percent the conservative newspaper *El Mercurio*, left Chile to become an international vice-president of Pepsi-Cola Corporation in New York. From the United States he lobbied the Nixon administration for assistance in blocking the Allende government (see Zeitlin and Ratcliff 1988, 66, 224, 252–57).

18. This percentage decline was not simply a reflection of a rapid increase in public investment. Stallings's data (1978, 248) show that real public investment did increase modestly in 1973, but real private investment dropped sharply from 260 million escudos of 1965 in 1970 to approximately 93 million escudos of 1965 in 1971. This decline appears to be quicker and sharper than that in Peru, where the private sector was still responsible for 40.8 percent of gross fixed capital formation in 1974 (though FitzGerald [1976, 84] estimates that only one-third of this was from local capitalists).

19. This point is difficult to document, but it is often made in the literature on this era. See, for example, de Vylder (1976, 62) and Bitar (1986, 204).

20. Indeed, there was some support for the UP coalition within the privileged classes prior to 1970. According to electoral surveys by Eduardo Hamuy in Greater Santiago, for example, 20 percent of those classified as in the bourgeoisie voted for the Socialist/Communist coalition in 1964. This was slightly higher than the 18 percent managers/professionals and somewhat below the 27 percent petty bourgeoisie who voted for the left in that election. These figures are cited in Stallings (1978, 244).

21. Although personally committed to restricting expropriations according to the original plan, Allende repeatedly gave in to pressures from more radical elements in order to maintain unity within the coalition and avoid breaking with his own political party. Most graphically, in early 1973 he rejected the Millas Project, named for the new economic minister Orlando Millas, which would have returned fifty small- and medium-sized firms to their former owners. After the workers in these firms, encouraged by the Socialist party and Movimiento de Acción Popular Unitario, went out on strike, Allende authorized the retention of these firms (de Vylder 1976, 239 n. 51). The pace of expropriations, the apparent lack of control over the process at the top, and the fundamentally anticapitalist stance of many

UP leaders fed deep fears within the bourgeoisie. Although few of the 35,000 businesses and firms in Chile were taken, this violation of prior commitments stirred panic throughout the bourgeoisie and brought even nonhegemonic elites into the anti-Allende camp. In a self-criticism written following the 1973 coup, former UP minister Sergio Bitar condemned the UP for regarding these middle strata as "temporary, tactical allies" rather than a "strategic element" whose interests had to be considered seriously and responded to by the government (Bitar 1986, 211).

22. The president of COPROCO, the peak association of the old, elite business organizations, proclaimed two weeks before the coup, "I don't belong to any party, I'm not tied to any important economic group. I'm a commercial and industrial businessman of medium importance. . . . Right now the concern of the business organizations isn't about how to get more . . . but with fighting for liberty, the right to work . . . and the right to produce and distribute goods and services under a regime that respects the law and individuality" (El Mercurio, September 4, 1973, as cited in Campero 1984, 86–87).

23. Key economic elites, particularly the powerful Edwards family, were able to fan public fears about the loss of freedom and deepen the polarization of the society through alarmist news coverage in the powerful right-wing daily El Mercurio. Through a combination of pressure on those who wavered and ideological leadership, the opposition press mobilized widespread opposition among the privileged sectors. De Vylder (1976, 47) reports that two-thirds of all television, 95 percent of radio stations, 90 percent of newspaper circulation, and almost 100 percent of weekly magazines were opposed to the government. One of the weekly magazines, El Segundo, published the names of businesspeople who agreed to sell their holdings to the state, thereby pressuring owners to reject purchase offers and making it more difficult for the government to successfully negotiate the takeover of private businesses.

24. For a discussion of the evolution of "notable families" in Latin America during the 1750–1880 period, see Balmori, Voss, and Wortman (1984).

25. Ecuador may provide another example. Well into the twentieth century, Ecuadorean business leaders tended to be well organized and participated in a series of private sector organizations that served as social as well as economic networks. Powerful cámaras de producción were set up by the state in the 1930s, and private sector membership was legally required. Small- and medium-sized businesses failed to form their own associations and generally followed the lead of the large-scale producers (Hurtado 1980, 180). Drawing on a study by the Comité Interamericano de Desarrollo Agrícola, Hurtado (1980, 53) notes that "the board of directors of the Chamber of Agriculture of the Sierra between 1937 and 1962 contained four presidents of the Republic, fifty-one national deputies or senators, twenty-one cabinet members, and twenty-nine others who occupied important public posts of various types. . . . In the presidential elections of 1968, two of the five candidates, one Liberal, the other Conservative, had served on the board of directors of agrarian associations." Unlike most Latin American bourgeoisies, the Ecuadorean elite faced little challenge to its political preeminence, even into the

1960s, as limits on the franchise excluded roughly half of the adult population (Hurtado 1980, 349).

26. The *matanza* of 1932 wiped out close to 1 percent of the population (Anderson 1971, 135).

27. One political party, the Partido Acción Renovadora, was officially proscribed in the 1960s for including a proposal for the expropriation of private land in its platform (Ramírez Arango 1985, 102).

28. According to de Sebastián (1986, 34), the Asociación de Cafetaleros was also allowed to control 36 percent of the stock in the Central Reserve Bank when it was founded in 1934.

29. A modest process of crop diversification began in the 1940s with the introduction of cotton and later with sugar cane; industrialization was promoted with 1952 legislation giving tax exemptions for the import of capital goods and with the creation of state investment institutes to finance industrial investment (Jiménez 1986, 13–14). Indeed, the average annual industrial expansion rate (5.7 percent) outpaced agricultural growth (4.5 percent) in the 1950–62 period (Bulmer-Thomas 1987, 7).

30. The powerful Asociación de Cafetaleros de El Salvador was allowed to acquire 40 percent of the stock in this bank, and the Asociación de Ganaderos de El Salvador another 20 percent (Baloyra 1982, 13).

31. See also Baloyra (1982, 25); and Dunkerley (1988, 343–49).

32. They were responsible, by one account, for 17 percent of manufacturing, 26 percent of commerce, and 31 percent of the service sector (Sevilla 1985, 18, table 10). Drawing on data for 1978–79, Sevilla (1985, 15) defines medium-sized as those operations with an annual production value of 1–5 million colones (US$400,000–$2 million at the then prevailing exchange rate) in manufacturing, gross earnings between 500,000 and 5 million colones (US$200,000–$2 million) in services and commerce, or land size between 50 and 100 hectares in agriculture.

33. ANEP was composed of the Coffee Association (which claimed 40,000 members in the early 1980s), the Chamber of Commerce, the Salvadoran Industries Association, the Banking Association, the Chamber of the Industry of Construction, the Cotton Producers Cooperative, the Association of Producers of Sugar, the Association of Processors and Exporters of Coffee, the Chamber of Tourism, and other regional affiliates (Ramírez Arango 1985, 97–98; Crosby 1985, 26). In 1980, it claimed 31 affiliates and a membership of over 50,000.

34. The reaction of the landed elite to the agrarian reform proposal of the military government in 1976 indicates the breadth of the elite's control and the intensity of its resistance to change. Proposed by military president Molina in 1976, the plan to distribute 59,000 hectares in the eastern cotton-growing region to 12,000 peasant families would have provided ample USAID-financed compensation at market prices (Baloyra 1982, 56; Jung 1980, 17). ANEP, representing agricultural producers, industry, and commerce, responded immediately by publicly denouncing the measure and mobilizing its membership in opposition. In a series of newspaper announcements, ANEP carried on a hot exchange with the Molina

government, condemning the government's "totalitarian stance" and "absolute intransigence" and reminding them of their "obligation to listen." The government, in its own newspaper announcements, responded that "the act of listening should not be confused with the action of obeying" (Baloyra 1982, 57–58). In spite of this bravado, within weeks the government began backing away from the plan. To bolster its position, the more extreme right-wing elements in ANEP formed the Frente Agrario de la Región Oriental, a militantly violent organization. This revived a long tradition of right-wing elites employing violence and financing death squads to eliminate those who challenged them.

35. Private sector leaders were not long involved. The first junta included Mario Andino, local manager of the Philips Dodge wire company owned by the de Sola family. Andino was viewed as an ANEP representative by Christian Democratic party leader José Napoleón Duarte, who publicly demanded the exclusion of all private sector representatives on the junta before the Christian Democrats would agree to join the government in January 1980. A second prominent private producer, Enrique Alvarez, a large landowner and former minister of agriculture, briefly served the new government in 1979 as the minister of agriculture before resigning to join the leadership of the Frente Democrático Revolucionario. He was subsequently assassinated.

36. This phase authorized the expropriation of properties over 500 hectares and the allocation of these estates to the resident labor force in the form of cooperatives. As in the agrarian reform program in Mexico, Peru (except in the highland and high-jungle region), and Chile, landowners were allowed to retain a substantial reserve—in this case 100–150 hectares, depending on soil quality. Phase I land was to be compensated with twenty-year bonds for inventories and land, at 6 percent interest, based on 1976–77 declared tax value. There is evidence to suggest that around 10 percent of the affected landowners had overestimated the value of their land, presumably to increase their access to bank credit. Many others, however, had underestimated the land value in order to reduce their property taxes. For them, the compensation provided was unacceptably low. The bonds themselves were also unattractive and traded at 55–62 percent of their face value. The government's willingness to accept the bonds in lieu of payment for some types of taxes, however, did give them a certain worth. In the end, almost half of the Phase I estates (238 properties) were acquired at market rates instead of rates based on declared tax value (Strasma 1990, 10).

37. According to data in Thiesenhusen (1989, 10–11) this would be more land to a higher percentage of the rural population than any other land reform program in Latin America except that of Bolivia. Thiesenhusen's data indicate that the Bolivian agrarian reform program affected 83.4 percent of the agricultural and forest land of the country, and benefited 74.5 percent of the "farming families."

38. In its 1990 census, the Proyecto de Evaluación y Planificación Agrícola of the Salvadoran Ministry of Agriculture reported that thirty cooperatives had been abandoned. See Strasma (1990, 25).

39. Recognizing this problem, the Duarte government modified the terms of

repayment for land recipients in 1986, reducing interest rates from 9.5 percent to 6 percent and extending the repayment period from up to thirty years to up to fifty years (Strasma 1990, 5, 11–12).

40. Payment for the banks was made in government bonds at 9 percent interest with five-year maturity. Not included in the nationalization were the foreign banks, which were now legally prohibited from accepting deposits (though in practice they continued to do so), savings and loan institutions, and the Banco Hipotecario. In his study of the nationalized banking system, Valdés (1989, 792 n. 3, 806) suggests that the latter may have been spared because it is commonly regarded as being in the public domain already, though in fact it is still largely owned by the coffee and livestock associations, and because of the mediation of its former president and, subsequently, Salvador's provisional president, Alvaro Magaña. Initially the state was to control the nationalized banks, but after some unspecified period of time, 49 percent of the stock was to be sold off—20 percent to bank workers and 29 percent to other buyers (Valdés 1989, 792). To prevent reconcentration of ownership, individuals were allowed to buy no more than 1 percent of the stock and could purchase stock in only one bank (Valdés 1989, 806).

41. According to Orellana's (1985, 15, table 5) study, for example, shareholders in the Banco Salvadoreño, the country's oldest and one of the largest banks, were paid 17 percent more than face value per share and 49 percent more than the book value established by the evaluation commission. In a few banks, however, fictitious loans that had been authorized to allow for capital flight were deducted from the portfolio, and some shares were compensated at 50 percent of face value.

42. Many agrarian reform beneficiaries were still excluded from the banking system. In 1984–85, 70 percent of Phase III land recipients received no credit, nor did almost a quarter of the Phase I cooperatives (80 of 338) (Valdés 1989, 800–801).

43. Coffee processors, on the other hand, were paid a straight processing fee determined by the state, and in some ways may have benefited from the new program. On the other hand, processors lost their ability to adjust their charges with different clients or to participate directly in the lucrative export trade.

44. On income calculations by efficiency levels, see the discussion of the USAID report "The Coffee Situation," San Salvador, March 8, 1984, in López (1986, 19). According to López's (1986, 34) calculations, in 1985, INCAFE earned the equivalent of 350 colones per quintal in its coffee transactions and paid producers only 220 colones. When international prices soared in 1986, the gap widened still further, with the state earning 1,000 colones per quintal and paying producers only 400 colones.

45. As early as 1984 the Salvadoran Ministry of Agriculture and Livestock estimated that 43 percent of the area planted to coffee had been effectively abandoned (meaning literal abandonment or the curtailment of active production labors like fertilizing, pruning, etc.), affecting varying amounts of the crop (from 98.7 percent of coffee land in Morazán to 20 percent in La Unión). In the crucial Santa Ana province, 47.6 percent of the coffee cultivation had been abandoned. See discussion in

López (1986, 25–26). International prices for Central America's "mild" coffee fell from $1.35 in 1988 to $.89 in 1990 (CEPAL 1990b, 30, table 12).

46. All of the organizations affiliated with ANEP opposed the reforms. Some were, however, more confrontational than others. The Asociación de Cafetaleros (formally known as the Asociación Salvadoreña de Café) was probably the most ferocious opponent; the Asociación Salvadoreña de Industriales, in contrast, maintained direct communication with Duarte in private conferences until May 1981, when pressure from other business leaders prompted them to suspend the meetings. Duarte attempted to build bridges to ANEP leaders, reportedly offering to name one of their leaders as minister of economic affairs in December 1980. In a formal, written counterproposal, ANEP leaders refused the offer unless they were also given a position on the junta plus the opportunity to select the ministers of foreign trade, agriculture, treasury, and labor and the Central Bank president (Ramírez Arango 1985, 156–58). Duarte declined their request.

47. For example, Dr. José Antonio Rodríguez Porth, president of the Chamber of Commerce, chaired ARENA's advisory council and played a major role as intellectual architect of the ARENA program and as a campaign fundraiser. He was named minister of the presidency in the Cristiani government but was assassinated soon after, on June 8, 1989.

48. Recent studies by Paige (1993) and Wolf (1992) indicate shadings of difference had developed by the end of the 1980s between ARENA "hardliners" and "softliners." Paige notes that the election of Cristiani represents not simply the return to power of the old coffee elite (represented by the Asociación Salvadoreña de Café) but the ceding of power to the faction of the coffee elite that is most tied to processing and industry (represented in the Association of Processors and Exporters of Coffee), a newer, more exclusive association founded in 1961. The leaders of the latter sector, he argues, have come in recent years to express partial support for the concept of democracy. Based on his interviews with elites, however, he concluded that neither sector associated democracy with social and economic rights, suggesting an important continuity within the elite establishment.

49. The annual per capita GDP decline during the crucial 1980–82 period was 10.5 percent (1980), 9.2 percent (1981), and 6.6 percent (1982) (CEPAL 1986, 2).

50. As in El Salvador, the reform initiative in Ecuador, which was introduced by the military during the 1972–76 oil boom, was largely stillborn. Most of Ecuador's large agricultural producers deftly sidestepped the agrarian reform laws. The 1973 legislation, which authorized expropriation of estates with less than 80 percent of their land in use, gave owners two years within which to comply. This measure only pushed owners to increase the intensity of their land use or divide unused lands. According to estimates by Zevallos (1989, 55), estates of more than 500 hectares occupied roughly 30 percent of agricultural land in the early 1970s and continued to occupy 20 percent at the end of the decade. Only 9 percent of all agricultural and forest land was affected by the various agrarian reform laws issued, and probably only 5–6 percent of all land was actually shifted to new hands

(as opposed to just titling land to current users), making it one of the least comprehensive agrarian reform programs in Latin America (Thiesenhusen 1989, 10; Zevallos 1989, 50).

The reform military's efforts to trim the power of economic elites by denying their traditional voting rights on government economic boards and mandating the registration of unincorporated family firms triggered fierce reaction on the part of the Ecuadorean private sector. Leading private sector organizations launched a forceful campaign of denunciation and opposition to blunt the reformist program. A weary and divided military finally called elections. Reformers elected in 1979 were soon supplanted by a unified right, and business leader Febres Cordero won the presidency in 1984. Much as in El Salvador, the Ecuadorean capitalists pursued "democratization" as an alternative to reform and succeeded in blunting the reform initiative when they returned to power. See Conaghan (1988).

51. Some analysts, such as Gary Wynia (1990), reserve the term "populist" to describe the personalistic movements led by Brazilian president Getúlio Vargas and Argentine president Juan Perón in his early phase. Indeed, Hamilton (1982, 138–39) contends that the postrevolutionary development of Mexico does not fit entirely in the populist model because the classical populist experiences of Brazil and Argentina did not mobilize the rural masses or include extensive agrarian reform. Yet most analysts of Mexican politics find the populist label appropriate. To differentiate between the Mexican and Peruvian forms of populism and their more moderate, industrial counterparts in Argentina and Brazil, I shall use the term "revolutionary populism" here to describe the former.

52. David W. Walker (1986, 227–28) illustrates the decline, focusing on the Martínez del Río family.

53. General and, subsequently, President Alvaro Obregón's landholdings, for example, reportedly expanded from 1.5 to 3,500 hectares after the revolution (Hamilton 1982, 68). Most postrevolutionary economic elites, however, had already acquired some significant assets during the *porfiriato*, though those resources certainly declined. As Camp (1989) points out, the best predictor of membership in the economic elite after 1917 is membership in that elite prior to the revolution.

54. Cárdenas expropriated a total of 811,157 hectares during the 1934–40 period compared with only 783,330 in the previous years of the revolution (Wilkie 1970, 194).

55. Land grants were given in the form of *ejidos* or communal holdings, based on a landholding pattern derived from tenancy practices of indigenous communities.

56. For example, with the reform of Article 78 of the Labor Code, a constitutional provision calling for payment to workers for the seventh day of the week was implemented, automatically raising wages approximately 17 percent (Hamilton 1982, 148).

57. The Mexican regime avoided the standard plague of populist governments: large deficits and inflation (Dornbusch and Edwards 1991). Increased government spending to support new social programs and expanded agricultural credit contributed to fiscal deficits, but these were offset somewhat in the Cárdenas era by

declining military outlays. The portion of the government budget spent on agricultural credit soared to 9.5 percent in 1935 and then stabilized at an average of 3.5 percent for the remainder of the *sexenio*, whereas the military's portion declined from between 30 and 53 percent in the 1920s–1930s to a low of 15.8 percent in 1939 (Wilkie 1970, 102, 139, 166). A modest deficit did emerge in the government budget in 1936 and became a recurring feature in the decades that followed (NAFINSA 1981, 304.) The deficit was financed internally by drawing overdrafts at the central bank (Medina 1974, 269).

58. Lázaro Cárdenas, *Los Catorce Puntos de la Política Obrera Presidencial* (México, D.F.: P[artido] N[acional] R[evolucionario], 1936), 48, as cited in Wilkie (1970, 73). See also Martínez Nava (1984, 85).

59. Drawing on data compiled by the Confederación de Cámaras de Comercio e Industria, Medina (1974, 271) reports that capital flight increased from 46 million pesos (US$12.8 million) in 1934 to 250 million pesos (US$69.4 million) in 1937 before tapering off in 1938. Direct foreign investment from U.S. investors dropped over 25 percent during the 1936–40 period (Wilkie 1970, 265).

60. See also Martínez Nava (1984, 113).

61. In 1936 new legislation was approved that required all firms worth more than 500 pesos (approximately US$143) to participate in trade associations. These organizations would be united in a single peak confederation under the jurisdiction of the secretary of the national economy. See Hamilton (1982, 196). In 1941, separate chambers of industry and commerce were reestablished.

62. There is some debate about the character of CANACINTRA. Analyzing this institution in the 1940s, Mosk (1954) presents it as an authentic private sector organization composed of revolutionary, nationalistic entrepreneurs. Shafer (1973), on the other hand, writing in the 1970s sees it essentially as a representative of the state in the guise of a private sector organization.

63. See Alcázar (1970, appendix 1, 106). By the 1970s, however, as the renewed populism of the Echeverría administration triggered greater private sector hostility, COPARMEX's membership increased, rising from 13,000 to 18,000 during the decade (Camp 1989, 164). Heredia (1991, 78) found that the number of regional affiliates of COPARMEX rose from 22 in 1978 to 64 (including 6 in Mexico City) in 1990. See also Bravo Mena (1987).

64. A 1982 public opinion poll conducted by the PRI concluded that only 17 percent of industrialists and 22 percent of company presidents professed membership in some political party. In contrast, 30 percent of the general public identified themselves as members of a political party. See Camp (1989, 139).

65. See the discussion in Camp (1989, 157). Camp acknowledged that it is hard to know what representational bias emerged in these business associations, but he found frequent allegations in his interviews with business leaders that leadership in these organizations tended to be weighted in favor of representatives of the largest firms. Unlike other Latin American countries such as Peru, where leading capitalists did not seek leadership positions in large business associations (Durand 1988b, 274), in Mexico they often did. See also Luna (1992, 4).

66. According to Lomnitz and Pérez-Lizaur (1987), Pablo Gómez broke with family tradition to invite a prominent general to become his daughter's godfather in 1939 (p. 39). Political alliances of this type allowed his branch of the family to prosper during this era. The two industrial concerns he inherited in 1925 were expanded into a complex of thirty-six factories by the time he died in the early 1960s (p. 109) His branch of the family continued to maintain friendships with political leaders, establishing social relationships and regular contact with subsequent Presidents Alemán, López Mateos, and Díaz Ordaz (pp. 200–201).

67. The Monterrey group emerged under the leadership of Isaac Garza and Francisco G. Sada. Starting with a brewery founded in 1890, their descendants expanded into glass, steel, packing, chemical production, and banking. For a detailed history of the Monterrey group from 1890 to 1940, see Saragoza (1988). Periodic tensions between this group and the government erupted even though personal friendships sometimes emerged, as in the case of Eugenio Garza Sada and Luis Echeverría (see Saragoza 1988; Basáñez 1990, 105).

68. Debate about the role of the bourgeoisie in Peru's revolution has been intense. Some analysts argued that the revolution was directed by the industrial bourgeoisie and foreign capital and was designed to serve their interests (Dore and Weeks 1977). Others, like FitzGerald (1976, 93–102), interpreted the revolution as an exercise in state capitalism in which the state attempted to counter the foreign and domestic bourgeoisie by becoming the central national entrepreneur itself. Stepan (1978, 290–317) viewed it as a failed effort to institutionalize a relatively autonomous state that would promote national development.

69. For nonirrigated land the maximum was set at 300 hectares for the coastal region and the amount of land necessary to maintain 5,000 sheep (or their equivalent in other species) in the highland or high-jungle region. See McClintock (1981, 60 n 34).

70. Thiesenhusen's (1989, 10–11) figures differ modestly. He found that 39 percent of the agricultural and forest land was transferred, between 1969 and 1982, to 30 percent of the farming families.

71. See also Becker's (1983, 187–89) analysis of the directorships of mid-size mining operations and their linkages with individuals from the agrarian oligarchy.

72. In a 1968–69 survey of 179 industrialists in medium- and large-sized firms, Wils (1975, 148) found 52 percent were descendants of first or second generation immigrants. Even in the largest firms, only 31 percent of the owners were from oligarchical families (p. 145).

73. According to data obtained by McClintock (1981, 47 n 16), fewer than 5 percent of the bonds were reinvested in this fashion. Bamat (1978, 140) points out that between 1969 and March 1976, investments approved for finance with the agrarian reform bonds amounted to only 4.4 percent of the total value of the bonds, and nine of the nineteen projects approved were actually for hotel construction rather than industrial activities. The prime beneficiary of this program was the Grupo Romero, which lost cultivated land on five large estates but was able to substantially expand its industrial and financial holdings. According to Reaño and Vásquez Huamán

(1988, 101) 61 percent of the funds administered in the Fondo de Financiamiento y Promoción de Empresas Industriales went to the Romero group.

74. According to FitzGerald (1976, 87), there were 3,000 state development projects under way in 1973; 150 were major, involving programmed investments of over 50 million soles.

75. Foreign capital's shares were to be reduced to a maximum of 49 percent by 1986. Following the August 1975 countercoup of Morales Bermúdez, these requirements were relaxed. The revised Industrial Communities Law adopted in late 1976 reduced the portion of the industry to be given to workers to 33 percent and gave the shares directly to the individual workers instead of the industrial communities. Foreign owners were given some options that included the retention of their stock if they chose not to participate in the benefits of the Andean market (Stepan 1978, 276–77). Peru eventually agreed to pay $150 million in compensation for U.S. firms that had been expropriated (Stepan 1978, 259).

The Peruvian private sector was also affected by these reforms, but much less so. A few local firms were shifted into the state sector, and major daily newspapers were turned over to groups representing different social sectors. But in many cases these changes were the result of bankruptcy, not expropriation. Only one big local capital group, the Prado consortium, lost its assets, and a series of Prado enterprises shifted under state control, including the Banco Popular and textile, paper, fertilizer, and cement factories (FitzGerald 1976, 33). This group went bankrupt, partly as a result of the crash of the fishing industry following overfishing and changing ocean currents.

76. Although some foreign firms were expropriated or had losses, others prospered. Becker's (1983, 97–165) account of the Peruvian mining sector, for example, contrasts the histories of two major mining companies. Cerro de Pasco was an internally divided foreign-owned operation that dominated the mining sector. When it decided to use Peruvian profits to expand operations in Chile, Peru's traditional rival, the company was expropriated. In contrast, Southern Peru Copper devised an expansionary investment plan that converged with the state's nationalist development program. In the latter case, the state not only refrained from expropriation but supported the negotiation of an international loan package to finance the expansion of the company.

77. Becker's (1983) work analyzes the development of a "new bourgeoisie" in Peru that supported the new state policy. This reform-oriented bourgeoisie was composed of managers and administrative personnel who were "knowledge-based" rather than "ownership-based" (p. 238). Becker's study may overemphasize the power of a managerial elite, since the lack of ownership limits this sector's ability to direct the industry over the long run. This work does, however, highlight proreform commitments even among relatively privileged members of that society.

78. The word *national* was dropped from its name. Other forms of pressure used against the association included forcing the society's stridently oppositional president to remain in exile for a year following a trip abroad. See Stepan (1978, 121).

79. In 1974 the SNI pushed for the creation of a United Front for the Defense of

Private Property to coordinate an industrywide response to the nationalization of the fishing industry. Fearful of the regime's response, leaders soon backed off, and this effort fizzled. Three years later, seven private sector organizations succeeded in creating the Unión de Empresarios Privados del Perú, but the association lasted only six months before it was dissolved (Durand 1991, 5–6).

80. According to Durand (1988b, 271–73), at the top of the pyramid are found a small number of "family clans" who attained prominence with the destruction of the oligarchy and whose position was fortified by the military regime's nationalistic policies. These top economic groups had investments in multiple sectors of the economy, including the country's major banks, and generally had some associative link with foreign capital. Beneath this group was a second layer of large- and medium-sized capitalists who, unlike the first group, were generally involved in only one or two economic sectors. Since their economic base was narrower, they were more vulnerable to shifts in state policy and more hostile to the reforms.

81. The state portion of gross fixed capital formation rose from 30 percent in the 1964–68 period to 50 percent in 1974–76 (FitzGerald 1979, 150). Private investment, already low at 10.8 percent of GDP in 1964–68, now dipped to 8 percent of GDP in 1969–76, and FitzGerald (1979, 151–52) estimates that foreign capital provided two-thirds of that amount.

82. Many of the reforms were substantially reduced in 1976 following the Morales Bermúdez countercoup in 1975 and ended altogether following the 1980 election and return to power of President Belaúnde Terry.

83. The willingness of the Peruvian bourgeoisie to support unorthodox economic measures was demonstrated again during the early years of the Alán García presidency (1985–86), when they rallied to his side and supported his economic reactivation plan. That approval collapsed with the subsequent bank nationalization in July 1987 (Durand 1988b).

84. This kind of mutual accommodation is not found exclusively in revolutionary populist regimes. Considerable segmentation and partial accommodation of the bourgeoisie were also found in Jamaica during the early years of the first Michael Manley government (1972–80). As with the other cases we have explored, much of the initial reform in Jamaica was directed against foreign capital. The target was the foreign-owned bauxite industry, where a unilateral increase in the bauxite levy raised state revenues from bauxite sevenfold. This measure was popular even with Jamaican capitalists, in part because of the foreign exchange windfall it produced (Stephens and Stephens 1986, 79). When expropriation of local elites occurred, it was generally in the form of a state takeover of failing businesses, such as the collapsing sugar estates and hotel industry. The government was constrained in its agrarian reform efforts by a constitutional requirement of full compensation at market rates for expropriated landowners. As a consequence, its land reform efforts were also modest.

Although the evidence is not conclusive, the Jamaican commercial sector organized in the Chamber of Commerce, whose economic interests and opportunities were most sharply and immediately curtailed by the Manley government's import restrictions, may have gone most quickly into the opposition (Keith and Keith 1985, 94–96; Stephens and Stephens 1986, 98, 350). Exporters affiliated with the JEA, on the other hand, were relatively favored by a government that was chronically strapped for foreign exchange. As in the Peruvian case, this sector tended to be more supportive of the new government and at times formally endorsed government initiatives (Stephens and Stephens 1986, 194).

By 1976, however, the various segments of the private sector were beginning to converge in opposition to the regime. A new peak organization, the Private Sector Organization of Jamaica, was founded to allow the private sector to confront the regime more effectively. Although the state-business relationship deteriorated in the final years, established divisions within the Jamaican elite and the Manley government's alliance strategy made the defection of the bourgeoisie a more gradual process in Jamaica than it had been in either Chile or El Salvador.

Chapter 2

1. The first law to support coffee cultivation was actually passed in 1835 but was not implemented during those turbulent years. Additional legislation was passed in 1847 exempting producers with more than 2,000 trees from taxes and both owners and workers on coffee estates from being pressed into military service. See Burns (1991, 232).

2. This legislation was passed in 1877 but was implemented more vigorously in the 1880s and 1890s. Vogl Baldizón (1985, 15–19, 355–60) describes how his father, a German immigrant who had come to Nicaragua in 1888 to manage a German import house, accepted the offer and built a farm in Matagalpa, where he met and married his Nicaraguan wife. Vogl reports that around 200 foreigners, mostly of German and U.S. origin, settled in the Matagalpa region at this time.

3. The Nicaraguan banking system emerged relatively late, by regional standards, and was largely foreign controlled. The Banco Nacional de Nicaragua (BNN) was founded by the Nicaraguan government in 1912, but foreign investment bankers Brown Bros. and J. and V. Seligman & Co. exercised their option to buy 51 percent of bank stock during debt negotiations the following year. The bank, which functioned as Nicaragua's central bank, was incorporated in the state of Connecticut; the majority of the bank's directors were from the United States. Control over the bank was not returned to the Nicaraguan government until 1940. See Hill (1933); Walter (1993, 12–13); and Wheelock Román (1980b). Coffee export was monopolized by the Compañía Mercantil de Ultramar, which was jointly held by the BNN and some of its principal stockholders (Paige 1989, 102).

4. Nicaragua remained a poor country, even by regional standards. As late as 1950, real per capita income in Nicaragua was ranked second-lowest in Latin America, with only Haiti falling below it (Bulmer-Thomas 1991, 249). In terms of its GDP, Nicaragua was clearly the regional laggard, steadily falling behind the

rest of Central America through the 1920–60 period (see Bulmer-Thomas 1987, 308–9). Only in the 1960s, when the growth rate in Honduras fell behind that of Nicaragua, did Nicaragua move out of the region's production basement.

5. The degree of state involvement in the Nicaraguan economy during the Somoza period has been a matter of dispute. Some analysts see the Nicaraguan state as primarily passive, nondevelopmental, and largely inactive in economic management. Gary Wynia's (1972) study of planning policy in the 1950s and 1960s, for example, emphasizes the regime's fundamental economic conservatism. José Luis Medal's (1985) study of central bank policy during this era also adopts this interpretation, finding the regime's credit, monetary, and balance of payments policies were left in the hands of conservative central bankers. Bill Gibson, analyzing fiscal and monetary policy during the Somoza era, labels state policies as "classically liberal" (1987, 27). According to these analysts, the state generated only modest revenues, took on a limited number of development tasks, lacked a coherent planning capacity, and largely turned the economy over to the forces of the international market. Its passivity was striking even by regional standards and won the praise of the most orthodox economic analysts in the international lending agencies.

Yet, the Nicaraguan state was not inert during this period, and several analysts (Biderman 1982; Walter 1993) have called attention to the regime's strategic interventions into the economy. These analysts have argued that the regime's economic involvement reflected ambitions that extended beyond mere personal enrichment and had an impact on the overall direction of national economic development. According to Jaime Biderman, by the 1950s the state played an important role in escalating the pace of capitalist development in Nicaragua, particularly in the cotton, beef, sugar, tobacco, rice, and banana sectors (1982, 80–127). Knut Walter (1993) takes this argument a step further, arguing that the capacity and resilience of the Somoza state have been seriously underestimated. He claims that, while other Central American dictatorships were toppling in the 1940s and 1950s, the Somoza dynasty proved politically agile and developmentally competent, consolidating its political base while it promoted infrastructural development that fostered rapid capitalist development in the subsequent decades.

6. The expansion in cotton land came primarily through the reduction in unimproved pastureland used for traditional cattle grazing in the Pacific coastal plain (Baumeister 1983). In addition, economically and legally vulnerable peasant staples producers were displaced from estate lands to which they had traditionally had access. With the rising profitability of cotton, owners now put these lands into more intensive cultivation. Gould's (1990, 85–181) study of rural mobilization in the Chinandega region (1912–79) documents the multiple ways in which peasant access to land was reduced.

7. The state supported the takeoff of the cotton sector in other ways as well. In the 1950s, these included funding of port facilities in "El Tamarindo" (*La Gaceta*, Decree #154, January 10, 1956); the classification of the vegetable oil industry as a "First Category Industry," thereby providing tax and tariff concessions for the

cottonseed oil sector (*La Gaceta*, Decree #16, March 3, 1956); and an increase in the exchange rate received by cotton exporters from C$6.60:$1 to C$7:1 as long as prices remained below US$31.50 (*La Gaceta*, Decree #18, November 21, 1956). See Navas Mendoza et al. (n.d.[a], 4–5).

8. Occupational information about the ninety-four founding members of ANSCA, for example, shows that forty of these members (43 percent) listed an urban profession (lawyer, industrialist, etc.) as their primary occupation (ANSCA n.d., 31–33).

9. Baumeister (1984b, 8, 32) reports that in El Salvador in the early 1960s 34 percent of the coffee and 52 percent of the cotton were produced on "large multi-family estates," whereas in Nicaragua estates of that size were responsible for only 20 percent and 31 percent, respectively, of production. The percent of cotton land held in medium-sized estates in Nicaragua (defined here as 50–500 mz.) surged from 26 percent in 1952 to 60 percent in 1963 and remained over 50 percent in the early 1970s. See also Bulmer-Thomas (1987, 354 n 18).

10. Whereas coffee yields in El Salvador in 1950 averaged 640 kg./hectare, Nicaraguan yields averaged 275 kg./hectare (Bulmer-Thomas 1987, 154, 156–57). See also Warnken (1975, 14).

11. Foreign loans for the development of the livestock (beef and milk products) sector came primarily from the World Bank and the IDB. These loans included $3.25 million from the World Bank in the 1950s to purchase agricultural equipment, open new lands, improve pastures, and acquire breeding stock. In the 1960s the IDB took over this financing, providing $1.1 million to acquire breeding stock and $9.1 million for the expansion of pastureland; the construction of fences, wells, troughs, drinking pools, silos, corrals, and dipping facilities; and programs to improve livestock health (Williams 1986, 97). Local banks also supported this effort. In 1962 the BNN became a development bank, and its credit gradually began to shift toward long-term (more than eighteen months) loans, many of which were for cattle development. The bank's first project as a development bank was a 1965–67 cattle-raising program (Lethander 1968, 358).

12. The cattle sector focused primarily on beef exportation, but a secondary interest in milk production developed. A 1959 FAO study concluded that Nicaragua had the greatest capacity in Central America for exporting milk due to the abundance of land in the interior that, for reasons of topography, was ill-suited to other crop cultivation (FAGANIC 1982, 6). To promote this idea, the regime launched Plan Camabocho, a three-year campaign to build 450 km. of feeder roads in Matagalpa, Boaco, and Chontales. In September 1969 PROLACSA, a joint venture between the Swiss company Nestlé and the Somoza government, was initiated. This firm became a major milk processor and eventually exported powdered milk (FAGANIC 1982, 6b).

13. The number of cotton gins increased to twenty-six, and their capacity expanded notably. Secondary industries were created for processing vegetable oil and balanced animal feed from cottonseed. New export houses sprang up to channel Nicaraguan cotton into the international market. By 1974 seventeen export houses

purchased Nicaraguan cotton. Fifteen were agents of international cotton firms and two were Nicaraguan-based firms (Baumeister 1983, 46–50).

14. Concessions were provided for industrialists on the importation of construction materials, capital goods, energy, maintenance equipment, and raw materials, and taxes were reduced 50–100 percent. The law developed a priority system in which new industries received more concessions than old, and those categorized as "fundamental" received more relief than those labeled "useful" (*convenientes*).

15. At the beginning of the 1950s several Central American ministers of economy approached ECLA with a request for information about regional integration. They were invited by ECLA to form an economic cooperation committee to study the issue. Five meetings were held between 1952 and 1957 to review studies on regional integration and draft regional treaties. This work culminated at the end of the decade in the approval of the Multilateral Treaty of Free Trade and Central American Economic Integration in 1959. This treaty, approved by all Central American countries except Costa Rica, established a list of 200 items to be traded without restrictions in the region and set integration goals for the next ten years (Wynia 1972, 45–46). These developments laid the foundation for the CACM. Under the rules of the CACM, import duties were cut sharply to facilitate regional trade. Gary Wynia (1972, 89) found that import duties dropped quickly in most of the region, declining from 20 percent of import value in 1960 to 12 percent in 1966 for the region as a whole. Nicaragua's drop was even sharper, falling from 20 percent in 1960 to 10 percent in 1966.

16. AID, Report to Congress, FY 1965, p. 45, as cited in Dosal (1985, 91). Disappointed by the collapse of cotton and coffee prices in the late 1950s, the regime began searching for an alternative economic strategy. The U.S. government agreed to finance a study of the economic options Nicaragua might pursue and contracted a report from the International Cooperation Administration. This report included a number of recommendations that were designed to foster industrial development. Perhaps the most important was the proposal that an industrial investment corporation be formed to provide long-term loans for industry (Lindeman 1961, 2–3). Several USAID projects also helped provide infrastructure needed for industrialization. For example, USAID supported the expansion of ENALUF by offering financing for U.S.-made generating plants. This program was designed to expand access to electrical energy in rural areas, but the growth of ENALUF facilitated industrial growth as well. The ENALUF rate structure favored industrial clients, providing them with electricity at less than one-third the rate charged rural residential customers (Dosal 1985, 85).

17. See also Brundenius (1987, 85–92); Rosenthal (1982, 21–26).

18. The BANAMER group grew out of a series of enterprises associated with the Ingenio San Antonio, then Central America's largest sugar mill, and its parent company, Nicaragua Sugar Estates, Ltd. The company was founded in 1890 by Italian merchant F. Alfredo Pellas in conjunction with several elite families from Granada and was backed by English investment. Favored with a liquor mo-

nopoly during the Zelaya presidency, the firm expanded rapidly. See Nicaragua Sugar Estates (1953); Gould (1990, 22–45). The bank was founded in 1952 under the leadership of Silvio F. Pellas (Strachen 1976, 9–10).

19. BANIC was founded in 1953 by a group of León and Chinandega investors under the leadership of Eduardo Montealegre. To prevent the concentration of resources and control, BANIC was designed so that no one investor could hold more than 10 percent of the stock. See Strachen (1976, 11, 16).

20. Strachen's (1976, 27) business respondents identified a total of twenty-one firms in the BANAMER group and sixteen in the BANIC group.

21. For a fuller discussion of Somoza family assets as of 1978, see IHCA (1978, 1:319–24).

22. Strachen (1976, 13–14), for example, finds only one prominent entrepreneur, Manuel I. Lacayo, involved in business ventures with both BANIC and the BANAMER group.

23. I would label this system quasi-corporatist because it deviates in several respects from the conventional corporatist arrangements. (See Schmitter 1974 on the concept of corporatism). For one, the typical tripartite structure was not employed, since there was no counterpart labor organization; labor representatives generally did not participate in these deliberations. Furthermore, because the private sector organizations were late to develop and often ephemeral in Nicaragua, no one organization emerged with an effective representational monopoly.

24. Three of the fifteen founding members were generals. Walter (1993, 107) notes that tensions with cattle ranchers in Chontales and Boaco led Somoza to end the subsidy to the association in 1940 and reassign some of its functions to the Ministry of Agriculture.

25. Three private sector organizations (ASGANIC, the Cámara Nacional de Comercio e Industria de Managua, and a coffee growers' association, the Asociación Agrícola de Nicaragua) were authorized to recommend representatives for the seven-person board (*La Gaceta*, October 29, 1940). Each of these associations was entitled to submit a list of seven candidates for its position on the board, and Nicaragua's president then made the final selections.

26. The regime's institutional partners in INFONAC were vaguely defined, giving Somoza García the greatest flexibility in selecting his private sector allies. One representative was to be drawn from agricultural and the other from industrial activities. Both were to be chosen by the president from a list submitted by "representative national associations," or, failing that, at the president's own discretion.

27. Following World War II, during a period in which he was attempting to cling to power despite substantial domestic and U.S. opposition, Somoza first cozied up with labor, passing progressive labor legislation and cultivating labor support. In spite of this, the regime had to resort to massive fraud to win the 1947 election. Since the labor strategy had certain costs and limited payoff, Somoza shifted again to favor capital by the late 1940s. See Gould (1990, 46–64) for further discussion.

28. Two of the seven representatives were to be chosen from a list drawn up by the Asociación de Industriales de Nicaragua. This association emerged from

a 1957 split in the Cámara de Comercio de Nicaragua. As momentum began to build for industrial expansion in the 1950s, a number of industrialists decided that they needed a separate association to address their specific concerns. A group of twelve industrialists founded the organization and quickly began to recruit more members. In spite of the opposition of the Cámara de Comercio, the group had secured enough support by the early 1960s so that congress reformed the 1934 Ley General de Cámaras de Comercio and granted legal status to the new association in 1965 (CADIN 1975, 2–3).

29. Torres-Rivas (1989, 9, 128) offers this characterization of the Somoza regime, sketching parallels between the Somozas and a "grand vizier" who gives resources to court favorites in order to solidify their loyalty. Drawing on Max Weber's work, Paige (1989, 107) defines this sultanic system as one in which "public authority" is construed as "private prerogative."

30. The Somoza family members or the managers of their properties were also among the top officials in the Cámara Nicaragüense de la Industria Pesquera, the Asociación de Productores de Arroz de Nicaragua, and the Cooperativa Arrocera, S.A. See INDE (1975) for a directory of officials in these organizations, and Austin (1972, 4:14–20) for a discussion of the rice sector.

31. At the 1959 meeting of the ASGANIC general assembly, for example, representatives of BNN, BANIC, BANAMER, and the Bank of London were present (Minutes of the meeting, February 26, 1959).

32. The rest of the beef slaughterhouse industry was also largely controlled by the Somoza family. By the 1970s three of the other six export quality slaughterhouses were controlled either by Somoza (through companies such as CARNIC) or close family members (through Amerrisque, for example, in which his sister, Lilian Somoza de Sevilla Sacasa was a prominent member) (Ballard 1985, 30; Interview, FAGANIC, August 14, 1987).

33. In a rare exception to the rule, a coalition of groups across several sectors formed the Comité de Acción Cívica in 1959 to pressure the government to provide an emergency response following a sharp economic downturn. This organizational effort was particularly successful in the cotton sector, where meetings drew over 1,000 planters (Fiallos Oyanguren 1968, 160). In response the regime granted a number of concessions to cotton producers, including an eight-year suspension, with no interest payments, of their loan obligations (*La Gaceta*, Decree #440, August 28, 1959) and a special C$40 per mz. subsidy. These emergency measures prevented the collapse of both cotton production and the Nicaraguan banking system.

34. Concerns about their economic erosion, for example, helped to galvanize the cotton growers in León to form ANSCA in 1962. This growers' cooperative was designed to be an alternative source of agricultural inputs, the preferred processing and ginning agent, and the negotiator for the export of the fiber. See ANSCA (n.d.). Cotton growers in other regions soon followed suit, establishing cotton cooperatives in Managua, Chinandega, Masaya, and Nueva Segovia.

35. Through the first half of the 1970s the portion of the internal beef price re-

ceived by producers dropped steadily. By 1975 producers received only 47 percent of the final price, whereas processors and intermediaries retained the remainder (Ballard 1985, 32).

36. A peak association is a national-level organization, made up of regional and sectoral associations, that assumes the role of representing that whole segment of society.

37. Acuña (1991) and Weyland (1992), for example, see the size and heterogeneity of business as a surmountable barrier if the other conditions are propitious, and point to the successful establishment of a peak association in Mexico, where the bourgeoisie was highly heterogeneous, to demonstrate the point. It should be noted, however, that the Mexican bourgeoisie continued to be highly fragmented and politically divided in spite of the creation of a peak organization, the Consejo Coordinador Empresarial, in 1975. See Luna et al. (1987) for discussion of the continuing political cleavages in the Mexican elite.

38. According to INDE's second *Informe general de actividades* (1966?, 5), 45 percent of its members were in commerce, 25 percent were in industry, and the remaining 30 percent were in financial institutions, services, professions, etc. The organization began with forty members in 1963 and grew to seventy-six in 1965 mainly through personal recruiting by existing members.

39. In the 1972–78 period, INDE received an average of 60 percent of its funding from international donations (calculated from INDE, *Informe anual*, various years).

40. INDE's activities included ideological orientation, promoting education and training, conducting planning studies, and lobbying the Nicaraguan government. In 1964 it distributed radio and TV programs from other Latin American countries on the evils of communism. With INDE's support, INCAE, an affiliate of the Harvard Business School, was persuaded to locate its main campus in Nicaragua. INDE's Fondo de Préstamos para Universitarios provided funds to send Nicaraguan students to study at INCAE, the UCA, and the UNAN, as well as to attend conferences abroad. The organization also promoted worker vocational training centers and training in "nonpolitical" unionism. Several of these early initiatives were later formalized through the creation of special programs under INDE management, including Educrédito (founded in 1966), which provided scholarships, and the Fundación Nicaragüense de Desarrollo (founded in 1969), which sponsored basic community development projects and rural cooperatives. See INDE (1965, 1966?, 1975).

41. INDE provided a training ground for Nicaragua's future political-economic leadership. The Consejos Ejecutivos of INDE and its affiliates, the Fundación Nicaragüense de Desarrollo and Educrédito, included representatives who would become prominent political actors in the 1980s. Some became Sandinista officials, like Dionisio Marenco, Sandinista minister of SPP, and Pedro Antonio Blandón, director of the Fondo Internacional de Reconstrucción. Others, including Alfonso Robelo and Adolfo Calero, followed more circuitous routes, first taking positions within the Sandinista government and later becoming prominent contra leaders.

42. Affiliated organizations and the number of members in each are as fol-

lows: ACBN (140); Asociación de Distribuidores de Vehículos Automotores (18); ASGANIC (500); Asociación de Instituciones Bancarias de Nicaragua (7); Asociación de Productores de Arroz de Nicaragua (45); Cámara de Comercio (330); CADIN (338); Cámara Nicaragüense de la Construcción (76); Cámara Nicaragüense de la Industria Pesquera (15); INDE (89); Sociedad Cooperativa Anónima de Algodoneros (226); and Sociedad Cooperativa Anónima de Cafeteros (2,000). See INDE (1975) and CADIN (1975).

43. In the report on the associations that founded COSIP, three organizations (INDE, CADIN, and the Asociación de Distribuidores de Vehículos Automotores) noted that they had no representation on any government board or agency. In contrast, ACBN and the Cámara de Comercio reported having representation in two or more government agencies, and ASGANIC and the Cámara Nicaragüense de la Industria Pesquera reported having general access to government officials. See "Directorio del COSIP," in INDE (1975, 1–20).

44. Until COSEP's bylaws were modified in 1988, INDE's president automatically became the president of COSIP/COSEP.

45. After years of low prices that caused heavy losses for producers, cotton prices began to rise in the early 1970s. Nicaraguan producers were presented with offers to buy the 1973–74 harvest at the startling price of US$30–40 per qt. oro. Unaccustomed to such high offers, growers moved quickly to sign futures contracts. In the months that followed, Nicaraguan producers watched while the high profits they had anticipated were steadily eroded as many of their costs more than doubled. International prices continued to climb far above the prices growers had accepted early in 1973, reaching US$80 per qt. oro in September. According to Baumeister (1983, 67), the earnings of a grower with 500 mz. of cotton could vary by over US$200,000, depending on the month of 1973–74 in which he or she sold the crop. When growers turned to the Somoza government for support in renegotiation of the contracts, they were rebuffed; instead of deciding in favor of Nicaraguan producers, Somoza aligned himself with foreign intermediaries. In March 1974 he issued a decree requiring producers to hand over at least 70 percent of the contracted cotton at the contracted price (Cruz and Hoadley 1975).

46. Following protests by independent cattle producers, Somoza finally pushed ASGANIC to open its membership and revise its statutes. At a dramatic meeting of the association's general assembly in 1975 that was attended by its honorary president, Anastasio Somoza Debayle, ASGANIC president and Somoza relative Oscar Sevilla Sacasa presided over an internal reorganization of the association (Minutes from April 9, 1975, meeting). The reorganization expanded the Junta Directiva from nine to twelve members, creating three new positions that were filled by reform-oriented members. In spite of these changes, ASGANIC remained an exclusive, elite association.

47. Somoza agreed to send a delegate to participate in this church-mediated dialogue, but only if it were postponed until after the local elections in February 1978. INDE leaders accepted this delay, but members of Los Doce rejected the proposal.

48. Los Doce included Emilio Baltodano Pallais (manager of Café Soluble,

Inc.), Fernando Cardenal (Jesuit priest and professor at the UCA), Ernesto Castillo Martínez (lawyer and bookstore owner), Ricardo Coronel Kautz (director of the livestock division of the Ingenio San Antonio and agricultural engineer), Arturo Cruz (economist with the IDB in Washington, D.C.), Joaquín Cuadra Chamorro (lawyer with BANAMER and Nicaraguan Sugar Estates, Ltd.), Miguel D'Escoto (Maryknoll priest and then communications secretary for the World Council of Churches), Carlos Gutiérrez Sotelo (dental surgeon), Felipe Mántica Abaunza (member of the board of directors of BANAMER and manager of a supermarket chain, who subsequently withdrew from the group), Sergio Ramírez Mercado (prominent writer and FSLN activist), Casimiro Sotelo F. (architect), and Carlos Tunnerman Bernheim (former rector of UNAN).

49. See Edmisten (1990). UDEL was formed in 1974 by a coalition of parties that were boycotting the September elections in which Somoza's presidency was renewed for seven more years.

50. The signatories of a February 4, 1978, communiqué supporting the continuing strike were INDE; CADIN; the Cámara de Comercio de Nicaragua; the Cámara Nicaragüense de la Construcción; the Cámara de Agentes Aduaneros, Almacenadores y Embarcadores de Nicaragua; the Cooperativa de Algodoneros de Managua; the Organización Nicaragüense de Agencias de Publicidad; the Asociación de Distribuidores de Vehículos Automotores; the Asociación de Ferreteros de Nicaragua; the Asociación Nicaragüense de Ingenieros y Arquitectos; the Sociedad Cooperativa Anónima de Cafetaleros de Nicaragua; the Asociación Nacional de Anunciantes de Nicaragua; ACBN; Federación de Sociedades Médicas de Nicaragua; Cámara de Ingenieros y Arquitectos Consultores; and the Asociación Nicaragüense de Distribuidores de Petroleo (INDE 1978).

51. Although the FAO contained members closely aligned with the FSLN, it generally represented an establishment reform movement. The twenty-one signatories of its founding program included such figures as Rafael Córdova Rivas of UDEL, Adolfo Calero Portocarrero of the Partido Conservador Auténtico, Sergio Ramírez Mercado of Los Doce, and Alfonso Robelo Callejas of the MDN. The FAO's program called for the reorganization of the military; an end to corruption; the termination of human rights abuses; the release of political prisoners; freedom of expression and organization; profit sharing; agrarian reform; improvements in health care, housing, and public transportation; price controls; the adoption of a literacy plan; tax reform; local government autonomy; and free elections. See FAO, "Programa Democrático del Gobierno Nacional del Frente Amplio Opositor," in IHCA (1978).

52. The three original sectors in UPANIC were given the greatest representation, but all affiliates secured some voting strength. The UPANIC board of directors was composed of CAAN (6 members), FAGANIC (6), UNCAFENIC (6), ANAR (2), ANPROBA (2), ANPROSOR (2), ASCANIC (2), and FONDILAC (2) (UPANIC n.d.).

53. Two members of the Junta Directiva broke off and formed a new association. Headed by Ernesto Salazar, one of the reformers who had joined ASGANIC during the 1975 reorganization, a new Federacion de Asociaciones de Ganaderos de Nicaragua (FAGANIC), was established (Minutes of ASGANIC's meeting, May 11, 1979).

FAGANIC was set up by the ACBN, the dissident wing of the ASGANIC, and regional representatives from Boaco, Camoapa, Chontales, Granada, Jinotega, Matagalpa, Rivas and Zelaya. See *La Gaceta*, August 21, 1980.

Chapter 3

1. On the argument linking high-ranking Sandinistas to the traditional elite families, see Stone (1990, 37–40); Vilas (1992).

2. See also the amplification in Decree #38 issued August 8, 1979 (CIERA 1989, 8:251–53).

3. State trade monopolies were established for cotton, coffee, sugar, banana, beef, and nontraditional exports.

4. See Brinton's (1938) classic work on the stages of revolution and the internal divisions that shape the process.

5. In 1975 the FSLN leaders divided and three factions emerged: the Guerra Popular Prolongada tendency, led by Tomás Borge, Henry Ruiz, and Bayardo Arce; the Tendencia Proletaria, led by Jaime Wheelock, Luis Carrión, and Carlos Núñez; and the Tendencia Insurreccional, or Terceristas, led by Daniel Ortega, Humberto Ortega, and Victor Tirado. Each faction inclined toward a different insurrectional strategy. The Terceristas, who were most eclectic in their tactics, least ideological in their recruiting strategy, and most optimistic about the prospects for immediate success, built the largest following drawing on spontaneous support that arose in the wake of national guard abuses. The three factions reunited in March 1979. See FSLN (1990a).

6. Four of the nine members of the FSLN national directorate assumed ministerial responsibilities: Humberto Ortega was minister of defense; Tomás Borge was minister of the interior; Jaime Wheelock added the Ministry of Agriculture to his portfolio as director of the Ministry of Agrarian Reform; and Henry Ruiz became minister of planning. The number of seats in the Consejo de Estado was increased from 33 to 47; 12 of the 14 new slots were assigned to pro-FSLN organizations (Booth 1985a, 191).

7. The "Análisis de la Coyuntura y Tareas de la Revolución Popular Sandinista," popularly known as the 72-Hour Document, summarized the conclusions of the September 21–23, 1979, meeting by naming the "sell-out bourgeoisie" as "the main instrument of the counterrevolution" (FSLN 1990b, 91).

8. On the FSLN internal structure, see Gilbert (1988, 41–78).

9. Under the leadership of Jorge Salazar, UPANIC attempted to recruit among small producers, particularly *cafetaleros* in the Matagalpa region. According to records of the Asociación de Cafetaleros de Matagalpa, this effort raised membership in their association (then named the Cooperativa de Cafetaleros) to over 7,000 in 1980 (interview, Asociación de Cafetaleros de Matagalpa, August 16, 1986; see also Christian 1986, 202). Following Salazar's death, UPANIC's recruitment efforts among small producers fizzled.

10. Expropriated under Decreto #759 were Santa Mónica, S.A.; Inversiones

Comerciales, S.A.; Corporación Plaza España, S.A.; Constructora Habitacional, S.A.; Sociedad General de Inversiones Urbanos, S.A.; Promotora Terramica, S.A.; Valle Gothel, S.A.; Sociedad General de Turismo, S.A.; Museo y Cultura, S.A.; AMCASA; Jabonería Prego, S.A.; Fábrica de Productos Lácteos "La Perfecta"; Fábrica de Helados "La Perfecta," S.A.; Industrial Ganadera de Oriente, S.A.; and Matadero San Martín. This group included two of Managua's most important shopping complexes as well as several large family-owned industries.

11. The government agreed to compensate expropriated land with payments in bonds based on declared tax value for the last three years. Compensation, however, was not required if the land had been abandoned (although in practice compensation was sometimes provided if the finding in the case was "administrative abandonment," i.e., the estate was no longer being administered productively but the owner had not departed the country) (interview, Mireya Molina, former director, MIDINRA, Tenencia de la Tierra, October 1, 1990). Land that was sharecropped or given out in a service-for-labor arrangement could be expropriated if the estate was larger than 50 mz. in the Pacific region or 100 mz. elsewhere. (See CIERA 1989, vol. 8; Deere et al. 1985; Mayorga 1990.)

12. See IHCA (1981). Some of the signatories who were out of the country or who fled into embassies for protection avoided prison sentences, but three were convicted and sentenced to 210 days in prison. All were released within four months, a concession not granted to leaders of the left-wing Frente Obrero who were convicted on a similar charge during this time period.

13. Over time, the *campesinistas* divided into two camps: those who favored collective cooperatives (CAS) and those who, following the preferences of most peasants themselves, endorsed individual land ownership and, at most, the credit and service cooperatives (CCS). (See Deere et al. 1985.) As the contra war escalated, the latter group gained some political leverage. Programs of land titling, which gave legal title to squatters in the agricultural frontier, and for land redistribution to individual recipients, which gave land without the requirement that recipients participate in cooperatives, increased the number of individuals receiving land and other benefits in Nicaragua's agrarian reform program (Mayorga 1990). For much of the period, including even the later years, however, the general trend among *campesinistas* and in the distribution of land and credit was to favor the CAS over the CCS and individual claimants.

14. The Cuban government ultimately forgave Nicaraguan debt obligations (valued at an estimated $73.8 million) for the construction of the sugar mill, Victoria de Julio. (See Brundenius 1987, 103.)

15. Ricardo and Manuel Coronel Kautz, MIDINRA vice-ministers and twin brothers who had been educated in agricultural programs in the United States and Europe and had spent decades as top administrators at the ISA, were ardent defenders of the state-centered, high-tech model. See M. Coronel Kautz (1984); R. Coronel Kautz (1984); interviews, Ricardo Coronel Kautz, October 30 and November 2, 1990.

16. These included a rum manufacturing and distribution network, both a

national (BANAMER) and an offshore (BAC International Credit Corporation) bank, a national auto and auto parts distributorship, and a large cattle ranch. Information on the Grupo Pellas holdings comes from the MIDINRA *cédula de notificación* that accompanied the 1988 expropriation of ISA and its subsidiaries, and from interview, Nicaragua Sugar Estates, Ltd., September 21, 1990.

17. The state took over 264,448 mz. between October 1981 and December 1982 but redistributed only 134,234 mz. (Cardenal Downing 1988, 48).

18. For discussion of this issue, see Deere et al. (1985); see also Wheelock's speech to 400 directors of APP operations, reported in *Barricada*, March 7, 1985.

19. Twenty-four percent of the divested land was "idle" or "fallow" land, 19 percent was forested, 19 percent was unimproved pasture, and 9 percent was land designated as inappropriate for agricultural use. See Cardenal Downing (1988, 178).

20. Data on land use patterns on APP farms are consistent with this interpretation. During the period when APP lands were being transferred, the percent of land on APP farms that was idle dropped from 19 percent in 1981 to 14 percent in 1986 (CIERA 1989, 1:298).

21. Indeed, studies of sectoral production patterns indicate that the percent of national production that came from the state farm sector actually increased marginally between 1981–82 and 1986–87 from 21 percent of the total to 22 percent, even though the percent of the farmland held by this sector was dropping sharply (Baumeister 1988, 30; CIERA 1989, 1:332).

22. One of the country's main supporters of the large-scale state projects explained: "After 1983, our views became the central theme. It was like in an orchestra where there are several musical themes being played at the same time but there's one central one. That was ours" (interview, November 2, 1990).

23. This was the label applied disparagingly by critics like Martínez Cuenca (1990) to MIDINRA's large-scale agroindustrial projects.

24. See the discussion of development and investment planning in Kleiterp 1988; see also Argüello Huper and Kleiterp 1985.

25. MIDINRA's Dirección Superior (1984, 23) reported to the JGRN in early 1984 that 61 percent of MIDINRA's investment funds had gone to the state farm sector whereas coops and individuals had received 39 percent. Hard currency capital goods imports were even more narrowly targeted to the state sector. CIERA director Orlando Núñez Soto (1987, 142) found that 89 percent of the foreign exchange spent to import capital goods for the agricultural sector in the 1980–84 period went to the APP; 64 percent of these funds went to the sugar sector for the Victoria de Julio sugar mill.

26. Note that Baumeister's (1991, 15) estimates about land distribution by sector for 1988 deviate modestly from that published in CIERA (1989, 9:115), presented here as Table 3.2. The main difference is in the calculation about land held in large, private estates, which Baumeister estimates at 13.5 percent of agricultural land in 1988 instead of 7.5 percent.

27. Data in Table 3.3 cover only land acquired through the application of agrarian reform laws and not that obtained through Somoza expropriations, dona-

tions, or sales. Approximately 62 percent of the reformed land was acquired in the early confiscations that centered on the expropriation of the landholdings of the Somoza family and its allies. Roughly 31 percent of the reformed land was acquired through the subsequent expropriation of non-*somocista* landowners under agrarian reform legislation (interview, Mireya Molina Torres, former director of MIDINRA's Tenencia de la Tierra division, October 1, 1990).

28. Núñez Soto (1991, 392–402) concludes that this strategy was counterproductive, especially in the cattle region where muted class divisions made even small producers resent expropriations of elites.

29. See Wheelock interview, *Barricada*, April 25, 1986, and MIDINRA, División de Comunicaciones (1986, 4). According to Mireya Molina, around 100 of these confiscations (roughly 7 percent of the total) were reversed or partially reversed under appeal, and around 80,000 mz. were returned to former owners (interview, October 1, 1990).

30. See also Luciak (1987) for discussion of this negotiation process and how it fit into the agrarian reform initiatives of 1985.

31. The government's response varied from case to case and included increasing the payment, suspending the purchase, returning the property, agreeing to only lease the land, or declaring the deal closed as it was originally agreed upon. This wide variation in government responses contributed to the view among private producers that there was no consistent or principled policy being followed, and that everything depended on the particularities of the negotiation process (personal connections, bribes, political animosities, etc.).

32. Banks loans increased from C$2,522 million in 1978 to C$4,308 million in 1981 (CIERA/PAN/CIDA 1984, 41).

33. Medium- and large-sized producers are defined here as those with more than 50 mz. Land data are from Table 3.2.

34. Data presented in the Argüello Huper and Kleiterp investment study (1985, 68–69) show that private investment accounted for an average of 61 percent of all investment in the 1960–78 period. It dropped, after the revolution, to only 39 percent of the total in 1981–83. An open question here is whether or not the private sector, skittish about expropriation, even wanted to undertake serious long-term investments. Clearly part of the reduction in investment responded to the producers' unwillingness to take on these obligations or design projects that might win bank support. As the gap between the interest rates and the rate of inflation widened, however, and bank loans became virtual gifts, resistance to borrowing on the part of producers dissipated. See the discussion of this issue in the following chapter.

35. *Crédito bancario* clients and APP were charged the highest interest rates on their loans. For example, in the 1981–84 period, the standard interest rate charged to APP and medium- and large-sized producers was 17 percent, whereas individual peasant producers in the *crédito rural* program paid 13 percent, CCS members paid 10 percent, and CAS members were charged a low 8 percent (CIERA 1989, 1:261). Since the inflation rate was much higher than any of these interest rates (ranging

from 22 to 50 percent during this period), all bank clients received subsidies (CEPAL 1985, 2).

36. According to one rough calculation of the loan recuperation rate, repayment in the 1981–84 period averaged 56 percent in the small producer/coop program, 55 percent in the APP sector, and 90 percent in the regular bank program for the private sector (Enríquez and Spalding 1987, 117).

37. In this work, Baumeister defines medium- and large-sized producers as those private producers who were enrolled in the regular bank credit program. Large producers are those receiving bank credit for the cultivation of more than 100 mz. in agricultural products or more than 1,000 mz. for livestock. The remainder are classified as medium-sized producers.

38. Middle-sized is defined here as 50–500 mz. for cotton production, 200–1,000 qt. for coffee, and 200–1,000 mz. for cattle ranches (Baumeister 1984b, 12).

39. Thus Wheelock could describe with enthusiasm the sustained erosion of properties larger than 500 mz. In his introduction to CIERA's nine-volume summary work, *La reforma agraria en Nicaragua, 1979–1989,* Wheelock looks back on the decade of reform and observes, "Between the time of the triumph of the Revolution and the present, almost all of the agricultural production [units] with more than 500 mz., and a considerable portion of the cattle ranches of that size, have been expropriated for purposes of agrarian reform." He notes that only in Region V, the country's main cattle ranching area, did large properties continue to exist. In that region, 18 percent of the land was still held in properties larger than 500 mz. In the Pacific region and in the northern interior, however, only 5 percent and 4 percent, respectively, were still held in these large estates (CIERA 1989, 1:29–30).

40. More of the estates were expropriated for reasons of abandonment in 1986 than had been the case previously. In 1981–84, only 20 percent of the cases were charged with abandonment; 61 percent of the expropriations resulted from the charge that the land was idle or inefficiently used (Cardenal Downing 1988, 46). In 35 percent of the 1986 cases, however, abandonment was listed as the sole or first cause given for the expropriation. That the land was inefficiently used or idle was charged in 27 percent of the cases. In 14 percent of the cases, the owners were found to have illegally arranged a sharecropping or labor-for-service agreement with local peasants. The remainder of the cases (24 percent) were expropriated for reasons of public utility or for use in an agricultural development zone (MIDINRA, Dirección de Tenencia de la Tierra 1987).

41. According to his calculations, 53 percent of the land that was handed out came from state farms, and another 39 percent came from private estates larger than 500 mz.

42. The guaranteed price for rice rose from 55 córdobas per qt. (granz) in 1979/80 to 164 córdobas in 1981/82, while that for coffee remained static at 1,000 córdobas per qt. oro and that for cotton rose only from 600 córdobas per qt. oro to 840 (CIERA 1989, 1:268).

43. Reasons for this are complex. Rice production had developed rapidly in the 1960s and 1970s, and the private producers, some of whom were trained as engineers, had a strong commitment to maximize productivity. These producers tended to use their land fully and efficiently, unlike cattle ranchers or coffee producers, who often left much of their land idle. Furthermore, the type of soil appropriate for rice production was inappropriate for most other crops, so rice tended to be produced in regions where peasant land pressure was not high. Finally, this sector was ably led. Unlike many private sector organizations in Nicaragua, it did not adopt a highly confrontational strategy toward the Sandinistas. According to a comparative study of private sector organizations in Central America by Julio Sergio Ramírez Arango (1985, 364–78), ANAR adopted a "limited stakes strategy" in dealing with the government, taking a low public profile, emphasizing technical arguments, and taking a long-term view of the situation. This approach made it more effective in its negotiations with the regime than the six other Nicaraguan private sector organizations evaluated in that study.

44. Private rice producers affiliated with ANAR were also able, after some opposition from the government, to secure long-term investment credits with which to finance 50 percent of the costs of building a new rice seed plant. Furthermore, the proscriptions on private exporting were lifted for ANAR affiliates, who were allowed to market their own semolina (rice bran) in Costa Rica and retain the hard currency earnings thus generated (interviews, Mario Hanón, August 23, 1986; May 3, 1990).

45. Spoor and Mendoza (1988, 31) argue that large sorghum producers often had investments in the cattle or poultry sectors and also benefited from being able to use unsold portions of the sorghum crop in these related activities.

46. Indeed, even those producing export crops were able to take advantage of the government-run pricing system, especially when the export crop was also an input for the domestic food system, as in the case of cottonseed. When international cotton prices fell in the 1980s, the government provided subsidies that kept cotton production alive in Nicaragua. Trevor Evans (1987, 14) found that cotton production levels in El Salvador and Guatemala in 1984 were only 43 percent and 54 percent, respectively, of the production levels obtained in 1974–76. In Nicaragua, although cotton output had certainly declined, the 1984 production level was noticeably higher, reaching 67 percent of the 1974–76 level. Even when the evidence mounted that the cotton subsidies took a toll on the rest of the economy (Evans 1987, 19), the Sandinista government was slow to suspend them.

47. The term is derived from the verb *chapear*, meaning to clear or prepare the land for use. Baumeister (1988, 31) defines the term as a synonym for *plebeian*.

48. Núñez was a rough-hewn cattle rancher whose experiences as a revolutionary Christian led him into conflict with the Somoza government that resulted in his imprisonment and torture. He was released from prison as part of the exchange negotiated by the FSLN following the Christmas kidnapping of a group of local notables in 1974. After the revolution, he donated his property to the govern-

ment and became the MIDINRA regional delegate in the coffee-growing region of Matagalpa and Jinotega. In 1984 he formally left the government to take over the leadership of UNAG (interview, Daniel Núñez, May 6, 1990).

49. See the full page discussion of the meeting, with special inserts on the role of large producers, in the FSLN newspaper, *Barricada*, July 9, 1984.

Chapter 4

1. Argüello Huper and Kleiterp (1985, 60–65) also found that these projects overemphasized agroindustrial investment (especially the cattle sector) relative to the rest of the economy, used and produced little that was supplied by or absorbed into the rest of the economy, focused too heavily on exports, were launched without feasibility studies, and continued unchanged even after the evidence of their negative impact mounted.

2. Tax pressure (tax revenues as a percent of GDP) had risen from 11 percent in 1977 (FitzGerald 1984a, 5) to 18.4 percent in 1980. (See Appendix 2, Table A.3.) With the imposition of new taxes, the tax pressure continued rising to 30.7 percent of GDP in 1984 before the soaring inflation rates and delayed tax payments started to erode the revenues collected. See Lance Taylor et al. (1989, 15) for discussion of the "Olivera-Tanzi effect" and its impact in Nicaragua.

3. For example, authorized imports could be acquired in January 1988 for an average exchange rate of C\$536:US\$1 whereas exports earned, on average, C\$6,840:US\$1 (Hernández 1990, 5).

4. According to Arana Sevilla et al. (1987, 49), in 1986 35 percent of imports were raw materials and intermediate goods, with petroleum representing another 17 percent. Consumer goods, which were more restricted, represented 19 percent. Capital goods imports, so emphasized in the development model, composed another 20 percent of the total.

5. By 1985 84 percent of official external financing was provided by socialist countries (Stahler-Sholk 1987, 162).

6. In his 1990 book reflecting on this period, Martínez Cuenca reports repeated clashes with both Ruiz and MIDINRA head Jaime Wheelock. He describes what he viewed as the "distrust some FSLN leaders had of me and of the project that we pushed for from the Ministry of Foreign Trade" (Martínez Cuenca 1990, 99). In a subsequent interview, he described pressures he faced in meetings with members of the FSLN national directorate. After presenting his ideas for budgetary cuts or reallocations, he reported that he would be told, "You can proceed with that plan, or you can understand that we are at war" (interview, August 16, 1991).

7. For discussion of the 1985 measures, see Pizarro (1987); IHCA (1986).

8. See CIERA (1988, 302–19); IHCA (1988c, 16); *Latin American Economic Report*, 88–02 (February 29, 1988), 16.

9. For example, the price of gasoline increased by a factor of twelve and, as a result, interurban transportation prices were multiplied by six. See IHCA (1988c).

10. Indeed, costs did rise more rapidly for producers using "modern" technolo-

gies than those using traditional approaches. Utting found, for example, that maize producers whose production was mechanized had the lowest per-unit production costs among the different types of maize producers in 1983–84. Following price adjustments in 1988–89, however, this modern group had one of the highest such cost ratios. Their production costs in February 1990 surpassed official producer prices by 19 percent. Nonetheless, the production costs for maize rose quickly for all groups and were higher in February 1990 than official prices regardless of the type of technology employed. Of the three major staples analyzed by Utting, only beans and traditional (rainfed) rice production were profitable in early 1990 (Utting 1991, 28–30).

11. In December 1987, prior to the 1988 reforms, the top salary on the officially approved salary scale was eight times that at the bottom. Following the February 1988 reform, the top salary was fifteen times that at the bottom (Gutiérrez 1989, 177; Hernández 1990, 5).

12. See IHCA (1988c, 28–42; 1989, 48); Zalkin (1990, 60–61).

13. In 1984 only 16,000 mz. were transferred to individuals under the agrarian reform program. In 1985 and 1986 this increased to 143,000 and 138,000 mz., respectively. Although the amount of land transferred to cooperatives continued to surpass that transferred to individuals (coops received 180,000 and 199,000 mz., respectively, in 1985 and 1986), individual petitioners were less disadvantaged in those two years than they were in either the 1980–84 period or afterward in 1987 (when they received only 6,000 mz. compared with 172,000 mz. for the cooperatives). (See Cardenal Downing 1988; Mayorga 1991, 38).

14. For example, in the Valle de Sébaco vegetable processing plant project, cooperatives were integrated as producers of vegetables for processing. OAS project director Daniel Slutzky reported that eleven of the twenty ongoing projects incorporated cooperative production in their plans for 1987. (See discussion in CIERA 1989, 1:346–47.)

15. See interview with Ramiro Gurdián, *Nuevo Diario*, June 18, 1988, following the second round of structural adjustments. Some of the enthusiasm of this sector declined a few weeks later when Mario Alegría, director of INIESEP, COSEP's economic research arm, was arrested and convicted on charges of selling government economic data to the U.S. Embassy in Managua.

16. The data for 1988 do not include the case of the ISA, since that expropriation was subsequently converted into a sale. See details below.

17. Data for 1989 were provided by the Dirección de Políticas Agrarias, Instituto Nicaragüense de Reforma Agraria, August 1991.

18. See Decreto #333, "Ley Creadora de las Comisiones Consultativas de Política Agropecuaria," approved by the JGRN, February 29, 1980, in CIERA 1989, 8:130–33. This decree created commissions for producers of cotton, beef, milk, chicken and pork, rice, bananas, sugar, coffee, and basic grains. These commissions were to be composed of representatives of five government agencies (the Ministry of Agricultural Development, the Ministry of Planning, the Agrarian Reform Institute, either the Foreign Trade Ministry or the Internal Trade Ministry, and the

Ministry of Labor) plus a representative from the producers' association affiliated with UPANIC to speak for large producers, a representative of small producers, a representative of the Sandinista-backed ATC for rural laborers, and a second union representative from an unspecified labor organization.

19. See, for example, the minutes of the March 23, 1984, meeting of the "Comité de Cosecha" for cotton producers in Region II, and the "Convenio Salarial Relativo a las Actividades de la Rama del Desmote de Algodón," signed February 1, 1984.

20. In my sample, two members of the economic elite who were first cousins of Sandinista ministers, for example, noted that they had broken all communication with those ministers and refused to attend family functions at which the ministers were present. In the Nicaraguan case, one should not assume automatically that family connections imply privileged treatment or political affinity.

21. According to the MIDINRA official responsible for overseeing the commissions, industrialists were less inclined than agricultural producers to reject government attempts at technical consultation. The industrialists' greater experience in negotiating with the government for licenses and permits in the prerevolutionary period, plus their heavy consumption of imports requiring scarce foreign exchange, made them somewhat more accommodating (interview, Mary Jane Mulligan, directora de políticas económicas del MIDINRA, August 22, 1986; see also Dijkstra 1992).

22. The government did begin, in 1986, to supply some of the UPANIC associations with items needed for production. Since the dues collected by these organizations were often inadequate to meet their rising costs, these associations stayed afloat by selling government-supplied production inputs to their members. Curiously, at the time when the government and COSEP affiliates were most at odds, the government distribution policy helped these associations to both cover their costs and hold on to their membership. See Spalding (1988).

23. Decreto #347, April 18, 1988, reprinted in CIERA 1989, 8:181–87. Five commissions were set up, but the commissions for rice and for sorghum were later combined. The composition of the commissions varied slightly, but they all included an executive president named by Wheelock and representatives of the BND, the rural labor association ATC, and relevant state corporations (such as the Corporación Nicaragüense de la Carne and the Corporación Nicaragüense de la Leche in the Livestock Commission). See CNG (1989). The private sector was represented usually by four delegates from UPANIC affiliates and four delegates from UNAG, as well as relevant private processors (such as the owner of a top private cotton gin in the National Cotton Commission). Although Jaime Wheelock ultimately named those who would participate in these commissions, most were nominated by their respective associations. Even some prominent critics of the regime (like Matagalpan *cafetalero* Jaime Cuadra, who refused to attend the meetings) were named to these commissions.

24. Interviews, executive presidents of the National Coffee Commission, May 5, 1990; the National Cotton Commission, June 6, 1990; the National Livestock Commission, September 10, 1990; and the National Rice and Sorghum Com-

mission, May 7, 1990. See also the Foro Soció-Económico section, *Barricada*, January 15, 1990. Three of the four executive presidents were linked by family ties to large cotton families of León, helping the government to make connections with the agrarian elite.

25. Like most analysts, O'Donnell and Schmitter differentiate between political and economic *concertación*. Political *concertación* or pact making produced agreements governing the transition to pluralistic democracy in much of Latin America as the military began to withdraw from control over the executive. Social and economic *concertación* was often also attempted, sometimes as part of the drafting of a new constitution. O'Donnell and Schmitter argue that the latter was more difficult to achieve, given the economic disarray that was often part of the military's legacy and the absence of peak associations that could orchestrate the construction and enforcement of these pacts (O'Donnell and Schmitter 1986, 45–47).

26. Unionization reportedly increased from 11 percent of the salaried workforce in 1979 to 56 percent in 1986 (Stahler-Sholk 1992, 4).

27. Thirty key representatives participated, including Antonio Lacayo, the newly restored general manager of GRACSA, and Carlos Mántica, who managed 3,500 mz. of family cotton production and was one of the largest producers in the country. See *Barricada*, January 27, 1989.

28. See *Nuevo Diario*, January 26, 1989, and *Barricada*, February 4, 1989.

29. The assembly divided producers into eight groups, based on their primary product. MIDINRA vice-minister Salvador Mayorga nominated secretaries for each of the groups, alternately selecting between UPANIC and UNAG representatives. Delegates from UPANIC were named to head the cotton, cattle, and rice committees; UNAG delegates were selected for the coffee, basic grains, and sorghum committees. Each group drafted a series of recommendations and requests, which the government responded to on the second day of the conference (*Barricada*, April 21, 1989; interview, Mario Hanón, August 26, 1989).

30. According to Vilas (1990), some of the concessions made to cotton producers had not even been requested.

31. See "Gobierno responde a los productores," *Barricada*, April 21, 1989, and "Estímulo y garantía: ¡¡¡Todos a producir!!!," *Nuevo Diario*, April 21, 1989.

32. Ortega asked private growers to join the state in setting aside land for a national land bank for the landless, but this was to be done on a voluntary basis (*Nuevo Diario*, April 21, 1989).

33. See *Barricada*, May 23, 1989. Most members of the delegation were either affiliated with UNAG or were not affiliated with any organization. Two officials from UPANIC's dairy association, FONDILAC, however, accompanied the delegation, including the association's president.

34. See discussion of the media coverage in IHCA (1989, 50).

35. In my sample of ninety-one private sector leaders, forty-six (50.5 percent) noted that at least one member of their immediate family (spouse or children) had gone abroad to live at some point during the Sandinista period.

36. By the mid-1980s, a policy of exempting one son from active service for the families of medium- and large-sized agricultural producers was formalized, replacing a system of ad-hoc exemptions. The fear that overzealous military recruiters might spirit their sons off to war in one of the periodic roundups that occurred, however, prompted even many of those eligible for exemptions to send their sons out of the country.

37. In contrast with other hegemonic elites from the prerevolutionary period, the Pellas family had reached a modus vivendi with the Sandinista government, continuing in the early years to make investments and requesting in 1983, in correspondence with then U.S. ambassador Anthony Quainton, that the U.S. government's decision to cut off the Nicaraguan sugar quota be reversed. (See *Nuevo Diario*, May 11, 1983.) Although the government claimed that the production drop and unstanched decapitalization going on at the mill in 1988 mandated state intervention, the perception grew among private elites that the Sandinistas were unreliable even in dealings with their friends in the bourgeoisie.

38. This group was composed of Arnoldo Alemán, president of UNCAFENIC; Nicolas Bolaños, former president of UNCAFENIC and brother of former COSEP president Enrique Bolaños; and Jaime Cuadra, long-term president of the Asociación de Cafetaleros de Matagalpa. At a public meeting of coffee producers in Matagalpa in June 1989, these producers, among others, orchestrated a ringing critique of the regime and announced the withdrawal of UPANIC affiliates from the newly created national coffee commission, CONCAFE. Within days their estates were taken over by the regime on the grounds that they had conspired to organize an act of economic sabotage by urging coffee producers to halt production. See "Cafetaleros se retiran de CONCAFE," *La Prensa*, June 19, 1989; "Respuesta a saboteadores," *Barricada*, June 22, 1989.

39. A contract was signed with ISA owners in January 1989 in which the government agreed to pay $637,000 for the land surrounding the mill and $12 million for the ISA itself, making payments of $1 million a year for twelve years. The government failed to meet the payment schedule, and the Pellas family challenged the contract in 1990 after the UNO government was elected (interview, Nicaraguan Sugar Estates, Ltd., September 21, 1990).

40. The three affected producers refused the offer, not wanting to further the regime's electoral chances by allowing it to undo the damage it had done. These estates were finally returned to their former owners in the period of transition after the February 25, 1990, electoral defeat of the Sandinistas and before the April 25, 1990, inauguration of the UNO government (interviews, Nicolas Bolaños, August 25, 1989, and October 15, 1990; *La Prensa*, March 23, 1990).

41. By its own regulations, UPANIC could not technically expel representatives of constituent associations, and FONDILAC officers rejected the push to oust López from the presidency. López remained a member of the UPANIC directorate, but in practice his association was subsequently represented by his alternate (interview, Juan Diego López, February 20, 1990).

42. See "Ocho gremios se retiran de Comisiones Nacionales," *La Prensa*,

June 23, 1989; "Cafetaleros de Jinotega se mantienen en CONCAFE," *Barricada*, June 22, 1989.

43. See "Se reintegran a comisiones desobedeciendo al COSEP," *Nuevo Diario*, July 14, 1989.

44. On August 7, 1987, the presidents of the Central American countries signed the Central American Accord, widely known as Esquipulas II or the Arias Plan. This agreement prohibited support for irregular forces attempting to destabilize regional governments, called for the restoration of civil and political rights, and committed all five governments to democratic electoral processes.

45. Nicaraguan members were Dreyfus and Mayorga along with Orlando Núñez, director of CIERA, and Xabier Gorostiaga, director of CRIES.

46. The commission recommended a substantially increased flow of development assistance: $2.5 billion over a three-year period for the displaced and poor, and another $2 billion per year in general financial assistance for the next five years (Comisión Internacional para la Recuperación y el Desarrollo de Centroamérica 1989, 5).

47. See CORDENIC (1988). In addition to Dreyfus and Mayorga, the group included business leaders Felipe Mántica, Pablo Ayón, Filadelfo Chamorro, Carlos Reynaldo Lacayo, Antonio Lacayo, and José Francisco Rosales.

48. COSEP wags promptly labeled CORDENIC "COSEP-Héroes y Mártires" (a takeoff on the name used by the Sandinista-aligned CONAPRO-Héroes y Mártires), implying a political affinity between CORDENIC and the FSLN.

49. According to biographical information attached to the CORDENIC mission statement and released at the press conference announcing the formation of the group, members included graduates of McGill, Georgetown, MIT, Harvard, Yale, and the Sorbonne. Three were members of university advisory boards in Nicaragua, and four had at some point been full- or part-time university professors. They owned or were major stockholders in some of the country's largest commercial houses, distributorships, import-export businesses, and agroindustrial complexes. See CORDENIC (1988, Anexo 1).

50. In interviews in 1990, several of the private sector leaders affiliated with UPANIC organizations described participating in social gatherings with FSLN leaders in the last years of the Sandinista government. These informal interactions were generally viewed as a breakthrough that allowed producers to speak honestly and reduced their fear of the regime.

51. In 1984 COSEP leaders had been the prime force behind the creation of the anti-Sandinista Coordinadora Democrática, a coalition of COSEP plus several small unions and political parties. After naming their presidential candidate, IDB functionary Arturo Cruz, and mounting an unofficial campaign, the Coordinadora declined to formally register Cruz in the race, claiming that the conditions for a free and fair election were missing. According to Cruz, business leaders in COSEP were responsible for the decision to pull him from the contest (interview with Arturo Cruz, December 9, 1987; see also Gutman 1988).

52. For a fuller discussion of that election, see LASA (1984). Observer teams

were also sent from the British Houses of Commons and Lords, the Irish Parliament, the Dutch government, and Socialist International; their conclusions about the elections were generally positive. The abstention rate of 25 percent, however, suggested that some element of popular dissatisfaction was already present. See Oquist (1992).

53. After several rounds of balloting, Chamorro reportedly secured 6 votes from the 14 assembled party representatives in the coalition, passing Bolaños and Godoy, who received 4 each. In the final round of voting on the first day, Chamorro's vote had climbed to 7 but fell short of the required 10 votes for nomination. In the second day of meetings, representatives voted on alternative tickets, with Chamorro paired with either Bolaños or Godoy, and the second combination secured majority support (Taylor 1989).

54. The rift with Bolaños supporters and COSEP was smoothed over, but not eliminated, during the campaign when COSEP president Gilberto Cuadra was named to the inner circle of her personal advisers (*La Prensa*, November 24, 1989).

55. See "Sin Concertación no habrá estabilidad," *La Crónica*, January 3–10, 1990.

56. See *Barricada international* 9, no. 302 (October 14, 1989), for the report on the FSLN convention.

57. See *Barricada*, February 20, 1990, for example. The Nicaraguan electoral system used a party list system and proportional representation. Parties and coalitions presented candidates and alternates ranked in order of priority for each slot they contested. Although the inclusion of private producers in the FSLN list was prominently advertised, most of these candidates were alternates (13 of the 24 advertised in the above ad) or were ranked in the bottom half of their lists. Only 6 of these 24 producers on the FSLN slate were actually elected.

58. According to leaders of FAGANIC, the Sandinistas committed themselves to hand over IFAGAN, formerly the largest slaughterhouse in the nation, to FAGANIC. When the Somoza regime was toppled, some of ASGANIC's property had been transferred to FAGANIC, but the slaughterhouse had been retained by the state (interviews, FAGANIC, September 18, 1990).

59. In an article titled, "Productores reconocen al FSLN como única alternativa," *Barricada* (February 11, 1990) reported conversations with a series of other producers who had recently had expropriated land returned to them.

60. The reliquidation program had been a source of discontent in the sector. The June 1989 meeting at which UPANIC coffee leaders declared their withdrawal from CONCAFE was nominally called to allow a full discussion of this matter.

61. See, for example, Vilas (1990); Petras and Morley (1992, 128–37).

62. Two other, small parties, the Partido Social Cristiano and the Movimiento Unido Revolucionario, won one seat each.

Chapter 5

1. Respondents' views were coded on a five-point scale based on their answers to three questions: What is your opinion of the Sandinista government? What

would you say were the most positive aspects of the Sandinista government? What would you say were the most negative aspects of the Sandinista government?

2. See Anthony Downs (1957) and Gordon Tullock (1979) for pathbreaking work in the rational choice school.

3. Indeed, the motivations of elites in the other categories also reflect considerations beyond simple self-interest as well. Moral-political opponents who baited the regime, for example, were sometimes targeted for expropriation and harassment by police and security forces. Self-interest in those cases might call them to moderate their critique or adopt a lower profile. They eschewed that approach in favor of strident opposition that reflected complex political and philosophical commitments.

4. Of the ninety-one elite leaders I interviewed, twenty-four (26 percent) spontaneously described ways in which they had contributed to the insurrection and the support they had provided to the FSLN during the late 1970s.

5. Postelection survey findings reported by Paul Oquist (1992, 14) estimate that only 10 percent of those classified as owners and proprietors voted for the FSLN in the 1990 election. If this is taken as a baseline, private sector supporters of the FSLN would then be overrepresented in this study. Oversampling in this case may be justified as a way of gathering additional information about a particularly complex and anomalous subsector of the leadership population.

6. Because of these considerations, a purely statistical analysis of the data in this chapter may be problematic. Participants in this study are not a true random sample of the economic elite, but a carefully targeted population of private sector leaders. The contrasts among them are often subtle, and the numbers found in some categories are small. Pearson chi-square statistics are presented here for each table, but these figures should be evaluated with these considerations in mind.

7. Twenty of the respondents (22 percent) participated actively in the 1990 FSLN campaign. Five were FSLN candidates in the election, and another fifteen were involved as FSLN party activists. Reflecting the greater preponderance of opponents to the government among the respondents, forty of those interviewed (44 percent) became actively involved in the UNO campaign, six as candidates.

8. There is ongoing debate in Nicaragua about how to define a middle-sized and a large-sized producer, and no clear consensus has emerged (Molina and Quezada 1990). Ideally, classification schemes should include reference not only to the amount of land held but to the size of the workforce, land quality, type of technology employed, and other such variables. Unfortunately, in a country where there has been no national census for over two decades, such detailed information is not available. Even looking at a single criterion—size of landholding—there has been disagreement about how the parameters should be set.

The most exhaustive work on this topic was done by MIDINRA's research arm, CIERA (CIERA 1981). Recognizing the widely varying levels of return and complexity for different types of subsectors, strata definitions have generally been product specific. (See Appendix 2, Table A.4.)

CIERA definitions were used as a guide in determining strata classifications for the respondents in this survey. In actual practice, however, most of these respondents were engaged in several economic activities simultaneously, making it difficult to classify them by size. It was common, for example, for producers to combine agricultural production and cattle ranching, or to have an urban profession as well as an agricultural enterprise. As a result, a producer could be both a small coffee producer and a medium-sized rancher, or be a lawyer, a medium cotton producer, and a large cattle rancher. These concepts become even more problematic when producers had varying levels of participation in several farms. A producer might be the sole owner of one farm but one of three partners in another. Because of the endless kinds of combinations that emerged in practice, summary classifications here represent careful estimates.

9. The Pearson chi-square value for Table 5.1 is 3.02, and the observed significance level is only .93, indicating that the null hypothesis (producer strata and views on the FSLN government are independent) cannot be rejected.

10. Whereas 38 percent of the full sample were strongly opposed to the FSLN government, 55 percent of those with an immigrant history fell into that category. Sixty-seven percent of the full sample were large producers, whereas 80 percent of those who noted a recent immigration experience in their family history were so classified.

11. At the secondary level, prestigious Nicaraguan boarding schools such as the Jesuit-run Colegio Centroamérica were preferred by the elite, although a handful of the most prosperous participants in this study also completed their high school education in the United States.

12. The long history of semicolonial status and the trade and aid linkages in the Somoza era made economic elites highly attuned to the United States. Other countries where several respondents received their final degrees included Mexico, Spain, and other Central American nations.

13. In addition to those who received their highest educational degree in the United States, many others spent some time studying and working there. In this sample, a remarkable 42 percent reported living or studying in the United States at some point in their lives. Over one-third lived in the United States for more than a year; 18 percent of the respondents lived there for five or more years. In this sense, analysts like John Weeks (1987), who allege a strong cultural dependence on the United States by the Nicaraguan bourgeoisie, have some empirical basis for their claims.

14. Among university graduates, 100 percent of those educated in the United States were large producers at the end of the 1970s, whereas only 61 percent of those who graduated from Nicaraguan universities were in that category.

15. There was also a connection between being educated in the United States and support for a pure free-market economic model. Whereas only 29 percent of those educated in Nicaragua selected a pure-capitalism economic model when asked about their philosophical preferences, 42 percent of those educated in the United States did so.

16. The Pearson chi-square value for Table 5.2 is 7.79, and the significance level

is only .45. The Pearson chi-square value for Table 5.3 is 4.72, with a significance level of only .31. In neither case can the null hypothesis be rejected. A purely statistical analysis of these data can, however, be problematic, since the measure of association depends, to some degree, on how the variables are defined. If the statistical analysis in Table 5.3 is confined to only those private sector leaders with university educations who were either strongly or moderately opposed to the regime, for example, then the contrast between those educated at home and abroad appears more sharply. The Pearson chi-square value for this more focused analysis is 3.44, with a significance level of .06.

17. UPANIC leaders often charged that their affiliate associations were suffering a conscious erosion at the hands of the FSLN. Indeed, the Sandinista state did provide significant support for UNAG and encouraged producers to choose this alternative. Among other forms of state support given to UNAG, Luciak (forthcoming, chap. 3) reports that 25 percent of UNAG's budget came from FSLN donations. On the other hand, the government also provided some organizational support for UPANIC affiliates. It channeled goods like tires and special authorizations (*asignaciones*) to purchase jeeps or tractors through these groups as well, although not on a priority basis. The state trade monopsonies also served as the collection agency for membership dues of FAGANIC and CAAN, transferring a percentage of their members' earnings from the cattle slaughter and cotton export to these associations.

18. The Pearson chi-square value for this table is 54.09, with a significance level of less than .01, indicating that we can reject the null hypothesis (producer organization and views on the FSLN government are independent) at the 99 percent level of confidence.

19. COSEP reported a relatively modest membership in its agricultural affiliate in 1985, with 75 percent of the members in one of two livestock associations (FAGANIC or FONDILAC). (See Appendix 2, Table A.5.) The harsh exchanges between COSEP/UPANIC leaders and government officials, the general contraction of the large producer class, plus the confiscation of the properties of UPANIC president Ramiro Gurdián and COSEP president Enrique Bolaños, had a negative effect on COSEP's ability to recruit and retain members.

20. UNAG's membership reportedly rose to a total of 120,506 in 1987. (See Appendix 2, Table A.2.) Membership figures for both UNAG and UPANIC are subject to some question, since both organizations may have inflated these numbers in order to appear more representative of agricultural producers. Since over one-fifth of UNAG's members in 1987 were individual members who did not belong to any base structure, cooperative, or UNAG association, it is hard to know exactly what their affiliation in this organization entailed.

21. The UNAG leaders who had lived in the United States had also done so for a shorter period of time than their UPANIC counterparts. Whereas only 25 percent of the UNAG leaders who had lived in the United States had done so for more than one year, 94 percent of the UPANIC leaders who had lived in the United States had spent more than one year there.

22. Some producers, seeking maximum political advantage, joined both UNAG and the local UPANIC affiliate. Regional leaders sometimes turned a blind eye to the practice, seeing it as necessary in order to survive under the difficult circumstances that prevailed during the era. In general, however, such double affiliation was frowned upon, both for ideological reasons and because of the dangers of infiltration by political opponents (interview, UPANIC, June 21, 1990; interview, UNAG, May 6, 1990).

23. In some areas, local UNAG leaders worked so hard to persuade their members to accept their military draft responsibilities, for example, that UNAG was perceived as an extension of the military. This perception contributed to a tendency among producers in these zones to avoid contact with UNAG (interview, UNAG-Matagalpa, June 25, 1992).

24. Several members of the UPANIC-affiliated ADAL, for example, were supporters of the revolution and ran as FSLN candidates in the 1990 election. One FSLN candidate for the León municipal slate had been an officer in ADAL and its representative in the UPANIC directorate in 1988–89, and two ADAL members were FSLN candidates for the national assembly. ADAL was exceptional, however, among UPANIC regional associations in its relative tolerance for Sandinista supporters in its ranks. León was one of the few municipalities where FSLN support continued to be strong throughout the decade and where the FSLN won the 1990 elections. The broader base of FSLN support in León and the absence of a war front there fostered relative tolerance for those with Sandinista sympathies, even in UPANIC affiliates.

25. Although the patterns in Table 5.5 are notable, the contrasts between national and regional leaders are not stark or absolute enough to rule out the possibility of a random occurrence, especially for the UNAG leaders. The Pearson chi-square value was 7.2 with a significance level of .13 for COSEP leaders and 1.9 with a significance level of only .6 for UNAG leaders.

26. Members of UNAG received a number of benefits and resources. One UNAG leader from Masaya told of a time in 1986 when his land was invaded and he faced expropriation. With a letter from the head of his departmental UNAG office confirming his status as a activist in the association, he was able to stave off the expropriation bid and reclaim his land. UNAG also helped its membership to acquire basic agricultural implements (boots, machetes, barbed wire, etc.) at a time when these were scarce.

Some of this support, however, was contingent on the FSLN remaining in power and responding to UNAG requests. UNAG regional leaders throughout the country reported, in the months following the inauguration of the UNO government, a sharp drop in membership and activity. Indeed, a UNAG report on its membership in 1993 indicates that the total had fallen from 120,506 in 1987 (see Appendix 2, Table A.2) to 101,500 (UNAG 1993, 8). Medium- and large-sized individual producers were particularly likely to jump ship, leading one frustrated UNAG leader in Jinotega to conclude that they had only been "glued with spit" to UNAG.

27. This group includes those who appealed the process and eventually received some or all of the land back, who were eventually given a *permuta* or land ex-

change, or who were never formally expropriated but who lost some land in land invasions that were not checked by state action.

28. As with other factors discussed above, expropriation was not an isolated variable, unrelated to other considerations. Those who were expropriated were more likely, for example, to have been large producers in the late 1970s and to have been leaders of UPANIC organizations. A full 44 percent of those in this study who were large producers in the late 1970s underwent an expropriation, and most of these expropriations were hard (26 percent vs. 18 percent soft). For those who were medium-sized or small, however, only 16 percent and 20 percent, respectively, were expropriated, and all of these were of the soft variety.

Forty percent of the UPANIC leaders interviewed in this study were expropriated, and a relatively higher percentage of those expropriations were of the hard variety (24 percent hard and 16 percent soft). Only 19 percent of the UNAG leaders, on the other hand, were expropriated, and all of these were of the soft variety, with some or all of the land eventually returned or a land swap arranged.

These patterns suggest a complex interaction among the variables, in which the growing opposition of the most privileged elites combined with their marginalization from the Sandinista development model and contributed to expropriation decisions that in turn deepened their hostility to the regime. Conversely, more co-operative, "patriotic" producers who had smaller estates or supported UNAG were less likely to fall under the expropriation ax. This relatively favorable treatment in turn encouraged them to adopt a less negative appraisal of the regime.

29. The Pearson chi-square value for Table 5.6 is 6.2, with a significance level of only .63, indicating that we are unable to reject the null hypothesis (expropriation experience and views on the FSLN government are independent).

30. See Utting (1991) for a discussion of the sharp price decline experienced by Nicaraguan food producers following structural adjustment at the end of the FSLN era. According to Utting, the large producers, who were heavily dependent on irrigation and imported machinery, were even more negatively affected by cost increases associated with post-1987 adjustment measures than were peasant producers. In addition to the problems of rising costs as subsidies were eliminated, rice producers complained heartily about Soviet rice donations in 1987 and 1988, which undercut prices for domestically produced rice (interviews, July 26, 1989; June 23, 1990).

31. The percent registering either moderate or strong support for the regime was 8 percent for those private sector leaders whose primary product at the end of the 1980s was coffee, 23 percent for grains (rice, maize, or sorghum), and 29 percent for livestock (beef and dairy).

32. Major investments were defined as long-term investments in acquiring new land, building new infrastructure (roads, workers' housing, irrigation systems, etc.), acquiring purebred cattle for breeding, and making major machinery purchases. Minor investments referred to routine investments needed to maintain existing production levels (erecting fencing, maintaining terraces, purchasing steers for fattening, meeting traditionally established standards for aerial fumiga-

tion or crop fertilization). "No investments" was reported by those who made no long-term investments during the period and whose short-term investments fell substantially below their prerevolutionary norms.

33. The Pearson chi-square value for Table 5.7 is 9.5, with a significance level of .05, indicating that we can reject the null hypothesis (views on the FSLN government and investment level are independent) with a 95 percent level of confidence.

34. Prospective buyers had to secure permission from MIDINRA to purchase land before the sale could be completed. This policy was designed to prevent owners who had been informed of a pending expropriation from trying to sell the land to unsuspecting buyers. It also allowed the state to monitor and channel land acquisition patterns.

35. According to one producer who bought land regularly during this period, prices for range land in 1984 were one-tenth what they had been before the revolution or came to be again in 1990.

36. In contrast, strong supporters had a relatively low land purchase rate (only 23 percent did so). In most cases their workload in the government or their association left them little time to attend to production on the land they currently held; in one case, a strong supporter received land through an agrarian reform land grant, making additional land purchases unnecessary.

37. It is, of course, remarkable that any of the opponents acquired additional properties. This curious pattern is the result of several forces. For one, land purchase is not always a purely economic calculation. Faced with the prospect that family lands would be sold to outsiders following the death or emigration of a relative, even regime opponents might buy the land in an effort to keep it in the family. Furthermore, opposition leaders sometimes bought land in the early years of the revolution, before they became as virulently opposed as they were at the end. In one case, a private sector opponent bought land and invested heavily in its development, anticipating a contra overthrow of the Sandinistas. (In two additional cases not included in this calculation, private sector leaders reported purchasing land, but in Costa Rica and Venezuela, as these producers prepared for the possibility of emigration.)

38. A holding company called PMA managed the assets of the three major stockholders, the two foreign investors who founded GRACSA (U.S. textile executive Philip Lehner and Salvadoran business leader Mauricio Borgonovo) and the company's first general manager (Alfonso Robelo). Robelo sold his interest in the company before leaving the country and joining the leadership of the contra forces, but his prior involvement triggered the initial state intervention in GRACSA in 1982. The company was subsequently retained by the state for reasons of "social utility," because of its central role in national oilseed production. After the supreme court decided in its favor, ownership of GRACSA was returned to PMA (which had held 51 percent of the stock) in 1988, and Antonio Lacayo returned as general manager.

39. In all, twelve new companies were added to the GRACSA group during the 1979–90 period. These included a balanced feed industry, two cattle ranches, chicken and pork production facilities, soybean and African palm projects, a

shrimp farm, a peanut export and processing firm, a transportation firm, a heavy construction agency, and a machine maintenance shop (interviews, GRACSA, September 4, October 3, 11, 25, November 1, 1990, August 9, 1991; Spalding 1991).

40. Respondents were asked to compare their overall production levels in the 1986–89 period with those of the 1976–79 period. Percentage shifts were calculated from the data they provided. Changes were classified as an increase when production rose by over 25 percent and a decrease when it fell by more than 25 percent. Production levels were considered stable if they did not change by more than 25 percent.

41. The Pearson chi-square value for Table 5.8 is 10.7 with a significance level of .03, indicating that we can reject the null hypothesis (views on the FSLN government and production level change are independent) with a 97 percent level of confidence.

Chapter 6

1. The U.S. Congress authorized US$9 million to support a "democratic" election in Nicaragua in 1990. Most of these funds went to UNO-allied civic organizations and, indirectly, to the UNO campaign. See LASA (1990); Robinson (1992, 60–89).

2. On the role of USAID in neoliberal restructuring in Costa Rica, see Sojo (1991), and in Nicaragua, see Saldomando (1992).

3. The recent shift toward neoliberalism in Latin American nations undergoing a process of democratization suggests that the regime need not be formally authoritarian to undertake this economic change. Haggard and Kaufman (1992b, 278–80) argue, however, that the more fragmented and polarized democratic regimes, in which the governing coalition is continually shifting, find it more difficult to successfully implement neoliberal reforms.

4. See Przeworski (1991, chap. 4) on the dynamics of economic transition, which he argues apply to both the Latin American and the Eastern European reform efforts.

5. On the tension between neoliberal politics and democratic politics, see Sheahan (1991, 65–72).

6. Campero (1984, 298–320) traces the rise of the Consejo de la Producción, el Transporte, y el Comercio, a new peak association for small- and medium-sized businesspeople who were protesting the losses they suffered under the Pinochet regime in the early 1980s.

7. After eight years of warfare and general economic decline, the country had massive foreign aid needs. For 1991, the government required an infusion of $1 billion just to meet the arrears on its foreign debt and cover the balance of payments gap (Enríquez et al. 1991, 20–21). U.S. aid fell far short of what was needed to stimulate reactivation.

8. Of the amount programmed for 1992, an estimated $576 million was reportedly disbursed (Larson with Nitlapán-UCA 1993, 7, 9).

9. Whereas loans from multilateral organizations represented 21 percent of the total foreign aid package in 1991, loans from these organizations were expected to reach 39 percent of the total in 1992 (BCN, *Nicaragua Economic Report*, November–December 1991, 15).

10. Helms demanded a series of policy changes by the Nicaraguan government including the return of properties to Nicaraguans who had become U.S. citizens, the removal of high Sandinista officials from the police and intelligence agencies, and judicial reform. See the text of Helms's letter of June 22 to USAID Director, reprinted in *La Prensa*, June 27, 1992, and Republican Staff Report (1992). After a U.S. GAO report (1992) sharply questioned the State Department's finding that the Chamorro government was making progress in dealing with the property claims of 155 U.S. citizens, the State Department reversed its position on aid suspension and also began pressuring the Chamorro government for further reforms.

11. The head of the Sandinista police, René Vivas, was retired from command along with eleven other high-ranking officers. He was replaced by Fernando Caldera, previously a National Police commander and also a Sandinista. Responsibility for the police force was reassigned to a new Vice-Ministry for Citizens' Security in the Interior Ministry under civilian appointee and Sandinista critic Ronald Aviles. See "Nicaragua Leader Ousts Some Sandinista Police," *Chicago Tribune*, September 6, 1992; Shirley Christian, "Managua Seesaw," *New York Times*, September 8, 1992.

In addition to these reforms, the Chamorro government reestablished a program to review property claims (Decrees #46-92, #47-92, #48-92, and Presidential Accord #248-92) and initiated an indemnization process (Decrees #51-92 and #52-92) that offered payment in twenty-year bonds at 3 percent interest to those whose properties could not be returned. These bonds could also be used to purchase stock in profitable state enterprises (the telephone, water, and electric companies, the Montelimar resort, etc.) (WOLA 1992, 23–25; Larson with Nitlapán-UCA 1993, 41).

12. U.S. aid was suspended again following the May 1993 discovery of an arms cache in Managua that belonged to a supposedly disarmed faction of the Salvadoran Farabundo Martí National Liberation Front.

13. In addition to Lacayo, CORDENIC members included Francisco Mayorga, who briefly served as president of the BCN; Enrique Dreyfus, who served for a year and a half as foreign minister; and Francisco Rosales, who became minister of labor.

14. INCAE had been founded in 1964 by Central American business leaders with financial support from USAID and technical assistance from the Harvard University Business School. By 1990, INCAE's various Central American campuses had graduated 1,432 students with advanced degrees in business administration, had 2,937 graduates of its four-week training program for business executives, and had enrolled 66,333 participants in its executive seminars. See INCAE (1990?).

15. This group included Alfredo César, who had joined the Sandinistas in 1977 while he was general administrator for Nicaraguan Sugar Estates, Inc. Among his various posts, César had been president of the BCN in the early Sandinista period

before leaving in 1982 for Costa Rica. In 1985 he was one of six founding members of the Southern Opposition Bloc, the contra force operating out of Costa Rica. He became a director of the Nicaraguan resistance in May 1987 and returned to Nicaragua in 1989 to help run the Chamorro presidential campaign.

16. Chamorro took on the title minister of defense herself but allowed Humberto Ortega to remain in charge of the armed forces and, until September 1992, René Vivas to remain as head of the Sandinista police force.

17. These actors were not entirely isolated from the Nicaraguan political terrain. Several had prior ties to COSEP affiliates like CADIN. Some had, through CORDENIC, been involved in orchestrating a national dialogue since April 1988. INCAE's role in training MIDINRA personnel in management techniques had linked much of its staff directly to the policy process for several years. Some cabinet members, such as Minister of the Presidency Antonio Lacayo, had gone through long years of negotiations with the Sandinista regime (see Chapter 4). The tendency of the new economic team toward insularity, therefore, was reduced by the prior involvement of several members in the political bargaining process during the Sandinista era. Compared, however, with many other political contenders, these actors were relatively removed from the traditional rough and tumble of Nicaraguan politics.

18. See IHCA (1990) for a comparison of the "Azul y Blanco" program advanced by Bolaños and the final UNO program.

19. Mayorga was a Yale-trained economist who had worked at the BCN in the 1970s. He participated in the drafting of the Sandinista government's first Programa de Gobierno de Reconstrucción Nacional and did consulting work for the Ministry of Planning in the early years of the revolution. He left that position in 1982 and served as director of the Central American Bank of Economic Integration until 1985; he subsequently became a professor and administrator at INCAE.

20. In some cases, when the FSLN bench was not united or when opposition parties resisted, the FSLN government did withdraw or modify a piece of draft legislation. In general, however, the FSLN government either circumvented the legislature or relied on its solid legislative majority to assure passage of important measures. See Booth (1985b).

21. Early presidential decrees are compiled in República de Nicaragua (1990?b). On the use of presidential decrees for economic policymaking, see the interview with Finance Minister Emilio Pereira (1991, 4). On the conflict between Chamorro and César, and the continued use of presidential decrees, see Flakoll Alegría (1991, 4–5); Vickers and Spence (1992).

22. Note, for example, the low level of strike activity in the late 1980s, even though real wages in 1988 had fallen by one estimate to only 5 percent of what they had been in 1980 (Neira Cuadra and Acevedo 1992, 87). See also Luciak (forthcoming) on the relationship between the ATC and the FSLN. For a contrasting point of view on labor autonomy in the Sandinista era, see Stahler-Sholk (1992).

23. Foreign Minister Dreyfus was a past president of COSEP and Minister of the Presidency Lacayo had been a member of the board of directors of CADIN. Minis-

ter of Agriculture Roberto Rondón was one of the country's largest cattle ranchers and former president of FAGANIC. At his first meeting with UPANIC members after the inauguration, Rondón began his comments by noting that he was still a member of the board of directors of UPANIC and had been secretary of FAGANIC until only two weeks before (observation of meeting of economic ministers and UPANIC, May 10, 1990).

24. Of the forty producers interviewed in my study who were active participants in the UNO campaign, fifteen (38 percent) gave mixed or negative evaluations of the UNO government within seven months after the inauguration.

25. According to Wheelock Román (1991, 18), 80 percent of the agrarian reform titles extended by the Sandinista government before February 25, 1990, were only provisional. See also WOLA (1992); Enríquez (1991a, 47–48). In my interviews with producers, several mentioned returning for visits to their former farms and discussing the formation of joint ventures with the cooperative members who now held title to the land.

26. The Sandinista government reportedly extended 9,404 land titles between August 1989 and April 25, 1990, most of which were granted between the time of their electoral defeat in February and the inauguration of the UNO government in April. In his response to widespread allegations of corruption and abuse of power during the lame duck period, Wheelock Román (1991, 111–12) argues that only 292 of these titles represented entirely new grants. The rest were characterized as titles that had been granted previously but not formally issued, or as previously arranged land swaps (permutas) for properties that had been expropriated under agrarian reform laws.

The most controversial of the new titles were those for large tracts of land given to individuals closely tied to the Sandinista government. According to a Barricada study (Guillermo Cortes, "Resurge el latifundismo," Barricada, July 8, 1991) 18,000 mz. were titled to five families in the last days of the FSLN period, including two former MIDINRA vice-ministers. Some of the land titled in this fashion was area that pro-Sandinista producers had previously donated to the revolution and were now reclaiming. In other cases, however, the legal basis of the claim was weaker; following a public outcry and FSLN internal pressure, some of the land thus acquired was subsequently handed on to other claimants (interview, Jaime Wheelock, June 27, 1992; interview, Ricardo Coronel Kautz, June 30, 1992). See also Hernández (1991, 23–24) and "Destapan piñata agraria," La Prensa, June 25, 1991.

27. See also Enríquez (1991a, 48); Barricada, May 15, 1991; Cuadra (1992, 19–20).

28. CORNAP uses the term privatization to refer to any action that shifts responsibility for the firm out of its jurisdiction. The liquidation of fifty-one companies and the transfer of twenty-eight others (such as telecommunications and the airport) over to other state agencies are both classified in CORNAP data as privatizations.

29. See Gabriela Selser, "New Reduction for EPS," Barricada international 10, no. 330 (December 1, 1990), 14–15; Lt. Col. Oswaldo Lacayo's report to the national assembly's budget commission, summarized in Barricada international 13, no. 360

(April 1993), 7. Among those released in December 1990 were 5,000 officers who were granted severance pay equal to six months to one year of salary, urban lots for building houses, and access to technical training.

30. In addition to layoffs in the privatized state enterprises, by the end of 1991 5,700 civilian, central government employees had enrolled in this plan, including 3,000 from the state banking system and 2,700 from public services like education and health (CEPAL 1992b, 22).

31. The total civilian public sector workforce prior to this reduction, including the central government (68,390) and public enterprises (78,000), was 146,390 (Government of Nicaragua 1992, 17; CORNAP 1991, 6).

32. The new banks authorized were the Banco Mercantil, BANPRO, Banco de América Central, the Banco de Crédito Centroamericano, the Banco de Préstamos, the Banco Intercontinental, and the Banco de la Exportación (interviews, Alejandro Martínez Cuenca, July 1, 1992; Eduardo Montealegre, Gerente General, Banco de Crédito Centroamericano, June 26, 1992; Haroldo Montealegre, Gerente General, Banco Mercantil, June 22, 1992; Chale Espinoza, Gerente General, Banco de la Producción, June 29, 1992; and Francisco Sanabanda, Gerente General, Banco de Préstamos, June 29, 1992). See also Saldomando (1992, 82–94).

33. See Decree-Law #37-91, Decreto de Promoción de Exportaciones, issued August 21, 1991, and the subsequent Reglamento del Decreto de Promoción de Exportaciones, published in *La Gaceta*, April 2, 1992. The income tax exemption for nontraditional exporters began at 80 percent in 1992 and was scheduled to gradually decline to 60 percent in 1997 before ending in 1998. In addition, nontraditional exporters were also granted a negotiable and transferable tax benefit certificate for a six-year period (interview, Juan Fernando Ramírez, Director, Departamento de Promoción de Exportaciones, MEDE, July 2, 1992; Larios and Cordero 1992).

34. See the Ley de Inversiones Extranjeras, #27, June 19, 1991, and the Reglamento de la Ley de Inversiones Extranjeras, Decreto #30-92, June 10, 1992. To encourage the repatriation of flight capital, Nicaraguan investors who imported capital and registered it with the BCN received the same benefits as foreign investors (Government of Nicaragua 1992, 14). To encourage investment in offshore assembly, the president also issued the Decreto de Zonas Francas Industriales de Exportación on November 13, 1991, followed by its enabling legislation (*reglamento*) on June 10, 1992.

35. The maximum income tax rate dropped from 45 percent to 35 percent in 1991 and then was lowered further to 30 percent in 1992. See BCN, *Nicaragua Economic Report*, November–December 1991, 15. The vast majority of Nicaraguan workers were not required to pay income taxes since those with annual incomes of less than C$25,000 ($5,000) were exempt. This reform, therefore, benefited the relatively prosperous. See the detailed analysis of the changes in the tax code in Hüper (1992, 13–22). In addition to these tax rate reductions, a capital gains tax, a wealth transfer tax, and a bequest tax were eliminated (Government of Nicaragua 1992, 12).

36. See FIDEG, *Observador económico* 16 (April 1993): 9; Hüper (1992, 13). Ac-

cording to FIDEG, 54 percent of tax revenues were generated from taxes on fiscal products in 1991. See *Observador económico* 8 (August 1992): 6.

37. COSEP itself was not invited to participate, nominally because the government wished to involve direct producers and employers rather than association officials. The government may also have feared, correctly, that COSEP's periodic denunciations of the government's performance would make it less open to government sponsored negotiations and less likely to support the final agreement.

38. For statements of the bargaining positions of the government and the FSLN-aligned labor groups, see *Barricada*, October 22, 1990.

39. This figure was negotiated in hard bargaining. The representatives of FSLN-allied groups called for the distribution to workers of 50 percent of the assets in the remaining firms that were undergoing privatization. COSEP-allied employers called for a limit of 10 percent worker ownership in these enterprises. The government, attempting to strike a balance between the two, called for an arrangement in which workers would be given concessionary terms allowing them to acquire 15–20 percent of the assets of enterprises in their sectors. See *Barricada*, August 6, 1991; CIPRES (1991).

40. In what was quickly becoming a pattern, COSEP organizations ultimately refused to sign the *Concertación II* agreement as well. From the standpoint of COSEP leaders, the second agreement failed to deal adequately with the return of property illegally distributed by Sandinista leaders. See COSEP's full page ad in *La Prensa*, August 15, 1991. This session reopened the issue of urban and rural properties acquired by Sandinista loyalists during the *piñata* period between the electoral defeat and the inauguration. During this period, urban and rural properties, and even office equipment and vehicles in particular ministries, were dispersed among political loyalists. Following the *Concertación II* agreement, the anti-Sandinista majority in the assembly attempted to set up a review and payment requirement for these properties, but the combustibility of the issue and commitments made to the FSLN during the preinauguration negotiations led the president to intervene and veto the measure.

41. See "Year in Review 1991" in *Barricada international* 12, no. 345 (January 1992), 22–24; Stahler-Sholk (1992, 45).

42. Neoliberal regimes typically establish some poverty abatement program that, though not entirely consistent with the classical liberal ideology, is designed to attenuate economic dislocations and the resulting political opposition. The Chamorro regime adopted several such social programs. The government created, with USAID financing, small employment programs and public aid services for low-income urban dwellers (Government of Nicaragua 1992, 18–19). The most important of these programs, the Emergency Social Investment Fund (Fondo de Inversiones Sociales de Emergencia, FISE) was created in November 1990 by presidential decree (Ministerio de la Presidencia 1991, 40–41). FISE was a five-year public works program designed to put under- and unemployed people to work in community infrastructural development projects. According to the USAID program director in Nicaragua, Janet Ballantyne, this program had created 35,000 short-term jobs

by mid-1992 (interview, July 1, 1992). Given the extremity of the economic crisis in Nicaragua, however, this program had only a marginal impact. FISE became controversial because of allegations that it gave the UNO-dominated municipal governments access to patronage positions that could be traded for political support.

43. In addition to these industries, in the mining sector, workers opted to buy 100 percent control of four of the mines and form a holding company that all interested mineworkers, regardless of the mine they worked in, could buy into. Sugar workers negotiated participation ranging from 25 percent to 70 percent in four of the mills. Banana workers obtained 25 percent participation in the administration and marketing operations of BANANIC (interviews with FNT legal adviser, Alejandro Martínez Cuenca, July 1, 1992; FNT Secretary General Lucío Jiménez, June 23, 1992; Ramiro Gurdián, COSEP president, June 30, 1992). See also *Barricada*, June 26, 1992; Soza (1992, 39); Larson with Nitlapán-UCA (1993, 43).

44. In the cattle sector, for example, those who chose to accept this benefit were given ten-year loans at 6 percent interest with one year of grace. In the industrial sector, the government offered similar terms but a two-year grace period (interviews, Ricardo Coronel Kautz, former president of HATONIC, June 30, 1992; Iván Saballos, CORNAP, June 24, 1992). See also CORNAP (1991, 18); Gobierno de Nicaragua-CST, *Acuerdo*, February 2, 1993.

45. Sergio Ramírez accompanied the Chamorro government delegation to the Donors' Conference in Rome in June 1990, and Daniel Ortega accompanied the delegation to Washington, D.C., in March 1992 to support the government's bid for new foreign assistance.

46. The seven-person Junta Directiva of UPANIC, for example, was elected biannually by the members of the organization's Directorio. The Directorio in turn was composed of twenty-eight representatives of the organizations that made up the association, modestly weighted to give more voice to the larger or more economically powerful organizations. See Chapter 2, n. 52.

47. UPANIC took this opposition furthest when it published a communiqué endorsing the June 1992 suspension of U.S. aid to Nicaragua. (See its *comunicado* of June 11, 1992, published in *La Prensa*, June 21, 1992.) It took this step even though UPANIC's own members were to be one of the primary beneficiaries of the funds, which included $50 million in medium- and long-term credit for private producers in agriculture and industry. COSEP did not publicly endorse the suspension of the aid. It did, however, publicly and privately denounce the government following a series of land invasions and transportation stoppages in April 1992. See COSEP's "Comunicado de prensa" of April 30, 1992 (COSEP 1992a), and its unpublished but distributed "Posición de COSEP ante gobierno," May 4, 1992 (COSEP 1992b).

48. Several prominent UPANIC leaders were affiliates of the PLC, including former UNCAFENIC president and UNO mayor of Managua, Arnoldo Alemán; former president of UNCAFENIC and member of the national assembly on the UNO slate, Nicolas Bolaños; and Arges Sequeira, former representative to COSEP for UPANIC and president of both UPANIC and the Asociación de Confiscados until his

murder in November 1992. Although a participant in the UNO coalition, the PLC took issue with the Chamorro government on major social and economic issues and sought to drive the FSLN further from power.

49. A fourth bank authorized in 1992, the Banco de la Exportación, was being organized under the leadership of Ernesto Fernández Holmann, former general manager of BANAMER.

50. Even in this group, however, political accommodation was not uniform. Haroldo Montealegre, for example, who played a prominent role in pushing through the *concertación* accords, drafting the Chamorro government's economic policy proposals in late 1990 and 1991, and representing the government in negotiations with the World Bank and the IMF during this period, broke ranks in mid-1992 when he launched a campaign against the state bank system. As president of one of the fledgling private banks, Montealegre has been particularly vehement in his denunciations of the BND, the state bank competitor. See his article "An Economic Policy Nicaraguans Can Bank On," *Wall Street Journal*, April 24, 1992, and an interview with him in *Vistazo económico*, #481 (June 19, 1992): 1–4.

51. See "U.S. Support Is Sought for Coffee Limits," *New York Times*, March 26, 1992. See also the USAID consultant's report by CARANA Corporations and Sparks Companies (1991, 55–59).

52. Percentages presented here include only those who actually responded to the question. INCAE's data output from this survey includes only frequencies, and so it is not possible to determine which subsectors responded in what way. COSEP's prominent role in organizing these seminars may have attracted more disaffected producers and contributed to the widespread negative appraisals of the government found in the responses.

53. These producers, over half of whom were in the cattle, coffee, and cotton sectors, gave a positive assessment of the exchange rate stability (66 percent positive), selective tax reductions (52 percent positive on the reduction of the sales tax and 42 percent on customs tax reductions), and the Export Promotion Law (56 percent expected to benefit).

54. Favored responses on the presidential preference question were "There's no one to vote for" (27 percent), Arnoldo Alemán (16 percent), Enrique Bolaños (16 percent), and Alfredo César (9 percent).

55. See APENN (1991, 1–3); *La Prensa*, May 22, 1990; interviews, Samuel Mansell, president of APENN, May 6, June 23, 1990, and June 24, 1992.

56. Membership rose from the initial 40 in May 1990 to 192 in June 1992. Although expanding, APENN remained a highly selective organization. Selection criteria included the requirement that members have access to irrigation, an agricultural technician on their staff, financial ability to assume the risks, and a record of "labor discipline" on their farms (interview, Samuel Mansell, June 24, 1992).

57. These included Miguel Barrios, who had been director of MIDINRA in Regions I, VI, and II before taking over the management of the ISA after its 1988 expropriation; Pedro Antonio Blandón, who had been director of the Fondo Internacional para la Reconstrucción and of the Programa Alimentario Nicaragüense;

and Joaquín Cuadra, former president of the BCN. Barrios became the director of ECODEPA; the others served as project consultants for UNAG.

58. See Barrios Johanning (1992); interview, Circles Robinson, consultant, Relaciones Internacionales y Proyectos, UNAG, Matagalpa, June 25, 1992; Fernández Ampié (1992).

59. The idea of a UNAG bank pitted UNAG members against each other. The sharp cutback in state bank credit to small producers and cooperatives made the idea attractive to some UNAG leaders, but the problems of having to restrict UNAG bank loans and force repayment by economically precarious members raised problems that others were reluctant to take on. By 1993, however, UNAG leaders secured international financial backing and began this project. See UNAG (n.d.).

60. After their electoral defeat, FSLN leaders established a series of party-owned enterprises that were designed to provide employment and revenues for the party (*La Prensa*, July 16, 1990). These operations included several highly visible ventures like a new airline, the Central American Airline. Public outcry about how the FSLN had enriched itself in power, and the stunning failure of the new airline, soon precipitated a reconsideration of party-owned enterprises. Although the FSLN did retain a small number of businesses, such as a newspaper and radio stations, the plan to found a series of prominent enterprises had reportedly been largely abandoned by 1991 (interview, Jaime Wheelock, June 27, 1992). In spite of this shift, two of the new banks authorized by the Chamorro government, the Banco de Préstamos and the Banco Intercontinental, which were partly owned by former high-ranking FSLN government officials or allies, were commonly referred to as Sandinista banks, even though they were not actually owned by the FSLN party. Likewise, businesses that bought advertising space in *Barricada* were also commonly labeled Sandinista enterprises.

61. In addition to the sectors noted above, several other pockets of investment could be found. Some of the producers who flourished during the Sandinista era because of the boldness of their investment strategy or the privileges they received from the government used their accumulated resources as a springboard for diversification and expansion in the 1990s. The OCALSA group, for example, moved quickly to build a supermarket chain and acquire a fast-food franchise. By mid-1991 its investments extended to twenty-five companies in the import-export, distribution, and manufacturing sectors (BCN, *Nicaragua Economic Report*, June 1991, 3, 6–7).

Another entrepreneurial venture centered around BANPRO. BANPRO was organized by a politically and economically illustrious list of investors, some of whom were linked to Minister of the Presidency Antonio Lacayo. Bank president Pablo Ayón García had participated with Lacayo in CORDENIC; junta member Alfredo Marín worked with Lacayo at GRACSA and replaced him as GRACSA's general manager when Lacayo resigned to direct the Chamorro campaign. Bank vice-president Ernesto Balladares was also vice-president of CORNAP; junta member Pablo Vijil was minister of communication; and junta member Rafael Martínez was executive president of the CNG. Two critics of the government, COSEP president Ramiro Gurdián and former COSEP president Gilberto Cuadra, were also on the Junta Directiva of this bank. This broad-based bank marshaled the resources of 105 producer/share owners. Recognizing the historical importance of bank ownership to group development in Nicaragua, these investors were unwilling to depend on either the banks organized by the returning elite, the old state banks, or those being set up with the participation of prominent allies of the FSLN. Drawing on relatively modest individual investments, this group moved briskly to raise the mandatory $2 million required to apply for permission to open a private bank.

62. CEPAL (1992b, 4) estimates for 1990 classified 75 percent of the Nicaraguan population as poor and 42 percent as extremely poor. Un- and underemployment, which had risen to 39.9 percent in 1989, continued to climb, reaching 53.5 percent in 1991 (CEPAL 1992b, 33).

63. According to a careful study of the nontraditional export strategy in Latin America by Barham et al. (1992), common problems include environmental degradation, declining terms of trade for primary products, multinationalization of the export sector, and concentration of benefits in the hands of a small group. Questions have also been raised in the Costa Rican case about whether the amount of the subsidies provided to nontraditional exporters by the government exceeds the increased economic return they generate.

Chapter 7

1. See Schmitter (1974). It is possible, however, for strong, independent business associations to emerge even when they are set up by state decree if the state is essentially under the control of the economic elite. In that case, the distinction between state-created and elite-created associations is blurred.

2. Ironically, spontaneous organizational forms for the private sector may, on one hand, contribute to private sector capacity for confrontation with the state but also complicate the process of achieving class unity. In the Chilean case, COPROCO represented the six top private sector organizations, but the small- and medium-sized producers or those producers in less prominent sectors were excluded from this alliance. The sense that the top elite is preoccupied with protecting its own privileges, while nonhegemonic capitalists in the rest of the private sector were not admitted into those hallowed chambers, could actually contribute to disunity in the class. Organizational autonomy that produces rigid divisions by sector, firm size, or region may, therefore, undermine private sector cohesion. In this sense, state intervention may actually foster class unification, whereas spontaneous organization may not. Indeed, the 1972–73 fusion of the private sector proved transitory in Chile. Disgruntled by the economic hardships they faced under the military dictatorship in Chile relative to the top elites, medium- and small-sized businesses split off and formed their own peak association, the Consejo de la Producción, el Transporte, y el Comercio, in 1983. See Campero (1984).

3. The role of outside agents can be overstated. It seems unlikely that the Nixon administration's subsidies to *El Mercurio* or the October 1972 bosses' strike in

Chile, for example, could have forged a united private sector opposition if the domestic capitalist class did not see opposition to be in its interest. The image of Latin American bourgeoisie as a dangling puppet responding jerkily to every tug from the United States shows little insight into the character of the local elite. On the other hand, concerted foreign intervention can help local entrepreneurs to coordinate their efforts and sustain their own confrontation with the state. In that more limited sense, the U.S. government can help to forge and maintain a business consensus, as can the IMF when it adds external validation and the promise of resources to local elites' efforts to quash reform. At the same time, the U.S. government can also contribute to internal tension in a relatively cohesive bourgeoisie, as it did in El Salvador by supporting the Duarte government and refusing to confer legitimacy on the more reactionary D'Aubuisson faction of the Salvadoran right.

4. The regime also welcomed the 1988 formation of an alternative elite organization, CORDENIC, which differentiated its approach from the confrontational style of COSEP and looked for new forms of dialogue.

5. In some cases, such as Jamaica during the first Manley government, the use of class-based rhetoric and attacks on the bourgeoisie triggered a rise of the elite's threat perception, even though the actual reforms introduced by the government were modest and domestic property holders were little affected by expropriation. See Stephens and Stephens (1986).

6. The Manley government's decision to grant the Order of Jamaica award to the president of the Private Sector Organization of Jamaica in August 1978 served that purpose as well. See Stephens and Stephens (1986, 211).

7. Stepan's (1978, 292) relatively comprehensive definition of institutionalization combines both aspects. Institutionalization, he concludes, "implies that a regime has consolidated the new political patterns of succession, control and participation, has managed a viable pattern of economic accumulation, has forged extensive constituencies for its rule, and has created a significant degree of Gramscian 'hegemonic acceptance' in civil society." I have divided the concept into two parts, since institutionalization may not occur simultaneously in both areas. Indeed, there may be a tension between the two. Steps taken to assure a broad, stable mass constituency, for example, may pose a serious challenge to economic accumulation.

8. Even in the Mexican case, which is our most successful example of political institutionalization, the problems of interelite consolidation were enormous. The 1934 confrontation between outgoing *jefe máximo* Calles and incoming President Cárdenas over who would actually govern was resolved only after ten months of dispute and Calles's forcible expulsion from the country. Furthermore, the 1940 presidential election was characterized by violent confrontations with electoral competitors and allegations of extensive electoral fraud. See Cornelius (1973) on the process of regime consolidation in Mexico.

9. Scott (1989, 5) developed this idea to describe the "prosaic" or "first resort" techniques of resistance by the peasantry, but the analysis may be extended to economic elites when these elites are in the (relatively rare) position of being

politically subordinate. Of course, the business elite has a much larger arsenal of weapons to choose from than the peasantry.

10. Nationalist development projects can, of course, have the reverse effect and alienate the local producers. Conaghan (1988), for example, argues that the extensive penetration of local businesses by foreign capital in Ecuador fed intense local business opposition to the Andean Pact's decision to restrict ownership and profit repatriation by foreign firms.

bibliography

Abugattas, Luis. 1986. "Crisis de transición, asociaciones empresariales y partidos políticos: El caso peruano." Paper presented at the International Congress of the Latin American Studies Association, Boston, October.

Acuña, Carlos H. 1991. "Intereses empresarios, dictadura y democracia en la Argentina actual (O, sobre porqué la burguesía abandona estrategias autoritarias y opta por la estabilidad democrática)." Paper presented at the Conference on Business Elites and Democracy in Latin America, Kellogg Institute for International Studies, University of Notre Dame, Notre Dame, Ind., May 3–5.

Alcázar, Marco Antonio. 1970. *Las agrupaciones patronales en México*. México, D.F.: El Colegio de México.

Allahar, Antón L. 1990. "The Evolution of the Latin American Bourgeoisie: An Historical-Comparative Study." *International Journal of Comparative Sociology* (Netherlands) 31, nos. 3–4 (September–December): 222–36.

Anderson, Thomas P. 1971. *Matanza: El Salvador's Communist Revolt of 1932*. Lincoln: University of Nebraska Press.

ANSCA. n.d. *Memoria 1960–65*. Managua: Editorial Aurora.

APENN. 1991. *Boletín informativo*, November–December.

Arana Sevilla, Mario. 1990. "Nicaragua: Estabilización, ajuste y estrategia económica, 1988–89." *Cuadernos de pensamiento propio*, serie ensayos 18 (March): 9–62.

Arana Sevilla, Mario, Richard Stahler-Sholk, Gerardo Timossi D. and Carmen López G. 1987. "Deuda, estabilización y ajuste: La transformación en Nicaragua, 1979–1986." *Cuadernos de pensamiento propio*, serie ensayos 15 (November).

Argüello Huper, Alejandro, and Nanno Kleiterp. 1985. *Análisis del proceso inversionista nicaragüense de 1979 a 1985*. Managua: Fondo Nicaragüense de Inversion, October.

Arriagada, Genaro. 1970. *La oligarquía patronal chilena*. Santiago, Chile: Ediciones Nueva Universidad.

Arriola, Carlos. 1976. "Los grupos empresariales frente al estado (1973–1975)." In *Las fronteras del control del estado mexicano*, by Centro de Estudios Internacionales, 33–82. México, D.F.: El Colegio de México.

ASGANIC. 1975. "Informe a la Confederación Interamericana de Ganaderos (CIAGA)." Paper presented at CIAGA meeting, Toronto, Canada, November 12–15.

Austin, James E. 1972. *Marketing Adjustment to Production Modernization.* Montefresco, Nicaragua: INCAE.

Ballard, Patricia. 1985. "The Insertion of Nicaragua into the World Market for Beef: A Summary." Report presented at I Congreso Nacional Científico Agropecuario, Managua, June.

Balmori, Diana, Stuart F. Voss, and Miles Wortman. 1984. *Notable Family Networks in Latin America.* Chicago: University of Chicago Press.

Baloyra, Enrique. 1982. *El Salvador in Transition.* Chapel Hill: University of North Carolina Press.

Bamat, Thomas. 1978. "From Plan Inca to Plan Tupac Amaru: The Recomposition of the Peruvian Power Bloc, 1968–1977." Ph.D. diss., Rutgers University.

Banco Nacional de Nicaragua (BNN; after 1979, Banco Nacional de Desarrollo [BND]). *Habilitados (Algodón, Café, Ganadería, and Granos Básicos).* Various years.

Barahona, Amaru. 1989. *Estudio sobre la historia de Nicaragua.* Managua: INIES.

Barham, Bradford, Mary Clark, Elizabeth Katz, and Rachel Schurman. 1992. "Nontraditional Agricultural Exports in Latin America." *Latin American Research Review* 27, no. 2: 43–82.

Barrios Johanning, Miguel. 1992. "Que la rentabilidad sea la base: Informe para la Asamblea General ECODEPA (10 abril 1992)." *Productores* 13 (April): 19–22.

Barry, Tom. 1990. *El Salvador: A Country Guide.* Albuquerque: Inter-Hemispheric Education Resource Center.

Bartell, Ernest. 1991. "Business Perceptions and the Transition to Democracy in Chile." Paper presented at the Conference on Business Elites and Democracy in Latin America, Kellogg Institute for International Studies, University of Notre Dame, Notre Dame, Ind., May 3–5.

Basáñez, Miguel. 1990. *La lucha por la hegemonía en México 1968–1990.* 8th ed., expanded. México, D.F.: Siglo Veintiuno.

Baumeister, Eduardo. 1983. *El subsistema del algodón.* Managua: INIES.

——. 1984a. "Estructura y reforma agraria en el proceso sandinista." *Desarrollo económico* 24, no. 94 (July–September): 187–202.

——. 1984b. "La importancia de los medianos productores en la agricultura nicaragüense." Paper presented at the Latin American Studies Center, Cambridge University, Cambridge, England, September.

——. 1988. "Desarrollistas y campesinistas." *Pensamiento propio* 6, no. 52 (July–August): 26–31.

——. 1989. "El problema agrario y los sujetos del desarrollo nicaragüense." In *El debate sobre la reforma agraria en Nicaragua,* edited by Raul Ruben and Jan P. de Grott, 129–54. Managua: Editorial Ciencias Sociales.

——. 1991. "Estado y campesinado en el gobierno sandinista." Paper presented at the International Congress of the Latin American Studies Association, Washington, D.C., April 4–6.

Baumeister, Eduardo, and Oscar Neira Cuadra. 1986. "The Making of a Mixed Economy: Class Struggle and State Policy in the Nicaraguan Transition." In *Transition and Development,* edited by Richard R. Fagen et al., 171–91. New York: Monthly Review Press.

BCN. 1979. *Indicadores económicos* 5, nos. 1 and 2 (December).

——. 1981? *Informe anual 1978.* Managua: BCN.

——. 1990. *Informe económico 1989.* Managua: BCN.

——. 1992. *Indicadores de actividad económica* 2, no. 4 (May).

——. *Nicaragua Economic Report.* Various issues.

Becker, David G. 1983. *The New Bourgeoisie and the Limits of Dependency.* Princeton: Princeton University Press.

Belli, Pedro. 1968. "An Inquiry Concerning the Growth of Cotton Farming in Nicaragua." Ph.D. diss., University of California, Berkeley.

——. 1975. "Prolegómeno para una historia económica de Nicaragua de 1905 a 1966." *Revista conservadora del pensamiento centroamericano* 30, no. 146: 2–30.

Bendaña, Alejandro. 1991. *Una tragedia campesina: Testimonios de la resistencia.* Managua: Editora de Arte, S.A. y Centro de Estudios Internacionales.

Biderman, Jaime M. 1982. "Class Structure, the State and Capitalist Development in Nicaraguan Agriculture." Ph.D. diss., University of California, Berkeley.

Biondi-Morra, Brizio N. 1990. *Revolución y política alimentaria: Un análisis crítico de Nicaragua.* México, D.F.: Siglo Veintiuno.

Bitar, Sergio. 1986. *Chile: Experiment in Democracy.* Philadelphia: Institute for the Study of Human Issues.

Booth, John A. 1985a. *The End and the Beginning: The Nicaraguan Revolution.* 2d ed. Boulder, Colo.: Westview Press.

——. 1985b. "The National Governmental System." In *Nicaragua: The First Five Years*, edited by Thomas W. Walker, 29–44. New York: Praeger.

Booth, John A., and Mitchell A. Seligson. 1989. *Elections and Democracy in Central America.* Chapel Hill: University of North Carolina Press.

Borge, Tomás. 1982. "The Second Anniversary of the Sandinista Revolution." In *Sandinistas Speak*, by Tomás Borge, Carlos Fonseca, Daniel Ortega, Humberto Ortega, and Jaime Wheelock, 127–40. Edited by Bruce Marcus. New York: Pathfinder Press.

Bottomore, Tom, and Robert J. Brym. 1989. *The Capitalist Class: An International Study.* New York: New York University Press.

Bourricaud, Francois. 1966. "Structure and Function of the Peruvian Oligarchy." *Studies in Comparative International Development* 2, no. 2: 17–31.

——. 1970. *Power and Society in Contemporary Peru.* Translated by Paul Stevenson. New York: Praeger.

Bravo Mena, Luis Felipe. 1987. "COPARMEX and Mexican Politics." In *Government and Private Sector in Contemporary Mexico*, edited by Sylvia Maxfield and Ricardo Anzaldúa Montoya, 89–104. La Jolla: Center for U.S.-Mexican Studies, University of California, San Diego.

Brinton, Crane. 1938. *The Anatomy of Revolution.* New York: Vintage.

Brockett, Charles D. 1990. *Land, Power, and Poverty: Agrarian Transformation and Political Conflict in Central America.* Boston: Unwin Hyman.

Brundenius, Claes. 1987. "Industrial Development Strategies in Revolutionary Nicaragua." In *The Political Economy of Revolutionary Nicaragua*, edited by Rose J. Spalding, 85–104. Boston: Allen & Unwin.

Buchanan, Paul G., and Betts Putnam. 1992. "The Reconstruction of Bourgeois Hegemony in the Southern Cone: A Microfoundational Analysis." Unpublished manuscript, September.

Bugajski, Janusz. 1990. *Sandinista Communism and Rural Nicaragua*. New York: Praeger.

Bulmer-Thomas, Victor. 1987. *The Political Economy of Central America since 1920*. Cambridge: Cambridge University Press.

———. 1991. "Nicaragua since 1930." In *Central America since Independence*, edited by Leslie Bethell, 227–76. Cambridge: Cambridge University Press.

Burns, E. Bradford. 1991. *Patriarch and Folk: The Emergence of Nicaragua, 1798–1858*. Cambridge, Mass: Harvard University Press.

CADIN. 1975. "Evolución histórica, organización y actividades de la cámara de industrias de Nicaragua." Paper presented at the Mesa Redonda sobre el Papel de las Organizaciones de Empleadores en América Latina, Río de Janeiro, Brazil, July 14–22.

Cámara de Comercio de León. n.d. Untitled collection of laws. León, Nicaragua: n.p.

Camp, Roderic A. 1989. *Entrepreneurs and Politics in Twentieth-Century Mexico*. New York and London: Oxford University Press.

Campero, Guillermo. 1984. *Los gremios empresariales en el período 1970–1983: Comportamiento sociopolítico y orientaciones ideológicas*. Santiago, Chile: Instituto Latinoamericano de Estudios Transnacionales.

———. 1988. "Los empresarios ante la alternativa democrática." In *Empresarios y estado en América Latina*, edited by Celso Garrido N., 245–66. México, D.F.: Centro de Investigación y Docencia Económica, a.c., Fundación Friedrich Ebert, UNAM-Instituto de Investigaciones Sociales, Universidad Autónoma Metropolitana-Unidad Azcapotzalco.

———. 1991. "Entrepreneurs under the Military Regime." In *The Struggle for Democracy in Chile, 1982–1990*, edited by Paul W. Drake and Iván Jaksic, 128–58. Lincoln: University of Nebraska Press.

CARANA Corporation and Sparks Companies. 1991. *Framework for an Agribusiness Strategy in Nicaragua*. Vol. 2. Report for USAID/Nicaragua, October.

Cardenal Downing, Gloria. 1988. "Desarrollo y transformaciones en el agro nicaragüense (1979–1987)." M.A. thesis, Universidad Católica de Lovaine.

Cardoso, Fernando Henrique. 1967. "The Industrial Elite." In *Elites in Latin America*, edited by Seymour Martin Lipset and Aldo Solari, 94–116. New York and London: Oxford University Press.

———. 1972. *Ideologías de la burguesía industrial en sociedades dependientes (Argentina y Brasil)*. 2d ed. México, D.F.: Siglo Veintiuno.

Castillo Aramburu, Melba. 1988. "El papel de los empresarios industriales en la economía nicaragüense." In *Empresarios y estado en América Latina*, edited by Celso Garrido N., 97–120. México, D.F.: Centro de Investigación y Docencia Económica, a.c., Fundación Friedrich Ebert, UNAM-Instituto de Investigaciones Sociales, Universidad Autónoma Metropolitana-Unidad Azcapotzalco.

Castillo Ochoa, Manuel. 1988. "¿La formación de una clase?: Empresarios, política y estado en el Perú de 1987." In *Empresarios y estado en América Latina*, edited by Celso Garrido N., 185–206. México, D.F.: Centro de Investigación y Docencia Económica, a.c., Fundación Friedrich Ebert, UNAM-Instituto de Investigaciones Sociales, Universidad Autónoma Metropolitana-Unidad Azcapotzalco.

Castro, Vanessa, and Gary Prevost, eds. 1992. *The 1990 Elections in Nicaragua and Their Aftermath.* Lanham, Md.: Rowman & Littlefield.

CEPAL. 1984. *Notas para el estudio económico de América Latina y el Caribe, 1983: Nicaragua.* México, D.F.: CEPAL.

———. 1985. *Notas para el estudio económico de América Latina y el Caribe, 1984: Nicaragua.* México, D.F.: CEPAL.

———. 1986. *Notas para el estudio económico de América Latina y el Caribe, 1985: El Salvador.* México, D.F.: CEPAL.

———. 1987. "Balance preliminar de la Economía Latinoamericana 1987." *Notas sobre la economía y el desarrollo,* nos. 455/456 (December).

———. 1989. "Balance preliminar de la Economía Latinoamericana 1989." *Notas sobre la economía y el desarrollo,* nos. 485/486 (December).

———. 1990a. *Notas para el estudio económico de América Latina y el Caribe, 1989: Nicaragua.* México, D.F.: CEPAL.

———. 1990b. "Preliminary Overview of the Economy of Latin America and the Caribbean, 1990." *Notas sobre la economía y el desarrollo,* nos. 500–501 (December).

———. 1991. "Balance preliminar de la Economía de América Latina y el Caribe 1991." *Notas sobre la economía y el desarrollo,* nos. 519/520 (December).

———. 1992a. "Balance preliminar de la Economía de América Latina y el Caribe 1992." *Notas sobre la economía y el desarrollo,* nos. 537/538 (December).

———. 1992b. *Nicaragua: Evolución económica durante 1991.* México, D.F.: CEPAL.

Chamorro, Amalia, Francisco Navarrete, and David Dye. 1983. Untitled manuscript. Paper presented at INIES workshop, Managua, Nicaragua, June 10.

Christian, Shirley. 1986. *Nicaragua: Revolution in the Family.* New York: Vintage.

CIERA. 1981. "Las clases sociales en el agro." Managua: Mimeo.

———. 1988. "La reforma monetaria de 1988: Operación 'Mártires de Quilalí.'" In *El debate sobre la reforma económica,* 302–19. Managua: CIERA.

———. 1989. *La reforma agraria en Nicaragua, 1979–1989.* Vols. 1–9. Managua: CIERA.

CIERA/Programa Alimentario Nicaragüense (PAN)/Canadian International Development Agency (CIDA). 1984. *Informe final del Proyecto Estrategia Alimentaria.* Vol. 3, *Directorio de políticas alimentarias.* Managua: CIERA.

CIPRES. 1991. "El area propiedad de los trabajadores: Una nueva forma de propiedad social en Nicaragua." *Cuadernos del CIPRES,* no. 10, special issue (December).

CNG. 1989. *Memoria: Julio 1983–September 1989.* Managua: CNG.

Colburn, Forrest D. 1986. *Post-Revolutionary Nicaragua: State, Class, and the Dilemmas of Agrarian Policy.* Berkeley: University of California Press.

———. 1990. *Managing the Commanding Heights: Nicaragua's State Enterprises.* Berkeley: University of California Press.

Colburn, Forrest D., and Silvio De Franco. 1985. "Privilege, Production, and Revolution: The Case of Nicaragua." *Comparative Politics* 17, no. 3 (April): 277–90.

Coleman, William, and Wyn Grant. 1988. "The Organizational Cohesion and Political Access of Business: A Study of Comprehensive Associations." *European Journal of Political Research* 16, no. 5 (September): 467–87.

Colindres, Eduardo. 1976. "La tenencia de la tierra en El Salvador." *Estudios centroamericanos* 31, nos. 335–36 (September–October): 463–72.

————. 1977. *Fundamentos económicos de la burguesía salvadoreña.* San Salvador: Universidad Centroamericana Editores.

Collier, David, and Deborah L. Norden. 1992. "Strategic Choice Models of Political Change in Latin America." *Comparative Politics* 24, no. 2 (January): 229–43.

Comisión Internacional para la Recuperación y el Desarrollo de Centroamérica. 1989. *Pobreza, conflicto y esperanza: Un momento crítico para Centroamérica.* Durham, N.C.: Duke University Press.

Comité Económico del Gobierno de El Salvador. 1990. "El plan económico de ARENA." *Estudios centroamericanos* 45, nos. 495–96 (January–February): 109–11.

Conaghan, Catherine M. 1988. *Restructuring Domination: Industrialists and the State in Ecuador.* Pittsburgh: University of Pittsburgh Press.

————. 1991. "Hot Money and Hegemony." Paper presented at the Conference on Business Elites and Democracy in Latin America, Kellogg Institute for International Studies, University of Notre Dame, Notre Dame, Ind., May 3–5.

Conaghan, Catherine M., James M. Malloy, and Luis A. Abugattas. 1990. "Business and the 'Boys': The Politics of Neoliberalism in the Central Andes." *Latin American Research Review* 25, no. 2: 3–30.

Conroy, Michael E. 1984. "False Polarization?: Alternative Perspectives on the Economic Strategies of Post-Revolutionary Nicaragua." Paper presented at the Twenty-fifth Annual Convention of the International Studies Association, Atlanta, March 29.

————. 1990. "The Political Economy of the 1990 Nicaraguan Elections." *International Journal of Political Economy* 20, no. 3 (Fall): 5–33.

Conroy, Michael E., and Manuel Pastor, Jr. 1988. "The Nicaraguan Experiment: Characteristics of a New Economic Model." In *Crisis in Central America*, edited by Nora Hamilton et al., 207–26. Boulder, Colo.: Westview Press.

Contreras, Ariel José. 1990. *México 1940: Industrialización y crisis política.* 2d ed. México, D.F.: Siglo Veintiuno.

CORDENIC. 1988. "Misión y programa de actividades." Managua: Mimeo.

————. 1990. "Informe de actividades 1988–1990." Managua: Mimeo.

CORFO. 1989. *50 años de realizaciones 1939–1989.* Santiago, Chile: CORFO.

CORNAP. 1991. "Estrategia de privatización del gobierno de Nicaragua." Unpublished document, November.

————. 1993. "La privatización en Nicaragua: Resumen de ejecutoria y perspectivas." Unpublished document, March 9.

Cornelius, Wayne A. 1973. "Nation Building, Participation, and Distribution: The Politics of Social Reform under Cárdenas." In *Crisis, Choice, and Change: Historical Studies of Political Development*, edited by Gabriel A. Almond, Scott C. Flanagan, and Robert J. Mundt, 392–498. Boston: Little, Brown.

Coronel Kautz, Manuel. 1984. "Una estrategia para superar la dependencia y subdesarrollo." *Revolución y desarrollo* 2 (July–September): 9–15.

Coronel Kautz, Ricardo. 1984. "La normación del trabajo y el salario y la difícil situación de nuestras empresas estatales." *Revolución y desarrollo* 2 (July–September): 25–26.

COSEP. 1987a. "Breve narración de reunión de 10 de julio de 1987 MIDINRA y Ganaderos (FAGANIC y UNAG)." *Memorandum de la presidencia*, no. 19, July 30.

——. 1987b. Press release. April 29.

——. 1990. "Pronunciamiento." October 24.

——. 1991. "Comunicado." January 23.

——. 1992a. "Comunicado de prensa." April 30.

——. 1992b. "Posición de COSEP ante gobierno." May 4.

——. *Memorandum de la presidencia.* Various issues.

COSEP/INCAE/MEDE. 1992. "Encuesta nacional a empresarios privados: Algunos resultados preliminares." Unpublished document, May–June.

COSIP. 1974. "Conclusiones sobre el tema: Estrategia de desarrollo socio-económico para la década de los 70." Managua: Mimeo.

Crosby, Benjamin L. 1985. "Divided We Stand, Divided We Fall: Public-Private Sector Relations in Central America." *Occasional Papers Series*, no. 10. Miami: Latin American and Caribbean Center, Florida International University, April.

Cruz, Ernesto. 1974. "Estrategia de desarrollo para los años 70." Paper presented at the First Convention of COSIP, Managua, Nicaragua, March 1.

Cruz, Ernesto, and Kenneth L. Hoadley. 1975. *Necesidad de una política oficial sobre comercialización del algodón: El caso de Nicaragua.* Managua: INCAE.

Cuadra, Scarlet. 1992. "Worker's Property in Nicaragua: New Dilemmas Every Day." *Barricada international* 12, no. 349 (May): 19–21.

Cuadra Pasos, Carlos. 1967. "Los Cuadra: Una hebra en el tejido de la historia de Nicaragua." *Revista conservadora del pensamiento centroamericano* 17, no. 83 (supplement): 1–26.

Deere, Carmen Diana, Peter Marchetti, S.J., and Nola Reinhardt. 1985. "The Peasantry and the Development of Sandinista Agrarian Policy, 1979–1984." *Latin American Research Review* 20, no. 3: 75–110.

De Franco, Silvio, and Emilio Pereira. 1989. "Cómo perciben los gerentes el entorno centroamericano." *Revista INCAE* 3, no. 1: 27–36.

de Janvry, Alain. 1981. *The Agrarian Question and Reformism in Latin America.* Baltimore: Johns Hopkins University Press.

Del Campo, Santiago, et al. 1973. "The Clans of Chile." In *The Chilean Road to Socialism*, edited by Dale L. Johnson, 395–409. Garden City, N.Y.: Anchor.

de Sebastián, Luis. 1979. "El camino hacia la democracia." *Estudios centroamericanos* 35, nos. 372–73: 947–60.

——. 1986. "Consideraciones político-económicas sobre la oligarquía en El Salvador." In *El Salvador: Estado oligárquico y desarrollo económico-social, 1945–1979*, edited by the Centro de Investigación y Acción Social, 28–48. México, D.F.: Centro de Investigación y Acción Social, Cuaderno de Trabajo no. 6.

de Vylder, Stefan. 1976. *Allende's Chile: The Political Economy of the Rise and Fall of the Unidad Popular.* Cambridge: Cambridge University Press.

Dijkstra, Geske. 1992. *Industrialization in Sandinista Nicaragua: Policy and Practice in a Mixed Economy.* Boulder, Colo.: Westview Press.

Diskin, Martin. 1989. "El Salvador: Reform Prevents Change." In *Searching for*

Agrarian Reform in Latin America, edited by William C. Thiesenhusen, 429–50. Boston: Unwin Hyman.

Dore, Elizabeth, and John Weeks. 1976. "The Intensification of the Assault against the Working Class in 'Revolutionary' Peru." *Latin American Perspectives* 3, no. 2 (Spring): 55–83.

———. 1977. "Class Alliances and Class Struggle in Peru." *Latin American Perspectives* 4, no. 3 (Summer): 4–17. Special issue: *Peru: Bourgeois Revolution and Class Struggle*.

Dornbusch, Rudiger, and Sebastian Edwards, eds. 1991. *The Macroeconomics of Populism in Latin America*. Chicago: University of Chicago Press.

Dosal, Paul J. 1985. "Accelerating Dependent Development and Revolution: Nicaragua and the Alliance for Progress." *Inter-American Economic Affairs* 38, no. 4 (Spring): 75–96.

Downs, Anthony. 1957. *An Economic Theory of Democracy*. New York: Harper and Row.

Drake, Paul. 1973. "The Political Response of the Chilean Upper Class to the Great Depression and the Threat of Socialism." In *The Rich, the Well Born and the Powerful: Elites and Upper Classes in History*, edited by Frederic Cople Jaher, 304–37. Urbana: University of Illinois Press.

Dresser, Denise. 1991. *Neopopulist Solutions to Neoliberal Problems: Mexico's National Solidarity Program*. La Jolla: Center for U.S.-Mexican Studies, University of California, San Diego.

Dubois, Alfonso, et al. 1983. *El subsistema del azúcar en Nicaragua*. Managua: INIES-CRIES.

Dunkerley, James. 1988. *Power in the Isthmus: A Political History of Modern Central America*. London: Verso.

Durand, Francisco. 1982. *La década frustrada: Los industriales y el poder, 1970–80*. Lima: Centro de Estudios y Promoción del Desarrollo-DESCO.

———. 1988a. *La burguesía peruana: Los primeros industriales, Alan García y los empresarios*. Lima: Centro de Estudios y Promoción del Desarrollo.

———. 1988b. "Empresarios y política en el Perú: De la concertación a la estatización de la banca." In *Empresarios y estado en América Latina*, edited by Celso Garrido N., 267–86. México, D.F.: Centro de Investigación y Docencia Económica, a.c., Fundación Friedrich Ebert, UNAM-Instituto de Investigaciones Sociales, Universidad Autónoma Metropolitana-Unidad Azcapotzalco.

———. 1991. "Business Peak Associations in Latin America: The Case of Peru." Paper presented at the Conference on Business Elites and Democracy in Latin America, Kellogg Institute for International Studies, University of Notre Dame, Notre Dame, Ind., May 3–5.

Eckstein, Shlomo, et al. 1978. *Land Reform in Latin America: Bolivia, Chile, Mexico, Peru and Venezuela*. World Bank Staff Working Paper, no. 275. Washington, D.C.: World Bank.

ECLA. 1951. *Theoretical and Practical Problems of Economic Growth*. Santiago, Chile: ECLA.

Edmisten, Patricia Taylor. 1990. *Nicaragua Divided: La Prensa and the Chamorro Legacy*. Pensacola: University of West Florida Press.

Emmanuel, Arghiri. 1972. *Unequal Exchange: A Study of the Imperialism of Trade*. New York: Monthly Review Press.

Enríquez, Laura J. 1991a. "Agrarian Reform in Nicaragua: Its Past and Its Future." Paper presented at the Sixteenth International Congress of the Latin American Studies Association, Washington, D.C., April 4–6.

———. 1991b. *Harvesting Change*. Chapel Hill: University of North Carolina Press.

Enríquez, Laura J., and Rose J. Spalding. 1987. "Banking Systems and Revolutionary Change: The Politics of Agricultural Credit in Nicaragua." In *The Political Economy of Revolutionary Nicaragua*, edited by Rose J. Spalding, 105–26. Boston: Allen & Unwin.

Enríquez, Laura J., et al. 1991. *Nicaragua: Reconciliation Awaiting Recovery*. Washington, D.C.: Washington Office on Latin America.

Evans, Peter, Dietrich Rueschemeyer, and Theda Skocpol, eds. 1985. *Bringing the State Back In*. Cambridge: Cambridge University Press.

Evans, Trevor. 1987. "El algodón: Un cultivo de debate." *Cuadernos de pensamiento propio*, April.

FAGANIC. 1982. "Guía para informe de ganadería." Managua: Mimeo, August 4.

FAO. 1978. "Programa democrático del gobierno nacional." In *Nicaragua: Reforma o revolución*, by IHCA. Vol. 2. N.p.

Fernández Ampié, Guillermo. 1992. "A Silent War." *Barricada international* 12, no. 347 (March): 11–13.

Fiallos Oyanguren, Mariano. 1968. "The Nicaraguan Political System: The Flow of Demands and the Reaction of the Regime." Ph.D. diss., University of Kansas.

FIDA. 1980. *Informe de la misión especial de programación a Nicaragua*. Rome: FIDA.

FIDEG. 1993. "Diagnóstico de empresas privatizadas a favor de trabajadores." *Observador económico* 19 (July): 22–26.

———. *Boletín informativo*. Various issues.

———. *Observador económico*. Various issues.

FitzGerald, E. V. K. 1976. *State and Economic Development: Peru since 1968*. Cambridge: Cambridge University Press.

———. 1979. *The Political Economy of Peru, 1956–78: Economic Development and the Restructuring of Capital*. Cambridge: Cambridge University Press.

———. 1984a. "Problems in Financing a Revolution: The Case of Nicaragua 1979–1984." Working paper—Sub-Series on Money, Finance and Development, no. 14. Paper presented at Institute for Social Studies Workshop, The Hague, December 3–14.

———. 1984b. *Stabilization and Economic Justice: The Case of Nicaragua*. Notre Dame, Ind.: Kellogg Institute for International Studies, University of Notre Dame.

———. 1989. *Financing Economic Development: A Structural Approach to Monetary Policy*. Brookfield, Vt.: Gower.

Flakoll Alegría, Daniel. 1991. "César Legislates Instability." *Barricada international* 11, no. 341 (September): 4–6.

Fonseca, Roberto. 1989. "El derecho a quien lo tiene." *Análisis*, no. 3 (November): 27–29.

Font, Mauricio. 1990. *Coffee, Contention and Change*. London: Basil Blackwell.

Foxley, Alejandro. 1986. "The Neoconservative Economic Experiment in Chile." In *Military Rule in Chile*, edited by J. Samuel Valenzuela and Arturo Valenzuela, 13–50. Baltimore: Johns Hopkins University Press.

Frank, André Gunder. 1969. *Latin America: Underdevelopment or Revolution*. New York: Monthly Review Press.

FSLN. 1990a. "Acuerdos de Unidad (1979)." In *Sandinistas: Key Documents/Documentos Claves*, edited by Dennis Gilbert and David Block, 68–73. Ithaca, N.Y.: Latin American Studies Program, Cornell University.

———. 1990b. "Análisis de la Coyuntura y Tareas de la Revolución Popular Sandinista." In *Sandinistas: Key Documents/Documentos Claves*, edited by Dennis Gilbert and David Block, 74–110. Ithaca, N.Y.: Latin American Studies Program, Cornell University.

Furtado, Celso. 1976. *Economic Development of Latin America*. Cambridge: Cambridge University Press.

Gallardo, María Eugenia, and José Roberto López. 1986. *Centroamérica: La crisis en cifras*. San José, Costa Rica: Instituto Interamericano de Cooperación para la Agricultura and la Facultad Latinoamericana de Ciencias Sociales.

Gariazzo, Alicia, et al. 1983. *El subsistema del café en Nicaragua*. Managua: INIES-CRIES.

Gibson, Bill. 1987. "A Structural Overview of the Nicaraguan Economy." In *The Political Economy of Revolutionary Nicaragua*, edited by Rose J. Spalding, 15–42. Boston: Allen & Unwin.

———. 1991. "The Nicaraguan Economy in the Medium Run." *Journal of Interamerican Studies and World Affairs* 33, no. 2 (Summer): 23–52.

Gilbert, Dennis. 1977. *The Oligarchy and the Old Regime in Peru*. Ithaca, N.Y.: Dissertation Series, Latin American Studies Program, Cornell University.

———. 1980. "The End of the Peruvian Revolution: A Class Analysis." *Studies in Comparative International Development* 15 (Spring): 15–37.

———. 1985. "The Bourgeoisie." In *Nicaragua: The First Five Years*, edited by Thomas W. Walker, 183–99. New York: Praeger.

———. 1988. *Sandinistas: The Party and the Revolution*. London: Basil Blackwell.

Glade, William, ed. 1991. *Privatization of Public Enterprises in Latin America*. San Francisco: Institute for Contemporary Studies.

Gobat, Michel. 1991. "Soldiers into Capitalists: The Rise of a Military Bourgeoisie in Pre-Revolutionary Nicaragua (1956–67)." Unpublished manuscript, April 1.

Gobierno de Nicaragua-CST. 1993. *Acuerdo*. February 2.

Gonsalves, Ralph. 1977. "The Trade Union Movement in Jamaica: Its Growth and Some Resultant Problems." In *Essays on Power and Change in Jamaica*, edited by Carl Stone and Aggrey Brown, 89–105. Kingston: Jamaica Publishing House.

Gould, Jeffrey L. 1990. *To Lead as Equals: Rural Protest and Political Consciousness in Chinandega, Nicaragua, 1912–1979*. Chapel Hill: University of North Carolina Press.

Government of Nicaragua. 1992. "Nicaragua: Medium-Term Development Strategy, 1992–1996." Document presented at the Consultative Group Meeting, Washington, D.C., March 26.

Gudmundson, Lowell. 1983. "Costa Rica before Coffee: Occupational Distribution, Wealth Inequality and Elite Society in the Village Economy of the 1840s." *Journal of Latin American Studies* 15 (November): 427–52.

Gutiérrez, Roberto. 1989. "Los aspectos financieros del paquete de medidas de la reforma económica." In *Política económica y transformación social*, edited by CIERA, 157–94. Managua: CIERA.

Gutman, Roy. 1988. "Nicaraguan Turning Point: How the 1984 Vote Was Sabotaged." *Nation*, May 7, 642–45.

Haggard, Stephen, and Robert R. Kaufman. 1992a. "Institutions and Economic Adjustment." In *The Politics of Economic Adjustment*, edited by Stephen Haggard and Robert R. Kaufman, 3–40. Princeton: Princeton University Press.

———. 1992b. "The Political Economy of Inflation and Stabilization in Middle-Income Countries." In *The Politics of Economic Adjustment*, edited by Stephen Haggard and Robert R. Kaufman, 270–318. Princeton: Princeton University Press.

Hamilton, Nora. 1982. *The Limits of State Autonomy: Post-Revolutionary Mexico.* Princeton: Princeton University Press.

Haugaard, Lisa. 1991. "With and Against the State: Organizing Dilemmas for Grassroots Movements in Nicaragua." *Conference Paper*, no. 54. New York: Columbia University–New York University Consortium.

Heredia, Blanca. 1991. "Can Rational Profit Maximizers Be Democratic?: Businessmen and Democracy in Mexico." Revised version. Paper presented at the Conference on Business Elites and Democracy in Latin America, Kellogg Institute for International Studies, University of Notre Dame, Notre Dame, Ind., May 3–5.

———. n.d. "Ideas vs. Interests?: The Mexican Business Community in the 1980s." *Conference Paper*, no. 26. New York: Columbia University–New York University Consortium.

Hernández, Julio Ricardo. 1990. "El rol de los subsidios a la producción agropecuaria durante el programa de ajustes 1988–1990 en Nicaragua." Unpublished manuscript.

———. 1991. "Evaluación de la reforma agraria nicaragüense y caracterización de la nueva demanda campesina de tierra." Managua: Report for the Regional Office of the Food and Agriculture Organization, July.

Hill, Roscoe R. 1933. *Fiscal Intervention in Nicaragua.* New York: Paul Maisal.

Hirschman, Albert O. 1973. *Journeys toward Progress.* New York: Norton.

Hodges, Donald C. 1986. *Intellectual Foundations of the Nicaraguan Revolution.* Austin: University of Texas Press.

Hüper A., William. 1992. "Balance de las medidas fiscales 1992." *Observador económico* 3 (March): 13–22.

Hurtado, Osvaldo. 1980. *Political Power in Ecuador.* Translated by Nick D. Mills, Jr. Albuquerque: University of New Mexico Press.

Ianni, Octavio. 1975. *La formación del estado populista en América Latina.* México, D.F.: Ediciones Era.

IBRD. 1953. *The Economic Development of Nicaragua.* Baltimore: Johns Hopkins University Press.

———. 1981. *Nicaragua: The Challenge of Reconstruction.* Washington, D.C.: IBRD.

IDB. 1983. *Informe económico: Nicaragua.* Washington, D.C.: IDB.

IHCA. 1978. *Nicaragua: Reforma o revolución.* Vols. 1–3. N.p.

———. 1981. "The Case Regarding COSEP and CAUS Members." *Envío,* no. 6 (November 15).

———. 1986. "Slow Motion toward a Survival Economy." *Envío* 5, no. 63 (September): 13–38.

———. 1987. "Private Enterprise—Alive and Kicking in Nicaragua." *Envío* 6, no. 70 (April): 30–39.

———. 1988a. "Economic Reform: Taking It to the Streets." *Envío* 7, no. 82 (May): 12–33.

———. 1988b. "More on the Economy—And More Needs to be Done." *Envío* 7, no. 88 (November): 19–24.

———. 1988c. "The New Economic Package—Will a Popular Model Emerge?" *Envío* 7, no. 86 (September): 14–42.

———. 1989. "Nicaragua: From a Mixed Up Economy toward a Socialist Mixed Economy." *Envío* 8, no. 94 (May): 33–54.

———. 1990. "Two Faces of UNO." *Envío* 9, no. 108 (July): 24–37.

———. 1991a. "The Economic Plan's Feet of Clay." *Envío* 10, no. 125 (December): 22–25.

———. 1991b. "How to Get Foreign Aid: Making the Poor Pay Isn't Enough." *Envío* 10, no. 118 (May): 29–38.

———. 1991c. "Labor: Rural Workers Fight to Become Owners." *Envío* 10, no. 118 (May): 16–19.

———. 1991d. "Privatization: Left, Right and Center." *Envío* 10, no. 124 (November): 20–34.

———. 1991e. "Property: Inside the Property Debate." *Envío* 10, no. 121 (August): 23–27.

———. 1992a. "Economic Takeoff: The Little Train that Couldn't." *Envío* 11, no. 135 (October): 18–24.

———. 1992b. "The Foreign Debt: Lengthening the Chain?" *Envío* 11, no. 129 (April): 15–21.

———. 1992c. "The FSLN-Government Balancing Act." *Envío* 11, no. 131 (June): 3–9.

———. 1992d. "The Urban Recession." *Envío* 11, no. 128 (March): 36.

INCAE. 1990? "Reseña Histórica." Brochure.

INDE. 1965. *Informe general de actividades, informe económico.* Managua: INDE.

———. 1966? *Informe general de actividades, informe financiero, anexos 1965–66.* Managua: INDE.

———. 1975. *Informe anual de INDE y sus programas FUNDE y EDUCREDITO 1974.* Managua: INDE.

———. 1977. *Informe anual de INDE y sus programas FUNDE y EDUCREDITO 1976.* Managua: INDE.

———. 1978. *Informe anual 1977.* Managua: INDE.

———. 1979. *El sector privado en la insurrección 1979.* Managua: COSEP.

————. 1980. *Informe anual 1979*. Managua: INDE.

INIES. 1987. *Plan económico 1987*. Managua: INIES.

INIESEP. *Cuadernos empresariales*. Various issues.

Irvin, George. 1983. "Nicaragua: Establishing the State as the Centre of Accumulation." *Cambridge Journal of Economics* 7:125–39.

Jarvis, Lovell S. 1989. "The Unraveling of Chile's Agrarian Reform, 1973–1986." In *Searching for Agrarian Reform in Latin America*, edited by William C. Thiesenhusen, 240–75. Boston: Unwin Hyman.

JGRN. 1983. "Economic Policy Guidelines 1983–1988." Managua: Mimeo.

Jiménez, C. Edgar. 1986. "El estado, la industrialización y la oligarquía en El Salvador." In *El Salvador: Estado oligárquico y desarrollo económico-social, 1945–1979*, edited by the Centro de Investigación y Acción Social, 3–28. México, D.F.: Centro de Investigación y Acción Social, Cuaderno de Trabajo no. 6.

Jirón, Manuel. 1986. *¿Quién es quién en Nicaragua?* San José, Costa Rica: Ediciones Radio Amor.

Johnson, Dale L. 1968–69. "The National and Progressive Bourgeoisie in Chile." In *Dependence and Underdevelopment*, edited by James D. Cockroft, André Gunder Frank, and Dale L. Johnson, 165–217. Garden City, N.Y.: Anchor.

Jung, Harald. 1980. "Class Struggles in El Salvador." *New Left Review*, no. 122 (July–August): 3–25.

Kahler, Miles. 1992. "External Influence, Conditionality, and the Politics of Adjustment." In *The Politics of Economic Adjustment*, edited by Stephen Haggard and Robert R. Kaufman, 89–138. Princeton: Princeton University Press.

Kaimowitz, David. 1989. "The Role of Decentralization in the Recent Nicaraguan Agrarian Reform." In *Searching for Agrarian Reform in Latin America*, edited by William C. Thiesenhusen, 384–407. Boston: Unwin Hyman.

Kaufman, Robert R., and Barbara Stallings. 1991. "The Political Economy of Latin American Populism." In *The Macroeconomics of Populism in Latin America*, edited by Rudiger Dornbusch and Sebastian Edwards, 15–44. Chicago: University of Chicago Press.

Keith, Novella Zett, and Nelson W. Keith. 1985. "The Rise of the Middle Class in Jamaica." In *Middle Classes in Dependent Countries*, edited by Dale L. Johnson, 67–106. Beverly Hills: Sage.

Kleiterp, Nanno. 1988. "Implementing a New Model of Accumulation: The Case of Nicaragua." Paper presented at the Forty-sixth International Congress of Americanists, Amsterdam, Holland, July 4–8.

Kolko, Gabriel. 1963. *The Triumph of Conservatism: A Reinterpretation of American History, 1900–1916*. Glencoe, N.Y.: Free Press.

Larios, Francisco, and Manolo Cordero. 1992. *Nicaragua: La reforma tributaria de 1992 y la reestructuración de los incentivos para la inversión*. Managua: INCAE.

Larson, Anne. 1993. "Nicaragua's Real Property Debate." *Envío* 12, no. 138 (January–March): 39–52.

Larson, Anne, with Nitlapán-UCA. 1993. "Foreign Aid: Where Have All the Dollars Gone?" *Envío* 12, no. 143 (June): 4–10.

LASA. 1984. *The Electoral Process in Nicaragua: Domestic and International In-*

fluences. Report of the LASA Delegation to Observe the Nicaraguan General Elections of November 4. Austin: LASA.

——. 1990. *Electoral Democracy under International Pressure*. Report of the LASA Commission to Observe the 1990 Nicaraguan Election. Pittsburgh: LASA.

Leff, Nathaniel H. 1976. "Capital Markets in the Less Developed Countries: The Group Principle." In *Money and Finance in Economic Growth and Development*, edited by Ronald I. McKinnon, 97–122. New York: Marcel Dekker.

——. 1978. "Industrial Organization and Entrepreneurship in the Developing Countries: The Economic Groups." *Economic Development and Cultural Change* 26, no. 4 (July): 661–75.

Lethander, Richard W. O. 1968. "The Economy of Nicaragua." Ph.D. diss., Duke University.

Lindeman, John. 1961. *Incentives to Private Industry in Nicaragua (Report to the International Cooperation Administration [ICA])*. Washington, D.C.: ICA.

Lomnitz, Larissa Adler, and Marisol Pérez-Lizaur. 1987. *A Mexican Elite Family, 1820–1980*. Translated by Cinna Lomnitz. Princeton: Princeton University Press.

López, Roberto. 1986. "The Nationalization of Foreign Trade in El Salvador: The Myths and Realities of Coffee." *Occasional Papers Series*, no. 16. Miami: Latin American and Caribbean Center, Florida International University.

López Vallecillos, Italo. 1979. "Fuerzas sociales y cambio social en El Salvador." *Estudios centroamericanos* 34, nos. 369–70 (July–August): 557–90.

Loveman, Brian. 1976. "The Transformation of the Chilean Countryside." In *Chile: Politics and Society*, edited by Arturo Valenzuela and J. Samuel Valenzuela, 238–96. New Brunswick, N.J.: Transaction Books.

Lowenthal, Abraham F., ed. 1975. *The Peruvian Experiment: Continuity and Change under Military Rule*. Princeton: Princeton University Press.

Luciak, Ilja A. 1987. "National Unity and Popular Hegemony: The Dialectics of Sandinista Agrarian Reform Policies, 1979–1986." *Journal of Latin American Studies* 19, part 1 (May): 113–40.

——. 1988. "Grassroots Movements in Nicaragua: A Comparative Analysis of the Rural Workers (ATC) and Small Farmers (UNAG) Associations." Paper presented at the Fourteenth International Congress of the Latin American Studies Association, New Orleans, March 17–19.

——. (Forthcoming). *The Political Economy of Transition: The Sandinista Legacy*. Gainesville: University Press of Florida.

Luna, Matilde. 1992. "Las asociaciones empresariales mexicanas y la apertura externa." Paper presented at the Seventeenth International Congress of the Latin American Studies Association, Los Angeles, September 24–27.

Luna, Matilde, Ricardo Tirado, and Francisco Valdés. 1987. "Businessmen and Politics in Mexico, 1982–1986." In *Government and Private Sector in Contemporary Mexico*, edited by Sylvia Maxfield and Ricardo Anzaldúa Montoya, 13–44. Monograph series no. 20. La Jolla: Center for U.S.-Mexican Studies, University of California, San Diego.

McClintock, Cynthia. 1981. *Peasant Cooperatives and Political Change in Peru*. Princeton: Princeton University Press.

Malloy, James M., and Mitchell A. Seligson, eds. 1987. *Authoritarians and Democrats: Regime Transition in Latin America.* Pittsburgh: University of Pittsburgh Press.

Malpica Silva Santisteban, Carlos. 1974. *Los dueños del Perú.* 6th ed., rev. Lima: Ediciones Peisa.

———. 1989. *El poder económico en el Perú.* Lima: Mosca Azul Editores.

Mansbridge, Jane J., ed. 1990. *Beyond Self-Interest.* Chicago: University of Chicago Press.

Marchetti, Peter. 1989. "Semejanzas y diferencias en dos debates sobre el campesinado." *Encuentro,* nos. 37/38 (July–December): 35–46.

Martínez, Javier, and Eugenio Tironi. 1985. *Las clases sociales en Chile: Cambio y estratificación, 1970–1980.* Santiago, Chile: Ediciones Sur.

Martínez, Julia E. 1989. "La política de reforma agraria de ARENA." *Estudios centroamericanos* 44, no. 492 (October): 843–46.

Martínez, Julia E., and Aquiles Montoya. 1990. "Un año de política económica de ARENA." *Estudios centroamericanos* 45, nos. 500–501 (June–July): 427–38.

Martínez Cuenca, Alejandro. 1988. "Medidas para domar una economía desbocada." *Pensamiento propio* 6, no. 52 (July/August): 19–23.

———. 1990. *Nicaragua: Una década de retos.* Managua: Editorial Nueva Nicaragua.

———. 1992. "The State and the Market: The Case of Nicaragua." Unpublished manuscript, June.

Martínez Nava, Juan M. 1984. *Conflicto estado-empresarios en los gobiernos de Cardénas, López Mateos y Echeverría.* México, D.F.: Editorial Nueva Imagen.

Maxfield, Sylvia. 1987. "Introduction." In *Government and Private Sector in Contemporary Mexico,* edited by Sylvia Maxfield and Ricardo Anzaldúa Montoya, 1–12. Monograph series no. 20. La Jolla: Center for U.S.-Mexican Studies, University of California, San Diego.

Mayorga, Salvador. 1990. "1980–1990: Land Reform and Human Development in Nicaragua." Mimeo.

———. 1991. "1980–1990: Agriculture in Nicaragua." Mimeo.

Medal, José Luis. 1985. *La revolución nicaragüense: Balance económico y alternativas futuras.* Managua: Centro de Investigaciones y Asesoría Socio-Económica (CINASE).

MEDE. 1991a. *National Export and Investment Promotion Program.* Managua: MEDE.

———. [1991]b. *Nicaragua: Basic Information for the Investor.* Managua: MEDE.

Medina, Luis. 1974. "Orígen y circunstancia de la idea de unidad nacional." *Foro internacional* 14, no. 3 (January–March): 265–90.

Menges, Constantine C. 1966. "Public Policy and Organized Business in Chile: A Preliminary Analysis." *Journal of International Affairs* 20, no. 2: 343–65.

MIDINRA. 1989. "Marco Estratégico del Desarrollo Agropecuario." In *La reforma agraria en Nicaragua, 1979–1989,* by CIERA, 1:155–231. Managua: CIERA.

———. *Plan de trabajo.* Various years.

———, Dirección de Tenencia de la Tierra. 1987. "Consolidado general: 1986." Unpublished data, January 14.

————, Dirección Superior. 1984. "Informe de la gestión estatal del MIDINRA para la JGRN (1979–1984)." *Revolución y desarrollo* 1 (April–June): 15–37.

————, Division de Comunicaciones. 1986. "Transformación de la Tenencia de la Tierra para 1986." *Informaciones agropecuarias* 17 (June–July): 4.

Miles, Sara, and Bob Ostertag. 1989. "D'Aubuisson's New ARENA." NACLA *Report on the Americas* 23, no. 2 (July): 14–39.

Millett, Richard. 1977. *Guardians of the Dynasty*. Maryknoll, N.Y.: Orbis.

Ministerio de Cooperación Externa. 1992. "Cooperación externa 1991 y perspectivas 1992." Managua: Unpublished document, 13 February.

Ministerio de la Presidencia. 1991. "Programa nacional de desarrollo social y superación de la pobreza." Draft document. Managua: Presidencia de la República de Nicaragua, March.

MIPLAN. 1980. *Programa de reactivación económica en beneficio del pueblo*. Managua: FSLN.

————. 1981. *Programa económico de austeridad y eficiencia '81*. Managua: MIPLAN.

Molina, Carlos, and Freddy Quezada. 1990. "La estratificación del agro en Nicaragua." Managua: Mimeo.

Moore, Barrington, Jr. 1966. *Social Origins of Dictatorship and Democracy*. Boston: Beacon.

Mosk, Sanford A. 1954. *Industrial Revolution in Mexico*. Berkeley: University of California Press.

NAFINSA. 1978. *La economía mexicana en cifras*. México, D.F.: NAFINSA.

————. 1981. *La economía mexicana en cifras*. México, D.F.: NAFINSA.

Navas Mendoza, Azucena, Adonai Jiménez Alar, Luz Adilia Cáceres Vilchez, and Arnoldo Montiel Castillo. n.d.(a). "Algunos elementos para un análisis de los períodos críticos del algodón en Nicaragua." Managua: Mimeo.

————. n.d.(b). "Elementos para un análisis de los períodos críticos del algodón de los años 70 en Nicaragua." Managua: Mimeo.

Neira Cuadra, Oscar, and Adolfo Acevedo V. 1992. "Nicaragua, hiperinflación y desestabilización: Análisis de la política económica, 1988 a 1991." *Cuadernos de* CRIES, no. 21.

Nelson, Joan M., ed. 1990. *Economic Crisis and Policy Choice: The Politics of Adjustment in the Third World*. Princeton: Princeton University Press.

Nicaragua Sugar Estates, Limited. 1953. *El Ingenio San Antonio, 1890–1953*. Granada, Nicaragua: n.p.

Nolan, David. 1984. *The Ideology of the Sandinistas and the Nicaraguan Revolution*. Coral Gables, Fla.: Institute of Interamerican Studies, University of Miami.

North, Liisa. 1985. *Bitter Grounds: Roots of Revolt in El Salvador*. 2d ed. Westport, Conn.: Lawrence Hill.

Núñez, Daniel. 1985a (interview). "If the Peasantry Did Not Trust the Revolution, We Would Be Through." In *Nicaragua: The Sandinista People's Revolution*, edited by Bruce Marcus, 367–74. New York: Pathfinder Press.

————. 1985b (interview). "The Producers of this Country Support Our Revolutionary Government." In *Nicaragua: The Sandinista People's Revolution*, edited by Bruce Marcus, 359–66. New York: Pathfinder Press.

———. 1991 (interview). "Sin nosotros no habrá desarrollo económico." *Envío* 10, no. 111 (February): 10–13.

Núñez Soto, Orlando. 1981. *El somocismo y el modelo capitalista agroexportadora*. Managua: Depto. de Ciencias Sociales, UNAN.

———. 1987. *Transición y lucha de clases en Nicaragua 1979–1986*. México, D.F.: Siglo Veintiuno.

———, ed. 1991. *La guerra en Nicaragua*. Managua: CIPRES.

Ocampo, José Antonio. 1991. "Collapse and (Incomplete) Stabilization of the Nicaraguan Economy." In *The Macroeconomics of Populism in Latin America*, edited by Rudiger Dornbusch and Sebastian Edwards, 331–68. Chicago: University of Chicago Press.

O'Donnell, Guillermo. 1973. *Modernization and Bureaucratic-Authoritarianism*. Berkeley: Institute of International Studies, University of California.

O'Donnell, Guillermo, and Philippe C. Schmitter. 1986. *Transitions from Authoritarian Rule: Tentative Conclusions about Uncertain Democracies*. Baltimore: Johns Hopkins University Press.

Ogliastri-Uribe, Enrique. 1986. "Estado, empresarios, sindicatos, trabajadores, administradores: Experiencias sobre gerencia y revolución en Nicaragua." Paper presented at the Thirteenth International Congress of the Latin American Studies Association, Boston, October 23.

Oquist, Paul. 1992. "Sociopolitical Dynamics of the 1990 Nicaraguan Elections." In *The 1990 Elections in Nicaragua and Their Aftermath*, edited by Vanessa Castro and Gary Prevost, 1–40. Lanham, Md.: Rowman and Littlefield.

Orellana, Víctor Antonio. 1985. "El Salvador: Crisis and Structural Change." *Occasional Papers Series*, no. 13. Miami: Latin American and Caribbean Center, Florida International University.

Ortega, Marvin, and Peter Marchetti. 1986. "Campesinado, democracia y revolución sandinista: Notas sobre los límites y posibilidades de la democracia en una sociedad rural atrasada." Managua: Mimeo.

Ortega S., Daniel. 1989. *Programa económico 1989*. Managua: Presidencia de la República.

Paige, Jeffrey M. 1987. "Coffee and Politics in Central America." In *Crises in the Caribbean Basin*, edited by Richard Tardanico, 141–90. Political Economy of the World-System Series, no. 9. Beverly Hills: Sage.

———. 1989. "Revolution and the Agrarian Bourgeoisie in Nicaragua." In *Revolution in the World System*, edited by Terry Boswell, 99–128. New York: Greenwood.

———. 1993. "Coffee and Power in El Salvador." *Latin American Research Review* 28, no. 3: 7–40.

Pasos, María Isabel. 1990. "Nuevas modalidades de dirección." *Análisis* 5 (January): 10–14.

Pastor, Robert A. 1987. *Condemned to Repetition: The United States and Nicaragua*. Princeton: Princeton University Press.

Pereira, Emilio. 1991 (interview). "Fiscal Reform Measures Reverse Economic Decline, Spur Expansion." In BCN, *Nicaragua Economic Report*, 1, no. 7 (September): 4–5.

Pérez, Andrés. 1992. "The FSLN after the Debacle: The Struggle for the Definition of *Sandinismo.*" *Journal of Interamerican Studies and World Affairs* 34, no. 1 (Spring): 111–39.

Pérez, Ernesto. 1992. "Comportamiento del comercio exterior de Nicaragua en 1991." *Revista de economía agrícola*, no. 4 (March): 3–15.

Pérez Piñeda, Carlos. 1985. "Propuesta teórica para el estudio de la burguesía en el subsistema ganadero nicaragüense." Paper presented at the IV Congreso Nicaragüense de Ciencias Sociales, Managua, Nicaragua, August 30-September 1.

Petras, James. 1969. *Politics and Social Forces in Chilean Development.* Berkeley: University of California Press.

Petras, James, and Morris Morley. 1992. *Latin America in the Time of Cholera.* New York: Routledge.

Phillips, Peter. 1977. "Jamaican Elites: 1938 to Present." In *Essays on Power and Change in Jamaica*, edited by Carl Stone and Aggrey Brown, 1–14. Kingston: Jamaica Publishing House.

Pilarte D., René, Vilma Ubau H. and Elías Guevara. 1988. "Evolución y resultados de las políticas económicas en el sector agrícola." *Boletín socioeconómico* 10 (November–December): 9–17.

Pizarro, Roberto. 1987. "New Economic Policy: A Necessary Readjustment." In *The Political Economy of Revolutionary Nicaragua*, edited by Rose J. Spalding, 217–32. Boston: Allen & Unwin.

"Popular Unity's Programme." 1973. In *The Chilean Road to Socialism*, edited by J. Ann Zammit, 255–84. Sussex, England: Institute of Development Studies.

Poulantzas, Nicos. 1978. *Classes in Contemporary Capitalism.* Translated by David Fernbach. London: Verso.

Pryor, Frederic L. 1991. "Third World Decollectivization: Guyana, Nicaragua, and Vietnam." *Problems of Communism* 40, no. 3 (May–June): 97–108.

Przeworski, Adam. 1991. *Democracy and the Market: Political and Economic Reforms in Eastern Europe and Latin America.* Cambridge: Cambridge University Press.

Purcell, John F. H., and Susan Kaufman [Purcell]. 1976. "El estado y la empresa privada." *Nueva política* 1, no. 2 (April–June): 229–50.

Ramírez Arango, Julio Sergio. 1985. "The Political Role of the Private Sector Associations of Central America: The Cases of El Salvador, Nicaragua and Costa Rica." Ph.D. diss., Harvard University.

Ramírez Mercado, Sergio. 1982. "Los sobrevivientes del naufragio." In *Estado y clases sociales en Nicaragua*, edited by the Asociación Nicaragüense de Científicos Sociales, 65–87. Managua: CIERA.

Ratcliff, Richard Earl. 1974. "Capitalists in Crisis: The Chilean Upper Class and the September 11 Coup." *Latin American Perspectives* 1, no. 2 (Summer): 78–91.

Reaño Alvarez, Germán, and Enrique Vásquez Huamán. 1988. *El grupo Romero: Del algodón a la banca.* Lima: Centro de Investigación de la Universidad del Pacífico.

Reid, Stanley. 1977. "An Introductory Approach to the Concentration of Power in the Jamaican Corporate Economy and Notes on its Origin." In *Essays on Power and Change in Jamaica,* edited by Carl Stone and Aggrey Brown, 15–44. Kingston: Jamaica Publishing House.

Reinhardt, Nola. 1989. "Contrast and Congruence in the Agrarian Reforms of El Salvador and Nicaragua." In *Searching for Agrarian Reform in Latin America,* edited by William C. Thiesenhusen, 451–82. Boston: Unwin Hyman.

República de Nicaragua. 1990a. *Acuerdos de la concertación económica y social y la política exterior del gobierno de Nicaragua.* Managua: República de Nicaragua.

———. 1990?b. *Leyes y decretos (25 de abril–2 de agosto).* Managua: n.p.

Republican Staff Report to the Committee on Foreign Relations, United States Senate. 1992. *Nicaragua Today.* Washington, D.C.: U.S. Government Printing Office.

Reynolds, Clark W. 1970. *The Mexican Economy: Twentieth Century Structure and Growth.* New Haven: Yale University Press.

Rivera Urrutia, Eugenio. 1986. "Foreign Debt and Financial Assistance: The Case of Central America." *Occasional Papers Series,* no. 17. Miami: Latin American and Caribbean Center, Florida International University.

Robinson, William I. 1992. *A Faustian Bargain: U.S. Intervention in the Nicaraguan Elections and American Foreign Policy in the Post–Cold War Era.* Boulder, Colo.: Westview Press.

Rosenthal, Gert. 1982. "Principales rasgos de la evolución de las economías centroamericanas desde la posguerra." In *Centroamérica: Crisis y política internacional,* edited by the Centro de Capacitación para el Desarrollo (CECADE) and Centro de Investigación y Docencia Económicas (CIDE), 19–38. México, D.F.: Siglo Veintiuno.

Ruben, Raul, and Jan P. deGroot, eds. 1989. *El debate sobre la reforma agraria en Nicaragua.* Managua: INIES.

Ruccio, David F. 1987. "The State and Planning in Nicaragua." In *The Political Economy of Revolutionary Nicaragua,* edited by Rose J. Spalding, 61–84. Boston: Allen & Unwin.

Ruchwarger, Gary. 1987. *People in Power: Forging a Grassroots Democracy in Nicaragua.* South Hadley, Mass.: Bergin & Garvey.

Ruiz, Henry. 1980. *El papel político del APP en la nueva economía sandinista.* Managua: Secretaría Nacional de Propaganda y Educación Política del FSLN.

Saldomando, Angel. 1992. *El retorno de la AID: El caso de Nicaragua.* Managua: CRIES.

Salgado, René. 1987. "Economic Pressure Groups and Policy-Making in Venezuela: The Case of FEDECAMARAS." *Latin American Research Review* 22, no. 3: 91–105.

Saragoza, Alex M. 1988. *The Monterrey Elite and the Mexican State, 1880–1940.* Austin: University of Texas Press.

Schmitter, Philippe C. 1974. "Still the Century of Corporatism?" In *The New Corporatism: Social-Political Structures in the Iberian World,* edited by Fredrick B. Pike and Thomas Stritch, 85–131. Notre Dame, Ind.: University of Notre Dame Press.

Schneider, Ben Ross. 1988–89. "Partly for Sale: Privatization and State Strength in Brazil and Mexico." *Journal of Interamerican Studies and World Affairs* 30, no. 4 (Winter): 89–116.

Schoultz, Lars. 1981. *Human Rights and United States Policy Toward Latin America.* Princeton: Princeton University Press.

Scott, James C. 1976. *The Moral Economy of the Peasant: Rebellion and Subsistence in Southeast Asia.* New Haven: Yale University Press.

———. 1989. "Everyday Forms of Resistance." In *Everyday Forms of Peasant Resistance,* edited by Forrest D. Colburn, 3–33. Armonk, N.Y.: M. E. Sharpe.

Selser, Gabriela. 1990. "New Reduction for EPS." *Barricada international* 10, no. 330 (December): 14–15.

Sen, Amartya K. 1990. "Rational Fools: A Critique of the Behavioral Foundations of Economic Theory." In *Beyond Self-Interest,* edited by Jane J. Mansbridge, 25–43. Chicago: University of Chicago Press.

Sequeira, Carlos Guillermo. 1981. "State and Private Marketing Arrangements in the Agricultural Export Industries: The Case of Nicaragua's Coffee and Cotton." Ph.D. diss., Harvard University.

Sevilla, Manuel. 1985. "La concentración económica en El Salvador." *Cuadernos de pensamiento propio.* Managua: INIES.

Shafer, Robert Jones. 1973. *Mexican Business Organizations: History and Analysis.* Syracuse, N.Y.: Syracuse University Press.

Sheahan, John. 1991. *Conflict and Change in Mexican Economic Strategy.* La Jolla: Center for U.S.-Mexican Studies, University of California, San Diego.

Sholk, Richard. 1984. "The National Bourgeoisie in Post-Revolutionary Nicaragua." *Comparative Politics* 16, no. 3 (April): 253–76.

Silva, Eduardo. 1992. "Business Associations, Neoliberal Economic Restructuring, and Redemocratization in Chile, 1973–1991." Paper presented at the Annual Meeting of the American Political Science Association, Chicago, September 3–6.

Silva Herzog, Jesús. 1975. *Lázaro Cárdenas: Su pensamiento económico, social y político.* México, D.F.: Editorial Nuestro Tiempo.

Skocpol, Theda. 1979. *States and Social Revolutions: A Comparative Analysis of France, Russia and China.* Cambridge: Cambridge University Press.

———. 1980. "Political Response to Capitalist Crisis: Neo-Marxist Theories of the State and the Case of the New Deal." *Politics and Society* 10, no. 2: 157–201.

Smith, Peter. 1979. *Labyrinths of Power: Political Recruitment in Twentieth Century Mexico.* Princeton: Princeton University Press.

Sojo, Carlos. 1991. *La utopía del estado mínimo: Influencia de AID en Costa Rica en los años ochenta.* Managua: CRIES.

Soza, Roberto. 1992. "Un nuevo sector económico de base popular." *L'Avispa*, no. 8 (January–February): 33–44.

Spalding, Rose J., ed. 1987a. *The Political Economy of Revolutionary Nicaragua.* Boston: Allen & Unwin.

——. 1987b. "State-Private Sector Relations in Nicaragua: The Somoza Era." Paper presented at Midwest Latin American Studies Association Meeting, Chicago, November 6–7.

——. 1988. "The Agricultural Bourgeoisie and the Nicaraguan Revolution." Paper presented at the Fourteenth International Congress of the Latin American Studies Association, New Orleans, March 17–19.

——. 1991. "Preliminary Report on GRACSA." Unpublished manuscript, August.

Spoor, Max. 1987. *Datos macro-económicos de Nicaragua (1960–1980).* Managua: UNAN Facultad de Ciencias Económicas, Depto. de Economía Agrícola.

——. 1989. "Reforma económica y crédito rural en Nicaragua (1988–89)." Paper prepared for the Fifteenth International Congress of the Latin American Studies Association, San Juan, Puerto Rico, September.

Spoor, Max, and Orlando Mendoza. 1988. "Agricultural Price Policy in Transition: The Case of Nicaragua (1979–1988)." Paper presented at the Fourteenth International Congress of the Latin American Studies Association, New Orleans, March 17–19.

SPP. 1985a. "Bosquejo del plan económico 1986." Internal report, June.

——. 1985b. "Evaluación y perspectivas económicas 1985." Internal report, June.

Stahler-Sholk, Richard. 1987. "Foreign Debt and Economic Stabilization Policies in Revolutionary Nicaragua." In *The Political Economy of Revolutionary Nicaragua*, edited by Rose J. Spalding, 151–68. Boston: Allen & Unwin.

——. 1988. "Stabilization, Destabilization, and the Popular Sector in Nicaragua, 1979–87." Paper presented at the Fourteenth International Congress of the Latin American Studies Association, New Orleans, March 17–19.

——. 1990. "Stabilization Policies under Revolutionary Transition: Nicaragua, 1979–1990." Ph.D. diss., University of California, Berkeley.

——. 1992. "Labor/Party/State Dynamics in Nicaragua: Union Responses to Austerity under the Sandinista and UNO Governments." Paper presented at the Seventeenth International Congress of the Latin American Studies Association, Los Angeles, September 24–27.

Stahler-Sholk, Richard, and Max Spoor. 1989. "Nicaragua: Las políticas macro-económicas y sus efectos en la agricultura y la seguridad alimentaria." Paper prepared for a PAN/CADESCA/CEE Seminar, Managua, Nicaragua, August 25–27.

Stallings, Barbara. 1978. *Class Conflict and Economic Development in Chile, 1958–1973.* Stanford: Stanford University Press.

——. 1979. "Peru and the U.S. Banks: Privatization of Financial Relations." In *Capitalism and the State in U.S.–Latin American Relations*, edited by Richard R. Fagen, 217–53. Stanford: Stanford University Press.

——. 1989. "The Political Economy of Democratic Transition: Chile in the 1980s." In *Debt and Democracy in Latin America*, edited by Barbara Stallings and Robert Kaufman, 181–200. Boulder, Colo.: Westview Press.

———. 1992. "International Influence on Economic Policy: Debt, Stabilization, and Structural Reform." In *The Politics of Economic Adjustment*, edited by Stephen Haggard and Robert R. Kaufman, 41–88. Princeton: Princeton University Press.

Stepan, Alfred. 1978. *The State and Society: Peru in Comparative Perspective*. Princeton: Princeton University Press.

Stephens, Evelyne Huber, and John D. Stephens. 1986. *Democratic Socialism in Jamaica*. Princeton: Princeton University Press.

———. 1990. "Capitalists, Socialism and Democracy: An Analysis of Business Attitudes toward Political Democracy in Jamaica." *Comparative Social Research* 12:341–79.

Stephens, John D. 1979. *The Transition from Capitalism to Socialism*. London: Macmillan.

Stone, Samuel Z. 1983. "Production and Politics in Central America's Convulsions." *Journal of Latin American Studies* 15, no. 2 (November): 453–69.

———. 1990. *The Heritage of the Conquistadors: Ruling Classes in Central America from the Conquest to the Sandinistas*. Lincoln: University of Nebraska Press.

Strachen, Harry W. 1976. *Family and Other Business Groups in Economic Development: The Case of Nicaragua*. New York: Praeger.

Strasma, John. 1989. "Unfinished Business: Consolidating Land Reform in El Salvador." In *Searching for Agrarian Reform in Latin America*, edited by William C. Thiesenhusen, 408–28. Boston: Unwin Hyman.

———. 1990. "Reforming the 1980 Land Reform: An Analysis of Proposals to Consolidate Debts and Allow Beneficiaries to Decide on Land Ownership and Production in Land Reform Projects in El Salvador." Unpublished report to USAID, June.

Taylor, Chris. 1989. "In Search of the 'Aquino effect.'" *Barricada international* 9, no. 300 (September 16): 3–4.

Taylor, Lance, et al. 1989. "Report of an Economic Mission to the Government of Nicaragua." Report for the Swedish International Development Authority, April 5.

Teichman, Judith. 1981. "Interest Conflict and Entrepreneurial Support for Perón." *Latin American Research Review* 16, no. 1: 144–55.

Thiesenhusen, William C. 1989. "Introduction." In *Searching for Agrarian Reform in Latin America*, edited by William C. Thiesenhusen, 1–41. Boston: Unwin Hyman.

Torres, Rosa María, and José Luis Coraggio. 1987. *Transición y crisis en Nicaragua*. San José, Costa Rica: Departamento Ecuménico de Investigaciónes.

Torres-Rivas, Edelberto. 1989. *Repression and Resistance: The Struggle for Democracy in Central America*. Boulder, Colo.: Westview Press.

Tullock, Gordon. 1979. "Public Choice in Practice." In *Collective Decision Making: Applications from Public Choice Theory*, edited by Clifford S. Russell, 27–45. Baltimore: Johns Hopkins University Press.

UNAG. 1993. "La estrategia de desarrollo agropecuario en Nicaragua: Una visión desde la UNAG." Foro sobre una Estrategia de Desarrollo Agropecuario en Nicaragua. Managua: ESECA-UNAN, PNUD-BID, RUTA, CONAGRO, February 23.

———. n.d. *Banco del Campo, BANCAM, S.A.: Resumen del proyecto.* N.p.

———. *Productores.* Various issues.

UNO. 1989. "Programa de gobierno de la Unión Nacional Opositora." Managua: Mimeo, August 24.

UPANIC. 1985. "Acuerdo." July 2.

———. 1992. "Comunicado." June 11. (Published in *La Prensa*, June 21, 1992.)

———. n.d. "Directorio 1988–89." Unpublished document.

USAID. 1990. "Status of the USAID/Nicaragua Program." Unpublished report, September.

———. 1992. "USAID Programs in Nicaragua: A Brief Description and Current Status." Unpublished report, June 10.

———. 1993. "USAID Program in Nicaragua: A Brief Description and Current Status." Unpublished report, April 6.

U.S. Department of State. 1988. *Nicaraguan Biographies: A Resource Book.* Washington, D.C.: U.S. Department of State.

U.S. GAO. 1991. *Aid to Nicaragua: Status of U.S. Assistance to the Democratically Elected Government.* Washington, D.C.: GAO.

———. 1992. *Aid to Nicaragua: U.S. Assistance Supports Economic and Social Development.* Washington, D.C.: GAO.

Utting, Peter. 1991. *Economic Adjustment under the Sandinistas: Policy Reform, Food Security and Livelihood in Nicaragua.* Geneva: United Nations Research Institute for Social Development.

Valdés, Mauricio. 1989. "Reformismo y guerra: Una evaluación de la nacionalización bancaria de El Salvador." *Estudios centroamericanos* 44, no. 492 (October): 791–808.

Valenzuela, Arturo. 1978. *The Breakdown of Democratic Regimes: Chile.* Baltimore: Johns Hopkins University Press.

Vichas, Robert Paul. 1967. "External Financing of the Nicaraguan Development Experiment." Ph.D. diss., University of Florida.

Vickers, George R., and Jack Spence. 1992. "Nicaragua Two Years after the Fall." *World Policy Journal* 9, no. 3 (Summer): 533–62.

Vilas, Carlos M. 1986. *The Sandinista Revolution.* Translated by Judy Butler. New York: Monthly Review Press.

———. 1990. "What Went Wrong." *NACLA Report on the Americas* 24, no. 1 (June): 10–18.

———. 1992. "Family Affairs: Class, Lineage and Politics in Contemporary Nicaragua." *Journal of Latin American Studies* 24, no. 2 (May): 309–41.

Villanueva, Benjamín. 1985. "Changing Relations between the State and the Economy in Central America." *Occasional Papers Series*, no. 9. Miami: Latin American and Caribbean Center, Florida International University.

Vogl Baldizón, Alberto. 1985. *Nicaragua con amor y humor.* 2d ed. Managua: Ministerio de Cultura.

Walker, David W. 1986. *Kinship, Business, and Politics: The Martínez del Río Family in Mexico, 1823–1867*. Austin: University of Texas Press.

Walker, Thomas W., ed. 1985. *Nicaragua: The First Five Years*. New York: Praeger.

Walter, Knut. 1993. *The Regime of Anastasio Somoza, 1936–1956*. Chapel Hill: University of North Carolina Press.

Warnken, Phillip F. 1975. *The Agricultural Development of Nicaragua: An Analysis of the Production Sector*. Columbia: Agricultural Experiment Section, University of Missouri, Columbia.

Waterbury, John. 1992. "The Heart of the Matter?: Public Enterprise and the Adjustment Process." In *The Politics of Economic Adjustment*, edited by Stephen Haggard and Robert R. Kaufman, 182–220. Princeton: Princeton University Press.

Weeks, John. 1985. *The Economies of Central America*. New York: Holmes & Meier.

———. 1987. "The Mixed Economy in Nicaragua: The Economic Battlefield." In *The Political Economy of Revolutionary Nicaragua*, edited by Rose J. Spalding, 42–60. Boston: Allen & Unwin.

Weyland, Kurt. 1992. "The Dispersion of Business Influence in Brazil's New Democracy." Paper presented at the annual meeting of the American Political Science Association, Chicago, September 3–6.

Wheelock Román, Jaime. 1980a. *Frente sandinista: Hacia la ofensiva final*. Havana, Cuba: Editorial de Ciencias Sociales.

———. 1980b. *Nicaragua: Imperialismo y dictadura*. Havana, Cuba: Editorial de Ciencias Sociales.

———. 1983. *El gran desafío*. Managua: Editorial Nueva Nicaragua.

———. 1984. "El sector agropecuario en la transformación revolucionaria." *Revolución y desarrollo* 1 (April–June): 5–14.

———. 1985. *Entre la crisis y la agresión: La reforma agraria sandinista*. Managua: Editorial Nueva Nicaragua.

———. 1990. *La reforma agraria sandinista*. Managua: Editorial Vanguardia.

———. 1991. *La verdad sobre la piñata*. Managua: Instituto para el Desarrollo de la Democracia.

Wilkie, James W. 1970. *The Mexican Revolution: Federal Expenditures and Social Change since 1910*. Berkeley: University of California Press.

Williams, Robert G. 1986. *Export Agriculture and the Crisis in Central America*. Chapel Hill: University of North Carolina Press.

Wils, Frits C. M. 1975. *Industrialists, Industrialization and the Nation State in Peru*. The Hague: Institute of Social Studies.

Winn, Peter. 1986. *Weavers of Revolution: The Yarur Workers and Chile's Road to Socialism*. New York and London: Oxford University Press.

Winson, Anthony. 1985. "Nicaragua's Private Sector and the Sandinista Revolution." *Studies in Political Economy* 7 (Summer): 71–106.

WOLA (Washington Office on Latin America). 1992. "U.S. Policy and Property Rights in Nicaragua: Undermining the Search for Consensus." *Nicaragua Issue Brief*, no. 2 (December).

Wolf, Daniel H. 1992. "ARENA in the Arena: Factors in the Accommodation of the Salvadoran Right to Pluralism and the Broadening of the Political System." Memorandum presented to the United Nations Observers Mission in El Salvador, January 20.

Wright, Thomas L. 1982. *Landowners and Reform in Chile: The Sociedad Nacional de Agricultura, 1919–1940.* Urbana: University of Illinois Press.

Wynia, Gary. 1972. *Politics and Planners: Economic Development Policy in Central America.* Madison: University of Wisconsin Press.

———. 1990. *Politics of Latin American Development.* Cambridge: Cambridge University Press.

"Year in Review 1991." 1992. *Barricada international* 12, no. 345 (January): 20–22.

Zalkin, Michael. 1990. "The Sandinista Agrarian Reform: 1979–1990." *International Journal of Political Economy* 20, no. 3 (Fall): 56–68.

Zeitlin, Maurice. 1984. *The Civil Wars in Chile (or the Bourgeois Revolutions That Never Were).* Princeton: Princeton University Press.

Zeitlin, Maurice, and Richard Earl Ratcliff. 1988. *Landlords and Capitalists: The Dominant Class of Chile.* Princeton: Princeton University Press.

Zevallos L., José Vicente. 1989. "Agrarian Reform and Structural Change: Ecuador since 1964." In *Searching for Agrarian Reform in Latin America,* edited by William C. Thiesenhusen, 42–69. Boston: Unwin Hyman.

index